Central Banking in Turbulent Times

Central Banking in Turbulent Times

Francesco Papadia with Tuomas Välimäki

OXFORD
UNIVERSITY PRESS

OXFORD

UNIVERSITY PRESS

Great Clarendon Street, Oxford, OX2 6DP,
United Kingdom

Oxford University Press is a department of the University of Oxford.
It furthers the University's objective of excellence in research, scholarship,
and education by publishing worldwide. Oxford is a registered trade mark of
Oxford University Press in the UK and in certain other countries

First Edition published in 2018
Impression: 3

Published in the United States of America by Oxford University Press
198 Madison Avenue, New York, NY 10016, United States of America

British Library Cataloguing in Publication Data
Data available

Library of Congress Control Number: 2017952243

ISBN 978–0–19–880619–6

Printed and bound by
CPI Group (UK) Ltd, Croydon, CR0 4YY

Foreword

This is a classic central banking book. It is written by two authors who have been senior and highly experienced central bankers. Francesco Papadia was Director General for Market Operations at the European Central Bank (ECB) during the critical years of the Great Financial Crisis (GFC), and played a central role in managing the ECB's response to it. Tuomas Välimäki is Chief Economist at the Bank of Finland and a member of the ECB's Monetary Policy Committee.

The book is about central banking in recent decades, primarily about the roles and actions of the two main central banks, the ECB and the Federal Reserve System of the USA (the Fed). Chapter 1 recounts how the consensus view on the appropriate role of such central banks developed during the course of the Great Moderation (1992–2007), that is, that central banks should use a single instrument, the official short-term interest rate, to control a single objective, price stability, defined as an inflation target. In this process it was, incorrectly, assumed that the achievement of overall macroeconomic stability, and the self-interest of those involved in banking and financial markets, would quasi-automatically help to ensure financial stability also. So the financial stability aspects of central banking became diminished.

When the crisis first erupted in 2007/2008, central banks also found that their ability to achieve their primary task of maintaining price stability via changes in the official short rate became compromised. As money markets became dysfunctional, and everyone, including bankers, began to hoard liquidity, the standard means of controlling the overnight interest rate became less reliable, spreads between official rates and market rates widened abruptly, and soon, by early 2008, official short-term rates began to hit the zero lower bound (ZLB). Chapter 2, the main segment of the book, is about the onset of such problems, and how the two key central banks, the ECB and the Fed, responded to, and eventually overcame, such problems and difficulties, largely by the use of balance sheet adjustments and quantitative easing (QE). This provides a truly authoritative account of the main actions of these two central banks during the GFC, as might be expected since Papadia played such a central role in this exercise at the ECB. This key, and lengthy, chapter will be a precious source about central bank actions in the GFC for scholars for decades to come.

The experience of the GFC means that central banks are now saddled with two objectives: financial stability as well as price stability. The third, final, and shortest chapter, Chapter 3, is primarily about how to handle this role expansion. The authors briefly consider whether financial stability could be delegated to another authority, but, rightly, dismiss this, given the centrality of central bank liquidity provision in crises.

If one has two objectives, ideally one should have two instruments, in order to hit such objectives exactly, as in the Tinbergen principle. Chapter 3 is largely about the question whether the new concept of using macro-prudential measures can provide such a second instrument. The authors are doubtful, since such macro-prudential measures are relatively new, not fully tried, and uncertain in effect. If they do not work well enough, the central bank could be left with a dilemma, a potential trade-off. In such cases, could the central bank seek political guidance? But would that be consistent with central bank independence? Perhaps fortunately, we do not know what the future will bring, so we, and central bankers, are left with more than enough unanswered questions.

This is a book by central bank experts, about central bank policy actions, and it will be eagerly read by members of the central bank fraternity around the world. But the audience of those who will profit by, and enjoy, reading this book goes much wider. It will include all those interested in the causes, conduct, and consequences of the GFC; those studying money and banking; those in financial markets and institutions caught up in the GFC; and those who want to make sense of recent financial developments.

Charles Goodhart

Preface

This book has been written by two central bank insiders. Indeed, we have spent practically all our professional lives in a central bank. Nevertheless, when writing this book, we have tried to move beyond our insider perspective. Or, rather, we have endeavoured to look again at the information we have accumulated over our long years in central banks from a new perspective, seeking to exploit our depth of knowledge, whilst avoiding the limitations implicit in any specific professional experience. In order to achieve this new perspective, we make selective use of the available economic literature. References to this literature are used only as long as they help to better understand the economic developments with which we deal in this book: the analytical apparatus serves our narrative, not vice versa.

During the Great Recession, which started in August 2007 and entered its most acute phase in September 2008 with the failure of Lehman Brothers, we worked at the border between top decision-makers and markets. Our job was to provide options to policymakers, to design the various programmes, and to carry them out in the trenches. This put us at the centre of it all, close to decisions, but also on the front line, implementing actions, often taken in emergency situations, and monitoring how they affected financial markets and, most importantly, the real economy.

This experience has been in many ways exhilarating: we found ourselves in the middle of historic events, in institutions that were at the forefront of understanding the unfolding crisis and limiting its damages. The ensuing choices had critical repercussions, beyond the mere economic sphere, on the welfare of hundreds of millions of individuals. The catastrophic experience of the 1930s—when central banks failed to adequately fight the Great Depression and the debt crisis—forced central banks to be bold and act swiftly. They were compelled to look beyond the well-trodden paths they had followed before the crisis. There were also reasons, however, to be afraid, or at least conscious, of the risk of making serious mistakes. Critical decisions, not written in any monetary policy textbook, were swiftly made. In fact, many central banks pursued actions that would have been unthinkable before the crisis but would eventually find their ways into textbooks.[1]

Numerous actions taken by central banks would have previously been considered extreme and even potentially dangerous. There were no orientation tools available, no maps to guide us: we were in terra incognita. Blanchard (in Blanchard et al. 2016, p. 8) summarized what happened in an apt way: 'Central banks have experimented with and researchers have explored monetary policy, often in that order.' At the same time, we felt that society was placing an outsized burden on our institutions. Problems were dealt with as they arose, day by day, sometimes hour by hour. Still, we sensed we were working in the tradition of institutions adapting to historical developments, asked to serve society by using, in the best possible ways, the important tools and resources entrusted to them.

Frequent, rapid, and frank contacts and exchanges with market participants and central bankers in other jurisdictions were critical. These information channels helped us, and the institutions in which we served, to make decisions and to avoid being paralyzed by doubt. Market participants presented us with problems that went beyond their capacity to solve. In return, they helped us understand what was happening and find new solutions for various emergencies. With central bankers in other jurisdictions, we shared experiences about the problems facing us and, together, we looked for solutions, often requiring joint actions. The relationship was particularly close with the Fed, which had a much longer experience than the ECB as a central bank with a global influence. This, together with the fact that the Great Recession developed in two phases—the first with an epicentre in the United States and the second with an epicentre in the euro-area—explains why this book is concentrated on the experience of these two central banks. However, at times, we extend our analyses to include central banks in other advanced economies. Although this book does not look at the experience of emerging economies, a relevant observation is that the tools that appeared totally unconventional for central banks in advanced economies were instead familiar in the experience of emerging economies. This is not surprising, because the disturbed functioning of markets in advanced countries during the Great

---

[1] The sense of being surprised by one's own actions in central banks during the Great Recession was analogous to that described in 1831 by the Bank of England Member Jeremiah Harman in the Lords' Committee, quoted by Bindseil (2004): 'We lent . . . by every possible means, and in modes that we never had adopted before, we took in stock of security, we purchased Exchequer bills, we made advances on Exchequer bills, we not only discounted outright, but we made advances on deposits of bills to an immense amount; in short by every possible means consistent with the safety of the Bank; seeing the dreadful state in which the public were, we rendered every assistance in our power.' The same sense of having to go well beyond normal practices is well presented in chapter 18 in the memoirs of Ben Bernanke (2015a) 'For much of the panic, the Fed alone, with its chewing gum and bailing wire, bore the burden of battling the crisis. This included preventing the failure of systematically important institutions.'

Recession had some similarities with the functioning of less mature markets in emerging economies.

Our book is not an historical account of the Great Recession, or of any time before it for that matter. A number of very good books cover this area.[2] Our purpose is to show how the concepts and practicalities of central banks changed with the Great Recession and what conjectures we can make about their future developments.

---

[2] See, among others, Pisani-Ferry (2014); Brunnermeier, James, and Landau (2016); Bastasin (2015).

Acknowledgements

We warmly thank the many people who helped us with the preparation of this book.[3]

For the part of the book written by Francesco Papadia, Alessandra Marcelletti, Madalina Norocea, Piero Esposito, and Pia Hüttl efficiently prepared the vast empirical material presented. Christophe Beuve and Deborah Perelmuter gave useful advice on some issues relating to the Federal Reserve of the United States (Fed), with which he was less familiar than the European Central Bank (ECB). Ariana Gilbert-Mongelli revised the English and provided numerous suggestions regarding presentation. Carina Wörner revised the typographical layout and checked the references. For the part written by Tuomas Välimäki, Jarmo Kontulainen provided several useful comments, and Gregory Moore revised the English as well as contributing to the presentation.

Claudio Borio, Fabrizio Cacciafesta, Andrea Enria, Ivo Maes, Giangiacomo Nardozzi, and André Sapir were very generous with their comments. Patricia Mosser, Klaus Regling, Rolf Strauch, Guntram Wolff, Zsolt Darvas, Marcello Messori, and Franco Passacantando commented on various versions of the book. The Directorate General for Financial Stability of the ECB, led by Sergio Nicoletti Altimari, allowed us to use data published in the Financial Stability Review (FSR) of the ECB.

Presentations at the School of European Political Economy at Libera Università Internazionale degli Studi Sociali (LUISS), the National Bank of Belgium, the Bruegel Institute, the Federal Reserve Bank of New York, Waseda University in Tokyo, and the ECB helped in developing the reasoning presented in the book, in some cases identifying weak spots in its development. Lectures at Politecnico di Milano, Scuola Sant'Anna of the University of Pisa, the Goethe University in Frankfurt, and LUISS in Rome allowed both substance and form to be honed.

---

[3] Tuomas Välimäki wrote Section 2.1.4. Francesco Papadia wrote the rest of the main text. The authors of the boxes and appendices are indicated in the boxes and appendices. The different authors are exclusively responsible for the content of their writings.

Contents

Contents

List of Figures

List of Tables

List of Boxes

List of Contributors

Christophe Beuve is currently the Head of Bond Markets and International Operations Division in the Directorate General of Market Operations at the ECB. He joined the ECB in 1998 and has occupied various positions in the asset management and monetary policy implementation areas. Prior to joining the ECB, Christophe worked in the money and foreign exchange markets departments at the Banque de France. He also worked at the International Monetary Fund (IMF) for two years and at the Fed for 18 months.

Philippine Cour-Thimann teaches monetary economics at HEC and at the Paris Institute of Political Studies (Sciences Po). She is Principal Economist at the ECB where she has been working since 1999 in the areas of monetary, fiscal, and financial analysis. Between 2007 and 2014 she contributed to the design and implementation of monetary policy decisions in the global financial crisis. Prior to joining the ECB, she worked at CEPII, the French centre for international economics. Her current research interests are in the fields of monetary policy, and money and banking. She holds graduate degrees in engineering and economics.

Piero Esposito has been a researcher at the School of European Political Economy since September 2014. He has a PhD in economics from Sapienza University of Rome. Between 2011 and 2014, he was a post-doctoral researcher at Sant'Anna School of Advanced Studies in Pisa, and a researcher at Centro Europa Ricerche (CER) in Rome. Between 2009 and 2010, he was a post-doctoral researcher at the Institute of Economic Studies and Analyses (ISAE, now merged with ISTAT). His research focuses mainly on European economic policy, competitiveness, international trade, and applied econometrics.

Ariana Gilbert-Mongelli has a Master's degree in Public Policy from the University of Chicago. Previously she worked as a Research Associate at the Washington, DC, Office of Vanderbilt University's Institute for Public Policy Studies, among various other positions. Currently she resides in Frankfurt, where she is a freelance editor and writer.

Pia Hüttl is an Affiliate Fellow at Bruegel. Prior to this, Pia worked as a trainee in the Monetary Policy Stance Division of the ECB, and as a trainee in the Directorate-General for Economic and Financial Affairs of the European Commission. She holds a Master's degree in International Economics from the University of Rome Tor Vergata and a Master's degree in European Political Economy from the London School of Economics. Currently, she is a PhD candidate at the Berlin Doctoral Programme in Economics and

Management Science. Her research interests include macroeconomics, international economics, and European political economy.

Alessandra Marcelletti is a post-doctoral researcher at the Department of Political Science of University LUISS Guido Carli, and a Research Fellow at the School of European Political Economy—LUISS since January 2015. She holds a PhD in Economic Theory and Institution from the University of Rome Tor Vergata. Her current research interests include European economic policy, government policy and regulation of banks and financial institutions, and applied econometrics.

Francesco Papadia has nearly 40 years of central banking experience. Beginning with the founding of the ECB in 1998, and until 2012, he served as the Director General for Market Operations at the ECB. Prior to that, he held various positions at the Banca d'Italia and was Economic Advisor at the EU Commission. Currently he is Chairman of the Board of the Prime Collateralised Securities, Chair of the Selection Panel of the Hellenic Financial Stability Fund, Senior Resident Fellow at the Bruegel Institute, and a university lecturer.

Tuomas Välimäki is the Head of Monetary Policy and Research at the Bank of Finland. As the Bank's Chief Economist, he is a member of the ECB's Monetary Policy Committee. During his two decades as a central banker, he has also worked as a visiting expert at the ECB.

Introduction

Fundamental questions about the optimal set-up for central banks are examined in this book. In particular, we ask whether the model of an independent central bank devoted to price stability,[1] which affirmed itself in most advanced economies at the turn of the last century, is the final resting point of a long and complex development that started centuries ago. We dissect the hypothesis that the Great Recession has prompted a reassessment and a possible revision of that model.[2] The most important factors raising this issue number four. First, a renewed emphasis on financial stability as an explicit key objective to be pursued by a central bank has emerged, possibly vying for the first rank with price stability and causing potential dilemmas for the central bank, which would have to arbitrage between two different objectives. The dilemma arises because the implicit assumption that the pursuit of price stability would always coincide with that of financial stability was not verified during the Great Recession. Second, central bank action moved closer to fiscal policy, both in the United States (USA) and in Europe. Third, forceful central bank action, while needed to avoid even graver economic consequences, engendered moral hazard. Fourth, and connected to the previous point, in the euro-area, more general responsibilities, such as avoiding the demise of the euro, were thrown upon the central bank. Ultimately, we ask whether the traditional model has been irrevocably altered, as central banks have been required to take on new responsibilities. Are we entering, as Goodhart (2010) has hypothesized, the 'fourth epoch' of central banking?

This book is organized into three main chapters. Chapter 1 examines how central banks have evolved over the decades, showing that, historically, four objectives have vied for dominance in the central bank ranking of

---

[1] The issue of the so-called dual mandate of the Fed is examined in Box 1 (see Chapter 1).
[2] Claudio Borio (2014b) also examines this hypothesis and reaches a quite trenchant conclusion: 'Central banking will never be quite the same after the global financial crisis' (p. 191).

objectives: price stability, financial stability, economic growth, and the funding of the government. The prevalence of the price stability objective eventually resulted from the poor inflation control delivered by the monetary policy technology that substituted the gold standard, until monetary control was entrusted to an independent central bank devoted to price stability. The implementation of the principle of central bank independence was somewhat different between the USA and the euro-area, partly by design, partly by necessity. In fact, in Europe, the memory of the ravages of inflation and the absence of a strong partner for the central bank, such as the US Treasury, led to a stronger version of central bank independence. In institutional terms, this can be seen in the fact that in the euro-area, unlike in the USA, central bank independence has constitutional relevance.

The conceptual and empirical basis for the dominant central banking model *before* the Great Recession are herein illustrated. In essence, economic theory and actual economic developments showed that there is no permanent trade-off between inflation and growth: indeed, stable prices foster growth in the long run. This finding was the basis for the generalized prevalence of central banks dedicated to price stability and endowed with the independent, technical discretion to pursue this objective. In Europe, the long quest for monetary union eventually succeeded when, based on the example of the Deutsche Bundesbank, it was agreed that the basis of the monetary union should be price stability rather than the intrinsically flawed attempt to stabilize exchange rates.

The main components of the central bank model prevailing before the Great Recession are also presented in this chapter. The approach that Wicksell developed in the 1920s, in which the interest rate rather than any monetary quantity plays the critical role, is a fundamental component of that model. Inflation targeting, giving up the attempt to identify intermediate targets, is the way in which the predominant objective of price stability was operationalized. The Taylor rule (1993) moved Wicksell's main analytical point closer to an approach that can be used for practical policymaking. Finally, the corridor approach was developed as an effective and parsimonious way to control the interest rate. The validation of that model during the Great Moderation is also discussed. It is stressed, however, that financial stability did not fit easily within the then prevailing paradigm. This feature matched the illusion that advanced economies had graduated from financial and banking crises, but was also favoured by the complexity of the concept of financial stability and its intricate relationship with banking supervision and macro-prudential policy. The possibility of dilemmas between the pursuits of financial or price stability is also presented, stressing that such dilemmas were hidden as long as financial stability was the overlooked field in the action of central banks.

2

This chapter also looks at the so-called Great Moderation, which seemed to be the final validation of the central banking model that had come to prevail across much of the advanced world in the final decades of the last century. The chapter ends with an analysis of the macroeconomic, regulatory, financial, and intellectual causes of the Great Recession.

In hindsight, the Great Moderation and then the Great Recession conform pretty closely to the sequence of phases identified by Kindleberger in 1978, measured by Reinhart and Rogoff in 2009, and theorized by Minsky in 1986: an excess of credit growth is the most salient feature of the run-up to a financial crisis. This chapter also argues that the shift from the Great Moderation to the Great Recession closely fits the shift from a 'good' to a 'bad' equilibrium in the multiple equilibria model of Diamond and Dybvig (Diamond 2007). The use of this model facilitates explaining developments that would otherwise be impossible to understand, such as the disproportionate consequences of the relatively small, immediate causes of the American and the European phases of the Great Recession. The basic logic of that model is also consistent with the fact that central banks do not necessarily lose money when they intervene in a crisis if they price their intervention at a price intermediate between the one prevailing in the 'bad' equilibrium and the one that would have prevailed in a 'good' equilibrium.

Chapter 2 examines central banking *during* the Great Recession. In particular, the monetary policy and financial stability consequences of the Great Recession, as well as the central bank actions and communications to counter their detrimental economic effects, are discussed and assessed.

The most important monetary consequences are found in the rejection of three critical, if untold, assumptions of monetary control before the Great Recession: first, the ability of the central bank to closely control a short-term market rate; second, a fairly stable relationship between that short-term rate and longer/riskier interest rates that are more important for the real economy; third, the possibility of reducing, in all cases, interest rates as much as needed. The Federal Reserve of the United States (Fed) and the European Central Bank (ECB) reacted to these difficulties by developing one additional tool for their arsenal: balance sheet management. This development built on the previous experience of the Bank of Japan (Kuroda 2014), which had embarked on a zero interest rate policy in February 1999 and then on quantitative easing (QE) in March 2001. The large balance sheet increase allowed the Fed and the ECB to move onto their balance sheet part of the intermediation process that private markets were no longer capable of carrying out and to ease monetary policy even when the short-term interest rate had reached its lower bound. This chapter then illustrates the common features as well as the differences between the actions of the Fed and those of the ECB, as well as the fact that globalization has made countries increasingly interdependent, and thus central banks had to strengthen the global dimension in their actions to deal with the crisis.

In the most acute phases of the Great Recession, banks started to extensively hoard liquidity. This impeded the central bank's capability to quantify the level of liquidity that would allow the short-term interest rate to reach its target. The main response by the Fed, large-scale asset purchases, differed from that of the ECB, full allotment in liquidity providing lending operations. Yet the outcome was similar: the determination of the overnight rate of interest switched from a corridor approach to a floor system. With this change, central banks managed to restore their control over short-term rates. A decade after the start of the crisis, the interest rate paid on banks' reserve holdings on their central bank accounts is still the main policy instrument for both the Fed and the ECB.

The origins of the impairments in the monetary policy transmission in the USA and the euro-area differed one from another. First, the role of capital markets in monetary policy transmission was, and still is, by far greater in the USA, whereas banks dominate lending to the real sector in the euro-area. Second, the sovereign debt crisis, which hit several euro-area countries, heavily hampered credit creation in these jurisdictions. Consequently, the actions taken by the two central banks to restore impaired policy transmission also differed one from the other. The Fed initiated three types of policy actions outside its standard interest rate policy: (1) lender-of-last-resort-type lending to financial institutions; (2) bypassing the banking sector by providing liquidity directly to key credit markets; and (3) large-scale purchases of longer-term securities. The ECB facilitated banks' ability to continue extending credit by providing them with cheap funding at maturities up to four years. Concerning the impairments in the sovereign bond markets, the ECB conducted several smaller scale programmes until 2012, when the risk of a breakup of the euro-area emerged and the President of the ECB pledged to do 'whatever it takes to preserve the euro'. The Outright Monetary Transactions (OMT) programme, which operationalized that promise, can be seen as a key action in restoring the functioning of monetary policy in euro-area.

The severity of the Great Recession evidenced the power of the zero lower bound (ZLB) for monetary policymaking. When the room for traditional monetary accommodation was exhausted, the combination of forward guidance and QE proved to be an efficient approach to prevent a Great Depression-type of total meltdown in the USA and the euro-area. As a consequence, the focus of monetary policy shifted from short-term to longer-term rates and to the size of the balance sheet. The unconventional measures taken were efficient in enhancing economic developments and addressing the risk of a deflationary cycle. However, they have not been very effective in bringing the inflation and inflation expectations back to their targets. In some currency areas, including the euro-area, ZLB was also pushed down to negative territory. Yet it seems that the room for negative rates is not large enough to overcome the liquidity trap in practice.

The most important financial stability consequences of the Great Recession affected banks, whose intermediation ability was severely affected. The impairment was acute, but shorter, in the USA, because Fed and government actions were more forceful and timely, whereas in the euro-area the consequences were significantly more protracted. This chapter considers both 'dual-purpose' actions from central banks, that is, policy moves that dealt with both the monetary and the financial stability consequences of the crisis, and actions specifically targeted at financial stability. In particular, it examines two such actions: the Fed's stress test of 2009 and the ECB's Asset Quality Review (AQR) of 2014.

Together with the positive effects of central bank actions, this chapter also looks at the hits that they delivered during the Great Recession to the pre-crisis central bank model. The main problem is that the overlooked issue of financial stability returned with a vengeance, creating potential dilemmas for the central bank, which may have to take the political decision of arbitraging between financial stability and price stability. This chapter also documents how the large-scale purchases of government bonds by both the Fed and the ECB blurred the borders between monetary and fiscal policy. Furthermore, it argues that the help offered by the ECB and the Fed to banks and, in the euro-area, also to sovereigns, created moral hazard problems. Closely connected to this last point is the observation that the ECB had to take on the task of mutualizing those idiosyncratic shocks that, in the euro-area, could no longer be dealt with by the exchange rate. This chapter also puts forward the idea that the participation of the ECB in the so-called troika took it far away from its specific area of expertise and responsibility. The chapter finally notes that global responsibilities became more evident for both the Fed and the ECB, and that, as in previous episodes of crisis, the central bank moved closer to the government, raising questions about its independence.

The third and final chapter of this book examines the possible developments of central banking *after* the Great Recession. The scope of Chapter 3 is explicitly limited to the central banking world, as there is no attempt to extend it to the broader questions that the attack of the populists to the global liberal order is raising. Implicitly, it is assumed that this order will survive substantially unscathed and we are not seeing a repetition of the disastrous experience of the 1930s. If that were not the case, the issue of the possible changes to the central bank model dealt with in this book would be a small element of a much wider problem. Another limitation of this chapter is that it does not address the changes that technological developments, including blockchain technology, could force onto central banks. There are two reasons for this omission: first, this book concentrates on the consequences of the Great Recession; second, it is too early to have a clear view of what these changes could be.

Chapter 3 deals first with strategic and operational issues. It concludes that the interest rate will remain, in a Wicksellian mode, the dominant monetary policy variable, and that it will continue to be moved as a function of the inflation and the activity gaps, according to the general logic of the Taylor rule. So no significant change is expected on these two aspects. A discussion follows about possible adaptations of the inflation targeting strategy. Three proposals are, in particular, discussed: first, raising the inflation target from 2 to something like 4 per cent; second, moving from an inflation- to a price-level target; third, adopting a nominal gross domestic product (GDP) target. Costs and benefits of the different proposals are briefly considered and the conclusion is that it is not obvious that any of the examined proposals would deliver better monetary policy performance than the inflation targeting strategy that prevailed before the Great Recession and survived practically unscathed during it. While it is not excluded that one or the other change will be opportune in the future, it is argued that new empirical evidence and new analytical considerations will have to accumulate before coming to this conclusion.

On the operational side, the point is made that large amounts of liquidity will prevail for a number of years as the consequence of QE by the Fed and the ECB. Therefore, a quick return to the pre-crisis approach, in which the short-term rate was kept in the middle of the interest rate corridor, will not be feasible, because the weight of excess liquidity will continue to push the rate towards the floor of the corridor. The possible continued use of the balance sheet tool for monetary policy purposes could prolong this situation into the indefinite future. The question then arises whether this is a desirable permanent feature or only something to be tolerated for a while longer. On the basis of currently available evidence and analytical considerations, the interim conclusion is that a general 'parsimony' principle advises a central bank balance sheet as small as possible and thus a return to a situation without excess liquidity. However, it is also argued that this conclusion may be reviewed on the basis of new evidence and new analytical considerations.

Overall, the changes to the strategic and operational set-up that will prevail after the Great Recession are considered limited. In addition, such a set-up does not require institutional changes and is therefore easier to implement than that that would require such changes.

To examine the possible institutional adaptations of the central banking model after the Great Recession, Chapter 3 explores how wide the scope of responsibilities of central banks is likely to be in the future. During the crisis, monetary policy was pursued in significantly innovative ways, and the remit of central banks expanded because new responsibilities were thrown on them. This chapter discusses whether these developments will become permanent or will gradually be reabsorbed as the legacy of the Great Recession withers away. In addition, a new regulatory landscape has emerged as one of the long-term consequences of the crisis; this will have an important bearing on the financial and banking markets within which central banks will exercise their monetary and financial stability functions, and thus could impact the central bank model.

The analyses of the altered scope of responsibilities of central banks and of the new regulatory framework are used to present some ideas about which changes need to be made to the pre-crisis central bank model. The proposals put forward are of incremental rather than radical nature, even if they will definitely look excessive to those who believe that the pre-crisis model helped central banks to effectively deal with the consequences of the Great Recession. In addition, even if only incremental, some of the proposed changes would require a modification of the Federal Reserve Act and of the ECB Statute, which are formidable hurdles to be surpassed.

Two radical changes are presented and subsequently rejected in this chapter. The first such change would be a return to the model of a central bank that is integral part of, and therefore dependent on, the government. Such a return would ignore the historical experience, dating back to the First World War when the monetary technology implicit in the gold standard was abandoned, which shows the intrinsic difficulties of delivering price stability with a fiat currency managed by a central bank dependent on the government. The second radical change, considered unfeasible, would be a return to a narrow definition of the role of central banks, taking off their shoulders all the additional burdens that have been put on them during the Great Recession. While this option would be desirable in principle, better matching the operational independence of the central bank with a technical task such as preserving price stability, it would require developments in the environment in which the central bank operates that are unlikely enough to make it imprudent to count on them. Indeed, a return to narrow central banking would require positive developments in all the following six areas. First, the central bank should not be exposed to the risk of dilemmas, in which it would have to arbitrage between price and financial stability. Second, clearer borders should be re-established between monetary and fiscal policy, which would require, in turn, that central banks would not need to continue using their balance sheet as an additional tool to complement the interest rate. Third, central bank should no longer be put in the situation of having to choose between either allowing a crisis engendering serious economic damages or creating a degree of moral hazard, by helping agents, including governments, that have put themselves in dangerous situations. Fourth, specifically for the

ECB, it should be relieved of the responsibility to act as mutualizer of idiosyncratic macroeconomic shocks hitting members of the euro-area. Fifth, again specifically for the ECB, it should no longer be called to be part of the troika, agreeing general economic programmes for countries requiring financial assistance. Sixth, globally relevant central banks, like the Fed and the ECB, should find it easier to better incorporate the international consequences of their actions in their decisions. The probability of positive developments varies across the six aforementioned areas: very high in some but much lower in others. As a result, the joint probability of positive developments in all areas, which would be needed to maintain the pre-crisis model unchanged, is low: hence some adaptations of the model are required.

The proposed incremental changes fall in a (broadly defined) governance area. First, to solve possible dilemmas between price and financial stability that could not be dealt with macro-prudential measures, the central bank should ask a relevant political body, for example parliament, to arbitrage between the two objectives, and should pursue the prescribed one with the higher priority. Second, should large-scale interventions in government securities continue to be needed, blurring the borders between fiscal and monetary policy, special majorities and reporting requirements should apply. In the third area mentioned above, namely the moral hazard created by helping banks and, in the euro-area, sovereigns that had put themselves into a dangerous situation, no institutional innovation seems to be needed. After the substantial pain suffered by imprudent banks and sovereigns during the crisis, a determinate use of the attenuating measures already taken by the Fed and the ECB during the Great Recession, namely maintaining part of the cost of imprudent behaviour on banks and sovereigns as well as applying macroeconomic conditionality when supporting governments in difficulty, should be enough. Fourth, a solution to free the ECB from the task of having to offset the idiosyncratic shocks that would hit one or the other euro-area country should be found outside of the central banking area, in the completion of the design of the monetary union. Fifth, the participation of the ECB in the troika during the Great Recession has produced substantial confusion so that there should no longer be support for it in the future. Finally, the Fed and the ECB, building on the intense cooperation established during the Great Recession, should be able to better incorporate the consequences of their own actions on global conditions without the need of any institutional innovation in this specific area. However, cooperation, transparency, and continuous information sharing are critical to ensure various central banks will be able to effectively coordinate their actions, as they did during the Great Recession, to best respond to potential future crises.

1

Central Banking before the Great Recession

1.1 Changing Nature and Objectives of Central Banks

Central banks are peculiar institutions. Thus, it is not possible to characterize them in a way that would be right for all times and for all places. Their institutional characteristics have changed over time and vary across countries. Some central banks are very old: the Sveriges Riksbank, the central bank of Sweden, was founded in 1668, the Bank of England in 1694. Some other central banks, instead, are much more recent. For example, the Federal Reserve Bank (Fed) was founded in 1913, after two failed attempts at creating a central bank in the early nineteenth century: the Bank of the United States (1791–1811) and a second Bank of the United States (1816–1836). The European Central Bank (ECB) was only created in 1998, to launch the euro and bring about the monetary unification of the euro-area. The oldest central banks started as private companies and gradually acquired the characteristics of public institutions. Newer central banks, like the ECB, had from the start a clear public nature. Still, some central banks carry traces of their original private nature. For example, the District Banks that form the Federal Reserve System of the United States have some characteristics of a private company, each having a private-sector Board of Directors. The Banca d'Italia has as shareholders private banks and insurance companies and pays corporate taxes. The shares of several national banks, such as the Banque Nationale de Belgique, the National Bank of Greece, and, until recently, the Bank for International Settlements (BIS, commonly characterized as the central bank of central banks), are quoted on the stock exchange. The main monetary policy tools of central banks are of a private law, rather than a statutory, nature. Indeed, the compulsory requirement for banks to hold reserves at their respective central bank is the only notable exemption. Statutory tools are, instead, mostly used in supervisory activities by those central banks that have this responsibility. Some central banks—like the ECB, the

Fed, and the Swiss National Bank—dispose of substantial independence in pursuing their statutory objectives by means of monetary policy. Some other central banks—like the People's Bank of China and the Bank of England (until 1997)—are (or were, in the case of the Bank of England) subject to government control.

Moreover, the objectives of various central banks have changed over time. Price stability, financial stability, funding of the government, and growth/employment appear in different periods as the objectives of central banks, with diverse rankings and in various combinations (Fischer, 1995; Bordo, 2007, 2016; Reinhart and Rogoff, 2009; Goodhart, 2010; Hellwig, 2015) (see Box 1).

Box 1 COMPARING THE FED DUAL APPROACH AND THE ECB DOMINANT PRICE STABILITY OBJECTIVE

This box focuses on the Fed's and the ECB's monetary policy mandates, knowing that they also perform other duties related to, for example, payment systems or the supervision of credit institutions.

The key difference between the Fed's and ECB's monetary policy mandate is the triple (but dual in practice) objective for the Fed and the single goal for the ECB. However, there are more similarities than differences between the objectives of the two institutions.

Legal basis

The legal basis for the mandate of the Fed is different, from the hierarchy of rules perspective, from that of the ECB. The Fed's mandate is set in a law, the Federal Reserve Act approved by the US Congress in 1913 and last modified in 1977. The ECB's mandate is laid down in an international treaty, the Maastricht Treaty approved in 1992, and later in the TFEU approved in 2007.

Policy objectives

The Fed is assigned with three policy objectives while the ECB is responsible for a primary objective.

The US Congress has entrusted the Fed with the mandate to achieve three specific goals: 'maximum employment, stable prices, and moderate long-term interest rates' (Federal Reserve Act, Section 2A.1). In the USA, the focus is, in practice, on the Fed's dual mandate of price stability and maximum employment, as long-term interest rates are likely to be moderate when prices are stable.

According to Article 127 TFEU, the primary objective of the ECB is to *maintain price stability*. Without prejudice to this objective, the ECB supports the general economic policies in the EU with a view to contributing to the achievement of the objectives of the EU, such as full employment and balanced economic growth.

However, both institutions consider that the main permanent effect of monetary policy is on the price level while real activity can only be affected temporarily

(Yellen 2016).[1] Therefore, both the Fed and the ECB consider that the inflation rate over the longer run is primarily determined by monetary policy. This conclusion tends to put the price stability objective in a privileged position, also in the USA.

The former Chair of the Fed, Janet Yellen, wrote in 1996:

> In my view, the appropriate primary long-term goal for the Federal Reserve should be price stability, an objective which one no one would deny is within the power of the central bank to accomplish. (p. 1)

But then she added:

> [S]tabilization of output and employment is a second appropriate goal for the Federal Reserve . . . there is no conflict whatever between pursuing price stability as the primary long-term goal while simultaneously operating to help stabilize the economy's real economic performance' (pp. 3–4)

Hierarchy of objectives

In the legal formulation, the Fed's objectives stand on equal footing and are viewed as generally complementary, while the TFEU establishes a formal hierarchy of objectives for the ECB. Indeed, the Treaty assigns overriding importance to price stability. In the logic of the TFEU, price stability is the most important contribution that monetary policy can make to achieve growth and a high level of employment.

Monetary policy strategy

The ECB's monetary policy strategy was announced in 1998 and amended in 2003. It comprises, first, a quantitative definition of price stability; second, a two-pillar (economic and monetary) approach to the analysis of the risks to price stability.

In January 2012, the FOMC released a 'Statement on Longer-Run Goals and Monetary Policy Strategy', elaborating on its longer-run goals and its strategy for setting monetary policy. This statement is reviewed every year and was slightly amended in January 2016 to refer to the symmetry of the price stability objective.

Definition of price stability

Both the Fed and the ECB have provided a broadly similar definition of price stability that encompasses three features: quantification, time horizon, and symmetry.

The ECB has defined price stability as a year-on-year increase in the HICP for the euro-area, of below, but close to, 2 per cent over the medium term. The ECB added the qualification of 'close to 2 per cent in 2003 for three reasons: first, to provide a sufficient safety margin guarding against the risks of deflation; second, to take into account a possible measurement bias in the HICP; and, third, to recognize the implications of

(continued)

---

[1] However, discussing the evidence brought about by the Great Recession, Janet Yellen advanced the possibility that monetary policy could also affect growth in a sustained way because of the so-called 'hysteresis effect'.

Box 1 CONTINUED

---

inflation differentials within the euro-area. The ECB has formulated its objective in terms of headline inflation because it is the relevant measure of consumers' purchasing power and is consistent with the medium-term orientation of its monetary policy, which focuses on underlying inflation trends and looks beyond transitory developments.[2]

In the USA, the FOMC has defined stable prices as an annual rate of increase of 2 per cent in the price index for personal consumption expenditures (PCE) over the longer run. In practice, the FOMC focuses on inflation derived from the PCE index excluding food and energy (core PCE), as illustrated in the FOMC's Summary of Economic Projections. The reason for this exclusion is because food and energy items are highly volatile and their price changes are expected to correct over a short period of time. The core PCE is seen as a measure of underlying inflation trends and a predictor of future headline PCE inflation.

Both institutions have underlined that their objective is symmetric and that inflation above or below 2 per cent is inconsistent with price stability.

The FOMC did not define a numerical indicator for its employment goal, consistent with the belief mentioned that the maximum level of employment is largely determined by factors other than monetary policy. However, the FOMC members provide their projections for the long-run rate of unemployment four times per year in the FOMC's Summary of Economic Projections. The FOMC did not define moderate long-term interest rates in a numerical manner either, but consider, as mentioned, that this objective can be reached through anchoring longer-term inflation expectations at a level close to its inflation objective.

Benefits of the definition of price stability

Both institutions justify the publication of their definition of price stability by the benefits it brings in terms of guiding the public in forming their expectations of future price developments, anchoring longer-term inflation expectations, and ensuring transparency and accountability.

Sources:
ECB—Monetary Policy <http://www.ecb.europa.eu/mopo/html/index.en.html>
Federal Reserve—Conducting of monetary policy.

Christophe Beuve

The most basic tool available to central banks is the monopoly right to create a means of universal settlement (money in its most essential form) and thus to determine short-term interest rates. Over time, including during the Great Recession, there have been attempts to endow central banks with

---

[2] President Draghi recalled these features at the ECB's press conference on 20 January 2017. 'We define our objective first of all [...] over a medium-term horizon. That's the relevant policy horizon. Second, it has to be a durable convergence [...]. Third, it has to be self-sustained. [...]. Fourth, it has to be defined for the whole of the euro-zone. I think these are the four features that always characterised our objective.'

additional tools. Such attempts have often related to simultaneous endeavours to add new objectives to the scope of central banks. The non-interest-rate tools have included exchange controls, the utilization of direct credit controls, like the Corset in the UK and the Massimale sul Credito e Vincolo di Portafoglio (Maximum Credit Expansion and Portfolio constraint) in Italy, as well as the newer so-called macro-prudential tools and, especially during the Great Recession, the management of the size of the balance sheet. None of the additional tools has achieved the same potency and generality of the interest rate, which means that multiple objectives create the risk of policy dilemmas: To which of the four mentioned objectives should the use of the interest rate instrument be targeted? Several cases of dilemmas have emerged in the history of central banks. In the 1970s, stagflation created a dilemma between the need to increase interest rates to fight inflation versus the need to lower them to foster economic activity. Easing the funding of the government often led to risking, or actually losing, price stability. This happened in the USA, until the so-called Accord between the treasury and the Fed in 1951. It also happened in Italy until the so-called divorce in 1981, when the Banca d'Italia was freed from the obligation to buy the auctioned treasury bills that were not purchased by banks. Competing objectives led to the hyperinflation of the 1920s in Germany and other countries. The maintenance of ultra-low interest rates to fight the risk of deflation or too low inflation in the aftermath of the Great Recession is feared, instead, to feed financial instability.

In practice, the previously mentioned four objectives fluctuated in the ranking order of central banks. Eventually, one objective tended to assume pre-eminence above all others. The rule seems to be that the most pressing problem forces a particular objective to the top of the rank.

Price stability emerged as the dominant objective in many central banks towards the end of the last century. The long march leading to this result started after money had lost its inefficient and costly, but sturdy, link to gold around the time of the First World War. The monetary technology used since the abandonment of the gold standard appeared incapable of avoiding a high degree of instability around a trend loss in the purchasing power of money.[3]

To provide a historical perspective, Figure 1.1 presents the development of consumer price levels in Italy, the UK, Germany, and the USA from 1861 to 2016.

Figure 1.1 demonstrates that during the Gold Standard era—that is, until the First World War—there was no secular increase, or decrease, of price levels.

---

[3] The expression 'monetary technology' is borrowed from Papadia and Välimäki (2011) and covers all the aspects of a monetary policy model, from the most strategic to the most operational ones. In this sense, it encompasses the concept of 'monetary regime', which only includes the high-level components of monetary policy.

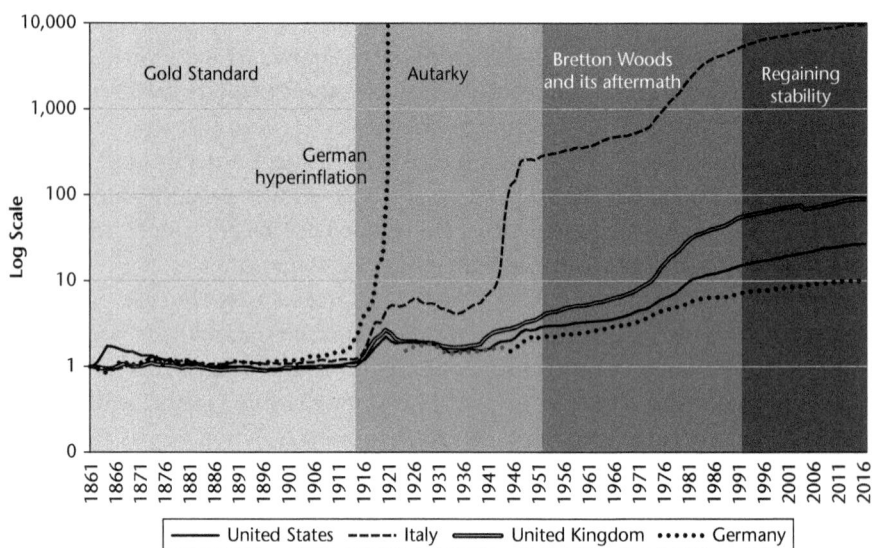

Figure 1.1 Consumer Price Levels in Italy, the UK, Germany, and the USA (1861–2016)

Source: Mitchell (1992); O'Donoghue, Goulding, and Grahame (2004); Italian National Institute of Statistics; OECD (2017); Main Economic Indicators data for recent times; Federal Reserve Bank of Minneapolis for US data.

Therefore, long-term price stability prevailed, even if there were large, medium-term price-level variations. Long-term stability, however, was lost after 1914, in the period characterized by economic and financial disintegration and the two world wars, which we denote as Autarky in Figure 1.1. This took place violently during the German hyperinflation in the 1920s, but also, albeit in less extreme form, in other countries. In Italy another extreme inflationary episode followed the Second World War. Moreover, price instability was also apparent in the 1970s and 1980s, especially in Italy and the UK, in the period following the demise of the Bretton Woods system. Only since the 1990s has there been a generalized recovery of price stability in advanced economies: until then, the monetary technology used after the abandonment of the gold standard was incapable of assuring it. The prominence of price stability among central bank objectives at the turn of the millennium thus results from decades-long dissatisfaction with the ability to properly control inflation.

Somewhat analogously, the emphasis on employment and growth among central bank objectives is clearly a consequence of the Great Depression. In particular, the awareness that the Fed had failed to counter the depression eventually led to identifying employment and growth as possible objectives. Nevertheless, it is not easy to find a period in which growth and employment really were at the top of the rank of objectives of central banks. A focus on employment and growth was most evident in the USA during the 1960s (Bordo, 2007), under the influence of Keynesian economics and counting on the stability of the Phillips curve. It was only in November 1977, however, when the US Congress amended the Federal Reserve Act, that the so-called dual objective (maximum employment and stable prices) was mandated on the Fed. Nevertheless, in practice, the price stability objective tended to prevail, because inflation was, and still is, seen as a monetary phenomenon at the end of the day, whereas monetary policy can hardly influence the long-term potential growth of an economy. Indeed, in 2012, the Federal Open Market Committee (FOMC) of the Federal Reserve noted that: 'the maximum level of employment is largely determined by non-monetary factors that affect the structure and dynamics of the labor market' (Plosser, 2013, p. 5).

In some cases, the funding of government budgets became the primary objective, at least de facto, when countries were under acute stress. This is seen in Figure 1.2, reporting the ratio of the size of the balance sheets relative to gross domestic product (GDP), for a number of central banks over a period somewhat longer than a century.

There are three peaks in the ratio. The first two, corresponding to the First and Second World Wars, are consistent with the inflationary developments displayed in Figure 1.1 and were determined by large-scale funding by the

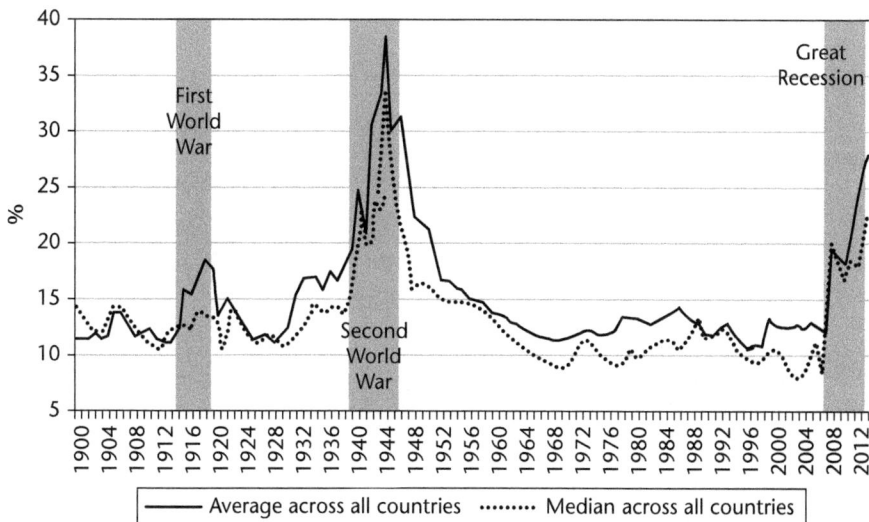

Figure 1.2 Size of the Central Bank Balance Sheets, as Percentage of each Country's GDP (1900–2012)

Source: This figure was drawn from data kindly provided by Professor M. Schularick. See Schularick, Ferguson, and Schaab (2015).

central bank of the government deficits. The peak is particularly high in the case of the Second World War, indicating the substantial financial and economic effort imposed on the nations at war. In addition, central banks were, during the First World War, still somewhat under the constraint of the gold standard, even if it was already fraying by that time. Interestingly, the third peak takes place during the Great Recession. According to this indicator, the Great Recession caused an economic stress of a similar order of magnitude as those caused by cataclysmic events like the two world wars.

Important differences obviously existed between the Great Recession and the experiences of the First and Second World Wars. First, during the Great Recession, it was not a necessity to fund national governments by monetary means that led to the very large increase of central bank balance sheets. Additionally, the recent huge expansion of central bank balance sheets did not bring about inflation; rather, the opposite risk of too low inflation has prevailed. Moreover, interest rates have declined even lower in the Great Recession than during the Gold Standard era, as can be seen in Figure 1.3, and indeed, in some cases, have even become negative. Whereas the need to finance wartime debt resulted in significant increases of inflation, the balance sheet expansions during the Great Recession should be seen as responses to deflationary developments in situations where the leeway of conventional monetary policy accommodation had been exhausted because of the nominal interest rates approaching zero. Interest rates as low as those prevailing in

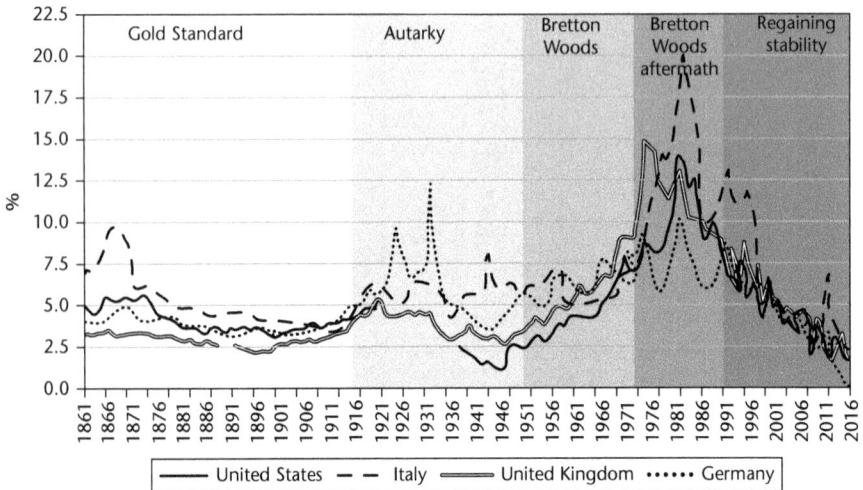

Figure 1.3 Long-Term Interest Rates in Italy, the UK, Germany, and the USA (1861–2016)

Source: Sylla and Homer (2005; Fratianni and Spinelli (2000). ECB Statistical Data Warehouse.

recent years are unprecedented. In fact, over the course of the last 150 years, interest rates have never been so low.

For the countries that have even longer time series one does not find nominal rates as low as those appearing during the Great Recession, even going back centuries.[4]

In Figure 1.4, long-term nominal interest rates are reported for two countries now in the euro-area, France and the Netherlands. Figure 1.5 gives long-term nominal rates for the USA and the UK. The two figures show that nominal long-term interest rates are at their lowest levels since

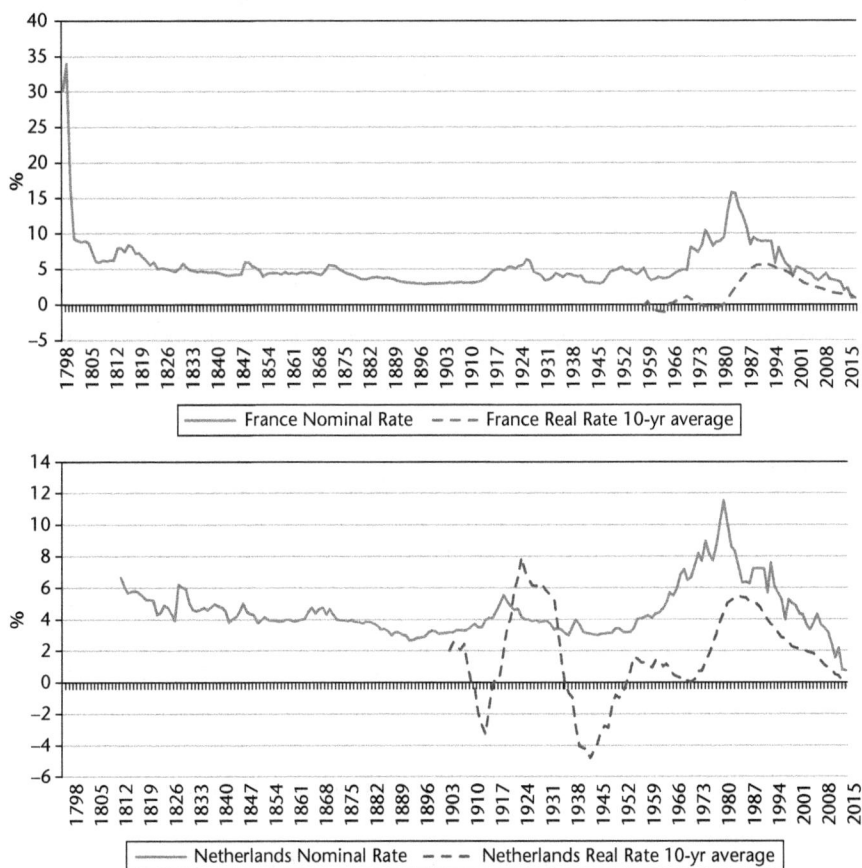

Figure 1.4 Multi-Secular Behaviour of Long-Term Interest Rates: France and the Netherlands (*c*.1798–2015)

Source: Sylla and Homer (2005); ECB Statistical Data Warehouse.

---

[4] The very long-term series presented here were analysed in Papadia (2016c).

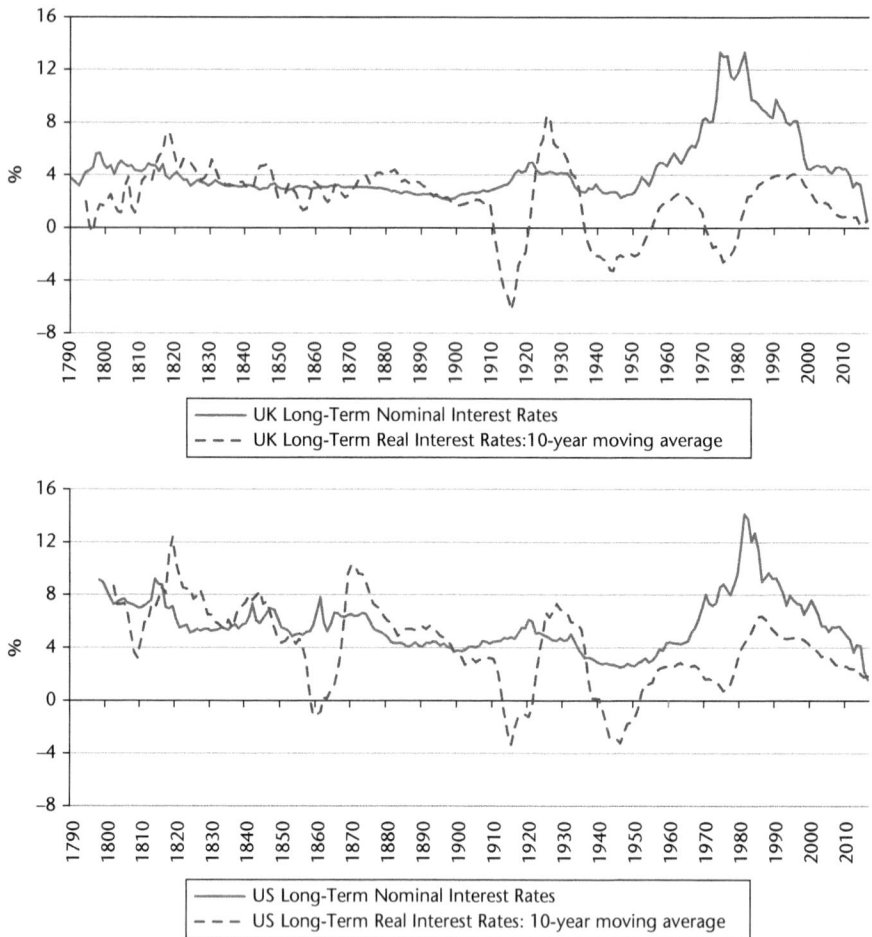

Figure 1.5 Multi-Secular Behaviour of Long-Term Interest Rates in the UK and the USA (*c*.1790–2015)

Source: Officer (2015). 'What Was the Interest Rate Then?' Available at: <https://measuringworth. com/>.

sufficiently accurate recordings were made, stretching back to the end of the eighteenth century.

The behaviour of real interest rates has been, for extended periods of time, different from that of nominal rates because of inflation developments. In a number of cases, in the UK, the USA, France, and the Netherlands, real rates were even negative. These low or negative real interest rates, appearing in periods with very high inflation, in most cases corresponded to wars or economic crises.

In the multi-secular perspective presented in Figures 1.4 and 1.5, another interesting phenomenon is evident: the exceptionally high level of nominal interest rates in the 1970s and 1980s, preceding the exceptionally low level in the mid-2010s.

One can try and see whether the two phenomena observed in the previous Figures—exceptionally high rates in the 1970s and exceptionally low rates now—are confirmed looking even further back in the past. Of course, the information on interest rates available for the last five millennia is scarce and imprecise. With some hesitation, historical data are reported in Figure 1.6, again using the data gathered by Homer and Sylla (1991).

Even looking back over the past 5,000 years, Figure 1.6 shows that it is hard to find interest rates below 1 per cent, let alone at zero. Going through Babylonian, Greek, Roman, Medieval, Renaissance, and modern times there are periods of low rates, but not as low as during the Great Recession.

Of course, a more in-depth review of historical records might reveal episodes of even lower rates. For instance, Giraudo (2016) reported that, in AD 33, Emperor Tiberius introduced zero interest rates in response to financial panic throughout the Roman Empire. Still, the overwhelming evidence is that rates are currently as low, or even lower, than they have ever been since interest rates started to be measured, millennia ago.

Table 1.1 shows a multi-secular average for the selected countries covered in Figures 1.4 and 1.5. The findings indicate that for around the last 230 years, the average long-term nominal rate across the four countries has

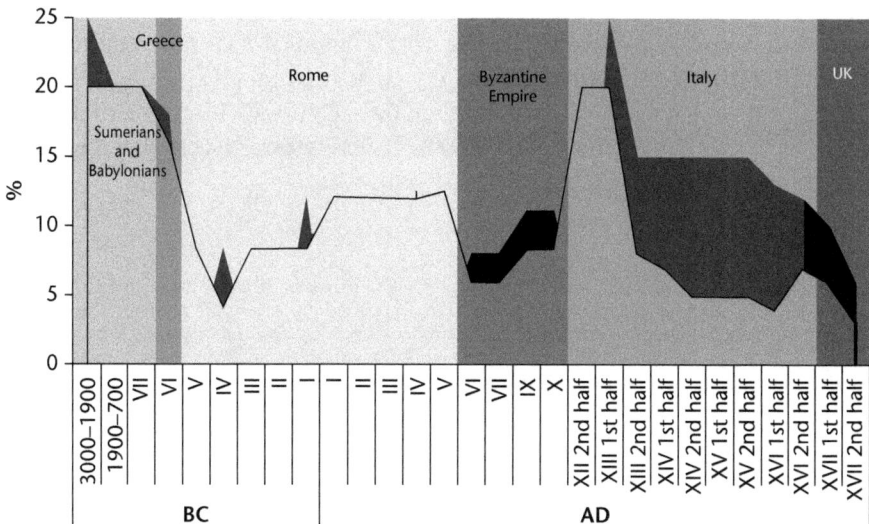

Figure 1.6 Nominal Interest Rates, Millennia Perspective (c.3000 BC–1700 AD)

Source: Sylla and Homer (2005); ECB Statistical Data Warehouse. Where available higher and lower rates are reported.

Table 1.1 Average of Short- and Long-Term Interest Rates between the Turn of the Eighteenth Century and 2015

	Long-term interest rate	Short-term interest rate
USA	5.74	3.21
UK	4.39	4.01
France	5.62	3.54
Netherlands	4.99	. . .[(*)]

Note: [(*)] Data not available.
Source: Officer (2015).

been about 5.5 per cent, whereas short-term interest rates have approximated 3.5 per cent. The difference between these figures indicates an average term premium of about 2 per cent. During the Great Recession, with both long-term and short-term interest rates approaching zero, we are, of course, far below historically prevailing averages.

Whereas price stability climbed in the priorities of central banks because of the persistence of high and variable inflation, financial stability, on the other hand, fell in the ranking of central bank objectives after the Second World War, as noted by Bernanke (2013).[5] This change in central bank priorities can also be explained by historic developments. As Bordo (2007) and Reinhart and Rogoff (2009) stressed, the Fed was created in 1913 to deal with the financial instability that had characterized the previous 80 years of American history, following two failed attempts to institute a central bank in the USA.[6] During the Bretton Woods period, and even after its demise, financial stability issues became less visible as tight regulation of the financial sector seemed to have dealt, once and for all, with banking crises, at least in advanced economies. This appears in Figure 1.7, which is drawn from Figure 13.1 in C. Reinhart and K. Rogoff, *This Time Is Different* (2009).[7] This figure suggests that systemic

---

[5] 'In particular, during much of the [post] World War II period, because things were relatively stable, because financial crises were things that happened in emerging markets and not in developed countries, many central banks began to view financial stability policy as a junior partner to monetary policy. It was not considered as important. It was something to which they paid attention, but it was not something to which they devoted many resources' (p. 121).

[6] 'After recurring bouts of financial panics and banking crises, and a particularly severe one in 1907, a clamour arose among policy circles and the business community that the United States was in need of serious banking and currency reform' (Reinhart and Rogoff, 2009, p. 48).

'As the opening line of the Federal Reserve Act clearly articulates, financial stability took centre stage in the initial mandate of the United States' central bank. While the Federal Reserve Act defined the supervisory duties of the Fed, there is no mention of a price stability mandate in the original version of the legislation. Indeed, the word inflation does not appear at all in the document. A full employment macroeconomic goal is not even remotely alluded to' (Reinhart and Rogoff, 2009, p. 48).

[7] The time series was kindly provided by C. Reinhart.

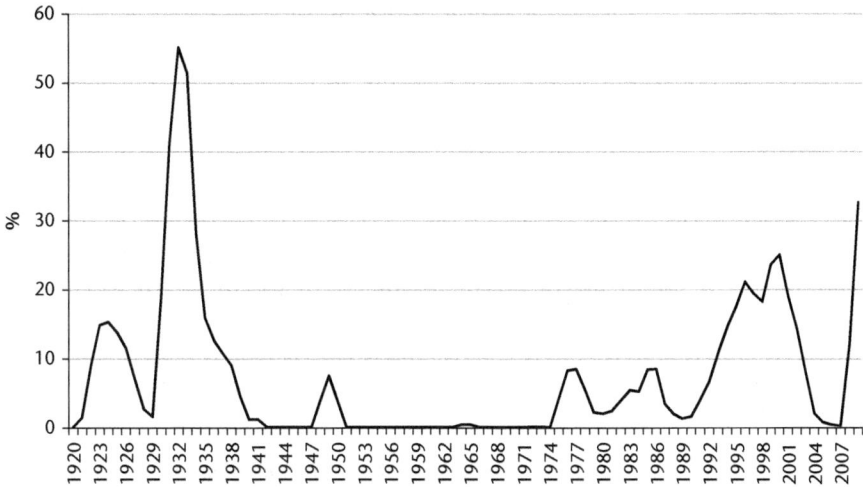

Figure 1.7 Share of Countries with Systemic Banking Crises (1920–2007)

Source: This figure was drawn from data kindly provided by Professor C. Reinhart from her book with K. Rogoff. Reinhart and Rogoff (2009).

banking crises were nearly absent for half a century between the beginning of the Second World War and the beginning of the 1990s.

In conclusion, the evidence of 'Shifting Mandates', as described by Reinhart and Rogoff (2013), extends beyond the Fed, as it is a characteristic of a number of central banks. This has led some authors, such as Goodhart (2010), to identify epochs in the history of central banks. It is difficult, however, to identify clear epochs that would apply across countries. It is fair to say, though, that at the end of the past century there was a predominant central bank model in the era that Goodhart defines as the 'Triumph of Markets from 1980 to 2007'. Section 1.2 will present this model.

1.2 Dominant Central Bank Model before the Crisis

The dissatisfaction with the monetary technology that followed the abandonment of the gold standard was presented in Section 1.1. In particular, it highlighted the difficulty of avoiding high variability and a secular trend of inflation, continuously eroding the purchasing power of money. This dissatisfaction served as the main motivation for the prevalence of price stability as a key objective assigned to central banks towards the end of the last century. This general motivation, however, can be articulated using four more specific factors.

The first factor was empirical evidence, according to which independent central banks devoted to price stability—like the Deutsche Bundesbank, created after the Second World War—controlled inflation better than central banks not sharing these characteristics (as seen previously in Figure 1.1). Barro and Gordon (1983) have provided the theoretical underpinning for this empirical result.

A second factor pushing price stability to the top of the objectives assigned to central banks is the evidence that the Phillips curve shifts towards a less favourable inflation–unemployment trade-off, along the theoretical analyses of Friedman (1968) and Phelps (1968), when economic policy seeks to reduce unemployment while accepting a higher rate of inflation (see Box 2).

Box 2 CHANGES IN THE PHILLIPS CURVE

The Phillips curve depicts the perceived inverse short-run relation between changes in prices and unemployment. Phillips (1958) observed that a lower level of unemployment was consistent with higher inflation in the UK between 1867 and 1957. Samuelson and Solow (1960) followed by showing similar patterns for the US economy.

The Phillips curve relation between the unemployment and the inflation rate was initially portrayed as a clear-cut downward sloping relationship, but this broke down in the 1970s with higher and more volatile inflation. The unemployment and inflation rates showed no correlation in the USA during the 1970–1999 period (Atkeson and Ohanian, 2000).

Samuelson and Solow further argued that the Phillips conjecture only prevails in the short run. Over the longer term, inflation expectations are internalized in wage negotiations and the natural level of unemployment is independent from changes in prices. Hence, money and monetary policy are neutral over the long term.

The natural (or non-accelerating inflation) rate of unemployment solely depends on factors such as demographics, technological change, and institutions. Despite the long-run neutrality of money, recent macroeconomic models assume prices to be sticky, thereby leaving room for the (expectations-augmented) Phillips curve to play a role.[8] The New-Keynesian Phillips curve employs a positive relation between current, past, and expected future inflation on one hand, and the difference between the economy's actual and potential output on the other.[9] Thus, a negative relation between inflation and unemployment is still assumed to prevail.[10]

The early experience with Phillips curve instability drove a shift to using changes in the inflation rate rather than inflation itself as the basis for the Phillips relation. When the unemployment rate was regressed against changes in the inflation rate in the period 1960–1983, Atkeson and Ohanian (2000) identified a non-accelerating inflation rate of unemployment (NAIRU) of 6 per cent for the USA. Inflation accelerates by 0.6 percentage points when unemployment falls to 5 per cent (i.e. 1 percentage point below the NAIRU). The slope of this kind of a Phillips curve implies an elasticity of changes in price or wage

---

[8] Phelps (1967) and Friedman (1968) both emphasized the role of expectations.
[9] The New-Keynesian Phillips curve has its roots in the works of Fischer (1977) and Taylor (1979).
[10] Mavroeidis et al. (2014) present a comprehensive survey of the New-Keynesian Phillips curve literature.

inflation to short-term changes in unemployment or the output gap. As the slope flattens, the 'sacrifice ratio' that the monetary policymakers face becomes larger, that is, a larger decline in the output gap is needed to achieve a certain reduction in inflation.

Notably, there is no theoretical basis that would explain why such a NAIRU Phillips curve should be considerably less prone to instability with changes in the economic environment and institutions than the original Phillips curve. Evidently, following the changes in the US monetary policy in 1984, the volatility of both inflation and the output gap decreased markedly. According to the 1960–1983 regression, a US unemployment rate of about 4 per cent was associated with a 1 percentage point increase in inflation over the following year. The 1984–1999 regression implies only a one-quarter of a percentage point increase in inflation (Atkeson and Ohanian, 2000).

The weakening of the relationship between inflation and economic slack from the 1980s to the early years of the new millennium is well documented in the literature.[11] A popular explanation attributes the flattening of the slope of the Phillips curve—that is, prices becoming less sensitive to changes in unemployment and output gap—to better anchoring of inflation expectations. This relates to the increased prominence of price stability as the ultimate goal of monetary policy, as well as acceptance of the notion of granting independence to central banks in setting the monetary policy stance.[12]

Whereas the forward-looking nature of inflation expectations seems to limit the policymaker's possibilities to exploit the relation between inflation and unemployment, at the same time it opens the door for forward guidance and expectations management as means for implementing monetary policy. Moreover, tighter anchoring of inflation expectations can reduce inflation persistence. This may be beneficial for the policymaker, because the lower the inflation persistence, the easier it is for the monetary policymaker to look beyond stochastic shocks as those stemming from, for example, changes in oil prices.

As explained by Carlstrom and Fuerst (2008a), the timing of reduction in inflation persistence and the flattening of the Phillips curve in the USA suggest that the change may be a by-product of adjustments in monetary policy. In 1983, the Fed started to react more aggressively to inflation, which seemed, erroneously, to have caused changes in relationships underlying the Phillips curve. In order to expand output towards the increased potential, an inflation-targeting central bank should ease its monetary policy in reaction to a positive technology shock that puts downward pressure on prices, that is, a behaviour that lessens volatility of the output gap. Under these circumstances, technology shocks have a smaller effect on inflation and the output gap, and increase the relative importance of mark-up shocks that shift the Phillips curve and imply a decline in the measured slope of the curve.[13]

Carlstrom and Fuerst (2008a) note that the estimated slope of the Phillips curve does not seem to be historically unusual after controlling for changes in the long-run trend inflation. Inflation persistence, on the other hand, seems to have declined considerably

(continued)

---

[11] See e.g. Staiger, Stock, and Watson (2001).

[12] Tighter anchoring of inflation expectations has been advocated as a justification for the flattening of the Phillips curve by e.g. Williams (2006), Mishkin (2007), and Roberts (2006).

[13] Shifts in the curve impede the estimation of the curve. It is hard to identify from the data whether various price–quantity observations represent movements along the Phillips curve or whether the curve itself has shifted. According to Carlstrom and Fuerst, the latter may well be the case. See Carlstom and Fuerst (2008b) for discussion of the importance of mark-up and technology shocks behind the shifts in the Phillips curve.

Box 2 CONTINUED

---

after changes in the Fed's monetary policy reaction function in 1983. Similarly, Roberts (2006) concludes that changes in monetary policy not only account for most or all of the reduction in the slope of the Phillips curve, but also for a large portion of the reduction in volatility of the output gap.

Another frequently used justification for a decline in the slope of the Phillips curve relates to globalization.[14] Wynne and Kersting (2007) and Ihrig et al. (2007) do not find a significant relation between openness of trade and the slope of the Phillips curve, but the International Monetary Fund (IMF) (2006) shows a significant negative relation between global value chains and the slope of Phillips curves in some industrial countries.

Zaniboni (2011) expects global measures of resource utilization to be increasingly important in determining inflation, as the importance of global markets increases in the price-setting decisions of firms. The evidence for this is mixed, however. Gamber and Hung (2001) and Borio and Filardo (2007) see a significant role for foreign output gaps, while Ihrig et al. (2007) argue that there is little support for the 'globe-centric' approach after controlling for domestic factors. Kohn (2008) and Yellen (2006) caution that globalization is a phenomenon that needs to be analysed carefully, and its influence on inflation and monetary policy should not be overstated.

Changes in the functioning of the labour market may also have brought about changes to the slope of the Phillips curve since the start of the Great Recession, in the euro-area in particular. Labour costs may adjust either via changes in wages or in employment. When the crisis started, labour markets in the euro-area were quite rigid in many countries. In particular, nominal wages were sticky to the downside.[15] Hence, in the early years of the crisis, the adjustment tended to materialize more via higher unemployment.

According to Holden and Wulfsberg (2014), nominal rigidities may have already started having an impact at levels above zero, and they depend heavily on labour market institutions. They argue that changes to the institutions in several euro-area countries during the Great Recession should impact the slope of the Phillips curve as the reforms increase the elasticity of wages and prices in relation to changes in the level of unemployment. On the other hand, they warn that a high level of structural unemployment reduces the downward pressure on wages stemming from unemployment, that is, the unemployment gap may be smaller than the unemployment numbers indicate.

Tuomas Välimäki

Basically, experience showed that the original Phillips curve result—showing a stable relationship between inflation and unemployment—was due to the fact that, in the data sample Phillips used, inflationary expectations were stable. However, the attempts, particularly in the 1960s, to move along the curve towards less unemployment eventually caused a shift of the curve to

---

[14] See e.g. Bean (2007).   [15] See e.g. Dickens et al. (2007) or Messina et al. (2010).

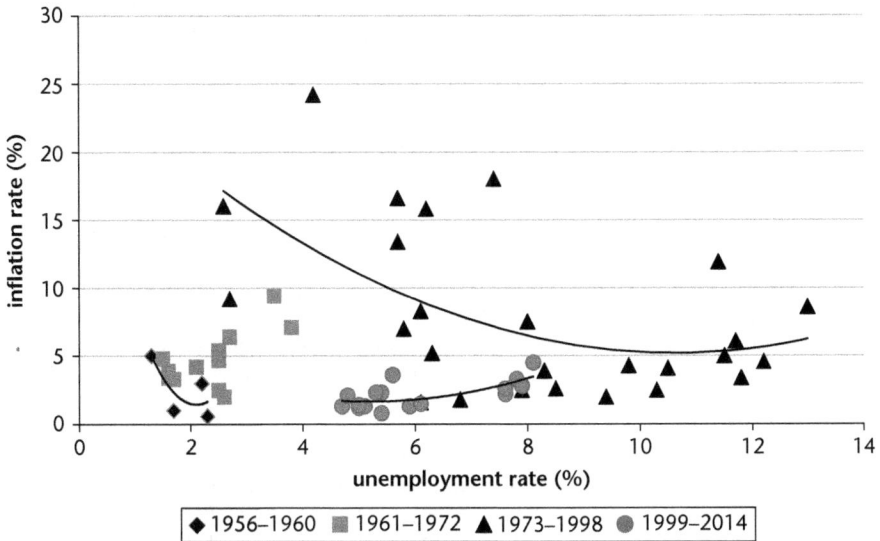

Figure 1.8 Inflation–Unemployment Trade-Off in the UK (1956–2014)

Source: OECD (2017), Main Economic Indicators (database); UK Office for National Statistics for data on unemployment rate until 1995.

the right, such that the damage to inflation was long term, whereas the gain in unemployment was only temporary. Figure 1.8 reports on the UK experience, where the favourable inflation/unemployment trade-off of the 1950s and 1960s gave way to the much less favourable outcome during the last three decades of the last century. A consequence of this finding was that, in line with the theoretical underpinning provided by Barro and Gordon (1983), an independent central bank devoted to price stability delivers better inflation control than a discretionary political process that is subject to running accommodative monetary policies prior to elections. Hence, as seen in Box 3, price stability is achieved without paying a cost in terms of reduced economic activity and higher unemployment. The relatively flat shape of the Phillips curve in the most recent period (1999–2014), with inflation around 2.5 per cent, shows that the constant inflation targets of central banks, anchoring inflationary expectations, became more important than unemployment in influencing inflation, and confirms the previous finding about the importance of anchored expectations delivered by an independent central bank.

The third factor leading to a gradual prevalence of the model of an independent central bank devoted to price stability was the growing awareness that, in the long run, volatile price developments hinder growth. Moreover, as the volatility of prices has been shown to grow with average inflation, a stable

---

Box 3 OVERCOMING INFLATIONARY BIAS THROUGH CENTRAL BANK INDEPENDENCE

The Bundesbank model, whereby an independent central bank devotes itself to stable, low inflation, has garnered considerable praise for providing price stability in the decades following the Second World War. The model today has many proponents, but independence per se would likely not have become the new orthodoxy in central banking without a boost from academic research on the inflationary bias of discretionary monetary policy.[16]

The theoretical underpinnings of central bank independence can be seen from three perspectives (Eijffinger and De Haan, 1996).

First, under the *public-choice argument* à la Buchanan and Wagner (1977), monetary policy decision-makers appointed by elected politicians face pressure to defer to the preferences of politicians. Such personal dependence risks exposing monetary policy to Nordhaus (1975) political business cycles. Elections might be preceded by calls for easier monetary policy to increase output briefly or provide tax cuts at the expense of increased inflation. This sort of inflationary bias could be overcome through appropriate procedures in appointing the monetary policy decision-makers. Such procedural protections include setting board terms of the central bank longer than the frequency of political elections and making such posts non-renewable, to reduce the incentive to align monetary actions with the short-term preferences of elected politicians. For example, ECB executive board members are limited to a single term of eight years.

Second, even if the personal independence of the monetary policymaker is procedurally protected, it only fulfils the basic prerequisite for independent monetary policymaking. The fiscal authority may still be free to allow budget deficits without influence from monetary policy considerations—the 'unpleasant monetary arithmetic' described in Sargent and Wallace (1981).

In a world where central bankers cannot affect the constraints on budget deficits, fiscal dominance emerges and the money supply eventually becomes endogenous. Here, the fiscal policymaker can be seen as the Stackelberg leader. As a Stackelberg follower, the monetary authority defers to fiscal decisions, and strives only to deliver a seigniorage stream sufficient to cover the deficit stream on the fiscal side. As there is an upper limit for the public's ability to absorb government debt, the government budget constraint at some point must be met with money creation. At the end of the day, when the fiscal authority gains the ability to determine long-run money supply, inflation becomes a fiscal phenomenon.

The Sargent and Wallace view, which puts fiscal and legal independence of the central bank at the forefront, assumes that the bank's ability to resist pressure to finance government deficits increases with its independence. The monetary authority can even assume the role of Stackelberg leader in policy coordination if there is a legal mandate that clearly forbids elected central bank officials from getting involved with monetary financing. Such legal protections are included in the TFEU, which prohibits EU central banks from having credit facilities with EU public entities or making direct purchases of debt instruments issued by public entities.

---

[16] For a thorough review of the issues relating to central bank independence, see Cukierman (1992). A comprehensive assessment of evolution of economics and political economy of monetary policy in recent decades is provided in Eijffinger and Masciandaro (2014).

The third theoretical perspective supporting the use of independence as a way to lower the monetary authority's inflation bias emerges from the time-inconsistency literature initiated by Kydland and Prescott (1977) and later turned into a monetary policy application by Barro and Gordon (1983).

The issue behind the dynamic inconsistency problem arises when the ex ante best choice for a future period is different from the ex post optimal choice after the period has started. Specifically, the monetary policy decision-maker may have incentives to inflate the economy to increase output once the rest of the economy (the public) has locked in its behaviour. Yet the desired impact on the output and employment can be acquired only if the inflationary impulse comes as a surprise. As long as the public behaves rationally in a forward-looking manner, it foresees the discrepancy between the monetary policymaker's ex ante promises and the ex post optimal actions. Hence, a discretionally operating monetary authority is unable to inflate the economy unexpectedly. Eventually the economy has higher equilibrium inflation without gains on the output front that would have been possible if the monetary policymaker had been able to commit to the ex ante optimal policy from the outset.

The standard time-inconsistency problem relates to the question of whether the policymaker should use rules rather than discretion. Once uncertainty is introduced into the economy, however, the task of designing a monetary policy rule that produces an optimal outcome is non-trivial.

Handing monetary policy power to an independent (apolitical) central bank may be thought of as a partial commitment method (Rogoff, 1985). Here, the key issue is whether the technocratic monetary policymaker takes a longer perspective than that of a typical politician. Other than because of differences in time preference, the monetary policymaking authority could be delegated to a central banker under orders to give higher subjective weight to stabilizing inflation over output.

Moreover, there are several ways to assure the conservativeness of the central banker's preferences. A simple approach is to impose a legal mandate spelling out goals for the central bank. The ECB's mandate unambiguously defines the preferences for various goals in lexicographic order. It clearly sets price stability as the primary policy goal, but grants the ECB a degree of goal independence. For example, the Governing Council of the ECB, operating under such a mandate, gets to define and quantify 'price stability'.

Another approach is to lock in central bank policies on maintaining price stability through a contractual arrangement between the government and the central bank decision-maker. Under the system in New Zealand, for example, the governor of the central bank can be dismissed if inflation exceeds 2 per cent. In the UK, if inflation moves away from the target by more than 1 percentage point in either direction, the governor must explain to the government the reasons for the deviation and the actions that the Bank of England plans to pursue in bringing inflation back into the target range. In such cases, the central bank is not independent regarding its inflation goal, but free to choose the instruments it will apply in meeting its inflation objective. Here, the central bank is said to have *instrument independence*.

Central bank independence is closely related to the concept of accountability, that is, assuming liability for failure. Accountability is needed whenever a public task, such as making monetary policy, is handed over to an independent non-elected body. The combination of independence and accountability necessitates transparency towards the government and the public. An independent central bank that is accountable for its performance must pay close attention to explaining and motivating its actions.

Tuomas Välimäki

and low rate of inflation is the best environment for sustained growth. As Figure 1.9 documents, using data pertaining to more than three decades and including 190 countries, per capita income grows faster when inflation is contained within moderate values. Moderate values are considered here

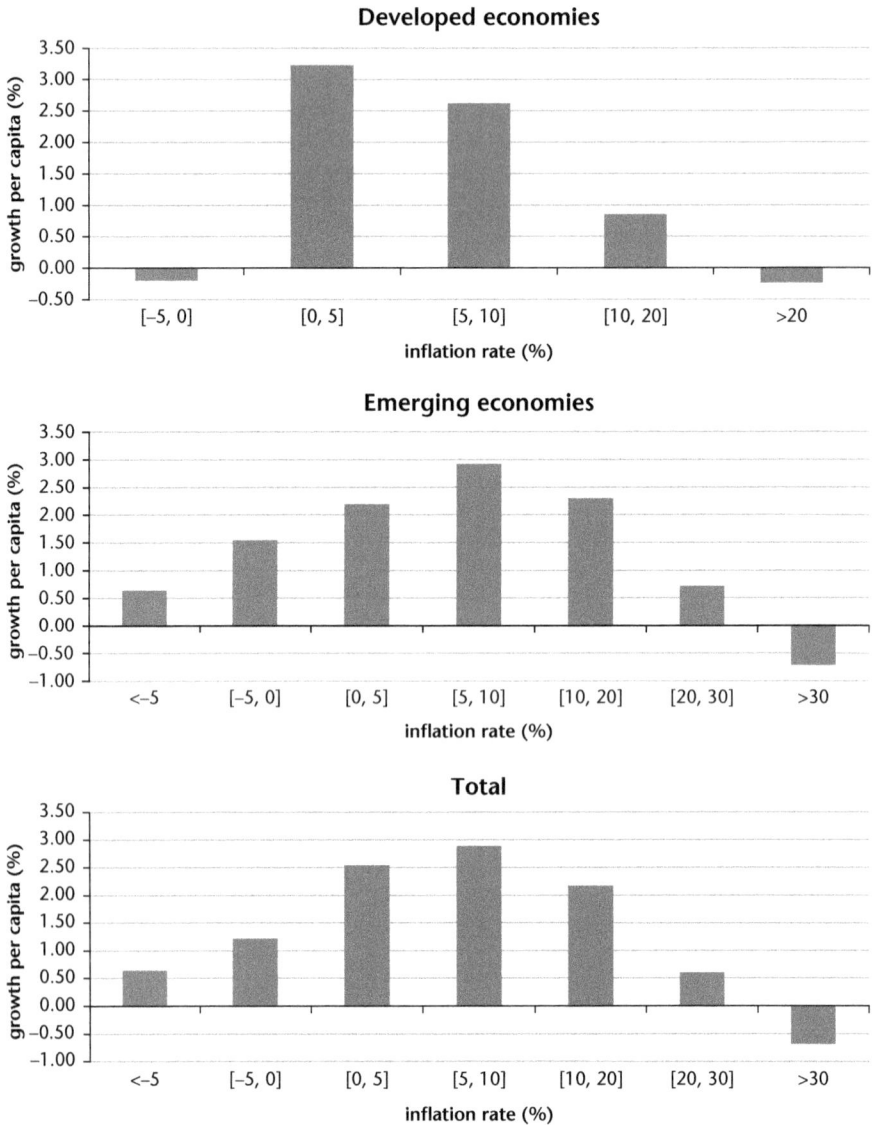

Figure 1.9 Distribution of Inflation Rates and Growth Per Capita (1980–2014)

Source: Author's calculations with IMF–World Economic Outlook data. The data refer to 36 advanced economies and 154 emerging economies for the 1981–2014 period.

between 0 and 5 per cent for developed economies, and between 5 and 10 per cent for emerging economies.

Even if, price stability cannot be seen as a sufficient condition to guarantee economic growth, it still favours growth. There are numerous costs of inflation that are, in the long run, obstacles to economic growth. These costs may come in the form of the so-called 'shoe leather' cost, due to the attempt to escape from the inflation tax by reducing money balances. In addition, unfair and unexpected redistributions of wealth between debtors and creditors, as well as between firms and workers, may also have negative impact on growth. Furthermore, the reduced ability of the price system to guide choices about consumption, investment, production, exports, and imports creates conditions whereby, in the long run, excessive inflation becomes an obstacle to growth (see Box 4).

Box 4 THE LONG-RUN EFFECT OF INFLATION ON GDP GROWTH

The long-run relation between inflation and growth has for a long time been a matter of debate.[17] In standard textbook models, like the aggregate demand–aggregate supply one, the effect of inflation on output depends on whether inflation is due to increasing demand or to shrinking supply. In the former case, the higher demand pushes up prices and quantities, whereas in the latter case price increases are associated with lower output, giving rise to stagflation phenomena.

In the economic models developed in the 1960s and 1970s, the argument that inflation reduces economic growth in the long run became prominent. The general idea was that high inflation has a negative effect on growth because of the uncertainty it adds to relative price changes. In periods of high inflation the signalling effect of relative price changes is weakened, leading to inefficient resource allocation and lower productivity dynamics (Lucas, 1973). In addition, uncertainty induces firms to postpone investments or to invest abroad, leading to a slowdown in the investment rate (Fischer, 1993). These arguments are grounded in the high inflation experience of the 1970s and 1980s and are based on the assumption that high inflation is an indicator of the governments' inability to stabilize the economy (Fischer, 1993).

This kind of literature acknowledges the possibility that, for relatively low inflation rates, the relation can be insignificant; however, its theoretical framework rules out the possibility of a positive 'optimal inflation rate'—defined as the one maximizing both the welfare of the representative consumer and macroeconomic stability. Standard models based on the non-neutrality of money find the optimal inflation rate to be either

(continued)

---

[17] In this box we consider only the long-run relation between inflation and growth. Short-run positive effects are associated with the inflation–unemployment trade-off derived from the Phillips curve. These effects are investigated in Box 2.

29

Box 4 CONTINUED

negative or zero (Schmidt-Grohe and Uribe, 2010). The former result is a consequence of the Friedman rule that states that, in a world with only nominal frictions as source of non-neutrality, the optimal inflation rate should be equal to the negative of the nominal interest rate. The optimal rate equal to zero is the result of non-neutrality due to sluggish price adjustment.

More realistic models introduce four channels through which low but positive inflation can be beneficial to growth, leading to a positive optimal rate. First, we focus on the zero lower bound (ZLB) for nominal interest rates. A positive inflation rate grants to the monetary authority room for manoeuvre on interest rates as stabilization tools (Summers, 1991). Second, in the case of zero inflation, relative price changes imply negative nominal price changes. With downward price rigidity such adjustments are costly. With a little positive inflation, relative price changes are facilitated (Tobin, 1972). This means that a positive inflation rate favours efficient relative price changes. Third, the measurement error implied in inflation estimates due to unobserved quality improvements and to the introduction of new products biases upward inflation measures. Standard inflation measures do not take into account price increases caused by quality improvements, leading to overestimation of consumer inflation by several decimal points (Schmidt-Grohe and Uribe, 2010). On a similar token, the introduction of new products in the basket used to calculate consumer inflation might lead to small upward biases in inflation estimates (Billi and Kahn, 2008). This latter effect is due to the fact that new products are usually introduced into the basket when they become of common use. For new technologies in particular, this means that the index does not reflect the massive price fall that these goods experience before becoming common, with the effect of biasing inflation estimates upward.

The fourth channel through which low but positive inflation can be beneficial to growth has to do with the costs associated with negative inflation, in particular for debt stabilization purposes. This is an important problem as deflation raises the real value of both public and private debt. This last argument is particularly important in light of both the current experience of European countries and of Japan. However, Borio et al. (2015) maintain that the costs of deflation are not high and they argue that this conclusion applies also to the deflation in the 2000s, following banks' balance sheet repair, once demographics are taken into account (per capita or per working-age population).

The empirical evidence does not provide precise conclusions on the optimal inflation rate, but tends to converge towards a low positive rate. The study of Billi and Kahn (2008) estimates a rate between 0.7 and 1.4 per cent for US PCE inflation during the Great Moderation to be optimal. Schmitt-Grohe and Uribe (2010) find that the optimal rate is either negative or insignificantly above zero. Due to the difficulties in identifying an optimal inflation rate, most of the studies focus on the estimation of threshold effects or non-linearities in the relation between inflation and growth. The estimates of threshold effect are based on the assumption that only after a certain level does inflation start to negatively affect long-run growth.[18] Most studies focus on developing countries because they usually set higher inflation targets, between 3 and 5 per cent, and are

---

[18] The threshold level does not necessarily coincide with the optimal rate but it provides an upper bound to it.

generally more subject to high inflation episodes. Among these studies, Bruno and Easterly (1996) find a negative relation between inflation and growth for rates above 40 per cent. However, Ghosh and Phillips (1998) find a negative relation even at rates around 10 per cent.

Among the studies on advanced economies, Kahn and Sendhadji (2000) estimate threshold effects for a sample of advanced and developing economies observed between 1960 and 1998, and find thresholds of 1 to 3 per cent for advanced economies and 7 to 11 per cent for developing ones. Above these levels inflation has a significant negative impact, whereas the effect is insignificant for rates below the threshold. Crespo-Cuaresma and Silgoner (2014) analyse the case of 14 EU countries before the creation of the monetary union and find two different critical levels for inflation: a first threshold at 1.6 per cent, below which inflation affects positively growth, and a second threshold of 15 per cent, above which the effect is negative and significant. Yet, when distinguishing between peripheral countries (Greece, Ireland, Portugal, and Spain, GIPS) and the rest of the EU, the second threshold for the latter group of countries falls to 3.5 per cent. This is explained by the catch-up of peripheral countries whose productivity increased at faster rates. Kremer, Bick, and Nautz (2013) find a slightly higher threshold for industrialized countries, around 2 per cent. Similarly, Ghosh and Phillips (1998) find that the relation between inflation and growth might be positive for rates below 3 per cent.

To sum up, the empirical literature finds optimal or threshold inflation rates in a range between 0 and 3.5 per cent for advanced economies. The choice of the optimal rate within this range then becomes a policy matter, depending on the specific prevailing economic conditions. A target rate is also useful to anchor the expectations of economic agents.

The relatively low estimates of the optimal inflation rate can be partially due to the fact that empirical studies consider a period including the stagflation era and the Great Moderation. The reduction of inflation has been associated with increased stability and higher economic growth, in particular during the years before the global financial crisis, when central banks were most effective in maintaining their 2 per cent target. Low thresholds might also be due to the theoretical models underlying the estimations, since they define the empirical specification used in the estimates. For example, most of the New-Keynesian literature gives little importance to the ZLB problem, as it considers welfare gains arising from low and stable inflation to overweigh the cost of hitting the ZLB (Coibion, Gorodnichenko, and Wieland, 2012). However, after the global financial crisis, interest rates have been around zero for a number of years in the USA and in the euro-area. This has forced central banks to use unconventional instruments, whose effectiveness in stimulating the economy is somewhat controversial.

The latter point is made clear by Ball (2014), who proposes a 4 per cent inflation target for the USA, based on the experience of the global financial crisis. The author shows that in 2009 the zero interest rate for the Fed funds was above the required level by 5 percentage points, leading to substantial costs. The same conclusion is reached by looking at Taylor-rule-consistent rates. As shown in Figure 2.7 in Chapter 2, the US interest rate in 2009 should have been between −4 per cent and −5 per cent. In addition, Ball criticizes the assumption of mainstream models that the ZLB is rarely hit. He shows that if the Fed had followed the 2 per cent rule for inflation, the ZLB would have been hit three times during the recessions that occurred between the early 1970s and the 1980s.

(continued)

Box 4 CONTINUED

The important question Ball raises is whether a higher inflation target would have reduced the size and length of the economic downturn, attenuating the reduction in the rate of investment to GDP, with negative effects on the rate of growth of potential output. More room for lowering rates during the recession, because of a higher inflation target, would not only have reduced the need to rely on QE but could also have increased its effectiveness.

This argument applies to the USA, where the rate stayed at the lower bound between 2009 and 2015. The three rounds of QE were indeed effective in bringing the economy out of the recession; however, low rates risked fuelling speculative activities in emerging as well as domestic markets. Again, with higher target inflation and thus higher policy rates this could have been partially avoided.

In conclusion, the issue is open whether it would be useful to raise the inflation target from its current level of 2 per cent. Two important, and contrasting, considerations have to be balanced here: first, the empirical evidence does not find any negative effect on growth from long-run inflation rates slightly higher than 2 per cent, for instance of 3 or 4 per cent. Second, there is a value in the fact that expectations and behaviour of economic agents have focused, after a long period of learning, on the specific 2 per cent value; it would not be simple to now move them to another value, however close, and the credibility of the new target may be affected by the change. The issue is further dealt with in Section 3.3.

Piero Esposito

The fourth factor leading to the model of an independent central bank devoted to price stability was not of an economic, but rather of an institutional and legal, nature. Any trade-off between different objectives affecting the social welfare of a country's citizens requires, in a democracy, political legitimacy. This is a prerogative of the government and the parliament, not of the central bank. For instance, if the short-term Phillips curve held constant when augmented with expectations, there would be a permanent trade-off between employment and inflation. Choosing between the two objectives would require a political judgement that the central bank, a technocratic institution, may not make. Hence, the consequence would be that the central bank should be directed in its action by the government. However, once a stable relation between inflation and employment vanishes, a trade-off between the two objectives reduces to an optimization problem with only one variable. When one objective, such as price stability, is assigned as the sole objective of the central bank, the need for a political choice disappears. Only the technical problem of the best way to achieve the objective remains, a role that an independent, technocratic institution is best able to carry out. In a way, the central bank is freed from the day-to-day discretional direction from the government but is fully dependent on the law (in the case of the euro-area, the Maastricht Treaty), which prescribes price stability as the dominant objective of the central bank.

Of course, solving the 'democratic deficit' issue becomes somewhat more difficult if one interprets the Fed mandate as a fully fledged dual one, in which price stability and maximum employment have comparable weights. The resulting 'balanced approach' would inevitably require some economic and political arbitrage between the two different objectives. It was mentioned in Box 1 that the similarities are more important than the differences and that, beyond the letter of the law, one can assume that the price stability objective also for the Fed takes de facto priority over the unemployment objective. In any case, the independence of the Fed is enhanced by a number of provisions, such as a long tenure for Fed governors and the largely independent district bank presidents. Still, one could interpret its institutional set-up as offering a lower degree of protection of its independence, because it could receive at any time directions from a political body, such as the US Congress.

The clearest example of the prevalence of the model of an independent central bank devoted to price stability was the agreement that the institution created to bring monetary union in Europe would be modelled on the Deutsche Bundesbank. One could say that the Maastricht Treaty gave an institutional basis, embodied in the ECB, to the de facto monetary leadership until then exercised by the Deutsche Bundesbank. (See Box 5.)

1.2.1 *Inflation Targeting*

The model of central banking prevailing towards the end of last century was not only specified in terms of institutional set-up and overall objectives, it also included a general agreement on the strategy to be pursued and even the gradual convergence towards a common operational approach.

In terms of strategy, the encompassing approach took the form of inflation targeting. Invented in 1990 in New Zealand, this approach gradually prevailed in advanced economies. Inflation targeting comes in many variants, but there are some basic components that distinguish it from other approaches.

Some central banks claimed that they did not follow inflation targeting, despite pursuing actions that essentially fell within that approach. A case in point is the ECB, which refused the name of inflation targeting for its monetary policy strategy. Nevertheless, as illustrated in Box 6, the ECB's two-pillar approach, particularly after the revision in 2003, can be considered a variant of a broad concept of inflation targeting. The essence of this approach is that the central bank either tightens or loosens monetary policy depending on whether it sees inflation rates in the medium run to be higher or lower

---

Box 5 THE 'SNAKE–EMS–ERM' EXPERIENCE AND DEUTSCHE BUNDESBANK LEADERSHIP

The most important dates of the Snake–EMS–ERM experience are presented in the following timeline.

A synthetic timeline

Aug. 1971   The dollar is no longer convertible at fixed price into gold.

Mar. 1972   The so-called Snake is created, linking the currencies of a number of European countries in an attempt to stabilize them.

Mar. 1973   The generalized fluctuations of currencies is decided in the so-called Smithsonian Agreements.

Jan. 1974   France withdraws from the Snake.

May 1975   France returns to the Snake.

Mar. 1976   France leaves the Snake again.

Mar. 1979   The European Monetary System (EMS) is created.

Apr. 1989   The Delors Report, the blueprint of monetary union, is completed.

Feb. 1992   The Maastricht Treaty is signed.

Sept. 1992   EMS crisis: Italian lira and British pound abandon the system; the currencies of Spain, Portugal, and Ireland are devalued within the system.

Aug. 1993   Another EMS crisis: the margins of fluctuation allowed in the system are increased.

May 1998   The European Council decides that 11 countries will adopt the euro.

June 1998   The ECB is formally established.

Jan. 1999   The euro is introduced.

The three decades between the early 1970s, when the Bretton Woods system broke down, and the creation of the euro, in the late 1990s, can be seen as a long, accident-prone, but eventually successful, attempt by European countries to stabilize their currencies. Indeed, Papadia and Saccomanni (1994) even date Europe's 'stubborn quest for monetary union' to the middle of the nineteenth century, stressing both the difficulties of this quest as well as the determination to pursue it.

Stability was initially sought on a bilateral basis, one currency against the other, that is, in terms of exchange rates. It required a few decades before the crucial progress was achieved to focus on the aggregate price level, that is, achieving price stability as the basis of monetary union.[19]

In Figure B.5.1, one sees the behaviour of the exchange rate that most significantly summarizes this history: the one between the Italian lira, the weakest among the currencies of the large European countries over three decades, and the Deutschmark, which functioned as the hinge of the system. In Figure B.5.1 the exchange rate between

---

[19] This point was forcefully made by Padoa-Schioppa in 1994: 'The monetary history of Western Europe between 1973 and 1993 can be seen as the history of the rise and decline of a Deutschmark system. This had begun to emerge with the Snake after the collapse of the dollar system. It was extended and consolidated in 1978 with the creation of the EMS... Few today would dispute that the new

the lira and the Deutschmark is reported on log scale, the two broken lines represent ± two standard deviations in the preceding three years around the spot rate.

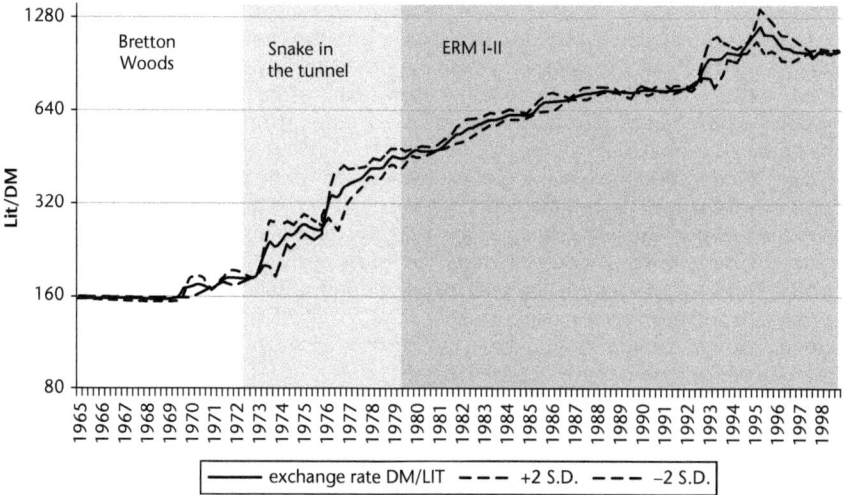

Figure B.5.1 Exchange Rate between the Italian Lira and the German Mark (1965–1998)

Note: the exchange rate is bracketed by two standard deviations above and below it, calculated over the previous three years.

Source: IMF–International Financial Statistics.

Three areas are distinguished in the figure: the first, corresponding to the final years of Bretton Woods, before the launch of the Snake, the second corresponding to the Snake, and the third corresponding to the Exchange Rate Mechanism (ERM) period. The figure highlights that at the beginning of the 1970s the lira started its trend depreciation against the German currency, which lasted practically uninterrupted until the second half of the 1980s, to be followed by a relatively short period of stability that came to an end at the beginning of the 1990s when the lira again depreciated sharply against the German currency. It was only at the end of the 1990s, just before the launch of the euro, that the exchange rate between the lira and the mark stabilized. The two standard deviation lines around the exchange rate followed a similar pattern, indicating stability in the Bretton Woods period, followed by persistent instability in the Snake and in the ERM period until the second half of the 1980s, followed by a few years of stability and then by the highest degree of

(continued)

monetary order brought about by the EMS with the help of the German currency contributed greatly to the extraordinary results achieved in the years that followed: the fall in inflation, the prolonged economic expansion, the development of intra-Community trade, and the completion of the internal market' (p. 15).

Box 5 CONTINUED

---

instability in the 1990s, until the lira returned to the ERM and then the euro was created in 1999.

The story of the exchange rate between the Italian and the German currencies confirms the difficulty of achieving exchange rate stability without a strong institutional basis: when this was no longer provided by the Bretton Woods system, decades of exchange rate instability followed, ending only with the creation of the euro.

Over the decades, there was a gradual recognition of the asymmetric nature of the European exchange rate arrangements. At the beginning, in particular with the Snake in 1972, but also in the initial years of the ERM, there was an attempt to build a fully symmetric system, considering all currencies equal, without privileging one over the others. This was apparent in the fact that a full grid of bilateral exchange rates was established and each central bank, independently of whether its currency was weak or strong, had to stabilize its exchange rate against all other currencies by means of interventions in the foreign exchange market.

Over time, however, there was increasing recognition that some currencies, in particular the Deutschmark, enjoyed a much better performance in terms of price stability than other currencies. Concurrently, price stability was establishing itself as the dominant objective of central banks. The Deutschmark, and therefore the Deutsche Bundesbank, gradually took a leadership role within the system.

The Deutsche Bundesbank leadership provided a temporary solution to the so-called 'inconsistent quartet' (Padoa-Schioppa, 1994), that is, the principle that it is not possible to simultaneously combine stable exchange rates, freedom of capital movements, national monetary policies, and free trade. In a slimmed-down version, the inconsistent quartet becomes a trio, with free trade dropping from the group. With capital account liberalization starting in 1987, the inconsistency of the quartet became even more evident. The temporary solution to the inconsistent quartet provided by the Deutsche Bundesbank leadership meant that all other central banks tended to follow its policies, thus giving up a national conduct of monetary policy. There was, however, an escape clause when one central bank did not manage to fully follow the Deutsche Bundesbank: realignments, whereby the central exchange rates of a currency in the grid were devalued. Indeed, the solution worked both ways: when a currency was too strong and the relevant central bank did not want to weaken it either through interventions or through a relaxation of monetary policy, it could revalue its central rates within the system. Realignments, however, were increasingly seen as undesirable and there was an attempt, not always successful, to reduce their occurrence.

In the ERM period, the emphasis progressively moved from stabilizing exchange rates towards stabilizing goods prices, mostly by managing interest rates. Thus, the policy focus moved from the external to the domestic side of monetary policy and to inflation. Moreover, interest rates and inflation in traditionally high inflation countries moved towards the lower levels prevailing in Germany, as can be seen, again for the Italian case, in Figure B.5.2. Indeed, after the peaks achieved between the end of the 1970s and the beginning of the 1980s, the difference between the Italian interest rate and inflation with respect to the same variables in Germany was irregularly but progressively reabsorbed, until the former reached values quite close to zero on the eve of the launch of the euro.

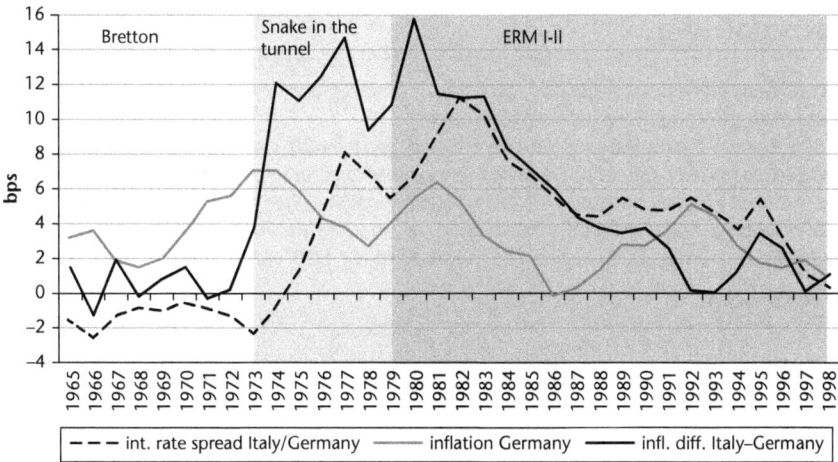

Figure B.5.2 Interest Rate Spread and Inflation Differential between Italy and Germany (1965–1998)

Source: European Commission, AMECO Database.

The move is even more remarkable as it was achieved at the time when Germany had returned to its inflation target, not higher than 2 per cent, after long periods in which it had exceeded it.

The enshrining of the Deutsche Bundesbank model as the basis of monetary union was decided, as mentioned, in Maastricht, when the eponymous treaty was approved in 1992. With that step it was decided to transform a national de facto leadership (which tried, with mixed success, through exchange rate constraints, to set the direction for monetary policy of the entire area) into an institutional set-up, establishing a unified monetary policy, embodied in the ECB and the euro.

The ERM did not completely disappear, however, as some non-euro currencies used the ERM to keep their currency stable against the euro. However, all participating countries, other than Denmark, eventually adopted the euro. Thus, the number of countries within the euro-area increased from 11 to 19, leaving only Denmark, in addition to euro-area countries, within the ERM.

The Maastricht Treaty, approved in 1992, cast in the Statute of the ECB all the characteristics credited with the success of the Deutsche Bundesbank. This includes protection against any temptation to fund, by money issuance, a government deficit. What had been in some circumstances the overriding objective of central banks was thus not merely demoted in importance, but actually prohibited. The growth objective was seen as mostly coincident with the price stability objective, given what experience had shown about the Phillips curve and the deleterious effect of inflation on long-term growth. The probability of conflicts between these two objectives was further reduced by the medium-term orientation of the price stability objective. However, if a dilemma appeared between price stability and growth, the logic was that the ECB should choose medium-term price stability, as the damage in terms of economic activity was seen as only temporary. Financial stability seemed to have been assured in advanced economies without any special action by central banks; after all, crises seemed mostly to affect emerging economies. Thus, the prevalence of the price stability objective was basically uncontroversial: the other possible objectives of the

(continued)

Box 5 CONTINUED

central bank were seen as redundant (growth), unnecessary (financial stability), or outright dangerous (funding of a national government).

The statute-based independence provided to the ECB can indeed be seen as fully fledged, as none of the national parliaments of the euro-area member states can change the mandate of the common monetary policymaker. Whereas a national parliament enjoys competence within its jurisdiction, a unanimous agreement between all EU countries is needed for changing the mandate of the ECB.

Francesco Papadia

Box 6 DIFFERENT VARIANTS OF INFLATION TARGETING

In 1990, New Zealand became the first country to introduce an explicit inflation target. It was soon followed by other advanced economies, including Canada and Australia. After the ERM crisis and the collapse of their exchange rate regimes, the UK, Sweden, and Finland joined the club in 1992 and 1993. By the end of the 1990s, inflation targeting had been adopted in over ten countries. That figure grew to almost 30 by 2008.

Three institutional elements are fundamental to this type of monetary policy framework: (1) the mandate for the central bank to aim for price stability and a quantification of a target for inflation; (2) central bank independence in pursuing its mandate and target; and (3) accountability, which calls for transparency and normally translates into making the inflation target public (Svensson, 2010).

A central bank that applies inflation targeting as its core monetary policy strategy uses various policy instruments to tighten or loosen economic and financial conditions to align inflation with its objective. Even if the central bank has a strong influence on price trends, economic developments and price changes can never be fine-tuned with such a precision to always meet the target. Moreover, no central bank applying inflation targeting could be regarded an 'inflation nutter'—the pejorative introduced by King to describe a policymaker interested only in stabilizing inflation (King, 1997). All central banks in advanced economies place weight on other economic variables such as unemployment and output. Using Lars Svensson's terminology, it would thus be correct to say that all inflation-targeting central banks are 'flexible' inflation targeters.

The degree of flexibility in applying the inflation-targeting regime varies with the credibility of the central bank. On the one hand, the more credible the central bank is, the more it can put weight on stabilizing other economic variables. On the other hand, the stricter the central bank is in pursuit of its inflation objective, the more credibility it gains.

As monetary policy affects the economy—and prices in particular—with a time lag, the setting of the monetary policy stance of an inflation-targeting central bank needs to be forward looking. Forward-looking monetary policy cannot be guided only by past or current economic variables. It needs to be based on forecasts, particularly the inflation forecast. Due to the central role given to forecasts in decision-making, they also impact the expectations of the public, thereby increasing their importance in monetary policy transmission.

According to King, the inflation forecast of an inflation-targeter can be seen as an intermediate target. In Svensson's terminology, inflation targeting is more appropriately called 'inflation-forecast targeting' or simply 'forecast targeting'. Some advanced inflation-targeting central banks promote *accountability* and *transparency*, publishing a forecast path for their policy instruments. New Zealand, again, was a forerunner on this front. Its central bank began to release the desired policy interest rate path in 1997. Norges Bank, the Sveriges Riksbank, and the Czech National Bank have since adopted this practice.

When the ECB's monetary policy strategy was being designed in the second half of the 1990s, a number of monetary policy strategies were considered. Many European countries had applied exchange-rate targeting prior to the monetary union, but this was rejected as inappropriate for a large and relatively closed economy like the euro-area. Practices of the Deutsche Bundesbank, applied before entering the monetary union, influenced the ECB's framework in many ways. However, one of the main reasons for not choosing German-style monetary targeting resulted from the considerable uncertainties about the empirical properties of money demand in the newly created currency area. But, as one did not wish to totally abandon the German tradition, and just jump to the inflation-targeting strategy that was gaining ground elsewhere, a two-pillar strategy was adopted. In this strategy, economic analysis is cross-checked with monetary developments (including both monetary and credit developments) within the euro-area.

Even if the ECB does not consider itself as an inflation-targeting central bank, its institutional features resemble those characterizing an inflation targeter. The TFEU clearly sets price stability, in a lexicographic mode, as the ECB's primary objective. The Governing Council of the ECB has defined price stability in quantitative terms, stating a numerical expression in terms of increases in consumer prices. Furthermore, the ECB has been granted independence in pursuing its mandate, which includes the freedom to choose the monetary policy instruments suited for the task. Finally, the ECB acknowledges the importance of forecasts in its decision-making, although the forecasts' role is downplayed by the fact that they are staff macroeconomic projections submitted to the Governing Council on an advisory basis.

Overall, the ECB is not all that different from inflation-targeting central banks. The more so considering the larger weight that financial variables, including money and credit, which are key ingredients in the second pillar, receive in the modern forecasting tools. Even so, it still is quite clear that the ECB cannot be regarded as an archetypal inflation-forecast-targeting central bank.

The Fed's top monetary policy-setting body, the FOMC, announced in January 2012 that the inflation rate over the longer run is primarily determined by monetary policy. Hence, the FOMC has the ability to specify a long-run goal for inflation (FOMC, 2012). The FMOC has also stated a 2 per cent inflation rate to be most consistent, over the longer run, with the Fed's statutory mandate. By announcing its inflation goal explicitly, the FOMC aimed at keeping longer-term inflation expectations firmly anchored, thereby fostering price stability and moderate long-term interest rates. This was also seen as enhancing the FOMC's ability to promote other objectives assigned to it, such as full employment.

The FOMC has clarified its monetary policy-setting role to the extent that it sees mitigating deviations of inflation from its longer-run goal and deviations of employment from full employment as generally complementary objectives. To differentiate itself from pure inflation targeters, the FOMC makes clear that when its inflation and employment objectives are not entirely consistent with each other, it will follow a balanced approach in promoting them, that takes into account the magnitude of the deviations and the potentially different time horizons over which employment and inflation are projected to return to levels judged consistent with its mandate (FOMC, 2012).

Tuomas Välimäki

than its objective. Inflation targeting recognizes that the link between monetary policy and price stability is imprecise and subject to lags. Other factors, such as raw material prices or exogenous wage pushes, have an influence on inflation in the short to medium run. The central bank must see past these disturbances and recognize that the effect of its own actions is not immediate, but requires a number of quarters before having a measurable effect. It is thus crucial to have a sense of what prices will do over the medium run and all possible tools have to be used to that effect. In the case of the ECB, the main tools that enter its eclectic judgement about inflation prospects are the following:

1. Outlook for economic conditions, hence the reliance on econometric forecasting models.
2. Inflationary expectations derived from market prices, in particular the comparison between inflation protected and straight bonds, or equivalently the break-even inflation derived from so-called inflation swaps.[20]
3. Inflation forecasts obtained from professional forecasters.[21]
4. Credit and monetary developments.

1.2.2 *The Neo-Wicksellian Approach*

The prevalence of inflation targeting was also due to the unsatisfactory experience with so-called intermediate targets. For quite a few years, especially in the 1970s, an attempt was made to deal with the imprecision and lags in the link between monetary tools and macroeconomic results by relying on some variable intended to react quickly and precisely to the monetary action, while also anticipating its consequences on the macro-economy. The basic idea behind assigning the price stability objective to the central bank is that it should stabilize the price of money expressed in terms of the aggregate of goods and services produced in the economy. In a way, having abandoned the gold standard after the First World War, the dominant objective of price stability has meant establishing, some 80 years later, a Consumer Price Index (CPI) standard. Central banks no longer have to stabilize the price of their currency against gold, but rather against all the goods and services produced in the economy, as summarized in the CPI or some other Aggregate Price Index (see Box 7).

---

[20] A comparison between protected and unprotected bonds gives a market estimate of future inflation. Break-even inflation is the implicit inflation rate in indexed bonds that allows its yield to equal that on a standard bond.

[21] ECB Survey of Professional Forecasters. Available at: <http://www.ecb.europa.eu/stats/prices/indic/forecast/html/index.en.html>.

Box 7 QUANTIFYING THE INFLATION TARGET

Former Fed chairman Alan Greenspan broadly defined price stability as a state where: 'the expected changes in the average price level are small enough and gradual enough that they do not materially enter business and household financial decisions' (Greenspan, 1989).

This vague description of the price stability objective may have been suitable for an institution with a dual mandate like the Fed in the 1980s and 1990s, but an inflation-targeting central bank needs a much more precisely defined target, because the target acts as the focal point for the anchoring of the public's inflation expectations. Moving to a quantified inflation target served this purpose and also helped increase the account-ability of the central bank. This is desirable feature for a central bank that has been granted independence in setting the monetary policy stance.

In the early 1990s, when inflation-targeting regimes started to gain acceptance, central banks had to select the inflation indicator that would be used both to objectify and quantify the target.

The choice between price indexes was not obvious. There was a trade-off between the coverage of the measure, its volatility and timeliness, as well as its familiarity with regard to the general public.

On one hand, the GDP deflator would include all domestically produced goods and services, on the other hand, it is normally available only quarterly with a considerable lag, and it is often subject to significant revisions.[22] The CPI is published without long lags, normally not subject to revision, and familiar to the public. However, headline CPI has potential issues as an inflation measure with regard to how it captures the effects of indirect taxes and subsidies, volatility related to components that vary—such as the prices of oil and seasonal foods—and the impact of interest rate changes. Central banks seeking to gauge underlying inflation pressures going forward typically exclude volatile components such as energy and other elements whose price changes may blur the usefulness of the measure from the headline figure.

Using a 'core inflation' measure as the target may also help the public to look through large temporary variations in relative prices to see the big picture. Hence, most of the first group of countries to adopt inflation targeting selected a modified CPI as their target measure. Mortgage interest payments, for example, were exempted from the target in Australia and Spain, while government-controlled prices and indirect taxes were excluded in Australia, Canada, Finland, and New Zealand. Departing from this approach, the UK initially opted for a retail price index instead of the CPI (Haldane, 1995).

The ECB currently uses the HICP as its relevant measure for defining price stability. The HICP is a headline inflation measure, compiled by Eurostat and the national statistical institutes in the euro-area, using Harmonised statistical methods. Even if the ECB seems to differ from the central banks that opted for modified measures of the CPI, the difference is mitigated by the fact that the ECB's inflation target is defined over the medium term. This gives the ECB leeway to look through, that is, not to react to, temporary volatility of its price measure stemming from the relative price changes of

(continued)

---

[22] On the choices between the price measures, see e.g. Yates (1995).

Box 7 CONTINUED

the more volatile CPI components. In the case of the Bank of England, the inflation target is currently expressed in terms of the CPI.

The Fed measures inflation in terms of annual changes in the price index for the PCE index. The PCE index, which covers a wide range of household spending, is produced by the Department of Commerce. Unlike the CPI, the PCE is said to avoid some of the upward bias and delivers a more consistent series over time (Board of Governors, 2000).

The quantitative objectives for the annual inflation rate chosen by the first group of inflation-targeting central banks were remarkably similar. Their choices differed, however, as to the nature of the target. The Bank of Finland was the only central bank in the first group of inflation targeters to announce an explicit percentage-point target for inflation. Others expressed their objectives as ranges of 2–3 percentage points. An argument in favour of target ranges relates to the ability of central banks to forecast inflation or bring about finely calibrated changes in the price level. Policy changes cannot be calibrated so precisely as to achieve an exact rate of increase in prices (Bank of Canada, 1991). Target ranges also help by mitigating the same issues that central banks address by exempting volatile items from the headline measure. However, the choice of applying target ranges does not come without a cost. The larger the range, the lower the chance of missing the target, of course, but it also dilutes the benefit from a quantified target. In essence, the policymaker's commitment becomes less binding. Thus, as long as the central bank's commitment to the target is credible, the strongest anchoring of inflation expectations comes from using a specific percentage-point target.

The difference between range and point targets is mitigated by the fact that central banks with a range target seem to aim at the mid-point of the range, so the ranges are described as having 'soft edges', whereby reaching a range boundary does not necessarily trigger discrete policy changes (Svensson, 2010).

When it comes to the numerical expressions for the target (or the range), New Zealand, as the first inflation-targeter, expressed its objective as a range between 0 and 2 per cent. Sweden and Canada opted also for a range of 2 percentage points, but at slightly higher level: 1–3 per cent. The Bank of Finland's point target at 2 per cent matched the medium-term inflation goal applied as the intermediate objective by larger European peers, including Germany, France, and Italy (Brunila and Lahdenperä, 1995).

Among the large central banks, the ECB's definition for price stability is implicitly stated as a range. It has defined price stability as a year-on-year increase in HICP below 2 per cent. As the expression referred to increases in the price index, it was interpreted as a target range of 0–2 per cent. In 2004, the ECB clarified its intentions by saying that, within this range, it aims to maintain inflation rate 'below, but close to, 2 percent over the medium term'.

Even if the ECB's definition for price stability is clearly a range of inflation outcomes, the clarification shaped the public's medium-term inflation expectations. By referring to the medium term, the ECB avoids having to fine-tune the inflation rate over very short horizons and can take into account the fact that the impacts of monetary policy are uncertain, state-dependent, and affect prices with a time lag. Moreover, the ECB frames its inflation target as a safety margin against deflation.

The ECB also acknowledges the potential measurement bias, that is, that the HICP may slightly overstate the true inflation, due, for example, to quality adjustments. In the case of the euro-area, a positive average inflation figure evidences the existence of inflation differentials across euro-area economies operating in different stages of economic development.

The FOMC notes that an inflation rate of 2 per cent is most consistent with the Fed's dual mandate for price stability and full employment. Of course, the Fed applies several inflation measures, including consumer and producer price indexes, when analysing price developments. Fed policymakers also examine a variety of core inflation measures that exclude volatile items such as food and energy to help identify inflation trends and underlying inflation pressures. The approaches taken by the Fed and the ECB may seem different on the surface; however, both excluding volatile components and assessing price developments over a medium term aim at the same goal: the central bank does not need to react to temporary changes in the headline inflation that are not likely to influence underlying inflation pressures going forward.

Over several decades, 2 per cent has become almost an international norm for inflation-targeting central banks. This increases the importance of the number as a focal point for price expectations globally, even if there are not necessarily compelling arguments in favour of this number compared to, for example, 1 or 3 per cent, as further illustrated in Section 3.3. The original choice of the target level traded off two arguments. On one hand, volatility of inflation (and inflation expectations) hampers economic development and volatility normally increases with the level of inflation—this would call for as low an inflation target as possible. Yet, on the other hand, prices in general, and wages in particular, are rigid to the downside. Thus, the inflation target should be high enough to provide leeway for the price mechanism to function, that is, relative prices to adjust without having a broad-based need for nominal prices and wages to be cut. Also, optimally, the sum of equilibrium real rate of interest and the average inflation should be high enough for nominal interest rates to normally be at a level that leaves standard monetary policy with room to manoeuvre. The lower the equilibrium real rate and the inflation target are, the closer the economy is to the ZLB on average. As the natural rate of interest (the equilibrium real rate) has been alleged to have come down over recent decades, the 2 per cent inflation norm has come under some pressure. Yet the burden of proof still rests on those who wish to modify the widely accepted norm, the changing of which could hamper the central banks' ability to set a credible anchor for price expectations, as further discussed in Section 3.3.

Tuomas Välimäki

The reasoning whereby the central banks stabilize the price of money in terms of all the goods and services consumed in the economy, that is, the CPI, immediately raises the observation that the CPI is only one of the ways to define the price of money. Another definition is the exchange rate, which expresses the price of money in terms of a foreign currency. Yet another expression for the price of money is the interest rate, where money is priced in terms of itself at a point sometime in the future. The exchange rate and the interest rate react more quickly to monetary policy changes and are continuously observable on financial markets, while having a final rendezvous with the rate of inflation. Therefore, there was an attempt to use one or the other as an intermediate target.

The problem with the exchange rate as an intermediate target is that it is only a relative measure of price stability: if a currency tends to appreciate compared to another, this only means that it has a lower underlying rate of inflation than the other currency, not that it is stable in terms of purchasing power.

The problem with the interest rate as an intermediate target is that it is the sum of two components: (1) the real rate of interest, that is, the compensation to be paid to an individual for giving up the use of money for a certain period of time; and (2) the inflation premium, that is, the compensation for the fact that the purchasing power of money changes over time. To complicate matters, the two components tend to be impacted in an opposite way by monetary policy. For instance, an easing of monetary policy will tend to increase the inflation premium, as more inflation will be expected over a somewhat longer maturity, but it will tend to reduce, at least in the short to medium term, the real rate of interest. As a result, the effect of monetary easing on the overall rate of interest is uncertain and the message to be derived from a change in the interest rate is therefore ambiguous.

Given that the two definitions of the price of money alternative to inflation, that is, the exchange rate and the rate of interest, did not provide suitable intermediate targets, an alternative was to consider the quantity of money as intermediate target: given a stable demand for money, supplying it in adequate amount should stabilize its price, that is, the rate of inflation.

This idea is in contrast to another clear characteristic of the central banking model prevailing before the Great Recession, namely the nearly exclusive focus of monetary control on short-term interest rates, consistent with the neo-Wicksellian approach. At the end of last century, the emphasis on quantities, which prevailed in the Friedmanian approach to monetary policy, was to be found only in some textbooks, not in actual policymaking.

The quantitative approach to monetary policy can be summarized by two quotations from Milton Friedman (1960). These quotations give the essence (but not the subtleties) of monetary policy as it stood before the predominance of the neo-Wicksellian school. Friedman's main idea was that quantities, as monetary aggregates, not prices in the guise of the interest rate, are the alpha and the omega of monetary policy:

i.   The links between Reserve action and the money supply are sufficiently close, the effects occur sufficiently rapidly, and the connections are sufficiently well understood, so that reasonably close control over the money supply is feasible, given the will. (p. 89)

ii. No substantial movements in the price level within fairly short periods have occurred without movements in the same direction in the stock of money, and it seems highly dubious that they could. Over long periods, changes in the stock of money can in principle offset or reinforce other factors sufficiently to dominate trends in the price level. (p. 86)

Even if the neo-Wicksellian school is in the ascendance (see, for instance, Florio, Lossani, and Nardozzi, 2011), the two ideas in the above quotations have not lost their appeal for some economists as well as for the layman. In the first quotation, one finds the basic idea that a central bank can control the money supply through the supply of reserves or base (or, more evocatively, high-powered) money. The cleanest example of this idea being put in practice by a central bank is the reserves targeting experiment the Fed undertook between 1979 and 1982, after Paul Volcker had become the Fed Chairman.[23] In the second quotation, one finds the other basic idea, that is, that there is a long-term stable relationship between the development of an appropriately chosen monetary aggregate and inflation.

Even in 2011, one could find a simplified exposition of these two ideas in one of the most popular intermediate macroeconomics textbooks, the one by Dornbusch, Fischer, and Startz (1994), surely not economists from a pure monetarist school. In the textbook, the first idea took the form of the money multiplier, according to which there is a constant, or at least an-easy-to-forecast, relationship between high-powered money and a relevant monetary aggregate. The second idea, which was presented more as a hypothesis than as a demonstrated empirical fact, took the form of a stable demand for money. According to the Friedmanian approach, changes in money market equilibrium are ultimately determined by reserve supply changes decided by the central bank and result, over the long run, in changes in the price level. The practical corollary of the two ideas is that the central bank can pursue price stability, in the medium term, by calibrating the issuance of high-powered money. Friedman even translated this into a simple rule: high-powered money should be issued in a way that it would lead to a constant 3 to 5 per cent growth for the relevant monetary aggregate.

In the euro-area, empirical facts provided mixed support to these two ideas before the crisis. The stability of money demand was assumed when the monetary policy strategy of the ECB was communicated in 1999:

The available empirical evidence suggests that broad monetary aggregates exhibit the properties required for the announcement of a reference value. [...] In the past the demand for euro-area broad money has been stable over the long run, [that] empirical evidence has been judged strong and robust enough for a reference value to be announced [...]. (ECB, 1999, p. 48)

[23] A finer historical analysis would be needed to ascertain whether the Fed really believed in a multiplier approach to monetary policy in Volcker's time or whether it followed an interest rate policy in disguise. A finer historical analysis could also establish whether the money multiplier ever enjoyed any practical success in central banks or whether it was to be found only in textbooks.

Subsequent empirical developments, however, did not confirm this statement. Indeed, the most exhaustive paper on money and monetary policy of the ECB (Fischer et al., 2008, p. 10), presented at a conference organized by the ECB, arguably to defend the 'Money pillar' in its strategy, concluded that: 'there is no reliable estimated money demand equation which covers the entire sample period'. Still, the paper argued that a complex, widely judgemental use of monetary variables helped—at least before the Great Recession—the conduct of monetary policy, including for the forecast of inflation over the medium to long run. Comments made at the conference showed that not every participant was convinced of the usefulness of monetary aggregates to forecast inflation. Still, probably quite a few would have conceded that a central bank should keep an eye on monetary developments while conducting monetary policy. In addition, probably a majority of participants would have agreed that it is much easier to find a relationship between the growth of monetary aggregates and inflation when both move away from low growth rates, such as those experienced with the euro, towards high growth rates, as happens in extremes during hyperinflations. This is the idea that Friedman expressed in 1960 when writing:

> While the stock of money is systematically related to the price level *on the average*, there is much variation in the relation over short periods of time and *especially for the mild movements in both money and prices* that characterize most of our experience and that we would like to have characterize all.
>
> (p. 87, emphasis added)

Monetary and credit aggregates not only lost, even before the Great Recession, much of their value as gauges for monetary policy, but did not even play an important role in detecting brewing financial instability risks. This was the case even if Borio and Lowe (2002 and 2004) had documented the properties of the difference between the credit-to-GDP ratio and its long-term trend (the so-called credit-to-GDP gap) as a handy early warning indicator for banking crises.

As regards the money multiplier, the experience of the Deutsche Bundesbank, before the Great Recession, seemed to be consistent with Friedman's analysis, as the money multiplier revealed a fairly predictable trend behaviour between 1980 and 1999 (see Box 8).

The experience of Germany in the two decades prior to the launch of the euro was not replicated, however, by either the ECB or by the Fed during the Great Recession. When base money started to display its explosive behaviour at the beginning of the Great Recession, in both the United States and the euro-area, any link to money and credit aggregates was lost, as can be seen in Figures 1.10 and 1.11.

Box 8 EMPIRICAL EVIDENCE FOR MONEY MULTIPLIERS

The main text illustrates the breakdown of any stable relationship between base money and money aggregates during the Great Recession: as bank reserves, the most variable component of base money, recorded huge and irregular growth rates, money and credit aggregates maintained an anaemic growth in the USA and in the euro-area (see Figures 1.12 and 1.13), as well as in some other advanced economies.

The melting down of the money multiplier must have surprised economists with a monetarist inclination: the Friedmanian approach to monetary policy was based on two assumptions: a close link between bank reserves and money supply, a stable relationship between price fluctuations and movements in the same direction of the stock of money. The latter is consistent with the quantitative theory of money, where the velocity of money is stable in the short run.

However, economists with more of a taste for economic history and very long time series should have recognized in the breakdown of the multiplier a phenomenon with a number of precedents. This box reviews historical episodes of instability in the money multiplier before the Great Recession in order to find lessons explaining the instability in this relationship, which many advanced economies' central banks have experienced during the Great Recession.

According to the traditional definition, the money multiplier represents the amount of broad money that is created after an injection of base money by the central bank. Broad money is created by commercial banks that use the base money to provide additional credit to the economy, after retaining a percentage of this money to fulfil their reserve requirement.

Following Beenstock (1989) we can express the money multiplier as follows:

$$m = \frac{1 + \alpha + \beta}{\alpha + \gamma(1 + \beta)}$$

Where:
α = the cash coefficient defined as the ratio of cash to deposits of the non-bank private sector;
β = the ratio of time deposits to sight deposits;
γ = the reserve ratio.

The monetarist assumption is that, in normal conditions, no major changes affect the parameters of this equation and the money multiplier is stable. In a weaker formulation the parameters change in a predictable way and the multiplier follows a stable path. In both cases base money can be used to predict total money supply and the inflation rate.

Contrary to the monetarist assumption, during the last 100 years there have been several cases in which the multiplier broke down, meaning that the relation between base money and total money supply suddenly changed and became unpredictable. The first example goes back to the Great Depression, following the 1929 crisis. Von Hagen (2009) shows that the money multiplier in the USA during the Great Depression contracted by 50 per cent. This was due to a massive increase in the cash coefficient α, caused by the bank run, whereas the reserve ratio β experienced more moderate changes, although it took several years to stabilize again.

(continued)

Box 8 CONTINUED

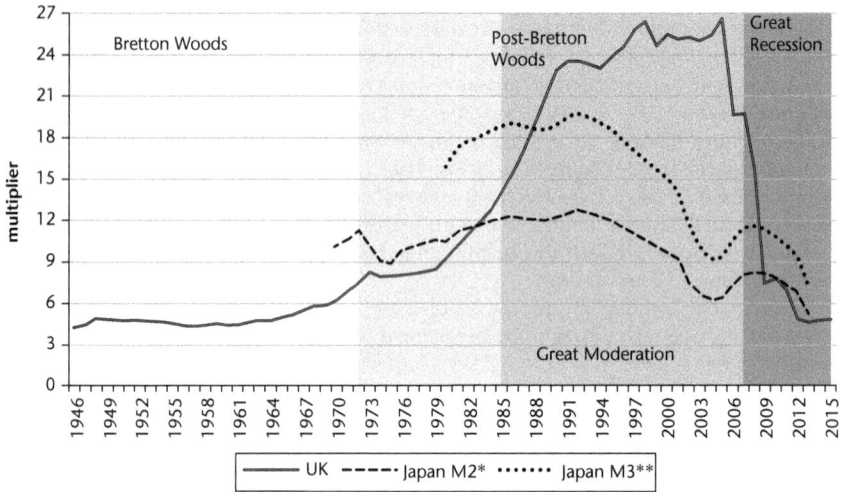

Figure B.8.1 Money Multipliers in the UK and Japan

Note: *data starts only in 1970; **data starts only in 1979.

Source: Bank of England, Bank of Japan.

In the UK, the money multiplier experienced major instability even before the Great Recession. Looking at Figure B.8.1 we can see that the multiplier remained mostly stable for a long period during the Bretton Woods period, whereas it turned to an increasing but quite predictable path at the beginning of the 1970s. According to Beenstock (1989), three factors contributed to this trend. First, the elimination of most credit controls and other distortions in the banking system following the 1971 reform caused a constant fall in the reserve ratio. More specifically, the increased competition induced banks to pay interests on time deposits, which skyrocketed in the following years. Second, the shift towards a fully floating exchange rate system contributed to a reduction in the demand for bank reserves. Third, the increased importance attached to monetary aggregates with the Thatcher premiership since 1979 affected money demand.

Another example of breakdown in the money multiplier can be found in the Japanese experience with the first QE, implemented between 2001 and 2006. The large increase in the monetary base led to a surge in bank reserves but without a correspondent increase of banks' balance sheets or, in particular, of broad money. Potential explanations for this behaviour were the zero interest rate and the deflationary tendencies associated with the prolonged lack of demand. However, the presence of huge amounts of toxic assets could have been the main cause behind the lack of increase in money supply, as banks used the additional liquidity to restructure their balance sheets, leading to what Richard Koo (2009) called a 'balance sheet recession'.

All these examples show that the instability of the money multiplier during the Great Recession crisis was not unprecedented. As shown by Von Hagen (2009), in the

USA the 'unconventional' expansionary monetary policy caused a reduction in the cash coefficient and a huge increase in banks' reserves. The latter replaced interbank loans that vanished as a consequence of the crisis. The increase in banks' reserves was also behind the irregular contraction of the multiplier in the UK and the euro-area. However, in the case of UK, the cash coefficient increased too. Von Hagen suggests this this was due to the increased preference for cash caused by distrust in the banking system.

According to Hoisington and Hunt (2013), these events are the obvious consequence of the economic context in which QE was implemented. When economies are over-indebted, interest rates are close to zero, and there are strong disinflationary tendencies, monetary policy finds it difficult to raise inflation. In the case of interest rates close to zero the opportunity cost of holding reserves goes to zero (Woodford, 2012a) and there will be a tendency to invest in speculative activities, which are riskier but more profitable. With limited bank capital, this policy has the obvious consequence of reducing traditional lending activities, and hence economic growth, as the banks' own capital does not change while risk-weighted assets increase.

Overall, the conclusion is that the money multiplier is not stable enough, on a long time horizon, for monetary policy to be confidently based on it: long spells of stable behaviour can give way to acute episodes of instability, jeopardizing the usefulness of this concept for policy purposes.

Piero Esposito

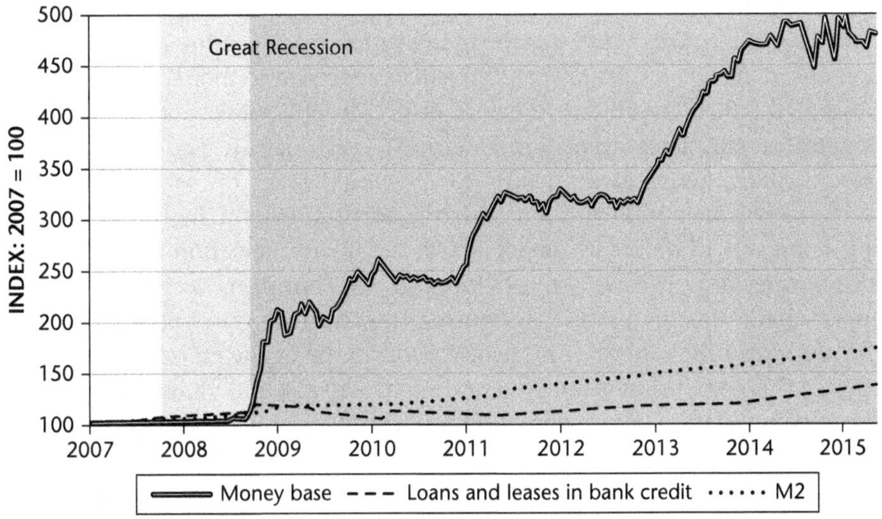

Figure 1.10 Components of the Money Multiplier in the Euro-Area, Index 2007=100 (2007–2015)

Source: Author's calculations with IMF–World Economic Outlook data.

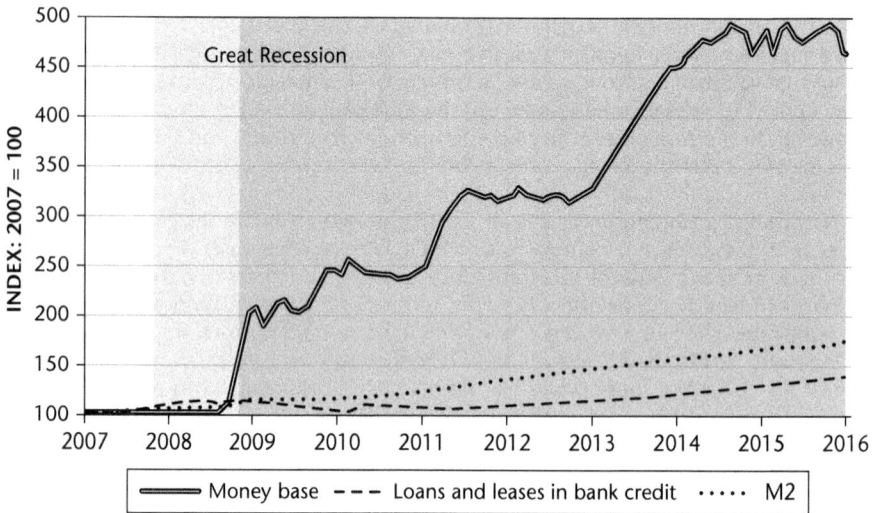

Figure 1.11 Components of the Money Multiplier in the USA, Index 2007=100 (2007–2016)

Source: Author's calculations with Board of Governors of the Federal Reserve System data.

Overall, even before the Great Recession, the empirical experience was not favourable to the conduct of monetary policy based on quantities. Instead, it was interest rates that received most attention, within central banks and outside of them. This trend was forcefully supported by an intellectual development, namely a return to the Wicksellian approach to monetary policy.

Bindseil (2004) documents the relatively short policy relevance of what he denotes as the 'Reserve Position Doctrine'. This doctrine prescribed, along Friedmanian lines, that monetary policy should focus on some variant of bank reserves held with the central bank. Bindseil convincingly argues that this approach to monetary policy was a temporary deviation from the old idea advanced by Wicksell, and before him by Thornton. According to this approach it is the interest rate, not one or the other monetary variables, that is the alpha and the omega of monetary policy. One of the empirical counterparts of this conclusion is the presentation by Papadia and Välimäki (2011) of the implementation of monetary policy of the ECB, which focuses on interest rates rather than on any monetary aggregate. Florio et al. (2011) take the original Wicksell idea as the basis for global monetary rules underpinning central bank collaboration.

Wicksell's (1935, pp. 192–193) basic idea is that there is, at every point in time, a natural interest rate, which is determined in the real side of the economy:

The rate of interest at which the demand for loan capital and the supply of savings exactly agree, and which more or less corresponds to the expected yield on the newly created capital, will then be the normal or natural real rate. It is essentially variable.

However, the monetary side of the economy (banks in Wicksell's presentation) also generates a rate of interest, namely the cost of loans, while the difference between the natural rate of interest and the loan rate determines the behaviour of prices. If the natural rate is lower than the rate fixed by banks on loans, there will be a tendency for prices to come down. The opposite will happen if the natural rate is higher than the rate on loans. In Wicksell's formulation, the mechanism bringing the two rates in equilibrium is inflation: too high a rate on loans will depress the economy, cause deflation, reduce the demand for loans and their cost; too low a rate on loans will have the opposite effect. In Wicksell's original formulation, the variability of the natural rate is higher than that of the rate on loans. The most common dynamic process, in his view, is that the natural rate changes and leads to changes in inflation, in turn bringing about a gradual corresponding change of the rate on loans. Wicksell describes as follows the process when the real rate is higher than the rate on loans:

> An increase in the real rate does not therefore immediately cause a corresponding rise in the bank's rates, but the latter remains unchanged for a time and with them the loan rates between individuals. The money rate therefore becomes abnormally low in relation to the real capital rate, and this naturally has just the same effect as if the money rate had been spontaneously reduced with an unchanged interest on capital—which seldom happens. Frequently commodity prices therefore rise continuously, business requires greater cash holdings, bank loans increase without corresponding deposits, bank reserves, and often bullion reserves, begin to fall and the banks are compelled to raise their rates somewhat, though this does not prevent the continuous rise in prices, until the interest rates have reached the level of the normal rate.   (Wicksell, 1935, p. 206)

The fact that the variability of the natural rate is higher than that of the rate on loans explains why 'rising prices very rarely coincide with low or falling interest rates, but much more frequently with rising or high rates' (p. 202), since a change in the natural rate is usually the first mover in the dynamic adjustment and the monetary rate only follows.

Following Bindseil (2004, p. 12), who was in turn adopting the diagram from Richter (1989), Wicksell's theory can be presented graphically, as in Figure 1.12.

This arbitrage diagram is the simplest possible model of an economy. On the left side we have the real sector, in which wheat today is transformed into wheat tomorrow, ideally by planting it today and then harvesting it tomorrow. Meanwhile, r is the natural rate of the economy, in Wicksell parlance,

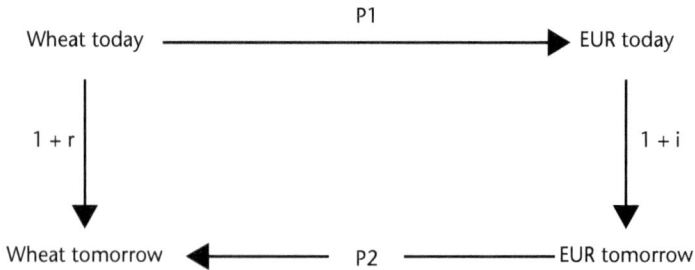

Figure 1.12 Wicksell-Richter Diagram
Source: Bindseil (2014, p. 12).

and can also be interpreted as the rate of growth of the economy. On the right side we have the monetary sector of the economy in which one euro today is transformed into $1+i$ euro tomorrow by investing it in the financial market. The upper part of the figure is today and the lower part is tomorrow. P_1 is the price of wheat today and P_2 is the price of wheat tomorrow. Arbitrage implies that the real and the monetary forms of investment must have the same return, which implies in turn that there is no inflation, that is, $P_2 = P_1$, and this is achieved when the rate of interest on money (i) is the same as the natural rate (r). One unit of wheat is sold today at price P_1 and invested in the money market. The investment will yield $P_1 (1+i)$ euros. This amount will be used to buy wheat at a price of P_2 which must result in an amount of wheat equal to $1+r$.

Arbitrage logic allows relationships between prices to be established by moving within the diagram from one good to another via different paths, indeed, by moving from 'Wheat today' to 'Wheat tomorrow' through different routes. One can show that in equilibrium:

$$1 + i_{real} = P_1(1 + i)/P_2 \tag{1.1}$$

Defining $(1 + \pi)$ as P_2/P_1, one obtains the Fisher equation:

$$(1 + i_{real}) = (1 + i)/(1 + \pi) \tag{1.2}$$

If the central bank manages to keep the money (nominal) interest rate, i, always equal to the real interest rate, i_{real}, no inflation occurs, i.e. $\pi = 0$.

1.2.3 Central Bank Reaction Functions and the Taylor Rule

The diagram in Figure 1.12 is a static arbitrage device, but, in reality, most of the time the economy is in complex, dynamic states of disequilibrium. Taylor's rules of different kinds can be thought of as dynamic versions of the Richter arbitrage diagram. In a dynamic disequilibrium situation, setting the optimal interest rate becomes more complicated—this is why central banks have large economic departments. Complicated issues also arise in identifying and measuring the relevant nominal rate and then deflating it to get the real rate of interest of the Taylor rule.

Simple as it is, the Taylor rule has provided both a descriptive as well as a normative rule concerning the basics of monetary policy in the USA and Europe.

The original Taylor rule had the following form:

$$r = p + 0.5y + 0.5(\pi - 2) + 2 \tag{1.3}$$

but can be rewritten, more intuitively, as:

$$r = 4 + 0.5y + 1.5(\pi - 2) \tag{1.4}$$

where:

$r =$ Federal Funds Rate (FFR);
$y =$ per cent deviation of real GDP from a target;
$\pi =$ rate of inflation over the previous four quarters;
$2 =$ desired level of the inflation rate;
$4 =$ nominal equilibrium interest rate when the activity gap and the inflation gap are 0 per cent.

The inflation gap parameter is the most important one in the equation; it must be higher than 1 for the economic system to be stable. This can be seen simply by noting that if the inflation parameter was lower than 1, the real interest rate would decrease as inflation grows above its desired level. Thus the central bank would impart additional stimulus just when it should withdraw it. The symmetrical problem would occur if inflation were lower than the desired level.

A comparison of the Taylor rule with the Wicksellian model reveals a basic analogy, but also two, relatively minor, differences.

The basic analogy is that, as can be seen from Equation 1.4, the behaviour of inflation depends on the difference between the monetary interest rate, on the left of the equation, and the natural nominal rate, equated to 4 (equilibrium real rate 2 per cent + target inflation 2 per cent) on the right side of the equation. In addition, inflation depends on cyclical conditions, as measured by the deviation of actual GDP from the target.

The two relatively minor differences between the Taylor rule and the Wicksellian model are, first, that, in the most common interpretation, the Taylor rule attributes more variability to the rate determined in the monetary side of the economy than to the natural rate, often assumed to be constant.[24]

---

[24] Taylor himself, in his 1993 paper, only considers the possibility of a changing natural rate when examining the specific case of the increase of rates on the occasion of German unification, not as an issue to be considered systematically when applying, 'not mechanically', the rule. Kohn (2012), instead, stresses that changes in the natural rate explain why the Taylor rule cannot be applied mechanically.

Second, the rate on the monetary side of the economy is fixed by the central bank in Taylor formulation, in the Wicksell approach it is instead fixed by commercial banks. Both differences presumably reflect the different monetary systems confronting Wicksell and Taylor. Wicksell carried out his analysis in a metallic money framework, in which the central bank had limited latitude to change interest rates, due to the need to maintain gold convertibility. Taylor, on the other hand, had in mind a fiat money system in which the central bank enjoys substantial discretion in fixing interest rates. In Figure 1.13 we find a partial confirmation of this interpretation looking at the historical experience of the USA, Italy, the UK, and Germany.

In fact, in the Gold Standard era, on average over the considered four countries, the real interest rate prevailing in the financial market, which is an empirical variable close to Wicksell's monetary rate, was less variable than the growth of income per head (a variable close to Wicksell's natural rate). In the post-Second World War period, instead, the variability of the real interest rate observed in the financial market was higher than that of income per head. This finding supports the view that the difference of emphasis between Wicksell and the Taylor rule lies in the different empirical behaviour of the natural and the financial rate confronting the two authors.

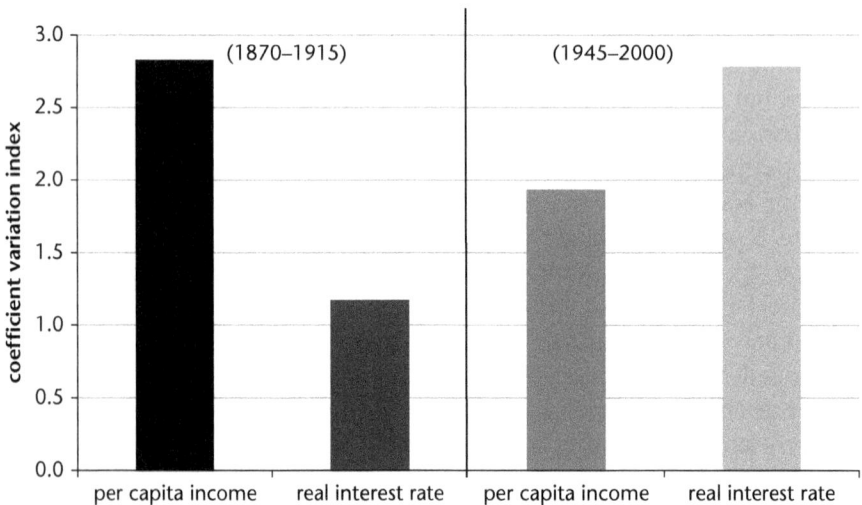

Figure 1.13 Variability of Aggregate Per Capita Income and Real Interest Rates: Average of USA, Italy, UK, and Germany (1870–1915 and 1945–2000)

Source: Author's calculations with Maddison project database. Available at: <http://www.ggdc.net/maddison/maddison-project/home.htm>.

Taylor (1993, pp. 195–214) was well aware that his proposed rule was only a first approximation to optimal policymaking:

> Good policy rules typically call for changes in the Federal funds rate in response to changes in the price level or changes in real income. An objective of the paper is to preserve the concept of such a policy rule in a policy environment where it is practically impossible to follow mechanically any particular algebraic formula that describes the policy rule. Even with many such modifications, it is difficult to see how such algebraic policy rules could be sufficiently encompassing.

Along the same lines, Yellen (1996, pp. 8–9), before becoming the Chair of the Fed, wrote:

> The Taylor rule has appealing properties as a normative description of how policy ought to be conducted. But as Taylor himself, and more recently Business Week, have noted, it does also a pretty fair job as a positive description of how policy actually has been conducted over the past decade or so. Let me immediately and emphatically stress that I do not favor mechanical adherence to the Taylor rule or any other rule.

Bernanke (2015b), the former Chair of the Fed, took very similar position:

> [W]ould it make sense, as Taylor proposes, for the FOMC to state in advance its rule for changing interest rates?
>
> No. Monetary policy should be systematic, not automatic. The simplicity of the Taylor rule disguises the complexity of the underlying judgments that FOMC members must continually make if they are to make good policy decisions.

Still Taylor's (1993) 'rule' became the benchmark for assessing monetary policy in the USA and in other countries (see, for instance, Hofmann and Bogdanova, 2012). Indeed, going well beyond Taylor's original formulation, there was some support in the US Congress to compel the Fed to follow the Taylor rule. Indeed, the US House of Representatives passed a bill in November 2015 calling for rule-based monetary policy, to the dismay of the then Chair of the Fed. Support for this initiative could come from the Trump administration. Taylor himself seems to have moved well beyond his initial position, supporting a harder form of monetary policy rule than he had initially proposed:

> The implication of this experience is clear: monetary policy should re-normalize in the sense of transitioning to a predictable rule-like strategy for the instruments of policy. Of course, it is possible technically for the Fed to move to and stick to such a policy, but the long departures from rules-based policy show that it is difficult.
>
> These departures suggest that some legislative backing might help. Such legislation could simply require the Fed to describe its strategy or rule for adjusting its policy instruments. It would be the Fed's job to choose the strategy and how to describe it. (Taylor, 2016, p. 137)

1.2.4 *The Corridor Approach*

The overall model of central banking prevailing before the Great Recession also extended to the operational domain. There, as documented by Papadia and Välimäki (2011, pp. 219–20), the so-called corridor approach, chosen by the ECB from the start, was eventually adopted also by the Fed, the Bank of Japan, and the Bank of England. The corridor approach 'is based on three fundamental components: an interest rate corridor, with a deposit and a lending facility at penalty rates, compulsory but remunerated reserves to be respected on average over a so-called maintenance period, and refinancing operations targeted at satisfying the liquidity needs of banks'.

The interest rate corridor of the ECB is represented in Figure 1.14.

The floor (deposit facility rate) and the ceiling of the corridor (marginal lending facility rate) establish the boundaries within which the interbank market rate can move. Indeed, no bank would want to lend at a lower remuneration than the one offered by the deposit facility, because the central bank is willing to take any amount at that rate. Symmetrically, no bank would want to borrow at a rate higher than that of the marginal lending facility, at which the central bank is willing to lend any amount

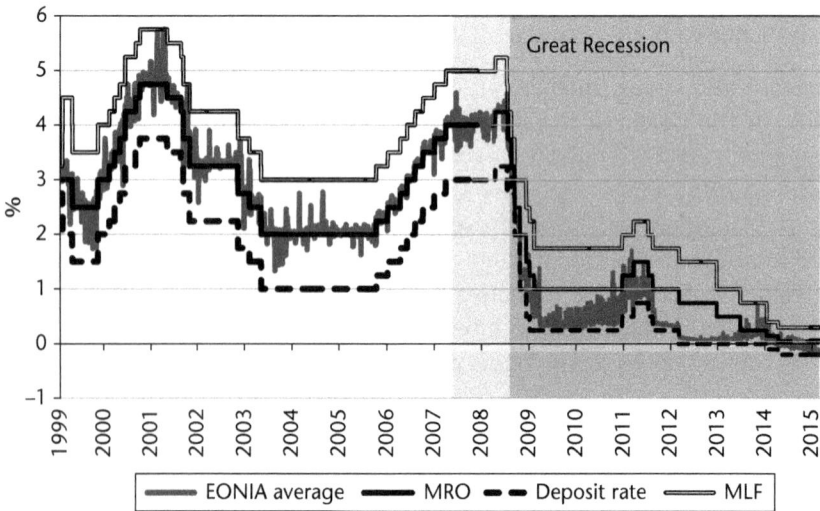

Figure 1.14 The ECB Corridor of Interest Rates (1999–2015)

Note: MRO—Main Refinancing Operations Rate; MLF—Main Lending Facility Rate; EONIA— Euro OverNight Index Average; Deposit Rate—rate on the deposit facility.

Source: ECB Statistical Data Warehouse.

against eligible collateral.[25] Fixing the corridor is a first tool to determine the level of market interest rates. However, as can be seen in Figure 1.14, this is only a first indication. If it was only the boundaries of the corridor that mattered, the market interest rate could be highly variable. Before the Great Recession, the ECB interest rate corridor was 200 basis points wide. The central bank sought and still seeks, however, a more precise control of the interest rate. This is obtained by regulating market liquidity. To understand how this is achieved, it is useful to introduce the general rule determining interest rates within a corridor system, as represented in Equation (1.5):

$$r^t = E_t(r^T) = P_l R^l + P_s R^s \qquad (1.5)$$

Where:

r^t = market interest rate on day t;

E_t = expectation operator based on information available on day t;

r^T = interest rate at the end of the maintenance period;

P_l = probability of banks having excess liquidity at the end of the maintenance period;

R^l = deposit facility rate, applied to the excess liquidity that banks deposit with the ECB;

P_s = probability of banks having excess liquidity at the end of the maintenance period;

R^s = marginal lending facility rate, at which banks may borrow overnight funds from the ECB.

Implicit in the equation is the martingale property, that is, that the rate of interest is the same on any day of the maintenance period and equal to that expected for the last day in the period.

If $P_1 = P_s$, the probability that banks will have an excess of liquidity at the end of the maintenance period is the same as the probability of having a deficit of liquidity. Such a 'reputational' equilibrium can be reached because the central bank credibly assures that, at the end of the period, there will be neither an excess nor a deficit of reserves. Moreover, with R^l and R^s symmetric around the policy rate, the market rate will (absent market imperfections) be at the policy rate all along the maintenance period. This is indeed what happened in the euro-area until the beginning of the crisis: the ECB provided liquidity according to the 'benchmark' approach, whereby enough liquidity was supplied to cover precisely the liquidity deficits of banks and required reserves (Papadia and Välimäki, 2011).

---

[25] The subtle issue of stigma, whereby a bank may prefer to borrow at a higher cost from the market instead of borrowing at a lower rate from the central bank, will be examined later in this section.

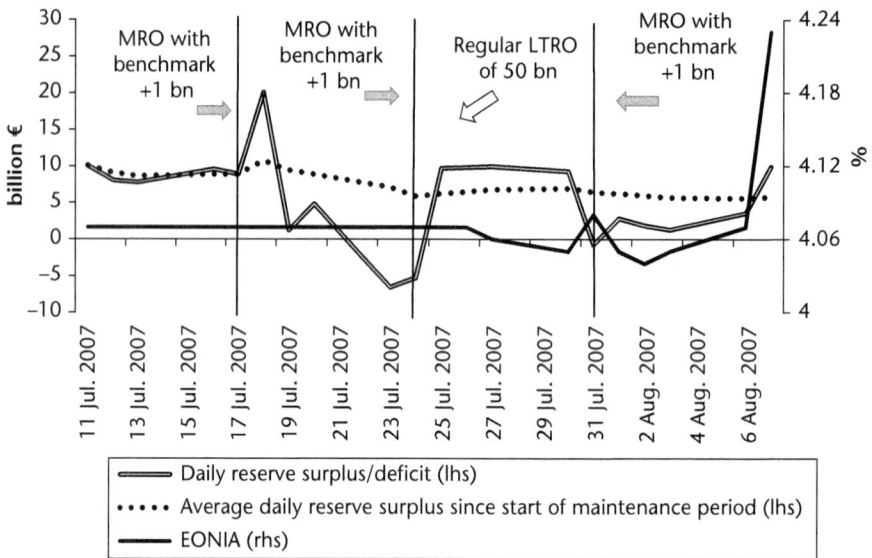

Figure 1.15 Liquidity and Overnight Interest Rate in the Euro-Area before the Great Recession (11 July 2007–6 August 2007)

Source: Author's calculations with ECB Statistical Data Warehouse.

Figure 1.15 refers to the last maintenance period before the beginning of the Great Recession, from 11 July to 7 August 2007. This four-week maintenance period was typical of the periods which preceded it: EONIA (Euro OverNight Index Average, the overnight interbank rate that used to be the operational target for ECB's monetary policy) is very close to the policy rate (i.e. the rate applied in the main refinancing operations (MRO) rate), indeed generally a few basis points constantly above it, except at the very end of the maintenance period, when the central bank could no longer regulate liquidity to offset autonomous factor shocks. Excess liquidity is maintained close to zero day after day and even closer to zero on a cumulative basis.

In normal conditions, the market rate stood halfway between the ceiling and the floor of the corridor, which was also the level of the MRO rate through which the ECB signalled its monetary policy stance. The benchmark amount of liquidity needed by the banks to fulfil the reserve requirements and satisfy the liquidity deficit was provided to the market with lending operations. The bulk of the liquidity needs were covered by the MRO. Yet, to fulfil the needs of smaller credit institutions, part of the provision of reserves was carried out with longer-term refinancing operations (LTRO), whose maturity was three months.

In addition to the lending operations, the ECB, with the national central banks acting as its agents, could have carried a wide range of operations. However, in practice, the ECB could maintain, before the crisis, short-term rates close to the MRO rate, in the middle of the corridor, having recourse only to the weekly MROs. The situation was different for the Fed, the Bank of Japan, and the Bank of England, which needed to intervene very frequently to regulate liquidity, even more than once per day. The ability of the EONIA to remain in the middle of the corridor, without daily interventions by the ECB, was due, in large part, to the functioning of the reserve requirements. These requirements oblige banks to maintain an amount of deposits with the Eurosystem in a given month proportional to the deposits they collected two months earlier from their customers. Because the compulsory reserves only have to be respected over a maintenance period (Papadia and Välimäki, 2011), banks can maintain a lower amount of deposits when there is little liquidity, offsetting this with higher amounts when liquidity is abundant. By so doing, banks operating in the euro-area automatically stabilize interest rates, without a continuous intervention by the central bank. Furthermore, because required reserves are remunerated with a market interest rate, banks have no incentive, as they had in the USA before the Great Recession, to try and reduce reserves. As a consequence, in the Eurosystem these reserves generally remained sufficient to provide a stabilizing interest rate buffer.

Because the ECB avoided providing excess liquidity, as mentioned, by matching the changing demand of liquidity by banks, that is, following the so-called 'benchmark' approach, the effect of excess liquidity on the overnight market rate was not visible before the Great Recession. In a way, the effect of excess liquidity was not visible because there was no excess liquidity (Papadia and Välimäki, 2011). This can be seen in the upper panel of Figure 1.16, reporting the scatter between excess liquidity and the spread between the EONIA rate and the deposit facility rate for the period 2000–2007, when the ECB had surpassed the complications that had appeared in the initial phase of implementation of the single monetary policy but had not been hit as yet by the uncertainty brought about by the Great Recession. In this upper panel there is no apparent relationship between excess liquidity and the spread between EONIA and the deposit facility rate; indeed, EONIA is scattered close to the middle of the interest rate corridor, which, in the period from 2000 to 2007, was about 100 basis points above the deposit facility rate. Furthermore, the cloud of excess liquidity was scattered around zero.

As will be discussed in Section 2.1.2, until it resorted to fully fledged quantitative easing (QE), the most important action of the ECB during the Great Recession was to allow banks to draw as much central bank funding as they needed, moving from auctions for its monetary policy operations with fixed quantity and variable rates to auctions with fixed rates and variable quantity. As the liquidity started to be determined by banks' demand in a period in which uncertainty was at its highest, banks drawing large amounts of excess liquidity resulted in overnight rates falling significantly below the MRO rate.

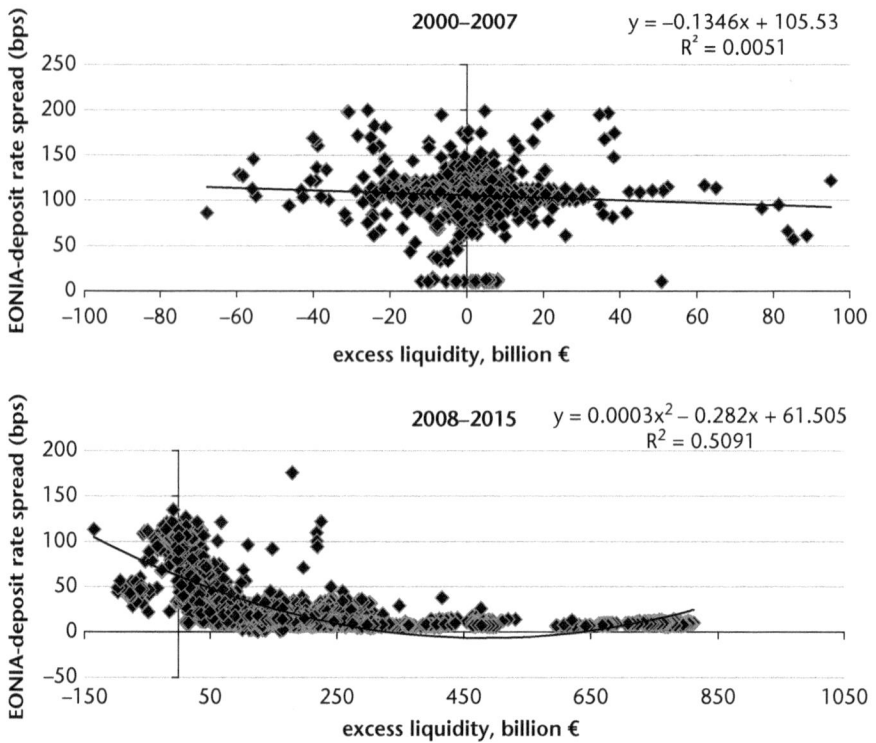

Figure 1.16 Spread between EONIA and the Rate on ECB Deposits and Excess Liquidity (2000–2007 and 2008–2015)

Source: Author's calculations with ECB Statistical Data Warehouse.

Empirically it can be seen in the lower panel of Figure 1.16 that, during the Great Recession, there is a clear, strongly non-linear relationship between excess liquidity, reaching much larger values, and the spread between EONIA and the deposit facility rate.

Figure 1.16 also shows that as excess liquidity moves away from around zero (where it concentrated before the crisis) to higher and higher values, the overnight rate moves down until it gets very close to the bottom of the corridor, that is, the rate on the deposit facility. It is also evident that the variability of rates around the interpolated line decreases as the amount of excess liquidity increases.

The decrease of elasticity from practically infinite to practically zero as well as the lowering noise as excess liquidity moves from zero to very high values match the theoretical explanation given in Equation 1.5. The large amount of excess liquidity prevailing during the Great Recession made the probability of an excess of liquidity practically certain at the end of the maintenance period. Therefore, $P_1 = 1$, which implies that Equation 1.5 reduces (again short of market imperfections) to:

$$r^t = E_t(r^T) = R^l \tag{1.6}$$

and the market rate will settle at the rate on the deposit facility.

In a corridor system, one can parsimoniously explain the fixing of the interest rate by the central bank in both 'normal' and 'crisis' times simply with Equation 1.5. The practical conclusion is that the question of 'how they do it?' (Friedman and Kuttner, 2011, pp. 1345–1433) (i.e. how do central banks change interest rates?) has an answer in two parts. First, the corridor is changed by altering the rates on the standing facilities, without any reference to liquidity. Then the position of the policy rate within the corridor depends on the supply of liquidity: if (strongly) in excess, the rate will gravitate towards R^l; if balanced, it will gravitate towards the policy rate, that is, the MRO rate in the euro-area; if insufficient, it will approximate R^s.

In the case of the Fed, the corridor approach was perfected only after the beginning of the Great Recession. Keister, Martin, and McAndrews (2008) described the interest rate fixation by the Fed (see Figure 1.17).

Before Congress approved legislation in 2006 authorizing the Fed to pay interest on reserves from 2008 onward (initially intended to begin after 2011), the Fed's way of fixing interest rates was actually a special version of a corridor system, with its bottom necessarily at zero. The position of the interest rate within the corridor depended on the supply of liquidity provided by the Fed, given the demand for reserves by banks. Demand depended, in turn, upon required reserves and excess reserves needed for payment purposes and to guard against undershooting reserve requirements. This corridor system,

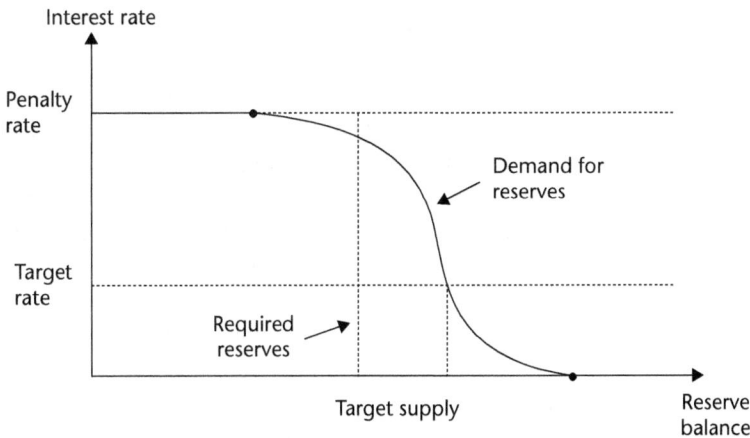

Figure 1.17 Fixation of Interest Rates in the USA
Source: Keister, Martin, and McAndrews (2008).

however, had three, interlinked, undesirable characteristics. First, as mentioned, the bottom of the corridor was necessarily at zero. Second, the width of the corridor changed with the level of the penalty rate (corresponding in the USA to the discount rate). Third, the central bank was not free to supply bank reserves according to its desire to favour smooth payments,[26] because liquidity had to be provided in exactly the amount necessary to achieve the targeted interest rate. This last drawback was particularly serious during the initial phase of the Great Recession, because the demand for liquidity grew enormously and the Fed desired to satisfy it, while also desiring to keep the policy rate sufficiently above zero. Symmetrically, the ability to separate the supply of liquidity from the interest rate is critical in exiting the zero interest rate policy—the policy which the Fed followed from December 2008 to December 2015.

The ability of the Fed to pay interest on reserves allowed it to deal with the three drawbacks mentioned. By separating the fixation of the interest rate from the provision of liquidity it was thus possible to have an interest rate different from zero while also providing abundant liquidity. Similarly to what happened at the ECB during the Great Recession, the corridor system employed at the Fed was the specific variant denominated 'floor system', as discussed in Bindseil's chapter in Mercier and Papadia (2011, pp. 5–114). According to this approach, the market interest rate is attracted by the interest on central bank deposits because of the large amount of excess liquidity.

It should be noted that the Fed corridor system differs from that of the ECB even after the US central bank was allowed to pay interest on bank reserves. In fact, Kahn (2010) notes that: 'Three issues in particular may limit the effectiveness of a corridor system in the USA—a soft floor, a porous ceiling, and a diverse decision-making structure.' The floor is soft essentially because there are a number of financial institutions holding large amounts of liquidity, in particular money market funds and the so-called government-sponsored enterprises like Fannie Mae and Freddie Mac, which do not have access to the Fed. Therefore, these institutions cannot deposit their liquidity with the Fed and are consequently willing to accept a lower remuneration from deposits held with private institutions. The ceiling is porous because of the 'stigma' still affecting borrowing under the discount window from the Fed. The January 2003 reform of the discount facility introduced a primary and a secondary lending facility, with the former establishing a ceiling for the

---

[26] Kashyap and Stein (2012, p. 48) summarize the function of bank reserves in payments and liquidity issues by a term y_{SVR}, which they define as the 'convenience yield on reserves', whereby the interest rate prevailing on the market for bank reserves is defined as $i = ior + y_{SVR}$, where ior is the interest on reserves, with the proviso that $y_{SVR} = 0$ for a very large supply of reserves.

overnight rate. Furthermore, the Fed expended great efforts to eliminate the stigma of borrowing under its discount facility. Still, the long tradition whereby it was only banks finding it difficult to borrow from the market—and thus seen as poor credit—which borrowed under the discount facility perpetuated the stigma on this kind of borrowing. As a consequence, banks were often willing to pay more than the discount rate in order to get liquidity from other market participants, thus avoiding the stigma of borrowing from the discount window. The 'diverse decision-making structure' to which Kahn refers, owes to the fact that the FOMC determines the FFR, that is, the policy rate, whereas the interest on reserves and the discount rate are fixed by a subset of the FOMC, namely the Board of Governors. Therefore, coordination between the two decision-making bodies is necessary.

Essentially, the soft floor and the porous ceiling, in the case of the Fed, depend on the persistent characterization of the discount facility as an ultima ratio source of liquidity, and on the fact that only a subset of financial institutions has access to the central bank. This latter characteristic was part of what Papadia and Välimäki (2011) defined as a 'narrow approach' to monetary policy implementation followed by the Fed before the crisis. This approach was also characterized by a collateral framework including only few types of securities that can be used as collateral for open market operations, by the small size of these operations, and by very low reserve requirements. While this approach served the Fed well in fixing the policy interest rate before the crisis, with liquidity demand mostly met through the money market, the broad approach, traditionally followed by the ECB, proved more robust to the changes in the implementation of monetary policy required during the Great Recession.

The interest rate control by the ECB apparently differs from that of the Fed. As it was seen, in the case of the ECB, it is explained in terms of the probability of banks finding themselves short or long of liquidity at the end of the maintenance period. In the case of the Fed, it is explained assuming a downward sloping demand for reserves within the interest rate corridor and the central bank calibrating the supply of reserves to bring the interest rate to the targeted level between the interest on reserves and the discount rate.

Basically, however, the same mechanism is at work for the two central banks: the position of the corridor defines the area within which liquidity supply will more precisely fix the policy interest rate.

This point is well clarified by Friedman and Kuttner (2011, p. 1348). They start their analysis by noting that there is no empirical evidence corroborating the traditional view of how central banks concretely set interest rates:

> How, then, do central banks set interest rates? The traditional account of how this process works involves the central bank's varying the supply of bank reserves, or some other subset of its own liabilities, in the context of an interest-elastic demand

for those liabilities on the part of the private banking system and perhaps other holders as well (including the nonbank public if the relevant measure of central bank liabilities includes currency in circulation).

In effect, the absence of empirical evidence of an interest elastic demand by banks of central bank reserves depends on three key factors:

1. The inverse, non-linear, relationship between central bank reserves and the interest rate only holds within the corridor.
2. If the central bank matches continuously the supply of reserves with their demand, as the ECB did with its benchmark approach, there is no apparent empirical link.
3. With reserve averaging in the course of the maintenance period, the link appears only on the last day of the maintenance period.

Thus, while the underlying link between reserves and interest rates does exist, as documented in the lower panel of Figure 1.16, it can be hidden by these three factors.

In conclusion, both the Fed and the ECB obtained major changes of short-term market rates of interest by moving the corridor. At the Fed this involved the discount rate and the interest on reserves. At the ECB this involved the rate on the deposit facility and the rate on the marginal lending facility. Then both central banks fixed the interest rate more precisely by using liquidity provision. Thus, if they would keep banks in a liquidity deficit situation, forcing them to borrow at the higher rate defining the ceiling of the corridor, the interest rate would move towards that rate. If, instead, they would supply liquidity abundantly, the interest rate would move towards the bottom of the corridor. This is, in particular, what both central banks did during the Great Recession (as will be seen more in detail in Section 2.1) to separate the provision of liquidity from the fixation of the interest rate.

1.3 The Unsettled Issue of Financial Stability

In the two previous sections, the neat and elegant central banking model prevailing before the crisis was described: an independent central bank pursues price stability within an inflation-targeting approach by moving interest rates according to some version of the Taylor rule, by means of an interest rate corridor and liquidity control. The model was applied with some variants in different countries but it was used widely, particularly in advanced economies.

What did not fit neatly within that model was an explicit role of the central bank in the pursuit of financial stability. Although it was the need to ensure financial stability that led to the establishment of some central banks, such as the Fed, this objective is treated in the statutes of various central banks more or less as an afterthought.

In the Maastricht Treaty, and in the Statute of the ECB, financial stability is only briefly mentioned, and only as it relates to banking supervision.

The most explicit formulation is found in Article 127.5 of the Treaty on the Functioning of the European Union (TFEU) (which is repeated in Article 3.3 of the Statute of the ECB):

> The ESCB shall contribute to the smooth conduct of policies pursued by the competent authorities relating to the prudential supervision of credit institutions and the stability of the financial system.

Article 25.1 of the Statute has a further reference to financial stability:

> The ECB may offer advice and be consulted by the Council, the Commission and the competent authorities of the Member States on the scope and implementation of Union legislation relating to the prudential supervision of credit institutions and to the stability of the financial system.

While Article 127.6 of the Treaty refers specifically to supervision:

> The Council, acting by means of regulations in accordance with a special legislative procedure, may unanimously, and after consulting European Parliament and the European Central Bank, confer specific tasks upon the ECB concerning policies relating to the prudential supervision of credit institutions and other financial institutions with the exception of insurance undertakings.

A common weakness of all these formulations is their vague nature: 'contribute to the smooth conduct', 'may offer advice', 'may ... confer specific tasks'. Such vague formulations did not provide a strong basis for the ECB to act on financial stability issues. Compare this with the strong formulation of the price stability objective: 'The primary objective of the European System of Central Banks shall be to maintain price stability.' Indeed, an extensive interpretation of Article 127.6 was required for the decision to grant supervisory powers to the ECB in 2012.

The complexity of defining financial stability adds to the weakness of the Treaty formulation. The ECB defines financial stability as follows:[27]

> Financial stability can be defined as a condition in which the financial system—comprising of financial intermediaries, markets and market infrastructures—is capable of withstanding shocks and the unraveling of financial imbalances, thereby mitigating the likelihood of disruptions in the financial intermediation

---

[27] ECB Financial Stability Review, December 2007, p. 9.

process which are severe enough to significantly impair the allocation of savings to profitable investment opportunities. Understood this way, the safeguarding of financial stability requires identifying the main sources of risk and vulnerability such as inefficiencies in the allocation of financial resources from savers to investors and the mis-pricing or mismanagement of financial risks. This identification of risks and vulnerabilities is necessary because the monitoring of financial stability must be forward looking: inefficiencies in the allocation of capital or shortcomings in the pricing and management of risk can, if they lay the foundations for vulnerabilities, compromise future financial system stability and therefore economic stability.

1. The financial system should be able to efficiently and smoothly transfer resources from savers to investors.

2. Financial risks should be assessed and priced reasonably accurately and should also be relatively well managed.

3. The financial system should be in such a condition that it can comfortably absorb financial and real economic surprises and shocks.

If anyone or a combination of these characteristics is not being maintained, then it is likely that the financial system is moving in a direction of becoming less stable, and at some point might exhibit instability.

Thus, 238 words were needed to define financial stability. Compare it with the neat 53 words needed to define price stability:

The ECB's Governing Council has defined price stability as a year-on-year increase in the Harmonised Index of Consumer Prices (HICP) for the euro-area of below 2percent. The Governing Council has clarified that, in the pursuit of price stability, it aims to maintain inflation rates below, but close to, 2percent over the medium term.

On the basis of the number of words needed to define the two concepts, we may conclude that that of financial stability is more than four times more complicated than that of price stability. Moreover, the pursuit of a complicated objective is necessarily more difficult than the pursuit of a simple objective, even if the two were put, which they were not, on the same level in the hierarchy of objectives. Add the 'fuzziness' in measuring financial stability, analysed by Borio and Drehmann (2009), and the complexity of the pursuit of financial stability is evident.

The last element proving the lower rank of the financial stability objective for the ECB is that the bank only began publishing a financial stability report in 2004, whereas it started, soon after its creation in 1998, to publish an Economic Bulletin.

The situation is different as regards the Federal Reserve System, but not so different that it would establish the prominence of financial stability in the hierarchy of objectives of the central bank. The Federal Reserve Act's official title is:

An Act to provide for the establishment of Federal reserve banks, to furnish an elastic currency, to afford means of rediscounting commercial paper, to establish a more effective supervision of banking in the USA, and for other purposes.

In this title we only find an explicit reference to bank supervision, which is only a part of financial stability. The Mission of the Fed, however, explicitly mentions financial stability:

The Federal Reserve System is the central bank of the USA. It was founded by Congress in 1913 to provide the nation with a safer, more flexible, and more stable monetary and financial system. Over the years, its role in banking and the economy has expanded.

Today, the Federal Reserve's duties fall into four general areas:

- conducting the nation's monetary policy by influencing the monetary and credit conditions in the economy in pursuit of maximum employment, stable prices, and moderate long-term interest rates
- supervising and regulating banking institutions to ensure the safety and soundness of the nation's banking and financial system and to protect the credit rights of consumers
- maintaining the stability of the financial system and containing systemic risk that may arise in financial markets
- providing financial services to depository institutions, the U.S. government, and foreign official institutions, including playing a major role in operating the nation's payments system.

The macroeconomic responsibility of monetary policy is better specified in the Act itself, while hinting at a monetarist approach:

The Board of Governors of the Federal Reserve System and the Federal Open Market Committee shall maintain long run growth of the monetary and credit aggregates commensurate with the economy's long run potential to increase production, so as to promote effectively the goals of maximum employment, stable prices, and moderate long-term interest rates.

There is no equivalent formulation in the Federal Reserve Act for the financial stability objective.

In conclusion, the maintenance of financial stability does appear as an objective to be pursued by the central bank in the statutes of both the ECB and the Fed, but in a weaker form than the macroeconomic objective of price stability and, in case of the Fed, maximum employment. This is not surprising, given that financial stability is a less well-defined concept in its borders and relationships with banking supervision and with the new entry, macro-prudential policy.

The demotion of financial stability in the rank of objectives of central bank did not meet universal agreement even before the Great Recession. Some voices still insisted, well before the crisis, that central banks should devote attention to financial stability issues, including supervision. In fact, Padoa-Schioppa wrote in 2004:

> Over the short span of my service as central banker . . . it was taken for granted that financial stability was a major responsibility of the central bank. Indeed, monetary policy, financial stability, and banking supervision formed a single composite, whose parts were difficult to disentangle.
>
> Now . . . one may wonder whether financial stability—a 'land in between' monetary policy and prudential supervision—still ranks among the tasks of a contemporary central bank. . . . the involvement in financial stability does, and should, remain even today, an important component of central banking.   (pp. 93–4)

As shown in Box 9, analogous points were made by Lamfalussy (as illustrated by Maes, 2010), Crockett (2000) and Borio (2003); indeed, these authors

---

Box 9 FINANCIAL STABILITY, BANKING SUPERVISION, AND MACRO-PRUDENTIAL POLICY: AN INTRICATE RELATIONSHIP

One of the difficulties of defining the responsibilities of central banks in the pursuit of financial stability is that the three concepts of banking supervision, and more generally micro-prudential action, macro-prudential policy, and financial stability have blurred contours. This is not surprising given that one of the components of the trio, macro-prudential policy, has only recently been added as a practical tool to deal with financial instability issues. Maes (2015) credits Lamfalussy for promoting, as far back as the late 1970s, the need to look at financial stability with a macro perspective, and mentions the influence of Minsky in the development of the concept of macro-prudential policy at the BIS: in the 'Lamfalussy Group's final report of 29 February 1980. The term "macroprudential supervision" was used six times, including three times in the conclusion' (Maes, 2010, p. 276).

Maes and Borio mention the public use of the term in 1986 by the BIS in the so-called Cross Report.[28] Borio (2009, p. 32), however, adds: 'it was only at the beginning of the new century that efforts were made to define the term more precisely, so as to derive more specific implications for the architecture of prudential arrangements'.

He added, furthermore, that: 'the usage of the term remains ambiguous'. Indeed, it is the financial and then economic crisis which started in 2007 that set in motion the full effort to develop the concept of macro-prudential policy, to clarify its relationship with financial stability and micro-prudential supervision, and to give operational content to it. In fact, it is only in the October 2009 Global Financial Stability Report of the IMF (IMF, 2009) that one finds frequent use (six times) of the term 'macro-prudential'. That term was, instead, used only once in the report of April 2007 and never in the reports between October 2007 and October 2008. Of course, the lack of

---

[28] BIS (1986).

conceptual clarity negatively affects any practical action: in many ways macro-prudential action is in its intellectual and, even more so, operational infancy. This is striking taking into account that the concept was first advanced, as mentioned, some forty years ago, and clearly articulated at the beginning of the 2000s (Crockett, 2000 and Borio, 2003). Such a long incubation has two, probably concurrent, reasons. First, the concept of macro-prudential policies is highly complex and thus not amenable to straightforward development and implementation. Second, conservatism prevails in central banks and other financial public institutions, standing in the way of new concepts.

A clear, but by no means unanimous, view about the relationship between financial stability and macro-prudential policy is assumed by the ESRB in its Flagship Report on Macro-Prudential Policy in the Banking Sector, of March 2014. According to this report, financial stability is the objective targeted by macro-prudential policy. Indeed, the ESRB even identifies four intermediate objectives of macro-prudential policy to be pursued whilst aiming at the final objective of financial stability.

> To make macroprudential policy operational, intermediate macroprudential object-ives need to be specified. The ESRB has identified four intermediate objectives relevant to the banking sector (ESRB/2013/1). These objectives act as operational specifica-tions to the ultimate objective of achieving financial stability. They aim at preventing/mitigating systemic risks to financial stability that follow from:
>
> - excessive credit growth and leverage . . . ;
> - excessive maturity mismatch and market illiquidity . . . ;
> - direct and indirect exposure concentrations . . . ;
> - misaligned incentives and moral hazard. (p. 7)

The same ESRB report illustrates the work being carried out to develop macro-prudential policy. However, in so doing, it also shows we are far from having a well-defined set of tools that can be precisely calibrated to target the four objectives in the quote and, eventually, the final objective of financial stability. The report clearly shows that we are just at the beginning of collecting empirical data and developing models and approaches that can help macro-prudential policy to reach the same kind of advance-ment that monetary policy reached long time ago.

Borio (2014a) argues, in contrast to the ESRB, that macro-prudential policy cannot, by itself, secure financial stability, and that a more holistic approach is needed, including not only bank supervision and macro-prudential policy but also macroeconomic pol-icies, such as interest rate control and fiscal policy. This conclusion is, in particular, borne out by what Borio (2015) calls the 'time dimension' of financial stability, that is, the succession of booms and busts that characterize the financial cycle, in an approach that is closely reminiscent of that underlying the analyses of Minsky (1986), Kindleberger and Aliber (2005), and Reinhart and Rogoff (2009).

The IMF puts forward the same idea that macro-prudential policy overlaps with other policies in the pursuit of financial stability. Indeed, the IMF views financial stability as interacting not only with monetary, fiscal, structural, and micro-prudential policies, but also with competition, crisis management, and resolution policies. Along similar lines, Brunnermeier and Sannikov (2014) argue that financial stability cannot be separated from price stability; thus monetary policy and macro-prudential policy tools are closely inter-twined, as both induce or restrict financial sector risk-taking. Consistency of the two policies is therefore essential. The BIS, in its 2014 Annual Report (AR) (BIS, 2014), as well as the ECB in its Financial Stability Review (FSR) of May 2013, develop similar arguments.

(continued)

Box 9 CONTINUED

According to Borio (2009) and the IMF (2013), the conceptual distinction between bank supervision and macro-prudential policy is clear. The perspective of macro-prudential policy, on the financial system as a whole, is very different from that of bank supervision, or more generally micro-supervision, which looks at financial firms in isolation. Borio has a nice analogy, drawn from investment theory, to clarify the difference between macro- and micro-prudential policy. The portfolio approach to investment shows that what matters is not the absolute risk and return characteristics of a single security, but the contribution that a security gives to the risk and return of a diversified portfolio. The correlations between the securities in the portfolio are thus the crucial variables. Analogously, the macro-prudential approach looks at shared exposures and common factors across institutions and hence focuses on the contribution of each financial institution to the stability of the overall system. A crucial consequence of this different approach is that for large financial firms risk is not a fully exogenous phenomenon that the individual financial institution has to manage, in analogy to the small country assumption in international economics, but rather an endogenous variable, which is influenced by the behaviour of financial firms.

The different perspectives of macro- and micro-prudential policies mean that there may be synergies but also conflicts between the two approaches. One obvious case of conflict appears during the bust phase of the financial cycle, when the prudent micro approach is to deleverage and sell assets whose risk has increased while the prudent macro approach recognizes that, when generalized, the sell and deleverage approach will give rise to fire-sale spirals, contributing to the crisis. Borio (2009) summarizes the uncertain relationship between the micro and the macro approach, concluding that stability in the former sense is neither a necessary nor a sufficient condition for the stability in the latter sense.

Francesco Papadia

---

established something like a 'BIS school' on the need to pursue both price and financial stability. This, however, did not represent the mainstream view before the crisis.

Overall, the lack of clarity surrounding the financial stability mandate in the statutes of the ECB and the Fed interacted with the low priority attributed to financial stability by central banks, to make financial stability a neglected field. Indeed, it came to temporary prominence only in special circumstances, for instance, the 1987 stock exchange crash, the attack of 9/11, and the passage to the new millennium.

While attention to the theme of financial stability was fairly low, some dramatic developments were taking place in the financial sphere. Padoa-Schioppa (2004) summarized them as follows:

- renewed instability;
- expansion of financial sphere relative to the real economy;
- technological progress;

- financial innovation;
- globalization;
- role of central banks.

Goodhart (2004—in Padoa-Schioppa, 2004) had a shorter, possibly complementary, list:

- more competition across sectors and across jurisdictions;
- the abolition of direct controls, part of a move towards freer markets.

While most policymakers and observers considered the financial stability implications of these developments only in episodes of stress, a chain of events was set in motion whose systemic consequences would be generally revealed only after the crisis had exploded. With hindsight, these developments followed a recurrent pattern. Three complementary books identify this pattern: Kindleberger (1978) offers a narrative of recurrent financial crises over the centuries. Reinhart and Rogoff (2009) provide enormous empirical material measuring all possible aspects of the crises, including their sources and consequences. Minsky (1986) offers a possible theory of endogenous economic instability.

Kindleberger and Aliber (2005) identified the common features of the sequence of manias, panics, and crashes—the hardy perennial, as they call it. According to these authors, the manias phase is started by an exogenous, positive shock, which hits the economy and leads to excessive profits, excessive debt (which obviously corresponds to excessive credit) much of it going across borders, too high asset prices (mainly for real estate and equities), abundant liquidity, and often buoyant economic activity, led by lending. The initial shock can be of a variegated nature, but often consists of a financial innovation or liberalization, which is eventually followed by a crisis. One relatively optimistic hypothesis explaining this sequence is that there is a learning process when a liberalization or innovation takes place. The innovation is at first poorly understood and inappropriately regulated, leading to a misuse or even abuse, possibly of a fraudulent nature. Then, at a certain point, the market wakes up and, in the panic phase, the process abruptly goes into reverse: credit and liquidity dry up, especially of the cross-border nature, asset prices plunge, economic activity moves from positive to negative rates of growth, liquidity evaporates, banks and other institutions fail or require very costly bail-outs, burdening the public budget, and, more often than, not the affected currency depreciates. In the words of Kindleberger and Aliber (2005, p. 62):

> Speculative manias gather speed through expansion of credit. Most increases in the supply of credit do not lead to a mania—but nearly any mania has been associated with rapid growth in the supply of credit to a particular group of borrowers.

Reinhart and Rogoff shone new light on the recurrent crises with time series and cross-section quantitative material.[29] In hindsight, it is surprising how the huge amount of data they collected had not received sufficient attention before their book. The insights derived from the data collected by Reinhart and Rogoff are as deep as their concepts and methodology are straightforward. The same observation can be made for the huge amount of narrative that is in the Kindleberger and Aliber book. In this sense, the two books are similar.

According to Reinhart and Rogoff (2009, p. 18):

> If there is a common theme to the vast range of crises we consider in this book, it is that excessive debt accumulation, whether it be by the governments, banks, corporations and consumers, often poses greater systemic risks than it seems during a boom.

Minsky (2008, pp. 230–1) went beyond illustrating recurrent crises to provide a theory explaining them. In so doing he identified three types of financing units: hedge, speculative, and Ponzi. First, hedge financing units involve 'cash flow from operating capital assets (or from owning financial contracts) to be more than sufficient to meet contractual payment commitments now and in the future'. Second, speculative-financing units involve 'cash flows to the unit from operating assets (or from owning financial contracts) to be less than the cash payment commitments in some, typically near-term, periods.... [but]...expected income receipts exceed the income (interest) payments on existing commitments in every period'. Third, Ponzi-financing units entail 'at least some near-term periods, the cash payment commitments on income account exceed the expected cash payment receipts on income account...so that the face amount of outstanding debt increases: Ponzi units capitalize interest into their liability structure'.

Minsky argues there are profit motives to move, in tranquil times, from hedge to speculative and finally to Ponzi financing, at which point the move is overdone and a crisis follows. His model therefore belongs, in Borio's 2011 categorization, to the endogenous variety, in which it is the financial system itself that generates the dynamics leading to instability and then to the crisis. In Minsky's model, as a consequence of the crisis, there is a return to hedge financing but then the process starts again. The crucial distinction between the three types of financing is given by the different needs of external funding, which is non-existent for hedge financing, present but not acute for speculative financing, and acute for Ponzi financing. Therefore, in Minsky's model,

---

[29] An analysis of bank credit booms over 170 countries for a period of half a century between 1960 and 2010 was carried out by Dell'Ariccia et al. (2012). Their analysis confirms that in one third of the cases in their sample credit booms are followed by financial crises.

debt developments are a crucial variable in progressively moving the economy from a non-crisis to a crisis situation. In this respect there is an evident common theme with the analyses of Kindleberger and Aliber (2005) as well as Reinhart and Rogoff (2009). Minsky thus goes much further in his theorizing to conclude that there is an intrinsic economic instability. This is, however, an extension of the theory that is not really needed in order to use Minsky's model as archetypal description of a financial crisis, fitting both the narrative of Kindleberger and Aliber as well as the empirical evidence of Reinhart and Rogoff.

In the euro-area there was one additional factor adding to the complexity of the financial stability issue. Monetary unification had left, consistently with the vague treatment of financial stability in the Statute of the ECB, the dominant responsibilities for financial stability at a national level. Enria (2011, p. 10), in his introduction to the Italian version of the book by Padoa-Schioppa, thus summarized this author's view (our translation):

> The red thread of all the essays in this book is the keen awareness of Padoa-Schioppa that, with monetary union, systemic risk had acquired a European dimension and required bolder institutional changes and more ambitious policies. The single currency and integrated money and financial markets needed the pursuit of public interest for financial stability at a higher level, namely the European one.

To put it directly in Padoa-Schioppa's words, the issue is:

> the novelty of abandoning the coincidence between the jurisdiction of monetary policy and the jurisdiction of banking supervision. Monetary policy embraces the twelve countries that have adopted the euro, whereas banking supervision remains national.   (p. 75)

Although these considerations look obvious now, they were, as mentioned, far from the focus of attention of central banks before the crisis. The importance of this factor as one of those contributing to the crisis will be examined in Section 1.4.3.

The limited attention to financial stability, however, hid the occurrence of dilemmas. To see why this is the case, one has to recall the Tinbergen (1952) result that, in a deterministic system, one needs as many tools as there are objectives, in order to avoid dilemmas. In a stochastic system, instead, as shown by Brainard (1967), the more tools there are relative to the number of objectives, the better it is. Given that, as argued, central banks basically had, at least before the Great Recession, just one tool—interest rates—giving them more than one objective would create potential dilemmas.

Dilemmas potentially faced by central banks are graphically illustrated in Figure 1.18. This adapts an approach used to illustrate possible dilemmas between fighting inflation and unemployment during the era of stagflation in the 1970s.

Quadrants II and IV denote no-dilemmas. For example, in quadrant II, inflation as well as risk appetite are too high and an increase of the interest rate is required. In quadrant IV, the opposite situation prevails. In quadrant I, there is, instead, a dilemma because inflation is too high, but there is too low risk appetite and therefore it is not obvious whether the interest rate should be increased or decreased. Symmetrically, in quadrant III, price and financial stability would require opposite movements of the interest rate because, in this case, inflation is too low, but there are also risks to financial stability coming from excessive risk appetite. According to White (2009), in quadrant III, the dilemma takes the 'clean versus lean' specific form: Should monetary policy be content to keep inflation in check and just 'clean' the consequences of the crisis once the mania phase is followed by the panic and crash phase? Or should monetary policy be tighter in the mania phase (when there are financial stability risks) than what is just needed to keep prices stable and 'lean against the wind' of excessive optimism, thus surpassing the prescriptions of inflation targeting? According to this latter interpretation, the central bank

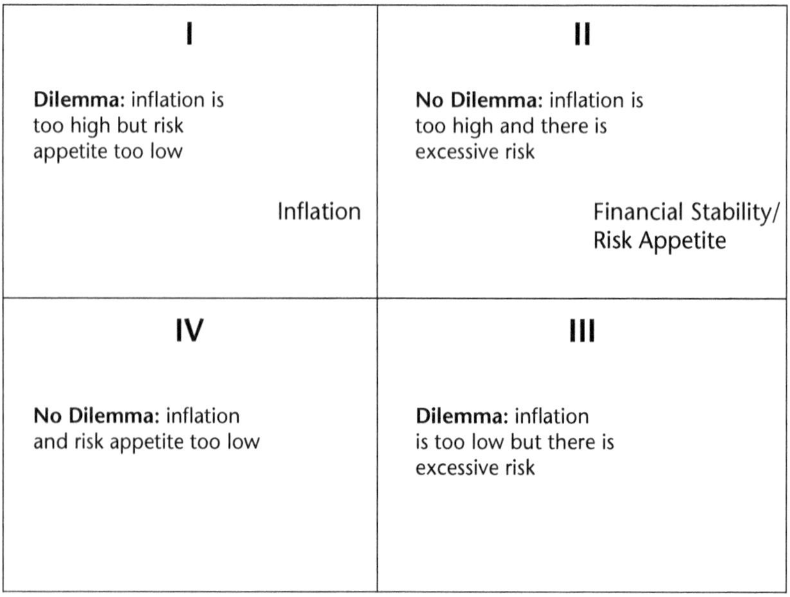

I	II
Dilemma: inflation is too high but risk appetite too low	**No Dilemma:** inflation is too high and there is excessive risk
Inflation	Financial Stability/ Risk Appetite
IV	**III**
No Dilemma: inflation and risk appetite too low	**Dilemma:** inflation is too low but there is excessive risk

Figure 1.18 Diagram of Central Bank Dilemma between Inflation and Financial Stability/ Risk Appetite

should, in the middle of market euphoria, keep a more guarded attitude and transmit sobriety to the market, tightening financial conditions.

Of course, no dilemma would occur if a new class of instruments, namely macro-prudential tools, could be assigned to financial stability, and if the instruments were sufficiently effective, leaving the interest rate exclusively assigned to price stability. Macro-prudential tools would preserve financial stability by acting on some parameters of the financial market. For instance, tools might include limiting the maximum share of the value of a house that can be covered by a mortgage (the so-called loan-to-value ratio) or increasing, under some circumstances, the equity banks have to keep against a given balance sheet size (the so-called dynamic capital charges).

There is neither agreement about the effectiveness of macro-prudential tools nor about the relative advantages or disadvantages of assigning interest rates exclusively to price stability and macro-prudential tools to financial stability. Using interest rates also for financial stability purposes has the advantage that it 'gets in all of the cracks'[30] (Stein, 2013, p. 17), meaning that it covers both banks and non-bank intermediaries. Assigning, instead, interest rates to price stability and macro-prudential tools to financial stability would have the advantage of potentially freeing the central bank from dilemmas. The issue is further complicated because, as argued by Brunnermeier and Sannikov (2014), the effects of the two classes of tools cannot be clearly separated. For instance, macro-prudential measures aimed at the maintenance of financial stability inevitably have an effect analogous to that of tightening monetary moves. The neat, if problematic, dilemma approach presented in Figure 1.18 is, in this perspective, simplistic as there is no clear separation possible between macro-prudential and monetary policies. Whatever resolution one gives to this conceptual controversy, de facto macro-prudential policy has not helped monetary policy to preserve financial stability, because the relevant tools were just not yet operationally available when the Great Recession hit.

Chapter 3 will examine how the situation has changed after the Great Recession. In particular, it will be assessed whether macro-prudential tools, a fairly recent invention, provide a way out of dilemmas. Here, it must be reiterated that central banks entered the Great Recession with an unclear responsibility about financial stability and without the support of macro-prudential policies. Indeed, macro-prudential policies started to mature as a consequence of the Great Recession and thus are more a tool to reduce the

---

[30] The full quotation is: 'while monetary policy may not be quite the right tool for the job, it has one important advantage relative to supervision and regulation—namely that it gets in all of the cracks. To the extent that market rates exert an influence on risk appetite, or on the incentives to engage in maturity transformation, changes in rates may reach into corners of the market that supervision and regulation cannot' (p. 17).

likelihood, or the intensity, of the next crisis rather than having been a tool to deal with the Great Recession. It is meaningful that the Flagship Report on Macro-Prudential Policy in the Banking Sector, issued by the European Systemic Risk Board (ESRB) in March 2014, proudly announced that: 'The EU is now ready to conduct macro-prudential policy' (p. 4), meaning that it was not ready until then. Indeed, it explicitly said:

> The new prudential rules for the EU banking system came into force on 1 January 2014. They provide Member States with a common legal framework that includes a set of macroprudential instruments. This structural innovation in EU policy-making was born out of the global financial crisis. (p. 4)

The Flagship Report also has a table (Table 1 on p. 5) with 13 examples of macro-prudential measures taken in Europe at national level: of the 13 measures, three were taken in 2010 and the other ten in 2012. The report confirms that, even at national level, macro-prudential measures were more an outcome of the crisis than a tool available when the Great Recession manifested itself. The same conclusion is reached by Akinci and Olmstead-Rumsey (2015), who note that the frequency of use of macro-prudential measures intensified during the Great Recession, as well as Cerutti, Claessens, and Laeven (2015), who recorded an increase of the macro-prudential measures taken in the euro-area from 11 in 2006 to 29 in 2013.

As will be seen more in detail in Section 3.4, macro-prudential policies are even less developed in the United States than in Europe.

1.4 Planting the Seeds of the Great Recession: Macroeconomic, Regulatory, Supervisory, and Intellectual Failings

1.4.1 *The Great Moderation*

Between 1985 and 2007, the volatility of American real growth and inflation was significantly less than in the previous decades (Figure 1.19).

The same phenomenon was recorded in the euro-area (Figure 1.20).

Instead, volatility between 1986 and 2007 remained high in emerging economies (Figure 1.21).

The higher stability in the advanced economies was sustained over two decades and led to the name Great Moderation being coined (see Box 10).

Bernanke (2012, p. 146) identified as possible causes of the Great Moderation: 'structural change, improved macroeconomic policies, and good luck'. He added: 'My view is that improvements in monetary policy, though certainly not the only factor, have probably been an important source of the great moderation.'

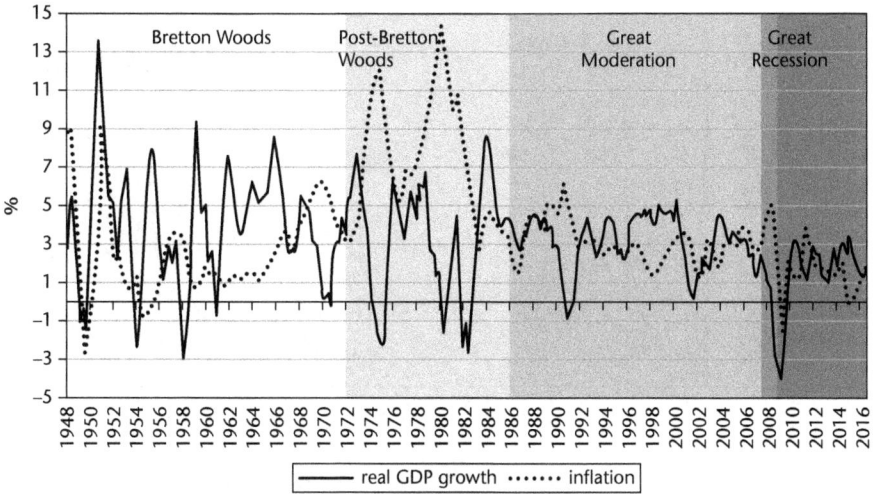

Figure 1.19 Inflation and Real GDP Growth in the USA (1948–2016)
Note: Consumer Price Index for all Urban Consumers and Real GDP.
Source: Federal Reserve Economic Data (FRED).

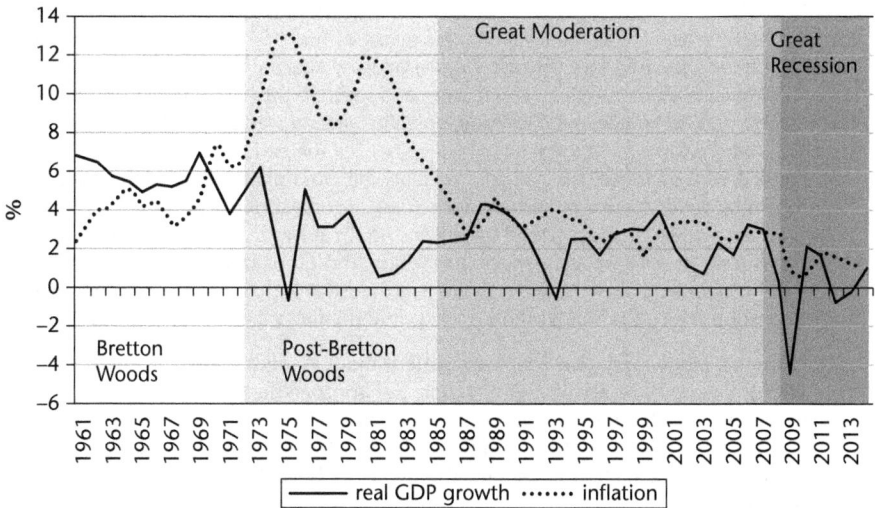

Figure 1.20 Inflation and Real GDP Growth in the Euro-Area (1961–2013)
Source: European Commission, Annual Macro-Economics Database (AMECO).

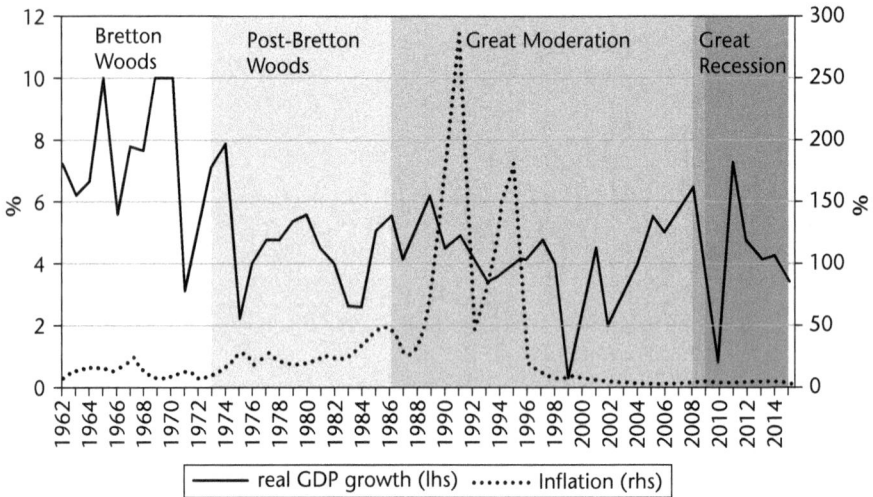

Figure 1.21 Inflation and Real GDP Growth in Emerging Economies (1962–2014)
Source: World Development Indicators, World Bank.

Box 10 CHARACTERISTICS OF THE GREAT MODERATION

The Great Moderation is empirically represented by the reduction in the volatility of the main macroeconomic aggregates, above all, output, employment, and inflation in advanced economies. A graphical representation is provided in Figures B.10.1 and B.10.2. In the first Figure we can see how the volatility of quarterly GDP in most advanced economies fell gradually from the peaks of mid-1970s to the years before the global financial crisis. This process was particularly sharp in the USA, where, after 1985, GDP growth volatility fell by seven times and reached the lowest levels among the major economies. In France and Germany, volatility already started to fall at the end of the 1970s, whereas the UK experienced instability until the early 1990s.

In Figure B.10.2 one sees that not only volatility fell, but inflation levels converged to the inflation target of the main central banks in advanced economies.

Several causes have been advanced to explain the Great Moderation. In the main text, attention is paid to the role of financial innovation and globalization as well as to the conduct of monetary policy. However, a more exhaustive list can summarize the main factors contributing to the stabilization of output and inflation in four categories.

1. Financial innovation and increased integration at global level (Dynan et al., 2006). Examples of financial innovation are improvements in the asset pricing, reduction of collateral requirements for household lending, and market development for corporate debt. In addition, global integration led to allocation efficiency. All these factors enhanced the ability of households and businesses to borrow funds.

2. Improved monetary policy in reducing the volatility of both inflation and real economic activity (Clarida, Galí, and Gertler, 2000). According to this

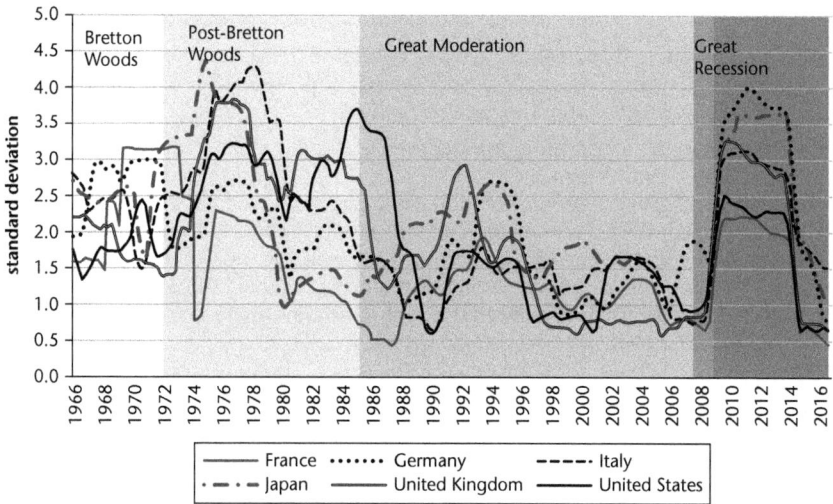

Figure B.10.1 Volatility of GDP in Selected Countries (Standard Deviation of Year-on-Year Growth in Percentage Terms—Five-Year Window)

Source: FRED.

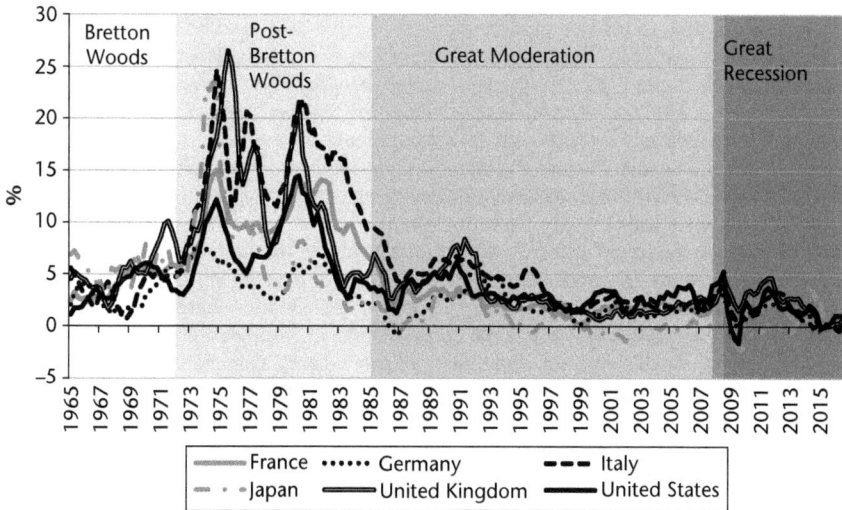

Figure B.10.2 Quarterly Inflation Rate, Year-on-Year (1965–2015)

Source: FRED.

(continued)

Box 10 CONTINUED

interpretation, the increased ability of central banks to implement inflation targeting helped to reduce both levels and variability of inflation rates, with similar effects on the level of output.

3. Technological advances in managing the supply chain (for example, Kahn, McConnell, and Perez-Quiros, 2002). This explanation is based on the evidence that volatility in the production of durable goods fell whereas that of sales stayed relatively constant. Technological improvements like the development of information and communications technology (ICT) technologies, increased flexibility in production, and better forecasting techniques (Summers, 2005) are examples of such advances. They all reduced the need to accumulate inventories as well as the risk of running into a shortage of inventories.

4. The 'good luck' assumption (see Stock and Watson, 2002), which suggests that the lower volatility during the Great Moderation was mostly the result of smaller shocks affecting the global economy. The strict version of this explanation simply states that the variance of all economic shocks fell uniformly during the Great Moderation. The weak version of the assumption states that volatility fell because of smaller shocks only in a subset of variables that are particularly relevant for output and inflation dynamics.

Most of the literature on the Great Moderation focuses on the USA (Clarida, Gali, and Gertler, 2000; Kahn, McConnell, and Perez-Quiros, 2002; Stock and Watson, 2002; Davis, 2008, Davis and Kahn, 2008; Galí and Gambetti, 2008). However, there are also a few analyses of other advanced economies (Summers, 2005; González Cabanillas and Rusche, 2008).

Studies pointing to the role of technological changes are based on the evidence that, in terms of growth accounting, most of the reduction in the volatility of output came from the production of durable goods, whereas the volatility of durable goods sales did not fall (Kahn, McConnell, and Perez-Quiros, 2002; Davis and Kahn, 2008). Such evidence provided a direct criticism to the explanation based on improved monetary policy. If the fall in volatility was the result of 'good luck' or improved monetary policy, the effect would have been uniform across sectors and no major differences should be observed between the volatility of production and that of sales. Instead, the concentration of volatility reduction in the durable goods production sectors suggests that factors related to changes in production processes played a role. In this respect, Kahn, McConnell, and Perez-Quiros (2002) provide an explanation based on the role of changes in inventory behaviour as a consequence of improvements in information technology (IT). Such innovation led to a more precise and faster reaction of production to demand changes. This conclusion is shared by Davis and Kahn (2008), who provide additional evidence on the dominant role of lower volatility in durable goods output in explaining the decrease in total output volatility.

Studies pointing to the role of improved macroeconomic policy do not neglect the contribution of technological advances in stabilizing output and inflation fluctuations, but emphasize the role of policies. The role of improved monetary policy was first stressed by Clarida, Gali, and Gertler (2000), who analysed the conduct of the Fed monetary policy before and after the leadership of Paul Volcker. The authors find that during the Volcker–Greenspan era the Fed raised both nominal and real interest rates in response to an increase in inflation expectations. In a basic Taylor rule framework this means that monetary policy actually stabilized inflation, whereas previously the increase affected only nominal rates, leaving room for bursts in inflation and output as a consequence of self-fulfilling expectations.

Galí and Gambetti (2008) compare the technological and the policy explanations by studying the co-movements among output, hours worked, and labour productivity. They provide evidence of the major role of policy improvements in the reduction of volatility. Their conclusion is based on two findings: first, that the contribution of technological shock—that is, supply-side shocks to labour productivity—on the volatility of output remained constant during the second half of the twentieth century; second, that the contribution of non-technological shocks—that is, shocks affecting productivity through aggregate demand—fell during the same period. Technology and non-technology shocks are identified in a structural vector autoregressive (VAR) framework based on the persistence of their effects: technology shocks are assumed to have a permanent effect on labour productivity whereas non-technology shocks are assumed to only have a temporary impact.

The authors recognize their result is consistent with positive effects of technological changes, especially in terms of better labour markets, as the volatility of technology shocks also fell. However, they give more weight to the policy explanation. In particular, they consider the lower contribution of non-technology shocks to output volatility to be the positive effect of the shift towards policies focusing on inflation stabilization and of the improved efficiency of fiscal stabilizers.

The focus on the US economy led scholars to interpret the international evidence in a single framework, with little effort to understand the different causes that may have affected the timing and speed of the Great Moderation in other countries. This view is challenged by Summers (2005), who argues that, since the reduction of volatility started at different times and proceeded at different paces, a common explanation does not fit all countries. By providing evidence on the G7 countries (Canada, France, Germany, Italy, Japan, the UK, and the USA), he concludes that technological advances and improvements in monetary policy are both fundamental in explaining the reduction of volatility. The technological story seems to fit the data for all seven countries while improvements in monetary policy do not matter for Japan. Little support is found for the 'good luck' explanation. The author does find some evidence that the volatility of oil prices might have played a role in Italy and Australia, but the evidence is not strong.

The analysis of González Cabanillas and Rusche (2008) provides interesting insights on the role of both monetary and fiscal policy in explaining the Great Moderation in the euro-area. They find that the correlation between interest rates and inflation increased in euro-area countries and interpret it as the result of improved counter-cyclicality in the conduct of monetary policy. As for fiscal policies, the authors argue that the increase in the size of government expenditure reflects an increase in both size and effectiveness of the automatic stabilizers in reducing volatility. Their econometric evidence confirms the role of these two factors as main determinants of the Great Moderation, alongside other factors such as the structural change towards services and innovations in product, labour, and financial markets. Their results also point to differences between the core and the periphery of the euro-area. The latter seem to have benefited the most from improvements in the conduct of both fiscal and monetary policy due to the fact that they were coming out of a period of severe mismanagement.

In conclusion, there is a general consensus that the Great Moderation in the USA and the other advanced economies was driven by several factors alongside the globalization

(continued)

Box 10 CONTINUED

---

process. The most important factors are a combination of improved monetary policy and technological changes. The reduction of the size of global shocks implied in the 'good luck' explanation finds little support. Monetary policy and macroeconomic policy in general seem to have been particularly effective in reducing volatility in the periphery of the euro-area. This can be considered a positive effect of the euro-area fiscal policy rules and the centralization of monetary policy. However, as stressed in the main text, the positive conditions experienced during the Great Moderation allowed the accumulation of imbalances within the euro-area, planting the seeds of the European crisis.

Piero Esposito

The brief description of the superior monetary policy technology to which Bernanke refers is the inflation-targeting strategy applied by independent central banks devoted to price stability, covered in Section 1.2.3. Bernanke also gave weight to a higher parameter in the 1980s for the inflation gap and a lower one for the output gap in the Taylor rule, consistent with the enhanced emphasis on price stability. The change, according to Bernanke, is that the coefficient on inflation in the Taylor rule has risen from something less than 1 before 1979 to a value significantly greater than 1 in the more recent period.

Further contributing to the superior economic performance during the Great Moderation was the globalization of the economy, in the sense of reduced importance of national borders for economic transactions, both real and financial. Particularly important in this respect was the integration of China, Central and Eastern European countries, and other emerging market economies (EMEs) in the global economy.

Goodhart, Pradhan, and Pardeshi (2015) set the integration of China and Central and Eastern European countries in a broader and longer lasting development, which they denote as the 'Global Demographic Sweet Spot' that prevailed between the mid-sixties and approximately until the beginning of the Great Recession. This development started with a favourable demographic trend in the mid-sixties, namely the fall of the dependency ratio, whereby the ratio of those in working age rose relative to the dependent young and old. This favourable trend was then forcefully sustained and intensified by the integration of China and Eastern and Central European countries into the world economy since the end of the 1980s, which made hundreds of millions of workers relevant for the equilibrium of the world economy and exercised an upward effect on growth and a downward push on inflation (Jaumotte and Tytell, 2007). This process also brought about, however, lower wages, income inequality, as well as lower productivity growth, since the labour/capital ratio increased.

According to Goodhart, Pradhan, and Pardeshi, the 'Global Demographic Sweet Spot' is reverting and demographics will turn from providing tailwinds into headwinds over the next decades. The importance of this projection for the future of central banking will be analysed in Section 3.5.

What can be further noted here is that globalization reduced volatility through a diversification effect. As the increase in the number of securities in a portfolio reduces (non-linearly) the variance of the portfolio, so the increase in the number of countries fully participating in the global economy should reduce its volatility. This effect, however, works at low frequencies, more as a background force than something that can explain cyclical developments. For instance, it should not be compared with the volatility that appeared with the beginning of the Great Recession.

While the world was enjoying the Great Moderation, macroeconomic and financial imbalances were growing. This phenomenon is in line with Minsky's view that imbalances grow in 'tranquil times',[31] as the financial system gradually moves from a situation in which 'hedge financing units' prevail towards one in which 'speculative financing units' are widespread, until finally it becomes a financial system full of 'Ponzi financing units'.

1.4.2 Macroeconomic Failings

Macroeconomic imbalances had different characteristics in the USA and in Europe, particularly in the euro-area, and these imbalances manifested themselves at different times. However, when, in 2010, the crisis moved on to Europe, the basic similarity between the American and the European experiences became apparent. The common dominant feature in the two areas was very high credit growth, often straddling national borders.[32]

The domestic dimension of the increase of credit in relation to income is visible in Figure 1.22. In the USA, the UK, and euro-area economies, with the partial exception of Germany, credit growth significantly exceeded that of income during the Great Moderation. The ratio between credit and income peaked around the beginning of the Great Recession and then declined.

---

[31] The expression 'tranquil times' is used in Minsky (1995, p. 203). The full quotation is: 'In tranquil times, as risk aversion attenuates, units which have established mutually profitable relations with bankers for the short-term financing of short-term positions find it feasible and prospectively profitable to introduce some short-term financing of longer term assets into their liability structure.'

[32] The IMF Global Financial Stability Report of September 2011 notes: 'among credit variables, annual growth of the credit-to-GDP ratio above 5 percentage points can signal increased risk of a financial crisis about two years in advance. This is especially so if credit includes direct cross-border loans from foreign financial institutions. Importantly, credit-based indicators are far more effective if combined with other variables, as this allows for a better understanding of the underlying cause of the increase in credit. This reduces the risk of inappropriate use of macroprudential policies when the expansion of credit is supporting healthy economic growth' (p. xi).

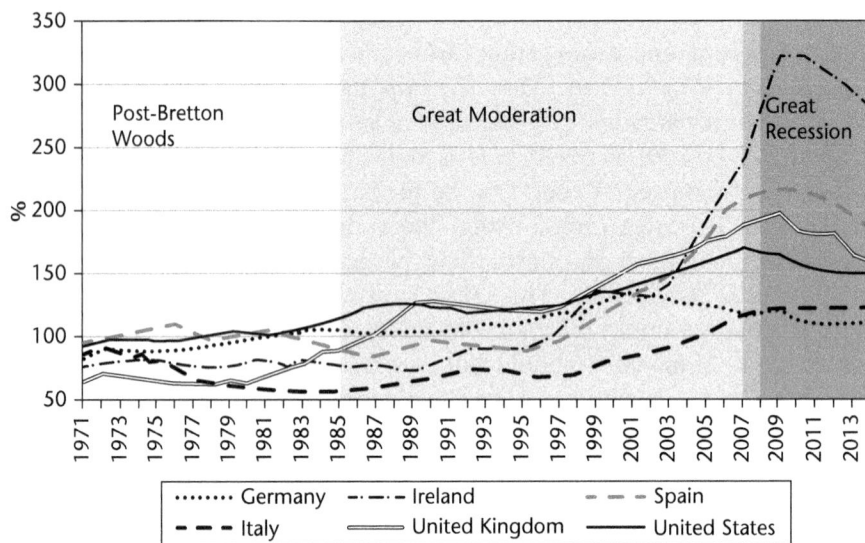

Figure 1.22 Ratio between Total Credit to Private Non-Financial Sector and GDP (1971–2013)

Source: Author's calculations with BIS data and European Commission, AMECO Database.

The ranking of countries in terms of the level of the peak broadly corresponds to the ranking of severity of the subsequent crisis: the countries in which the ratio between credit and income grew the most, such as Ireland and Spain, were most seriously hit by the crisis.

The global dimension of the increase of credit to income in the period preceding the Great Recession is visible, in particular, in the huge current account deficit of the USA, matched by the huge current account surplus of China since the end of the 1990s (Figure 1.23).[33] The specular behaviour of the two variables underlines the importance of the bilateral relationship between the USA and China and the common causes of changes in their current accounts. Like the ratio of domestic credit to GDP, seen in Figure 1.22, current account imbalances of the USA and China also grew significantly until the beginning of the Great Recession, but were partly reabsorbed in subsequent years.

Underlying these imbalances were the very meagre savings in the USA, unable to fund investment in that country, and huge savings in China, exceeding by far the exceptionally large investment. To a large extent, the

---

[33] The emphasis on the current account here and later in this section when examining the imbalances within the euro-area does not imply that only the net between capital inflows and outflows indicates excessive credit: gross flows can lead to financial stability issues even if they do not give rise to large net figures.

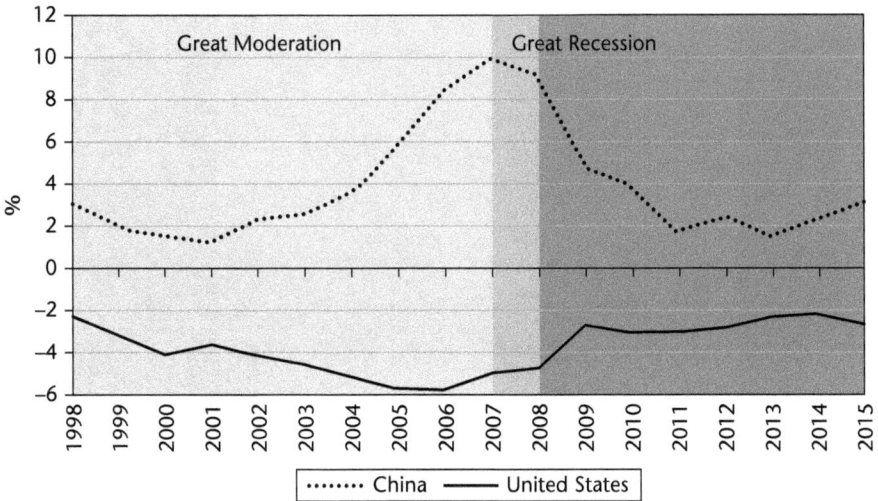

Figure 1.23 Current Account Balance in China and USA, Percentage of GDP (1998–2015)

Source: IMF–World Economic Outlook Database.

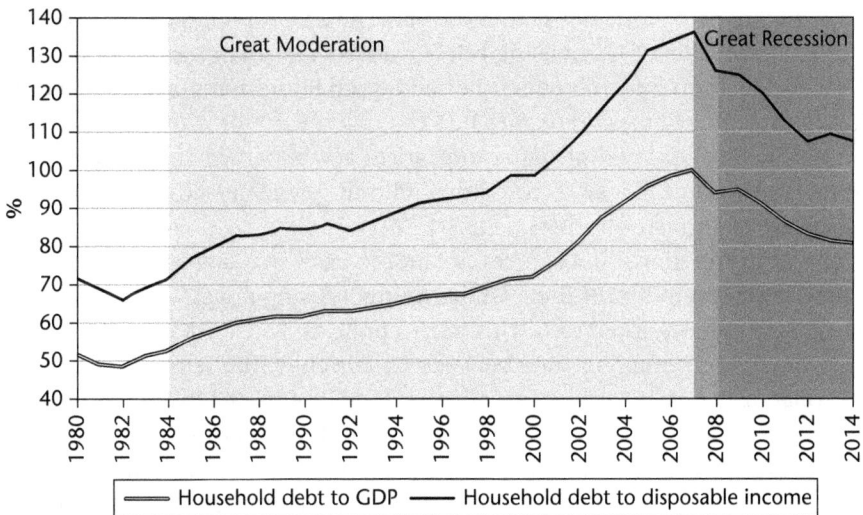

Figure 1.24 US Households' Debt, Percentage of GDP and Percentage of Disposable Income (1980–2014)

Source: FRED.

foreign debt of the USA corresponded to the debt of its household sector, which nearly doubled in per cent of GDP and of disposable income between 1980 and 2008 (Figure 1.24). Again, only with the beginning of the Great Recession was a partial correction achieved.

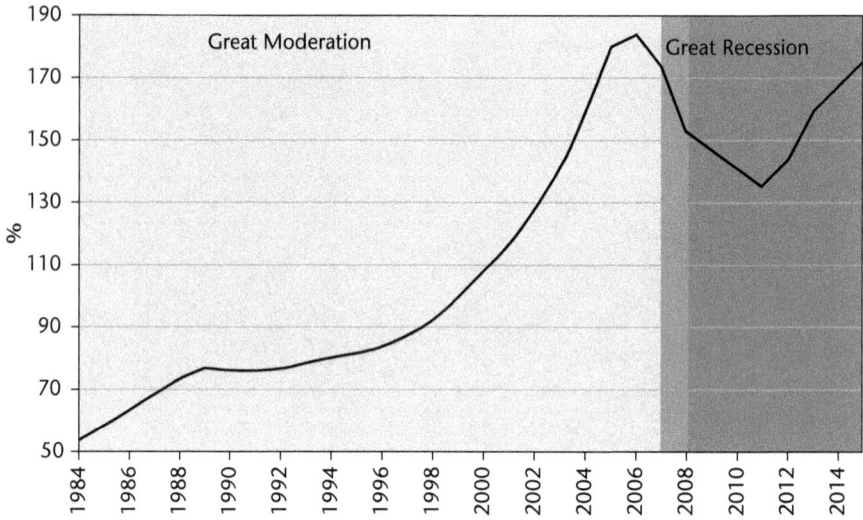

Figure 1.25 S&P/Case-Shiller US National Home Price Index (1984–2014)
Source: Standard and Poors.

The higher debt of the household sector in the USA was, in turn, interrelated with the explosion of US housing prices, which more than tripled during the Great Moderation and subsequently had a partial and temporary correction during the Great Recession (Figure 1.25).

The low level of volatility of equity prices accompanied the explosion of housing prices in the USA, before it would multiply by a factor of eight after the failure of Lehman Brothers (Figure 1.26).

Domestic and global imbalances, including excessive saving in China and excessive consumption in the USA, booming housing prices, and low equity volatility obviously interacted with macro policies. As China in practice had fixed the foreign exchange rate between its currency, the renminbi, and the US dollar, it maintained the competitiveness of its exports, thus contributing to a current account deficit in the USA. In turn, the negative contribution of net exports to aggregate demand in the USA was matched by expansionary fiscal and accommodative monetary policy. This resulted in the national savings rate in the USA deteriorating further. Emerging market countries, China in particular, entering rapidly into the global trade and production chains, contained price pressures. This further kept inflation low in advanced economies and hence facilitated maintaining low interest rates over a long period of time. Taylor (2012) argued that if monetary policy had followed his rule in the new century as it had in the previous 20 years, maintaining a stricter stance, things would have turned out much better. Indeed, in his view,

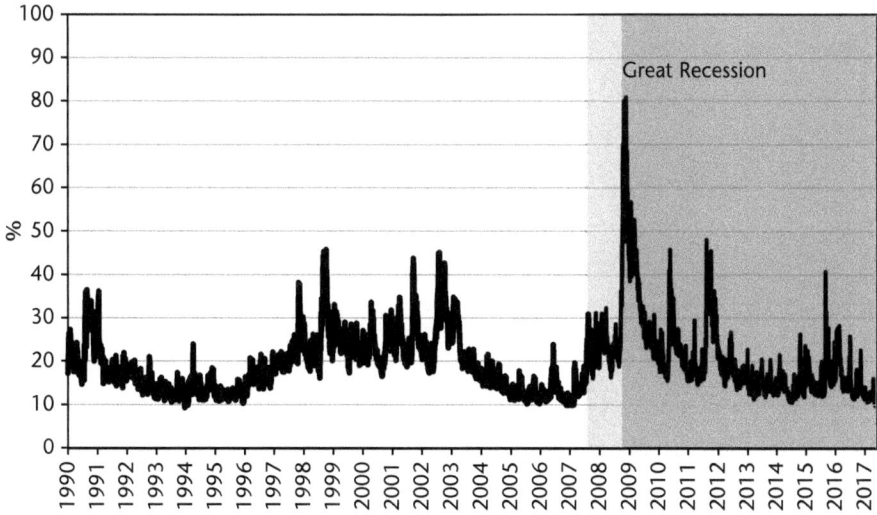

Figure 1.26 Volatility of Asset Prices in the USA (1990–2017)
Note: VIX measures market expectation of near-term volatility conveyed by stock index option prices.
Source: Chicago Board Options Exchange, CBOE Volatility Index.

if the Taylor rule had been followed, interest rates would have been 2 to 3 percentage points higher in the USA in some years and this would have mitigated the upswing, particularly in terms of housing prices, and, arguably, would have reduced the intensity of the crash. In his conclusions, in Europe adherence to the Taylor rule would also have brought about higher rates and a better macroeconomic performance.

In Europe, particularly in the euro-area, imbalances mostly took a different appearance from those in the USA; however, there were some fundamental analogies between the cross-country imbalances within the euro-area and the global mismatch of savings versus consumption.

Basically, during the Great Moderation and particularly before the launch of the European Monetary Union (EMU), a sharp decrease of nominal interest rates took place in the countries that, during the crisis, would be considered as peripheral to the euro-area. The introduction of the euro at the beginning of 1999 perfected this move. Indeed, the level of interest rates that had prevailed for a long time in core countries with a long history of price stability, especially Germany, came to prevail across the entire euro-area. This is seen in Figure 1.27, where yields for ten-year government bonds for the four largest economies of the euro-area, Germany, France, Italy, and Spain, are reported since 1980.

Here four different periods are clearly identified. First, there was the convergence period, which roughly coincides with the Great Moderation, starting in

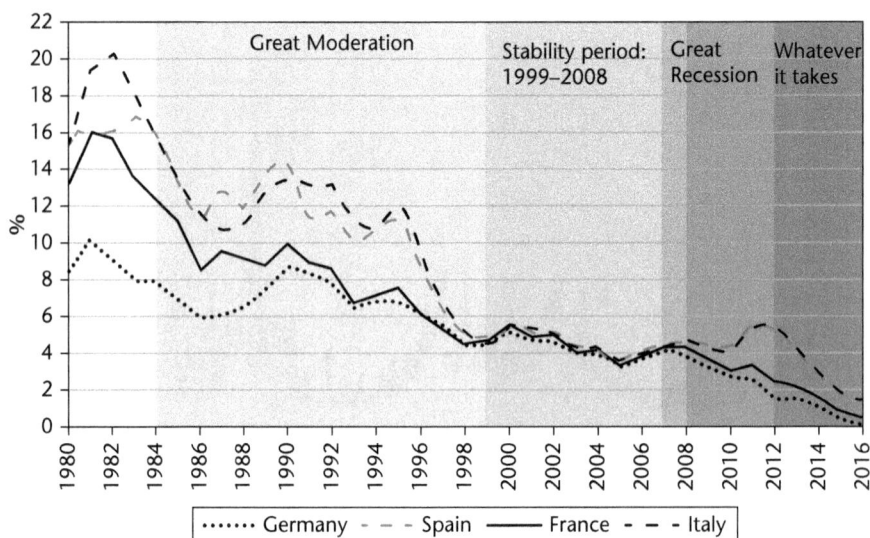

Figure 1.27 Ten-Year Nominal Government Bond Yields in Selected Euro-Area Countries (1980–2016)

Source: European Commission, AMECO Database.

the early 1980s, getting more obvious in the middle of the 1990s with the prospect of the single monetary policy, and eventually perfecting itself with the launch of the euro in 1999. Second, a period of stability ensued that lasted until the autumn of 2008. During this second period yields were practically the same for all euro-area sovereign issuers, because of the equalization of liquidity and credit premia, in addition to expected short-term rates. The most notable development in this period, concerning the euro-area sovereign spreads, was the increasing number of countries joining the single currency area. When the euro was launched there were 11 member states, by 2008 there were 15. The third period started with the Great Recession, after the fall of Lehman Brothers, and had its climax at the peak of the euro-area sovereign debt crisis, in the summer of 2012. The final period may be dated to start with the partial reabsorption of the tensions after the ECB President Mario Draghi delivered his famous speech in London in July of 2012, stating that the bank would do 'whatever it takes' to preserve the euro.

While, during the Great Moderation, interest rates in the periphery approached those in the core and followed them lower during the Stability Period, inflation did not adjust to the same degree, as shown in Figure 1.28, which reveals that for last years of the Great Moderation and for practically the entire Stability Period, inflation in the peripheral countries, Spain and Italy, remained higher than in the core.

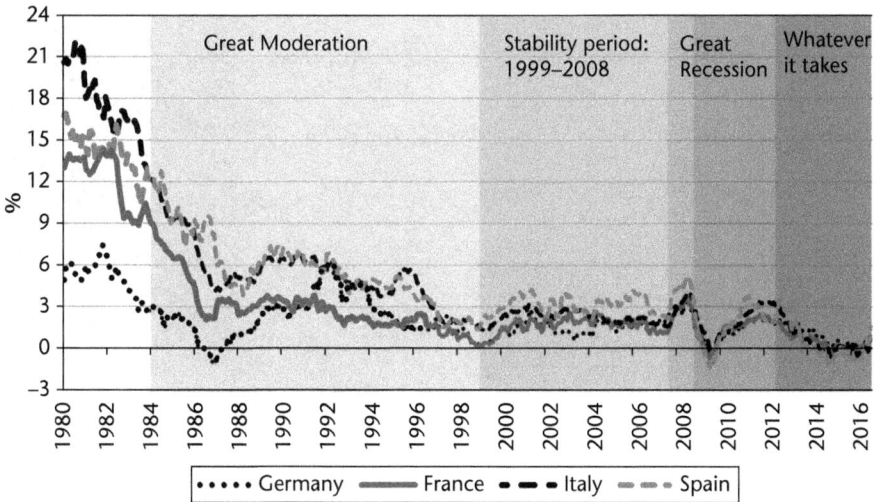

Figure 1.28 Consumer Price Inflation in Selected Euro-Area Countries (1980–2016)
Source: OECD (2017), Inflation (CPI) (Main Economic Indicators).

Overall, it seems that not all countries interpreted in the same way the inflation anchor the ECB was providing. Whereas the below, but close to, 2 per cent indicated a ceiling for price increases in some countries, in others this looked more like a floor.

An analogous phenomenon can be observed for survey-based inflationary expectations,[34] as reported in Figure 1.29. In this figure the imperfect convergence of inflation expectations between the periphery (simple average of Italy and Spain) and the core (simple average between Germany and France) in the Stability Period is illustrated.

The full convergence of nominal interest rates and the only partial convergence of inflation and inflationary expectations is consistent with an asymmetric behaviour between the financial and the real sector. The former, where interest rates are determined, adapted itself completely to the new monetary policy regime of low and stable inflation brought about by the introduction of the euro, managed by the ECB. On the contrary, in the peripheral countries the real sector, where inflation and inflation expectations are generated, adapted only partially to the euro. This result is reminiscent of the Dornbusch 'overshooting' effect (Dornbusch, 1976), whereby the exchange rate is more flexible than relative inflation and a monetary shock leads to an impact

---

[34] The derivation of quantitative inflationary expectations from surveys is presented in Appendix 2.

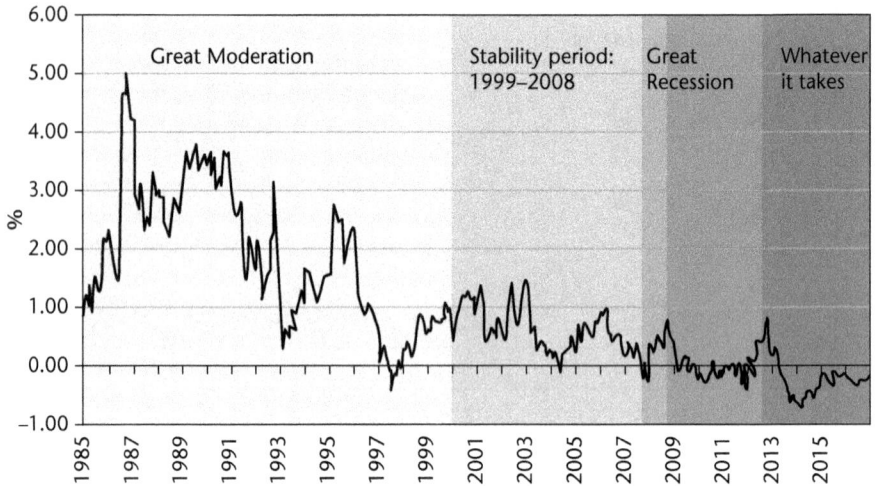

Figure 1.29 Difference in Estimated Inflation Expectations between the Periphery and the Core of the Euro-Area (1985–2015)

Source: Author's calculations based on the European Commission Business and Consumer Survey and OECD (2017), Main Economic Indicators (database). See Appendix 2.

depreciation of the exchange rate that is higher than the long-run depreciation, thus giving rise to a subsequent gradual exchange rate appreciation.

In the initial years of monetary union, the asymmetric behaviour between the real and the financial sectors determined lower real interest rates in the periphery than in the core of the euro-area, but then the relationship dramatically inverted during the Great Recession. This result can be seen in Figure 1.30: real rates of interest were much lower in the periphery than in the core of the euro-area starting in the final years of the Great Moderation and during the Stability Period. With the beginning of the Great Recession, however, a dramatic inversion occurred and real rates in the periphery surpassed those in the core. Both the lowering of the real rate before the Great Recession and its sharp increase during it was more extreme in Spain than in Italy: for instance, in the former country, the real rate moved from 3 per cent in 1999 to close to 0 in 2005–2006 and then up to 3.6 per cent in 2013.

In Figure 1.31 one sees a confirmation of the striking developments seen in Figure 1.30: only in the Stability Period were real interest rates calculated from estimated inflationary expectations lower in the periphery than in the core.

Figure 1.32 illustrates the same phenomenon in more compact form. In the periphery the nominal interest rate differential with respect to the core was higher than the expected inflation differential in both the Great Moderation and the Great Recession/Whatever it takes periods. However, the relationship

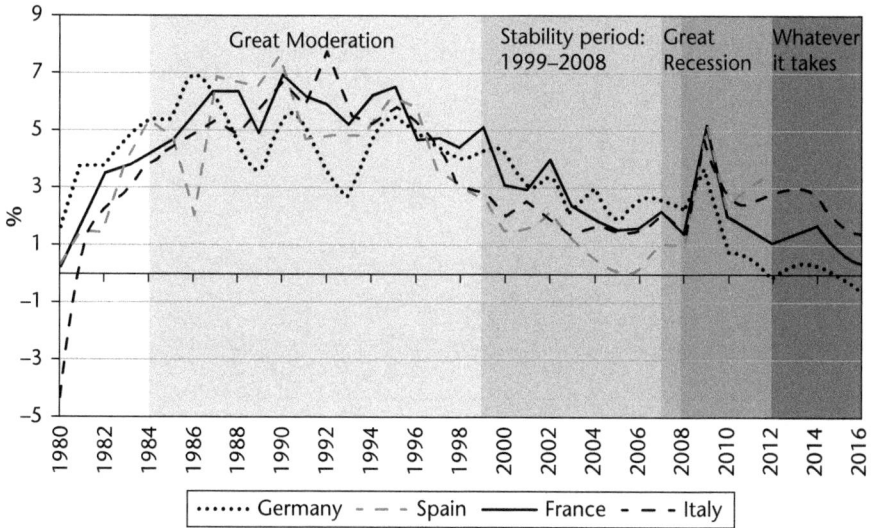

Figure 1.30 Ten-Year Real Government Bond Yields in Selected Core and Peripheral Euro-Area Countries, CPI Deflator (1980–2016)

Source: European Commission, AMECO Database.

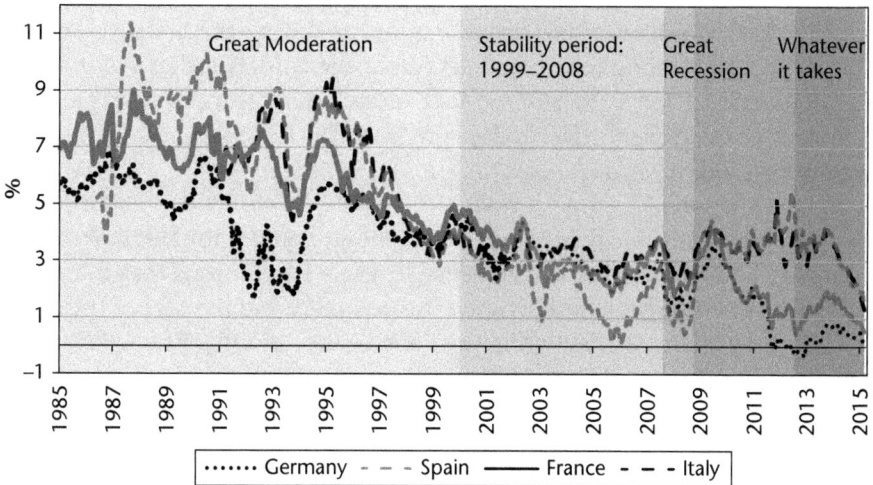

Figure 1.31 Real Interest Rates Calculated from Estimated Expected Inflation Rates, Selected Euro-area Countries (1985–2015)

Note: The real rates are calculated ex post, subtracting one year ahead inflation expectations at the time t from the nominal interest rates at time t.

Source: Author's calculations based on the European Commission Business and Consumer Survey and OECD (2017), Main Economic Indicators (database). See Appendix 2.

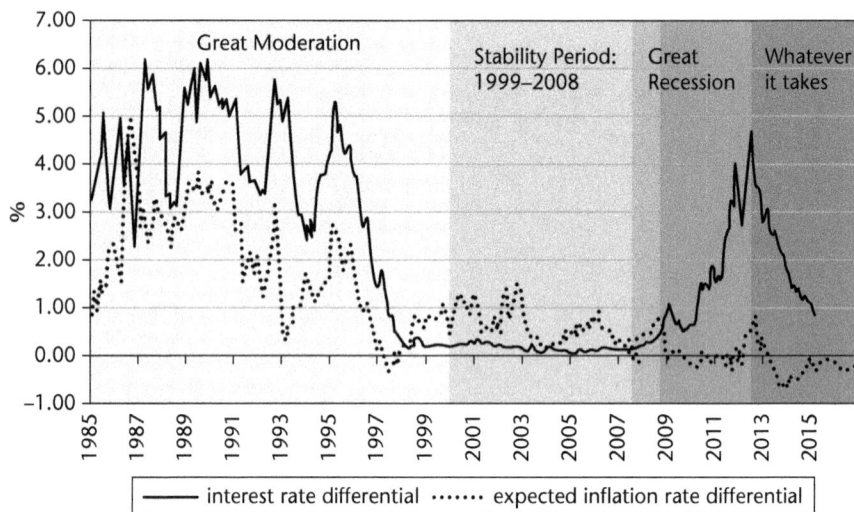

Figure 1.32 Expected Inflation vs Ten-Year Government Bond Interest Differentials between Periphery and Core of the Euro-Area (1985–2015)

Note: Both the expected inflation and the interest rate differential are calculated as the difference between core (simple average between Germany and France) and periphery (simple average between Italy and Spain).

Source: Author's calculations based on European Commission Business and Consumer Survey and OECD (2017), Main Economic Indicators (database). See Appendix 2.

between the two differentials was the opposite during the Stability Period, roughly corresponding to the first decade of the euro. Another way to look at this phenomenon is to observe that the real rate of interest was always higher in the periphery than in the core, with the only exception being the Stability Period.

Table 1.2 reports for three periods (1985–1997, 1998–2008,[35] 2008–2016), the average ten-year yield, inflation expectations, and real interest rates in the periphery and in the core. The evidence in Table 1.2 confirms that there was full interest rate convergence between the periphery and the core of the euro-area in the Stability Period, while the convergence of inflation expectations was less than perfect. Hence, unlike in the previous and subsequent period, real rates of interest were lower in the periphery than in the core during the Stability Period. During the Great Recession/Whatever it takes periods, as also shown in Table 1.2, there was instead full convergence of inflation and inflation expectations between the core and the periphery, but interest rates

---

[35] The Stability Period is made to start in 1998, since by that time the approximation of the euro had already led to a perfect alignment of interest rates.

Table 1.2 Average Ten-Year Government Bond Yield, Average Inflation Expectations, and Average Real Interest Rates

	1985–1997		1998–2008		2009–2016	
	Core	Periphery	Core	Periphery	Core	Periphery
Ten-year yield (%)	7.7	11.6	4.4	4.5	2.4	4.3
Inflation expectations (%)	2.0	4.0	1.1	1.7	0.9	0.8
Real interest rates (%)	5.7	7.6	3.2	2.8	1.5	3.5

Source: Author's calculations based on European Commission Business and Consumer Survey and OECD (2017), Main Economic Indicators. See Appendix 2.

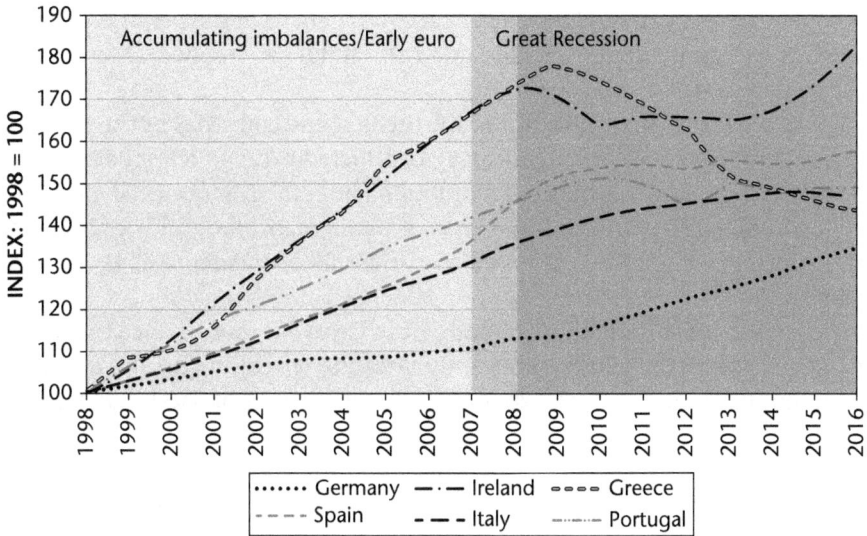

Figure 1.33 Compensation per Employee in Selected Core and Periphery Euro-Area Countries, Index 1998=100 (1998–2016)
Source: European Commission, AMECO Database.

diverged again, with those in the periphery significantly higher than those in the core.

The higher expected inflation in the periphery in the Stability Period was also visible in wages, which grew much faster than in the core, as seen in Figure 1.33. In the early years of the single currency, a decade after its unification, Germany was seen as the 'sick man' of Europe (*The Economist*, 1999). The German government reacted to this situation with a number of structural reforms, particularly in the labour market. After the so-called Hartz reforms (Siegele, 2004), it seemed only natural that inflation and wages in the periphery, affected by the inertia in adapting to the new monetary regime introduced by the euro, would exceed those in Germany. As a consequence, too little attention was paid to the substantial loss of competitiveness accumulating in the more vulnerable countries within the periphery. Only after the beginning of the Great Recession was there a partial convergence between wages in the periphery and those in Germany, as wages in the peripheral countries stabilized or decreased and wages in Germany began to climb more significantly.

The loss of competitiveness in the periphery contributed to large current account deficits that worsened until the onset of the Great Recession, when they were sharply corrected, as seen in Figure 1.34. The developments of savings-investment imbalances between the core and periphery in the euro-area ended up resembling those between China and the USA.

With the onset of the Great Recession, the private capital flows from the core that had easily funded the current account deficits of the periphery, since the euro had eliminated exchange rate risk, 'suddenly stopped' (Merler and Pisani-Ferry, 2012).

Before the Great Recession would hit them, some countries of the periphery, namely Italy, Greece, and Portugal, conducted fiscal policies that further contributed to large current account imbalances. This occurred because the favourable effect of the lower cost of public debt due to lower interest rates was not sufficiently exploited to correct fiscal imbalances, as seen in Figure 1.35.

The fiscal correction took place during the Great Recession, once the focus of the crisis shifted to Europe, but only after the recession and the decision to bail out banks had brought about a huge aggravation of fiscal imbalances.

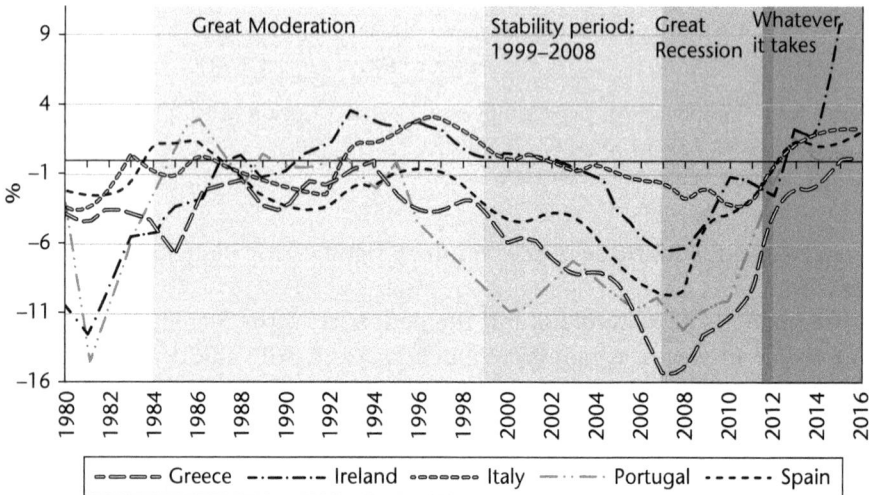

Figure 1.34 Current Account Balances in Euro-Area Peripheral Countries, Percentage of GDP (1980–2016)

Source: IMF–World Economic Outlook Database.

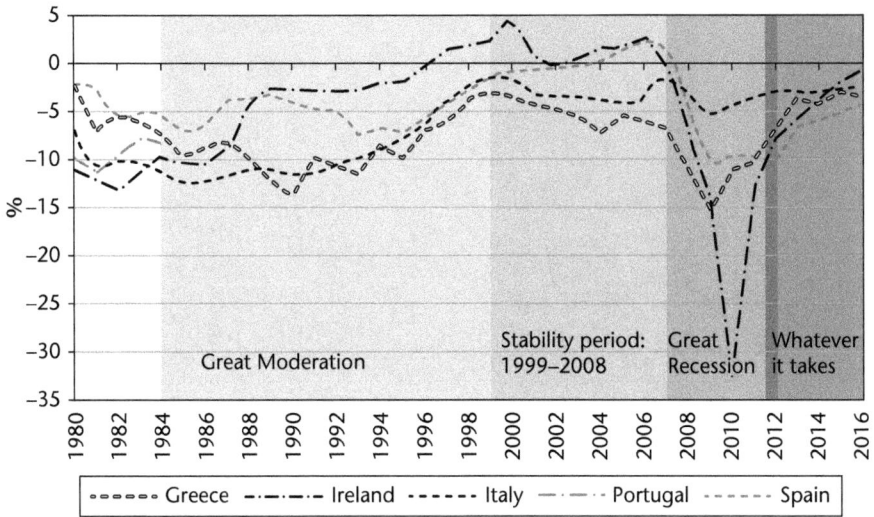

Figure 1.35 Budget Balances in Selected Euro-Area Peripheral Countries, Percentage of GDP (1980–2016)

Source: IMF–World Economic Outlook and European Commission, AMECO Database.

It was only since around the middle of the 2010s that fiscal balances in the periphery climbed closer to zero.

The inertia in lowering inflationary expectations in the periphery may have also contributed to fiscal deficits, as governments may have limited their correction efforts under the illusion that inflation would continue eating into the real value of debt, thus reducing its burden.

In Greece, Portugal, and, to some extent, Italy, the excessive credit took the form of large external borrowing as well as large public deficits and, eventually, debt. In some other countries, such as Ireland and Spain, the fiscal balance fully respected the Maastricht criteria at the onset of the Great Recession, with average deficit clearly below 3 per cent and the debt-to-GDP ratio lower than 60 per cent. However, somewhat similarly to the situation in the USA, real estate prices increased sharply, with house purchases and real estate projects being financed by bank lending. The low level of expected real rates fed the demand of funding to purchase real estate. Thus household debt increased sharply. In Ireland and Spain excessive debt took the form of heavy external borrowing and large indebtedness by the domestic private sector. This, however, duly transformed itself into public debt during the crisis, when, to avoid massive bank failures, governments bailed out the banks with public funds.

The excess of credit growth in the euro-area was visible not only in macro-economic imbalances, such as the current account and the budget deficits of the peripheral countries as well as the surpluses in core countries, but was also

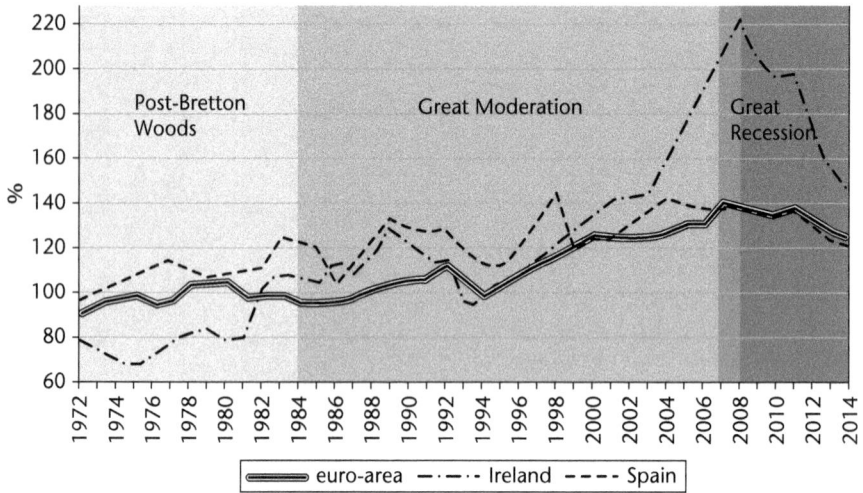

Figure 1.36 Ratio of Bank Loans to Deposits for the Euro-Area, Ireland, and Spain (1972–2014)

Source: FRED and International Financial Statistics of IMF.

manifest in the relevant banking sector balance sheets. Figure 1.36 presents the bank loan-to-deposit ratios of Ireland, Spain, and the aggregate euro-area. Loans grew faster than deposits, especially in the period of the Great Moderation. Increasing dependence on wholesale funding predisposed banks and entire national banking sectors towards funding risk, which also strengthened the links between the credit risk of the banks and that of their domestic sovereign. The strong correction in the loan-to-deposit ratio after the beginning of the Great Recession was particularly precipitous in Ireland, but took place, in less extreme form, also in Spain and in the entire euro-area.

Overall, the provided interpretation, based on the asymmetry between the financial and the real sectors of the peripheral economies, is quite powerful, because it can help explain a number of features in the shift from the Stability Period to the Great Recession: the dramatic inversion of the relationship between real interest rates in the periphery and the core, higher wages in the former group of countries up to the Great Recession, the deterioration and then the improvement of current account balances, the behaviour of budget deficits, the real estate boom and the heavy private-sector indebtedness in some peripheral countries, eventually also the strong increase of non-performing loans in the peripheral countries.

The same interpretation also lends itself to a happy-ending prognosis: the Great Recession would have offered a very painful and thus effective learning experience to peripheral countries, forcing them to adapt inflation and inflationary expectations to the stable monetary policy of the ECB, as the memory of the less stable monetary policies of their national central banks faded into the past. This conclusion is consistent with the fact that inflation and inflation expectations in the periphery has no longer deviated from those in the core since the beginning of the Great Recession, as was seen in Figures 1.28 and 1.29 as well as in Table 1.2. The experience in the first two decades of the euro could thus be interpreted as a one-off painful learning experience.

While excessive debt in the USA and in the euro-area had different manifestations, in both cases its development was consistent with the line of analysis pursued by Kindleberger and Aliber (2005), as well as Minsky (1986), and Reinhart and Rogoff (2009). The pattern of interest rates before and during the Great Recession is also consistent with the multiple equilibria approach. Risk and maturity premia were too low before the Great Recession, as the market took a complacent view of risk. As the crisis manifested itself, though, and the economy moved from a 'good' to a 'bad' equilibrium, spreads increased in a disorderly fashion, becoming significantly more variable.

This line of analysis helps in understanding the crisis that started in 2007, distinguishing the developments that led the economies into a dangerous zone, in which multiple equilibria phenomena can more easily arise, from the 'spark', that is, the specific event that ignited the crisis.

Indeed, the relatively recent theoretical advance about the possibility, under certain conditions, of multiple equilibria can give a deeper understanding to the sequence of manias, panics, and crashes of Kindlebergian tradition.

One notable feature of the financial crisis, evident in both its American and European phases, was the jerky movement of some critical financial prices, which are difficult to reconcile with a proportionate change determined by changes in fundamentals.

In the case of the USA, the financial price that most clearly displayed a sharp change was the spread between the uncollateralized dollar interbank lending rate (Libor, London Interbank Offered Rate) and the Overnight Index Swap (OIS) interest rate, which is very close to the collateralized—or repurchase agreement—interbank lending rate. This spread was limited before the crisis to around 25 basis points. In the summer of 2007 it started to grow, signalling growing market stress, but it was in October of 2008, just after the failure of Lehman Brothers, that it exploded in a matter of days to a peak of 250 basis points or more, as one can see in Figure 2.3 in Section 2.1.1.2. Similar developments were observed for the euro and the pound. The figures for the three currencies show a similar pattern, with a second peak in the summer of 2012, corresponding to the most stressed period in Europe. In the figures one also sees that the second peak was, understandably, higher in the euro-area than in the USA and the UK.

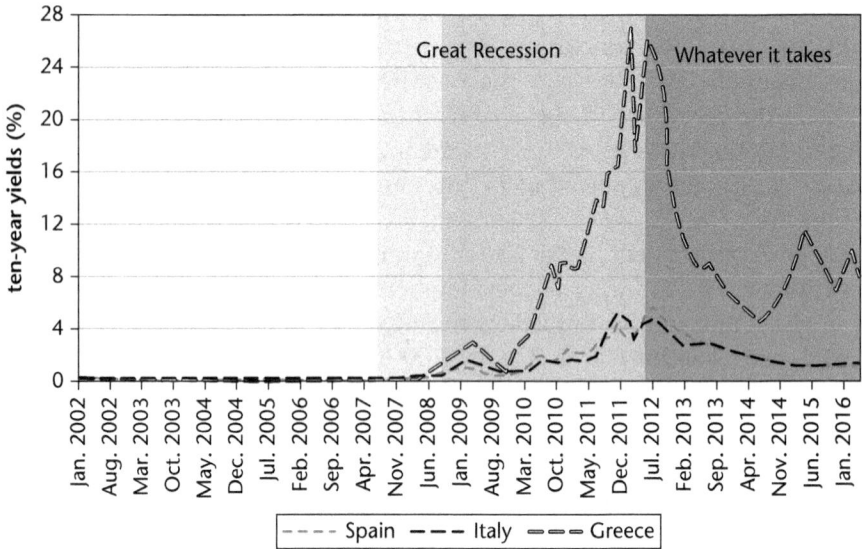

Figure 1.37 Spreads between the Sovereign Bond Yields of Greece, Italy, and Spain with Respect to Germany's Ten-Year Yields (2002–2016)
Source: Eurostat.

In the case of Europe, as seen in Figure 1.37, there was another financial price affected by the sudden stress: the differential between so-called peripheral and so-called core sovereign bond yields.

The case was most extreme in Greece, where the sovereign bond yield spread moved from 1.6 to 8.3 per cent between November 2009 and August 2010, following the revelation at the end of 2009 that the Greek fiscal deficit was much higher than previously communicated. In the following months the spread reached a peak of over 27 per cent. What is, however, more interesting is the opening of the spread for Italian and Spanish bonds, given that in these countries, unlike in Greece, there had been no observable change in fundamentals, thus denoting a pure contagion effect. In Italy, in particular, the spread increased by 370 basis points, from 1.5 per cent in April 2011 to 5.2 in November of the same year.

Although such sharp moves are difficult to reconcile with changes in fundamentals, they fit quite nicely with the idea that both the USA and the euro-area economy moved, at the start of the Great Recession, from a 'good' to a 'bad' equilibrium, as foreseen in the multiple equilibria model. This model was proposed by Diamond and Dybvig (Diamond 2007) to explain sudden shifts of banks from solvency to insolvency. The model, however, can easily be extended to corporations and sovereigns.

Analogously to banks, sovereigns can also encounter 'runs'. Such a scenario occurs if investors, at a certain point, doubt the ability of the government to repay its debt and ask for higher returns, until the return becomes so high that the sovereign's inability to repay debt becomes reality. However, governments, as banks, can reduce their vulnerability to changes in expectations by increasing their 'tipping point', as defined in Box 11. To use the multiple equilibria model for governments rather than banks one needs to make some, relatively minor, adaptations. Indeed, the concept of liquidity mismatch is not immediately applicable to sovereigns. In order to apply it, one can, without forcing reality too much, assume that government assets have infinite, or at least ultra-long, maturity, and are therefore practically illiquid. Accordingly, any increase of the debt, with whatever maturity, short of a perpetual bond, causes a mismatch between government assets and liabilities. Consistently, any increase of the debt of the government can be assimilated to an increase of the liquidity mismatch.

Box 11 MULTIPLE EQUILIBRIA AND THE GREAT RECESSION

The essence of the multiple equilibria model, as presented by Diamond in 2007, considers an entity (this can be a bank or a corporation, but also a sovereign) which can borrow at two different maturities: short-term borrowing is cheaper than long-term borrowing, but the entity can only invest in long-term assets. There are also two types of consumers/lenders: patient and impatient ones. The entity knows the ex ante distribution of lenders between the two types and decides its borrowing policy accordingly. Through the combination of its investment and funding policy, the entity provides liquidity to its lenders by incurring a liquidity mismatch. There will be an optimal level of liquidity mismatch, given the ex ante distribution of lenders between the two types, which maximizes return for both the lenders and the entity and is thus Pareto optimal. Such optimum, in which bank assets have a longer maturity than liabilities, is, however, open to a risk of runs if a so-called 'coordination failure' happens. Such event takes place if, for some reason, the patient lenders, which were in principle willing to lend the money to the entity for a longer period of time, start to fear that a certain share of other patient lenders would ask for an earlier redemption of their lending and would thus also 'run to the bank' to get their money before it is too late.

Multiple equilibrium models are often criticized because the move from 'good' to 'bad' equilibrium is assumed to have no identifiable cause and because they seem to break the correlation between fundamentals, on one side, and outcomes, on the other side. For instance, Morris and Shin (2000, p. 139) write:

Models that utilize such apparent indeterminacy of beliefs have considerable intuitive appeal, since they provide a convenient and economical prop in a narrative of unfolding events. However, they are vulnerable to a number of criticisms. For a start, the shift in beliefs, which underpins the switch from one equilibrium to another, is left unexplained. This runs counter to our theoretical scruples against

(continued)

Box 11 CONTINUED

---

indeterminacy. More importantly, it runs counter to our intuition that bad fundamentals are somehow 'more likely' to trigger a financial crisis, or to tip the economy into recession. In other words, sunspot explanations do not provide a basis for exploring the correlation between the underlying fundamentals and the resultant economic outcomes.

Krugman (2015) made a similar criticism, in more journalistic fashion.

These two criticisms are, however, only partially valid. As far as the criticism that equilibria shifts have no plausible causes, looking at the specific cases of both the USA and the euro-area during the Great Recession, one finds something of a cause for the shift from a 'good' to a 'bad' equilibrium. The problem is that the cause was just too small to produce, in a single equilibrium model, the catastrophic effects that followed: the subprime market was too small a sector of the US financial market to explain the meltdown which followed, and Greece was just too small a country in the euro-area to cause the fear that the full euro construction could be undone. But, however small, both the US subprime crisis and Greece were obviously large enough to ignite fears, which tipped the economy from a 'good' to a 'bad' equilibrium for countries in a vulnerable position.

Concerning the criticism that, with multiple equilibria, the link between fundamentals and outcomes is lost, it should be noted that such a link is preserved in the Diamond–Dybvig model, even if it is looser than in single equilibrium models. The link is introduced in the model through the 'tipping point' concept, defining the share of 'patient investors' that, because of a coordination failure, can cause a run, precipitating the economy from a 'good' to a 'bad' equilibrium. The tipping point in the model depends on the liquidity mismatch: the higher this value is, the lower the tipping point. Therefore, if there is high vulnerability of a 'good' equilibrium to a coordination failure on the lenders' side, then even a relatively small share of patient lenders that ask for their money back is sufficient to cause the switch to a 'bad' equilibrium.

Banks, or any other borrower, can limit the liquidity mismatch below the optimum to reduce the risk of a run. This is accomplished by offering a relatively lower return to impatient lenders and thus moving the borrowing towards longer maturities, increasing the 'tipping point' beyond which patient investors can ask for an early withdrawal. The new Basel regulation on the liquidity cover ratio and the net stable funding ratio can be seen as ways to increase the tipping point and make the liquidity situation of banks more robust.

Francesco Papadia

To apply this model to what happened in the Great Recession, one can see Germany as a prudent government that kept its debt and liquidity mismatch low. Germany therefore established a very high tipping point, so that it was very unlikely that investors would doubt its ability to repay its debt. As a consequence, the probability of a run was very low. Imprudent governments, such as those from the periphery, were, instead, highly vulnerable to a change of expectations. Thus, peripheral countries were close to their tipping point, because of a high, direct or indirect, debt, making the Greek spark sufficient to move them from a 'good' to a 'bad' equilibrium. Indeed, the multiple equilibria story does not absolve imprudent governments: if the governments in the periphery had had less debt, the Greek spark would have not led to a bad equilibrium; if the spark had not met large amount of flammable material the fire would not have developed as virulently as it did. Indeed, all the governments that moved from a 'good' to a 'bad' equilibrium had public debt problems, either directly (Greece, Portugal, Italy) or because bank debt was transformed into public debt during the crisis (Ireland, Spain). This means that one can still make policy recommendations even with multiple equilibria models: the more imprudent the borrowing behaviour, the more vulnerable a given country is to a shift of beliefs.

To simplify the reasoning, instead of having a continuum (the more a bank/country has a liquidity mismatch, the more likely are runs) one can say that there are safe zones (where the tipping point is high) and dangerous zones (where the tipping point is low). Prior to the crisis, peripheral countries such as Italy, Spain, Greece, Ireland, and Portugal were in dangerous zones; core countries, like Germany, the Netherlands, and France were in safe zones.

The multiple equilibria paradigm also helps to understand, when applied to the case of sovereign borrowers, which policies to carry out once there is a move from a 'good' to a 'bad' equilibrium. One can identify basically two different strategies: one hard, one soft. The hard strategy consists of changing fundamentals until the 'bad' equilibrium is ruled out. In macroeconomic terms this means repaying debt through fiscal austerity. This is a particularly hard strategy because to switch back from a 'bad' to a 'good' equilibrium requires a deep change in fundamentals. The soft strategy consists of trying to act on expectations of lenders to convince them that their money is safe and thus remedy the coordination failure. This attempt is easier to visualize as an outside intervention supporting the sovereign in difficulty, analogously to a public intervention bailing out a bank hit by a shift from a 'good' to a 'bad' equilibrium. This would, however, create the usual moral hazard problem that any 'bail-out' action causes.

In the case of the USA and the European Union (EU), a combination between the soft and the hard strategy was followed. In the USA, banks were forced to recapitalize, but expectations were also changed by programmes of public support, such as the Troubled Asset Relief Program and the financial support of the Fed, as it will be better seen in Section 2.2.2.2. Also in the euro-area, a combination between the two strategies was followed. Peripheral countries enacted a strong correction of domestic and external deficits, while a change in expectations was engineered by intergovernmental financial support and by the action of the ECB.

1.4.3 *Regulatory and Supervisory Failings*

There is now generalized, ex post, consensus that there was a robust role for regulatory and supervisory failings (Blundell-Wignall and Atkinson, 2008; Truman, 2009; De Larosière et al., 2009; Claessens, Kose and Terrones, 2010; Claessens and Kodres, 2014) leading up to the Great Recession. These failings took different forms in the USA and in the EU, but one can identify some common underlying factors. Possibly the most general failing was the insufficiency, indeed in some cases the total lack, of a macro approach in regulating and supervising finance:

> A key lesson emerging from the financial crisis that erupted in 2007 was the inadequacy of the institutional policy frameworks prevailing at the time to deal with the build-up and materialization of systemic risks. In particular, micro-prudential supervision proved to fall short by not accounting for the externalities associated with the activity of individual banks, i.e. their impact on the risk in the financial system as a whole.[36]

Although the concept of a macro-prudential approach was first advanced at the end of the 1970s and started to be developed at the end of the 1980s, it was not fully articulated until the beginning of the twenty-first century. Still, it is only after the crisis erupted between 2007 and 2008 that the concept started to be gradually applied in practice. Indeed, the lack of a macro approach in regulation and supervision was germane to the subsidiary role that financial stability had in the remit of central banks. While central banks naturally have a more holistic view of the financial system than any other institution, the low priorities and limited responsibilities they had in this field meant that they did not sufficiently contribute to a macro approach in regulation and supervision. In addition, while growth, inflation, and overall market functioning were key priorities for the Fed, the Fed policies in the supervisory area may have been short-sighted and thus further contributed to the national enthusiasm for broader homeownership, which required a relaxation of lending criteria. Low, or non-existent, lending standards in real estate business were a central part of the problem leading up to the crisis.

The insufficient attention to macro aspects of financial stability led, as a necessary consequence, to an underestimation of liquidity risk. After all, liquidity risk is an issue that can only be properly appreciated considering the financial system in its entirety, as opposed to individual institutions in isolation: liquidity is in essence a systemic variable, having to do with relationships among financial institutions rather than any characteristic of an individual institution.

---

[36] De Larosière Report and ECB Financial Stability Review, May 2013, Special Feature. Exploring the nexus between macro-prudential policies and monetary policy measures (p. 99).

Further consequences of the insufficient macro dimension in regulation and supervision were revealed. First, the inability to fully realize the danger that the sheer enormity and complexity of the shadow banking system was creating and the limited supervision and regulation of this sector. Second, the lack of awareness that the competition of the 'shadow banking system', favoured by a faulty risk assessment employed by rating agencies, was pushing banks to take more risks to compete with it (Truman, 2009). Thus, this failing actually appeared more as an indirect rather than a direct contribution to the crisis by the shadow banking system. Indeed, the De Larosière Report (De Larosière et al., 2013) notes that, contrary to expectations before the crisis: 'Concerning hedge funds, the Group considers they did not play a major role in the emergence of the crisis' (p. 24). Consistently, it states that:' It has been the regulated financial institutions that have turned out to be the largest source of problems' (p. 10).

Another general failing in regulation and supervision was the maintenance of a prevailing national approach to regulating and supervising an increasingly global financial industry. This is indeed the specific aspect of a more general phenomenon, which has seen the public sector continue working in a dominant national framework while the private sector, both in the financial and in the real domain, became increasingly global. This increasingly global nature of the financial industry led to a relative weakening of the public sector, which found it difficult to effectively produce international public goods, including global supervision and regulation. This kind of argument links up to the observation of Kindleberger (1988, p. 134), who connected the Great Depression to the absence of a hegemon capable of providing the international public good of macroeconomic stabilization:

> I originally suggested that the 1929 depression was allowed to run unchecked because there was no leading country able and willing to take responsibility for crisis management, halting beggar-thy-neighbour policies from 1930, and especially acting as a lender of last resort to prevent the serious run on the Creditanstalt in May 1931 spreading, as it did, to Germany, Britain, Japan, the USA, and ultimately the gold bloc.

Saccomanni (2008) and Rodrik (2011) apply the same analysis to more recent times.

The benefits of financial globalization were thus impacted by the limited provision of complementary global-oriented regulation and supervision. The specific form taken by globalization during the Great Recession was the ease and speed with which the crisis spread from one jurisdiction to the other (Claessens, Kose, and Terrones, 2010; Claessens and Kodres, 2014): in the first phase, it moved eastward from the USA to Europe, in the second phase it moved westward, from Europe to the USA.

The insufficient supranational approach to regulation and supervision took a specific, and more acute, character in the euro-area. While undoubtedly some progress in the euro-area had been achieved before the crisis to reach a supranational approach to supervision and, in particular, to regulation, this was still not commensurate with the degree of financial integration prevailing after the introduction of the single currency.[37] In addition, national regulators and supervisors in the euro-area often succumbed to the temptation, during the Great Recession, to become defenders of their 'national banking champions' instead of regulating and supervising them on an objective basis. Indeed, the 'bank nationalism' decried by Posen and Veron (2014) was the very opposite of the global approach that was unquestionably needed.[38]

Yet another failing in regulation was the inability, bordering on unwillingness, to properly regulate two financial innovations that substantially increased the margins of freedom of financial institutions, including banks: asset-backed securities and derivatives. Asset-backed securities were seen as a way to surpass the dualism between market- and bank-based financial systems, the first prevailing in the USA and the UK, the second prevailing in continental Europe. The bridge between the two models appeared to be the 'originate and distribute' intermediation approach, whereby banks originate loans that they then distribute to the capital market in the form of asset-backed securities. Derivatives were considered to be a tool that could efficiently transfer and redistribute risk within the economy to those better able to bear it and to maximize the opportunities for eliminating idiosyncratic risk by means of diversification. Ex post, securitization and derivatives played a similar role as bills of exchange in the Kindleberger and Aliber story, facilitating the increase in credit supply and leverage. What regulators and supervisors did not manage to do, however, was to assure a proper use of these two brilliant, but potentially dangerous, if abused, innovations. Asset-backed securities were an essential component in generating the excessive debt of US households to finance house purchases, giving rise to the subprime debacle. At the same time, they were the vehicle through which the subprime crisis crossed US borders, in particular in the direction of some European banks that invested heavily in these types of securities. As the De Larosière Report

---

[37] For a measurement of financial integration in the euro-area see the ECB Reports on financial integration as well as Figure 2.45.

[38] 'What can be described as "banking nationalism"—a continued reliance on national policy instruments to defend and promote national banking champions in an increasingly integrated European financial market—can be identified as a key reason why the financial crisis of 2007–08 had such a severe impact on Europe, despite having started in the United States. It also explains why, unlike in the United States, European policymakers were unwilling to resolve it and were unable to rapidly reestablish trust in their banking system.' The De Larosière Report refers, with milder words, to: 'Lack of frankness and cooperation between supervisors' (De Larosière et al., 2013, p. 42).

(De Larosière et al., 2013, p. 8) stipulates: 'Although securitisation is in principle a desirable economic model, it was accompanied by opacity which camouflaged the poor quality of the underlying assets. This contributed to credit expansion and the belief that risks were spread.'

According to this report, the abuse of the innovation of asset-backed securities was greatly facilitated by the poor performance of rating agencies that distributed with undue largesse, before the crisis, the top-notch credit assessment to securities that were violently downgraded when the crisis erupted.

A final failing was the difficulty of properly calibrating the capital requirements agreed in the Basel Committee for Banking Supervision. Blundell-Wignall and others identify in the Basel II agreement a specific factor leading to the crisis since it 'opened an arbitrage opportunity for banks that caused them to accelerate off-balance-sheet activity' (p. 4), particularly in the mortgage area. The De Larosière Report disputes this criticism, noting that, although the Basel I framework did not cater adequately for, and in fact encouraged, the pushing of risk-taking off balance sheets, this was partly corrected by the Basel II framework. What is beyond controversy is that the Basel agreements had difficulties in finding the right approach to weigh the risk of different bank assets in order to achieve an adequate risk-weighted asset aggregate. An acute difficulty, within this general problem, was the weighing of national government bonds, which eventually maintained a zero weight in the successive version of the Basel agreement. The negative consequence of the incentive given to banks to invest in government securities, especially those of their national government, was starkly revealed, as will be seen in Box 16 on the European Banking Union, during the European phase of the crisis. During this phase, the strong risk link between banks and their national governments created was rightly called a 'doom loop'.

1.4.4 *Intellectual Failings*

With the benefit of hindsight, it is surprising that the Great Recession was mostly unforeseen. The evidence of recurrent financial crises was there. Kindleberger had written his book in 1978, documenting, in a narrative fashion, the intrinsic, centuries-long instability of market economies. Borio (2012) recalled the long analytical tradition of studying financial cycles, fostered by Lamfalussy when he was first Economic Advisor and then General Manager of the BIS, between 1976 and 1993. In 1986, Minsky, developing ideas he had already put forward in the 1970s, sent a clear message about the vulnerability of market economies to financial crises and clearly detected the illusion, systematically denounced by Reinhart and Rogoff, that 'This time is different.' Indeed, Minsky (2008, p. 237) wrote: 'as a previous financial crisis recedes in time, it is quite natural...to believe that a new era has arrived.

Cassandra-like warnings...are naturally ignored in these circumstances.' Finally, the theory of multiple equilibria was available, which showed the economy was liable to sharp changes for minor causes once a country is in a dangerous zone because fundamentals have reached values that are consistent with both 'good' and 'bad' equilibria.

Of course, some economists warned about a possible impending crisis, especially those of the 'BIS school', such as White (2013) and Borio (2012). They represented, however, a tail in the distribution of opinions before the crisis. Given a sufficiently wide distribution of opinions, there will always be some economists who are eventually vindicated by events. The author of this chapter admits to only now seeing clearly, after having gone through the crisis, the intellectual failings contributing to the Great Recession. He indeed does not claim to have seen the crisis coming or having promptly understood its gravity and length. He is in good company though; indeed, he probably fits close to the median economist.

The full explanation of the intellectual failings contributing to the crisis goes beyond the boundaries of this book and would have to find the reasons why governments, regulators, market professionals (inside and outside of central banks), and monetary authorities had a part in them. Still, it is useful to signal one factor that helps explain the illusion that the Great Moderation was a permanent state of affairs and thus crises were, for advanced economies, a problem of the past: the insufficient integration between the fields of economics and economic history.[39] Economists, also because of data availability, tend to work with time series too short to capture secular phenomena, including deep crises. Economic historians often do not wish to make the effort to compare the narrative or the data of long, possibly very long, time periods with the supposedly constant 'laws of motions' that economists strive to identify and test. Often they prefer telling a specific story, relating to a given period and place, rather than trying to see how that specific story would fit into a more general interpretative scheme. This is now changing, partly because of the crisis, with the two disciplines converging one onto the other. Still, the lack of integration between economics and economic history contributed to the inability to see the crisis coming.

What White (2013) calls 'false beliefs' also impeded the awareness that imbalances were cumulating and would eventually lead to a crisis. For example, many, in particular in the UK and the USA, assumed, without proof, that risk would be appropriately distributed through derivatives so that any shock could be more easily absorbed and thus any intervention by the regulators would be inappropriate. In addition, various arguments were

---

[39] Maes (2014) made a similar point.

put forward, before the crisis, to defend the view that large international and domestic imbalances could be permanently maintained. Perhaps even celebrating a Great Moderation was a mistake: in doing so vigilance was compromised.

In the case of the USA, it was argued that globalization in financial and trade markets allowed larger cross-border lending and therefore wider current account deficits. In addition, it was maintained, defective financial systems in emerging economies led savers in those countries to place their investment in advanced economies, especially in the USA. Finally, the explanation was put forward that because the average return on external assets of the USA was higher than the average cost of its external liabilities, the American economy could sustain a large external debt.

In the case of the euro-area, the idea was that currency unification had dramatically increased capital mobility, having taken away exchange rate risk from intra-area capital movements. This allowed the funding, on a permanent basis, of larger current account deficits and the domestic imbalances that were behind them, be they fiscal deficits or excessive household debt.

However well argued, all these ideas turned out to be wrong with the advent of the crisis.

In conclusion, the build-up of imbalances and then the crisis appeared, ex post, fully consistent with the long-term pattern of manias, panics, and crashes, and then the shift from a 'good' to a 'bad' equilibrium. Indeed, the crisis was a sharp reminder that, while market economies are the only ones capable of freeing humanity from poverty, with its assortment of ills such as early mortality (especially infant mortality), malnutrition, and low literacy rates, they are also, unfortunately, prone to instability. What Reinhart and Rogoff (2009, p. 133) wrote is sobering: 'thus far, no major country has been able to graduate from banking crises'. It is also dispiriting that so many clever people did not resist the temptation to argue that: 'This time is different.'

The Great Recession had its first manifestation in August of 2007: however, its acute phase flared up with the bankruptcy, in September of 2008, of the investment bank Lehman Brothers, following the bankruptcy of Bear Sterns. These events occurred against the backdrop of a vulnerable financial market, which had been particularly aggressive in riding the boom. While some market observers, particularly in the USA, had advanced the idea that the failure of Lehman should be left to run its course, its consequences were dramatic. This is not the place to go through the tumultuous events that accompanied and followed the Lehmann bankruptcy, such as the serious crisis of the insurance firm AIG (American International Group). Nevertheless, one should at least note that the sharp drop in international trade and global GDP, which followed the Lehman event, had been unprecedented over the previous 60 years. Between 2007, the year before Lehman failure, and 2009, real growth fell by about 6 percentage points in both advanced economies (from + 2.8 to −3.4 per cent) and at global level (from +4.3 to −1.7 per cent). Growth then recovered between 2009 and 2010 by a similar amount. The decline and recovery of international trade was even more dramatic: in 2009 world trade fell by 22.3 per cent, whereas in 2010 it grew by 22 per cent, seeming to make up for the previous year's losses. Eichengreen (2010) documents that the crisis had a destructive potential commensurate with that of the Great Depression. He also asserts that it is plausible that fiscal and monetary policies impeded the potential of the recession to turn into an actual depression.

When the crisis that had its epicentre in the Unites States was ebbing, a new source of crisis emerged in the euro-area, with the revelation, in the autumn of 2009, that the Greek fiscal deficit was much larger than previously communicated. As it will be seen in Chapter 2, this developed over time into a potentially fatal crisis for the euro.

The actions of central banks, and in particular the Fed and the ECB, during the crisis are the focus of Chapter 2.

2

Central Banking during the Great Recession

The Great Recession delivered two blows to central banks. First, the monetary policy approach that had worked so well up to then was no longer adequate to deal with the changed circumstances. Second, the responsibility for financial stability, which until then had been belittled, was suddenly thrown onto central banks. This chapter examines these two developments in turn, assessing how serious the damage to the central bank model prevailing before the Great Recession was.

2.1 Monetary Policy

2.1.1 *Consequences of the Great Recession*

The Great Recession played havoc with the prevailing monetary policy approach employed by central banks until its onset. As seen in Chapter 1, this was based on three unacknowledged but critical conditions:

1. The central bank can tightly control its interest rate, that is, the rate chosen as the operational target.

2. There is a stable relationship, both for current and expected values, between the central bank rate and longer, riskier market rates, which have a much stronger direct impact on the macro-economy.

3. The central bank can either cut or hike its interest rate by any desired amount, depending on the circumstances.

In one or the other phase of the Great Recession one or more of these conditions no longer applied. First, central banks found that it had become more difficult to steer their dominant tool, namely the interest rate. Second, the relationship with longer and riskier rates had become very uncertain and thus the interest rate's previously estimated impact on the real economy and prices no longer held. Third, the lower bound for nominal interest rates constrained central banks' ability to reduce interest rates.

More specifically, control over the short-term interest rate became imprecise in the first phase of the Great Recession, as the banks' demand for liquidity could no longer be properly estimated and offset by central bank supply. In addition, the relationship between the short-term risk-free rate controlled by the central bank and those rates directly relevant for the economy underwent two episodes of extreme uncertainty and volatility. The first episode took place in the American phase of the crisis, after the bankruptcy of Lehman Brothers and the massive bailout of American International Group (AIG), in the autumn of 2008. The second episode came in the European phase of the crisis, after the revelations about the misreporting of Greek fiscal data in the autumn of 2009. Finally, the ability to reduce interest rates was severely impaired during the most advanced phase of the crisis, when the interest rate had already reached its lower bound, or moved close to it.

The way to visualize these developments is to consider the interest rate most directly controlled by the central bank as the hinge of the entire yield structure of interest rates. As seen in Chapter 1, the central bank steers the economy by changing its interest rate. These changes are then reflected in longer, more variegated interest rates along the maturity and risk dimensions. This is the starting point of monetary policy transmission, as these latter rates influence the behaviour of economic agents. With the crisis, the ability to set and maintain the hinge of the structure of rates at the desired level and to influence other rates along the maturity and risk curves were severely affected. Eventually, when uncertainty about the longer-term economic outlook escalated, the final part of the transmission, that is, from interest rates to real economy and prices, also changed considerably.

The difficulty of steering the central bank rate, the substantial uncertainty affecting its relationship with other, macro-economically more relevant rates, and the problems created by the so-called 'zero lower bound' (ZLB) or 'effective lower bound' (ELB) are illustrated in turn.

2.1.1.1 DIFFICULTY CONTROLLING THE INTEREST RATE

The first symptoms of the crisis were seen, already in August 2007, in the money market. The demand for liquidity grew significantly and irregularly as banks wanted to hoard liquidity for precautionary purposes, making demand for it much more volatile and harder to project. The European Central Bank (ECB) and the Federal Reserve Bank (Fed) tried to offset this by increasing the elasticity of liquidity supply, but they could not really calibrate it to offset the sharp changes in liquidity demand. As a consequence, the Euro OverNight Index Average (EONIA) in the euro-area and the FFR in the USA started to fluctuate significantly more than before the crises. The instability of the central bank rates grew disproportionately after the failure of Lehman Brothers. The reassuring conclusion before the Great Recession, that both central banks

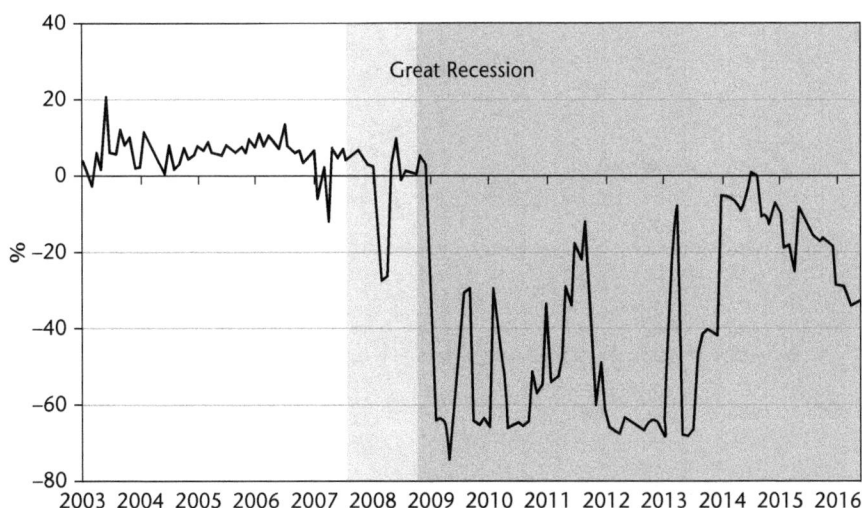

Figure 2.1 Spread between EONIA and the Rate on ECB MRO (2003–2016)
Source: ECB Statistical Data Warehouse.

could tightly manage their rate around the objective by means of the corridor approach (Papadia and Välimäki, 2011), was lost. It was only in the more advanced phase of the crisis, when central bank liquidity became overwhelming, that interest rates stabilized, this time not around the centre of the corridor but close to its bottom.

These developments are visible, in the case of the ECB, in Figure 2.1.

As evidenced in Figure 2.1, EONIA was quite stable at a level just above the rate applied in the main refinancing operations (MRO) until the summer of 2007. Then a first period of volatility followed, which intensified after October 2008, and lasted, with some pauses, until the beginning of 2014. At this point in time, central bank liquidity became so abundant that it gradually compressed the EONIA rate close to the deposit rate at which the ECB absorbs excess reserves from banks.

Also, in the case of the Fed, one sees that the very tight control that prevailed until the summer of 2007 was lost, at least until the end of 2012. At that time the Federal Funds Rate (FFR) stabilized at about ten basis points above the centre of the Fed target range (see Figure 2.2).

2.1.1.2 UNSTABLE RELATIONSHIP BETWEEN SHORT-TERM TARGET
AND LONGER-TERM/RISKIER INTEREST RATES

The first instances of the instability between the short-term target rate and riskier/longer-term interest rates appeared in the summer of 2007, but they sharply intensified after the failure of Lehman Brothers in mid-September 2008.

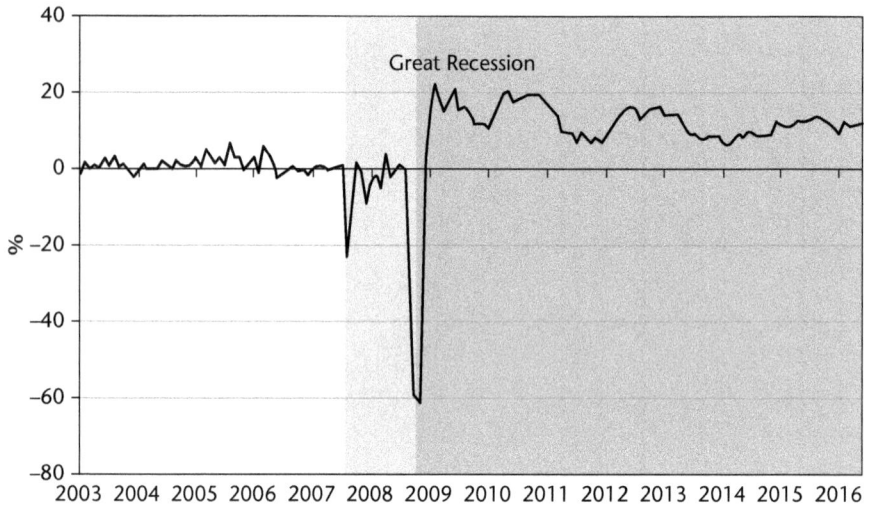

Figure 2.2 Spread between the FFR and the Target Rate* (2003–2016)

Note: *From December 2008 a Target range, with upper and lower bounds, replaced the target rate. The spread as from this date is measured with respect to the mean between the upper and lower bounds.

Source: Federal Reserve Economic Data.

The top panel of Figure 2.3 illustrates how a huge gap opened up between the Euro Interbank Offered Rate (Euribor) and the euro Overnight Interest Swap (OIS) index rate on various maturities for the euro. The same pattern also materialized in the spread between London Interbank Offered Rate (Libor) and the OIS rates for the dollar and the pound, in the second and third panels of Figure 2.3. In Section 2.2.1.3 this phenomenon will be considered in more detail, and its credit and liquidity risk components will be measured. Here, the emphasis is on both the explosion and the high variability of the spread.

Before the failure of Lehman Brothers, when the crisis had already started but was still in its initial phase, the spread was still contained. However, by the autumn of 2008, at the peak of the American phase of the crisis, the spread surged by 150 to 200 basis points, depending on the currency and the maturity. Before the crisis, a typical rate hike by the Fed or the ECB was 25 basis points. Therefore, the impact of this kind of jerk in the money market spreads onto the borrowing cost of economic agents is comparable to approximately six to eight normal rate hikes by a central bank. Furthermore, the spread occurred just when the crisis called for monetary easing rather than a tightening of financial conditions.

Figure 2.3 illustrates the common pattern but also the differences in the waves of stress in the euro-area, the USA, and the UK. As expected, the first wave of stress was more acute in the USA and the UK, whereas the second wave

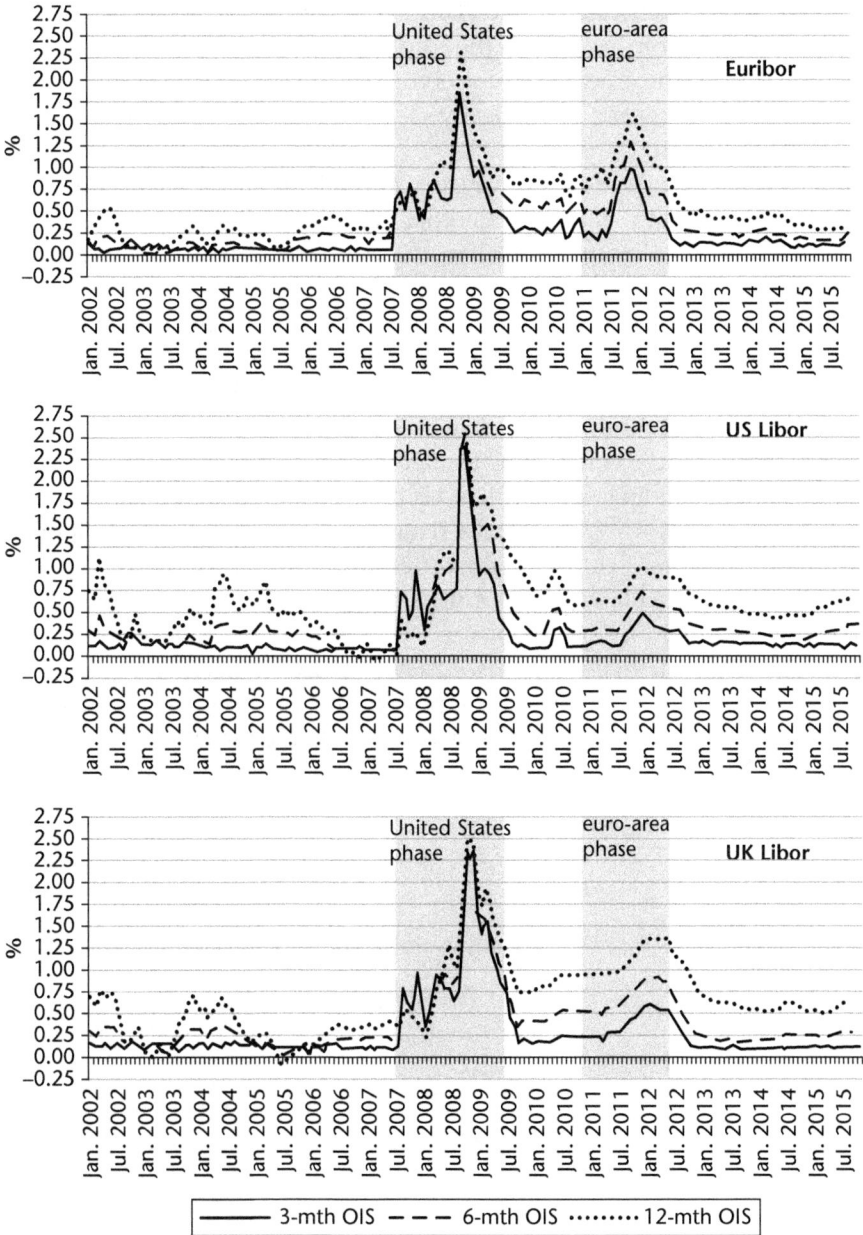

Figure 2.3 Spreads between Euribor, US Libor, and UK Libor over the OIS Rate (2002–2015)

Source: Bloomberg.

hit the euro-area particularly hard. This pattern shows that the epicentre of the crisis shifted from the USA to the euro-area. Notably, the stress appearing in Europe during the American phase of the crisis and the one appearing in the USA during the European phase clearly show the contagion that characterized the Great Recession.

The jump of the spreads between the central bank interest rate and other rates was common to practically all other markets. To further document this phenomenon, it is useful to analyse the developments of the spreads in another two cases.

Figure 2.4 shows the difference between the cost of bank loans up to 1 million euro in selected euro-area countries and EONIA, that is, the difference between the cost of bank loans and the central bank rate. Two phenomena are observable in the figure. First, in the aftermath of the failure of Lehman Brothers, the financial crisis started to affect the real economy via substantially increased bank-lending cost. This is visible as the increasing gap between bank lending rates across both core (France and Germany) and peripheral (Italy and Portugal) euro-area countries and the rate targeted by the ECB. Second, particularly in the European phase of the crisis, the cost of financing of small and medium-sized enterprises, which are the typical borrowers of small loans, increased substantially in peripheral countries compared to the core. In fact, at the peak of the crisis the cost of relatively small bank loans relative to the central bank rate had grown to over 7 per cent

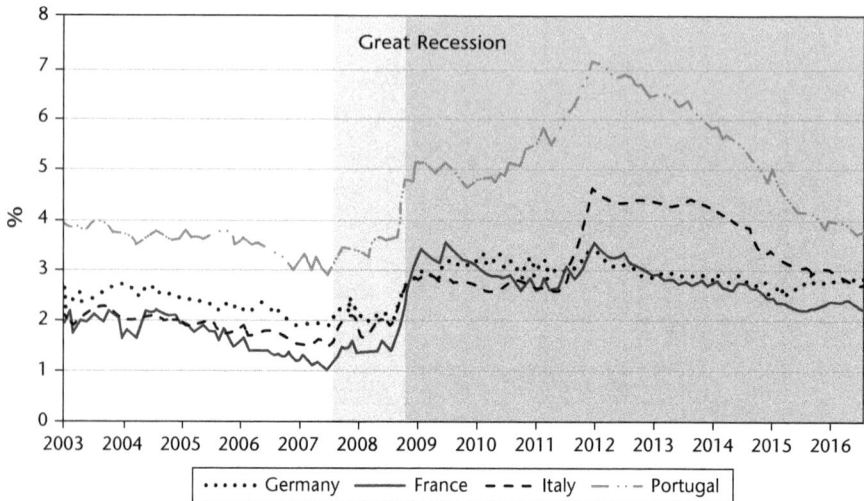

Figure 2.4 Spread between Interest Rates on New Loans up to Euro 1 Million and EONIA in the Euro-Area (2003–2016)
Source: ECB.

in Portugal and nearly 5 per cent in Italy, compared to less than 3.5 per cent in Germany and France.

Both phenomena reflected the impaired transmission of monetary policy, that is, the chain of links through which a given monetary policy move impacts the economy. The increase of lending rates relative to the central bank interest rate brought about a tightening of monetary conditions all across the euro-area, independently of—actually against—the policy of the central bank. The increase in the cost of bank lending in the periphery with respect to that in the core implied that monetary conditions had turned perverse, being tighter in the periphery, where the recession was deeper and more persistent, than in the core, where it was shallower and shorter. It was only some seven to eight years after the beginning of the Great Recession that the spreads of bank lending in the periphery converged back towards those in the core. However, the cost of bank lending in the core, relative to EONIA, showed no tendency to return to the levels prevailing before the crisis. Still, in 2016, bank loans remained some 100 basis points more expensive, relative to EONIA, than before the crisis, and thus monetary policy was less expansionary than the level of the overnight rate would have implied. A possible reason for this persistent effect could be the new liquidity ratios mandated by the Basel agreement.

In the USA the opening of a spread between the cost of bank lending and the rate controlled by the Fed was more contained and less persistent than in the euro-area. Figure 2.5 indicates that American banks recovered their ability to provide cheap credit to their borrowers more quickly than the European ones. Indeed, there was an increase of some 50 basis points between the cost of

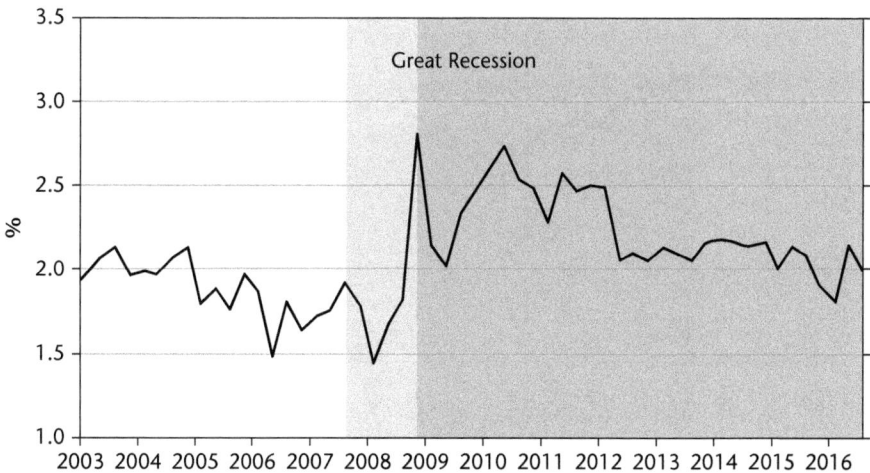

Figure 2.5 Spread between the Weighted-Average Effective Loan Rate for All Commercial and Industry Loans in the USA and the FFR (2003–2016)
Source: Federal Reserve Economic Data (FRED).

bank lending and the FFR just after the failure of Lehman Brothers in late 2008. However, by the first quarter of 2012 the spread had gone back towards 2 per cent, not far from where it was before the crisis.

Figure 2.6 depicts another manifestation of the opening up and instability of spreads in the euro-area. It shows the yields on government securities of the periphery, here represented by its two largest countries, Italy and Spain, and the yield on the ten-year German government bonds, as well as the ten-year OIS, giving the market expectation of the EONIA rate with a ten-year maturity.

This figure reveals that the yields of Italy, Spain, and Germany were aligned when the euro was launched in 1999 and until the beginning of the Great Recession. These yields were also aligned with the OIS, between 2005, the first date for which it became available, and the beginning of the Great Recession. But then a large spread opened up, particularly during the European phase of the crisis, between the yields in Italy and Spain, on one hand, and, on the other hand, the yield in Germany and the ten-year OIS. Thus, the ten-year yield of German government securities remained close to the long-term expectation of the ECB policy rate. But the yields of Spain and Italy significantly deviated from it. The perverse nature of monetary conditions is visible in the fact that, whereas yields in the core of the euro-area more than halved, from 4 to about 1.5 per cent between 2008 and 2012, in line with the expectation of the ECB interest rates as reflected in the OIS, those in Spain and Italy increased from 4 to nearly 6 per cent during the same period, tightening monetary conditions. It was only after the summer of 2012,

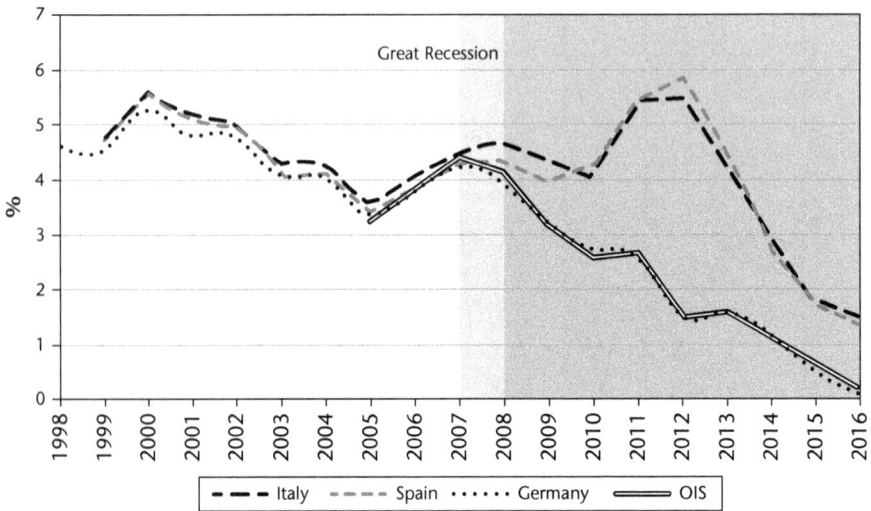

Figure 2.6 Yields on Italian, Spanish, and German Ten-Year Government Bonds and Ten-Year OIS Rate (1998–2016)
Source: Bloomberg and OECD (2017), Long-term interest rates (indicator).

when the ECB took stronger measures to fight the hiatus between the monetary conditions in the periphery and those in the core, as ECB President Draghi issued his famous pledge that the ECB would do 'whatever it takes' to preserve the euro, that the yield spread on the government bonds of Italy and Spain started to come down, getting closer to the OIS rate and to the German yield. Still, the spreads remained substantially higher than they were before the beginning of the Great Recession.

2.1.1.3 IMPAIRED ABILITY TO LOWER THE INTEREST RATE AS IT REACHED ITS LOWER BOUND

The possibility that the Taylor rule could result in a zero or negative rate of interest was not really considered until the Great Recession.[1] Consistently with the long time series discussed in Section 1.1, zero, and even negative, nominal rates of interest, have rarely, if ever, occurred in the history of humanity. Yet both the downward deviation of income growth from potential as well as the rate of inflation falling clearly below the central bank target implied that, according to the Taylor rule, nominal rates should have been brought into the negative domain during some phases of the Great Recession. According to the calculations reported in Figure 2.7, rates should have been lowered to about –4.5 per cent in 2009–2010 in the USA, and nearly –2.5 per cent in 2013–2014 in the euro-area.

Before experience demonstrated the contrary during the Great Recession, the prevailing view was that the central bank interest rates could not become negative. The reasoning was based on the fact that central banks issue two liabilities, banknotes and bank reserves, which are close substitutes. Since banknotes have intrinsically a zero nominal interest rate, any attempt to bring the return on bank reserves below zero would create incentives to arbitrage between the two assets, shedding bank reserves and hoarding banknotes. Of course, it was recognized that the substitutability between banknotes and bank reserves is not perfect, because there are storage, insurance, and transportation costs that affect banknotes but not bank reserves. These costs, however, were deemed to be low enough not to strongly affect the possibility of arbitrage, thus basically binding the interest rate on reserves to zero.

The experience of Denmark, Sweden, Switzerland, the euro-area, and Japan in the late phase of the Great Recession showed that, in practice, the interest rate on bank reserves could be made negative without immediately engendering overwhelming arbitrage through banknote hoarding. (See Box 12.)

---

[1] Woodford (2012b, p. 1) presents the problem as follows: 'Recent events have confronted many of the world's leading central banks with a situation that was regarded a few decades ago as merely a theoretical curiosity—a situation in which they have reached a lower bound on the level to which they are able to push overnight interest rates, despite an undesirably low level of capacity utilization, and low inflation or even fears of deflation.'

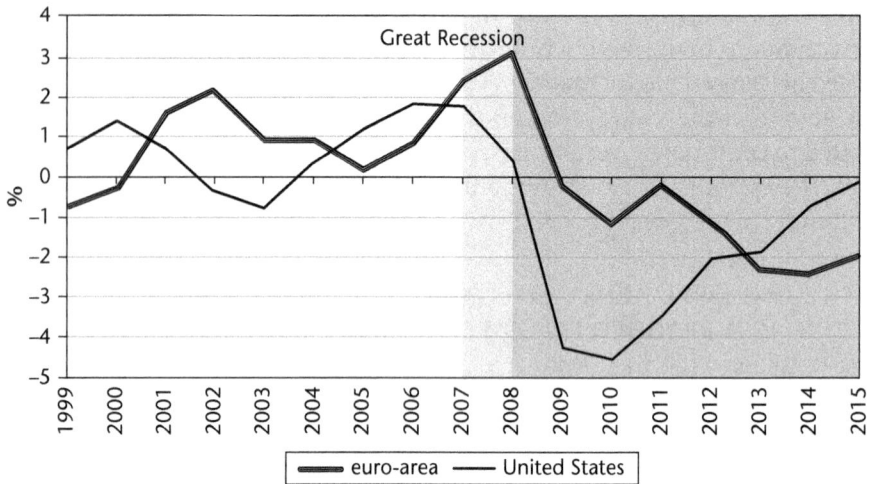

Figure 2.7 Interest Rate Consistent with the Taylor Rule for the Euro-Area and the USA (1999–2015)

Note: The Taylor rule interest rate is calculated using a parameter of 1 for the output gap and 1.5 for the inflation gap.

Source: Author's calculations with Eurostat, FRED.

Box 12 EARLY EXPERIENCES WITH NEGATIVE RATES

Before the Great Recession, central bank interest rate policies were assumed to have a ZLB. The thinking at the time was that official interest rates could no longer be cut when the risk-free short-term nominal interest rate reached zero. Cash was seen as a close enough substitute for central bank reserves and bank deposits that arbitrage opportunities would prevent negative short-term nominal rates.

The first central bank to break the ZLB barrier and redefine it as an ELB was Danmarks Nationalbank, following its historical deposit rate into negative territory in mid-2012. The Sveriges Riksbank, the SNB, the ECB, and the Bank of Japan followed suit.

The motives for a central bank to apply negative rates may stem from pressures on the external or internal value of its money. In the first case, when a central bank with a target rate or target range for its foreign exchange rate faces large capital inflows, it needs to sell its own currency on the Forex (FX) market or ease its monetary policy stance to stop the inflows. FX interventions may work for a while, but, if the pressure continues, the need to cut domestic interest rates relative to those of the target currency eventually materializes.

At the height of the European phase of the Great Recession in the summer of 2012, such developments occurred in Denmark, which was widely seen as a safe haven by euro investors.

The second justification for negative rates relates to the price stability objective. For example, the ECB applied negative rates and several other non-standard monetary policy measures to avoid deflation and raise below-target inflation expectations.

Sometimes the domestic and external motivations may be indistinguishable. In the case of the Sveriges Riksbank, inflation falling below the target was clearly the main motivation for going to negative rates, but the impact of the negative rates on the external value of the Swedish krona was likely the main channel through which the central bank expected negative rates to be transmitted to domestic inflation.

In the following, the experience of the Danish, Swedish, and Swiss central banks with negative interest rates is briefly reviewed. The ECB's experience with negative rates is dealt with in Section 2.1.4.3.2.

Denmark

Since the birth of the euro, Denmark has pegged its krone with a narrow deviation band against the euro.[2] Between August 2011 and July 2012, the height of the European phase of the Great Recession, Danmarks Nationalbank conducted large purchases of foreign exchange and cut its policy rate several times to thwart sustained foreign exchange inflows and the krone's tendency to strengthen against the euro (Jørgensen and Risberg, 2012). Following the ECB's rate cut in July 2012, Danmarks Nationalbank reduced the policy rate to −0.20 per cent to maintain the interest rate spread vis-à-vis the euro-area policy rate. It was the first time in modern history that a central bank had challenged the ZLB.

The Danish banking sector operates in a liquidity surplus vis-à-vis the central bank, so Danmarks Nationalbank relies on the issuance of certificates of deposit (CDs) as its main tool for steering short-term market rates. Using a carrot-and-stick approach, current account balances of banks with the central bank are not remunerated in Denmark. Banks have an incentive to convert their central bank reserves to CDs whenever the policy rate (i.e. the rate paid on CDs) is positive. When CDs pay negative interest, banks prefer to leave their reserves in their central bank accounts. In this case, the central bank converts balances exceeding an upper limit automatically to CDs. The limit for each bank depends on that bank's activity in the money market. These limits were hiked considerably when rates turned negative, because the central bank wanted to mitigate the burden of negative rates on banks. In other words, Danmarks Nationalbank mostly paid attention to *the marginal price* of reserves in the money market.

The success of the Danish experiment should be evaluated primarily in terms of FX developments, because the descent into negative rates was motivated by the need to defend a currency peg. The impact of the initial announcement of a switch to a negative policy rate was minor.[3] As 2012 wore on, however, the krone depreciated further.[4]

In any case, it is probably impossible to disentangle the impact of negative rates from the effect of the ECB's policy innovations in the summer of 2012.[5] As uncertainty over the future of the euro-area abated, the safe-haven flows to Denmark stopped and the

(continued)

---

[2] From 1982 to 1999, Danmarks Nationalbank had applied fixed exchange rate policy against German Deutschmark. In the euro era, a narrow, +/−2.25 per cent deviation band has been followed by the Danish central bank.

[3] The krone depreciated just 0.05 per cent on the day after the market participants realized that the central bank was ready to resort to negative rates to ease the pressure on its peg.

[4] The cumulative depreciation of krone against the euro was 0.3 per cent.

[5] These included the 'whatever it takes' speech by the ECB President on 26 July 2012 and the subsequent introduction of the ECB's OMT programme.

Box 12 CONTINUED

pressure on the currency was alleviated. Indeed, Danmarks Nationalbank was able to raise its policy rate to –0.1 per cent in January 2013, and returned to positive territory (0.05 per cent) in April 2014. Negative rates had to be reintroduced in Denmark in September 2014, again shadowing an ECB rate cut. In January and February 2015, after the ECB had announced the beginning of its PSPP (QE) and following the break-up of the Swiss currency peg against the euro, the Danish central bank rate was pushed further down in the negative domain as the CD rate was cut to –0.75 per cent.[6]

When the sole objective for monetary policy is to keep the FX rate stable, the policy rate has no role in adjusting to cyclical developments in the real economy. However, given that the spread between money market rates in Denmark and in the euro-area heavily influences the FX rate (Moselund Jensen and Spange, 2015), the pass-through from policy rate to the money market rates is central to Danmarks Nationalbank's ability to manage the krone's exchange rate. In this regard, the move to negative territory did not affect the potency of Danish monetary policy. Danmarks Nationalbank detected no indication of a weakened pass-through from policy rates to money market rates after they had been significantly reduced in early 2015. Short-term money market rates closely kept tracking the policy rate (Figure B12.1).

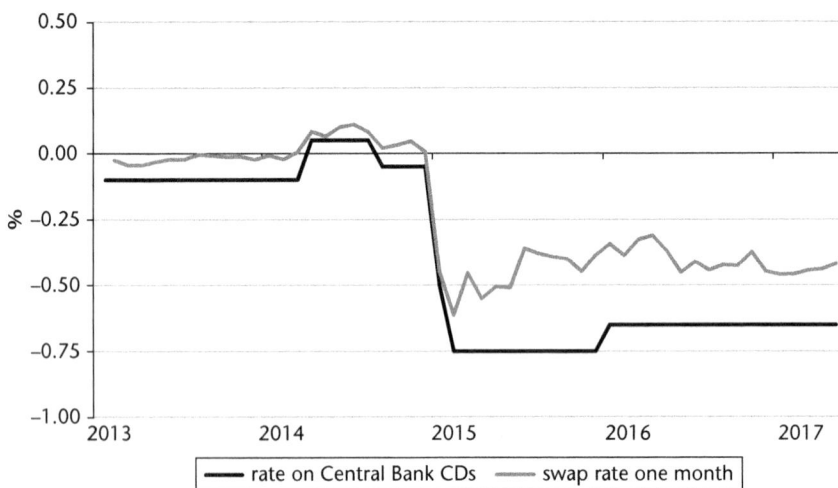

Figure B.12.1 Danish Policy Rate and One Month Swap Rate (January 2013–May 2017)

Source: Macrobond.

---

[6] The rate cut was accompanied by large foreign exchange interventions. In January and February 2015, they totalled DKK 276 billion, amounting to almost 14 per cent of Danish GDP. Danmarks Nationalbank says that its reaction function differs according to the direction of the pressures on its FX rate. It can prevent the krone from appreciating too rapidly by unlimited sales on krone, so there is no cap on interest when fighting against a capital outflow (Danmarks Nationalbank, 2015).

Additionally, the deposit rates applied by banks to insurance and pension funds continued to follow the developments in the money market, dropping to significantly negative levels in early 2015.

Regarding bank lending rates and deposit rates, Danmarks Nationalbank followed an asymmetric behaviour. Whereas the pass-through from policy to corporate and household deposit rates appeared to fall at low interest rate levels, the fact that the policy rate was positive or negative had a much smaller impact on the setting of bank lending rates (Kofoed Mandsberg, Lejsgaard Autrup, and Risbjerg, 2016; Figure B12.2). Even when the marginal cost of holding central bank reserves was −0.75 per cent for banks, households were generally exempt from negative deposit rates, and only about 30 per cent of non-financial corporates were subject to them. The reluctance of banks to impose negative deposit rates on households suggests the existence of a first-mover disadvantage and fear of a run to cash by depositors. No bank wants to be the first one to test the waters of negative deposit rates and risk their depositors fleeing to open accounts with their competitors. Moreover, even if all banks simultaneously shifted to negative rates, depositors could switch to holding cash, which again would be costly for banks. As household deposits rates continued to be non-negative in Denmark, no signs of unusual increases in the demand for cash emerged in 2016 (Danmarks Nationalbank, 2016).

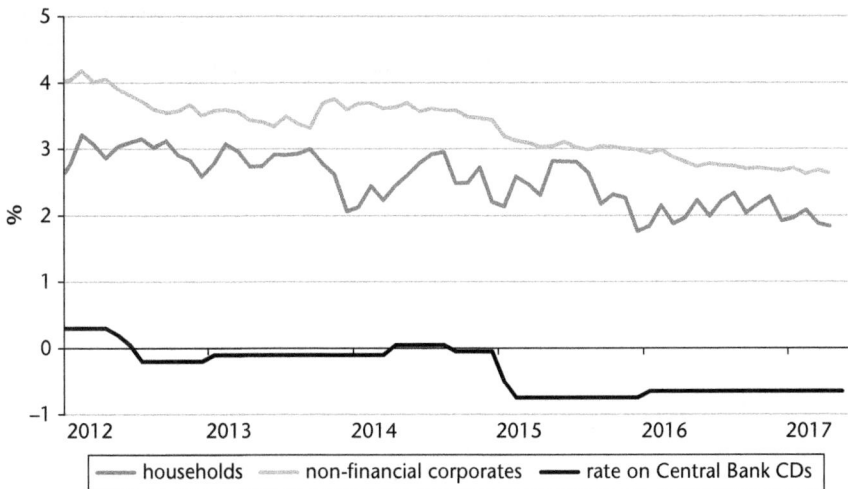

Figure B.12.2 Danish Policy Rate and Bank Lending Rates to Non-Financial Corporates and Households (January 2012–May 2017)
Source: Macrobond.

The pass-through of the negative rates to bank lending rates seemed to slow when the central bank defended its currency with negative interest rates. However, this could be explained by the unwillingness of banks to adjust their lending rates until the reduction could be seen to be long lasting.

(*continued*)

Box 12 CONTINUED

Sweden

The key policy rate, the repo rate, has been negative in Sweden since February 2015. The Swedish adoption of this innovation was motivated by two arguments (Riksbank, 2016).

First, the global interest rate level is reflected in the domestic rate level in a small, open economy like Sweden's. Moreover, policy rates in Sweden's key trading partners had already fallen to around zero. Thus, if domestic short-term rates much exceeded those of other countries, the Swedish krona would, *ceteris paribus*, appreciate. The rising external value of the domestic currency would then result in subdued economic activity and lower inflation.

Second and more importantly, Swedish inflation in early 2015 had remained below the monetary policy target for quite some time and longer-term inflation expectations had already trended downwards for about two years. Hence, the Sveriges Riksbank felt necessary to safeguard the anchoring role of the inflation target by adding to the monetary policy accommodation by cutting its policy rate (Riksbank, 2016).

As the accommodative stance must be passed through to market rates to be effective, cutting the policy rate to negative territory does not guarantee an increase in the stimulus. Still, the monetary policy transmission mechanism seemed to continue to function in Sweden despite the negative policy rate. The money market rates continued tracking the policy rate into negative territory (Figure B12.3). Similarly, lending rates to non-financial corporates in particular continued to move more or less in tandem with the policy rate, indicating that the transmission of monetary policy had not been hampered.

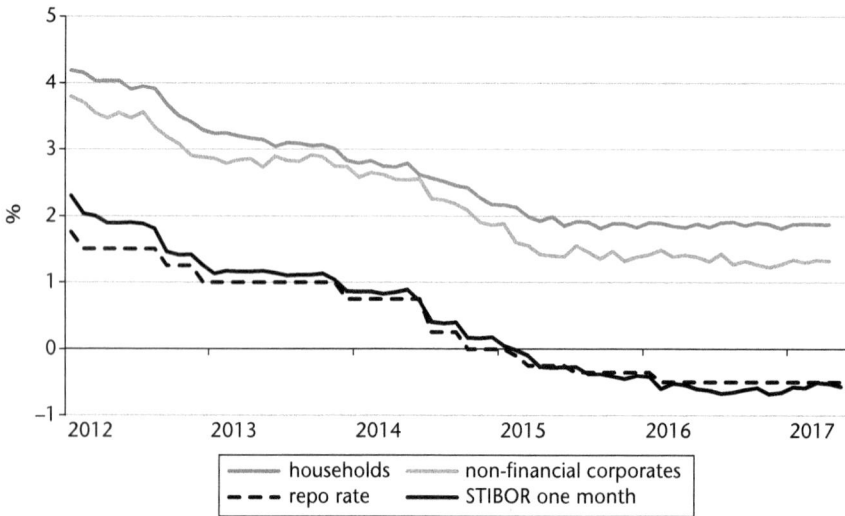

Figure B.12.3 Swedish Policy Rate (Repo), One-Month Money Market Rate (STIBOR), and Bank Lending Rates to Households and Non-Financial Corporates (January 2012–May 2017)

Source: Macrobond.

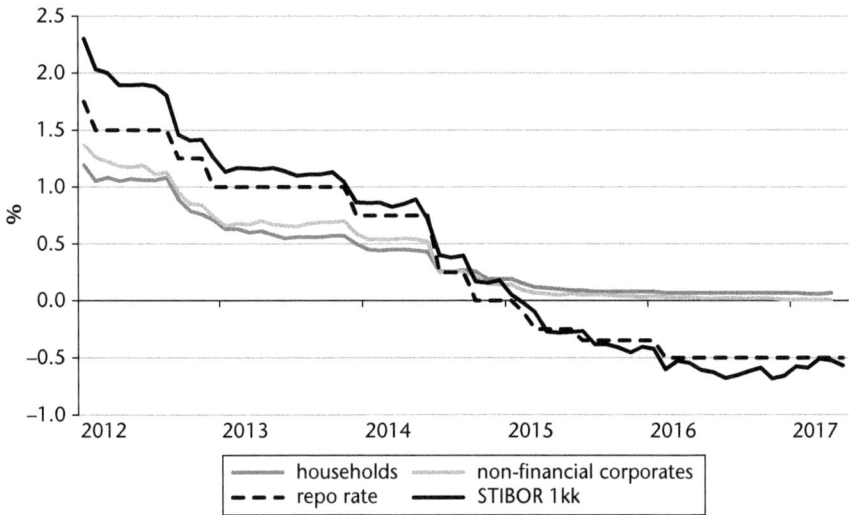

Figure B.12.4 Swedish Policy Rate (Repo), One-Month Money Market Rate (STIBOR), and Bank Lending Rates to Households and Non-Financial Corporates (January 2012–May 2017)

Source: Macrobond.

However, while the pass-through to lending rates broadly survived negative rates, the behaviour of deposit rates did change in response to the new situation (Figure B12.4). The pass-through from policy rates to interest rates paid on household and non-financial corporate deposits started to slow when the rate that the Riksbank paid on bank reserve deposits turned negative. Eventually, the link between the deposit rates and the policy rate disappeared when the deposit rates reached zero. Swedish households and many small and medium-sized non-financial corporates do not need to deal with negative deposit rates in practice, even though the policy rate has been negative for over two years.

Lower lending rates with unchanged deposit rates threatened to eat into the net interest income of Swedish banks. Some were able to compensate for this with declines in other funding costs and increasing their lending volumes (Figure B12.5). Furthermore, low interest rates helped maintain the asset quality for Sweden's big banks. The portfolio of impaired loans fell between 2012 and 2015, and credit losses remained stable despite increased lending to the public (Riksbank, 2015).

The Sveriges Riksbank did not detect significant changes in the volume of cash in circulation from the trend prevailing prior to the introduction of the negative rates. If anything, the downward trend in the holding of cash turned even more negative, probably connected to updating of some of the banknotes and coins in circulation. As the deposit rates for households and non-financial corporates mostly remained in positive territory, the stability in the demand for cash mostly shows that negative rates for over two years—and the policy rate at –0.5 per cent for over a year—did not result in banks switching from central bank reserves to increased holdings of vault cash.

(continued)

Box 12 CONTINUED

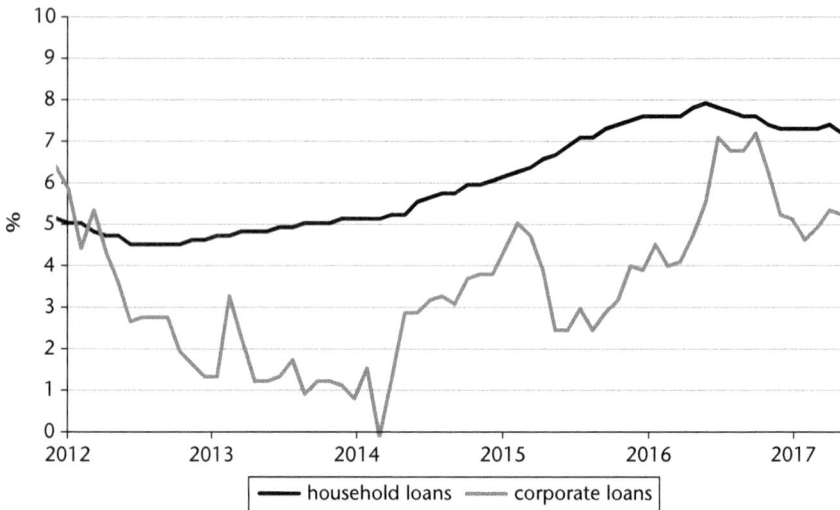

Figure B.12.5 Year-on-Year Changes in Bank Lending Volumes in Sweden (January 2012–May 2017)

Source: Macrobond.

Switzerland

Switzerland has followed the global trend in nominal and real interest rates over the past few decades. Thanks to its political stability, Switzerland enjoyed a safe-haven status, resulting in a negative interest rate spread vis-à-vis its main trading partners. Hence, Swiss interest rates were at relatively low levels even before the Great Recession. With the crisis, and especially since its European phase started, Swiss short-term rates fell close to zero.

The strong monetary accommodation provided by the ECB resulted in a narrowing of the interest rate differential between euro and Swiss franc money market rates during the European phase of the crisis. This, together with the safe-haven capital inflows, led to a significant appreciation of the Swiss franc. The SNB's mandate calls for ensuring price stability and, in so doing, taking due account of economic developments. Like the situation in Denmark and Sweden, the exchange rate is a key channel from interest rates to economic developments. To prevent major negative economic consequences from significant inflows of foreign capital, the SNB introduced a minimum exchange rate for the franc vis-à-vis the euro in September 2011.

When the ECB first introduced a negative deposit rate and was about to launch a significant QE programme, the exchange rate of the euro fell sharply against all major currencies. This made it much more difficult to maintain the minimum exchange rate against the euro.

In January 2015, the SNB decided to discontinue applying the cap on its euro exchange rate. In addition to easing pressures on franc appreciation beyond what was tolerable from the domestic economy's point of view, the Swiss central bank chose to lower the interest rate it pays on banks' sight deposits to –0.75 per cent.

In joining the club of central banks applying negative policy rates, the SNB went further with its policy rate than any of its peers had done. The SNB's negative interest rate re-established the negative policy rate premium between Switzerland and the euro-area. This, combined with SNB's willingness to intervene in the FX market, eased pressures on the Swiss franc (Jordan, 2016).

The pass-through from the policy rate to the short-term money market rates remained strong. The three-month Libor continued to track the policy rate closely even in negative territory. This did not mean that the monetary policy transmission in Switzerland was unaffected. The profitability of Swiss domestically focused banks had fallen significantly since the start of Great Recession due to the declining net interest rate margins (Zürbrygg, 2016).[7] Room for lower deposit rates was limited even at the outset, and lending rates followed the lower general interest rate level. Fortunately, the situation stabilized with the introduction of a negative central bank deposit rate. Domestically focused banks started to raise their long-term mortgage rates even as long-term market rates continued to fall. Profitability was further improved by the fact that the SNB exempted most bank sight deposits from the negative rate. (The negative rate is charged only when the volume of sight deposits exceeds 20 times the minimum reserve requirements.)

The Swiss example confirms not only that the ELB for short-term nominal rates lies below zero, but also that rates can be maintained in the negative territory for quite some time. It also shows, however, that there are limits to life in negative territory. Banks have increased their interest rates margins to maintain profitability, a move that operates against the credit channel of monetary policy. Negative rates have also functioned as a tool to influence the exchange rate rather than as a tool to relax funding conditions in the domestic economy. Finally, the SNB has lifted the burden on banks of having to pass the negative policy stance to retail deposits by internalizing a large part of the costs, by allowing quite substantial exemptions on negatively remunerated sight deposits.

Three major characteristics seem to apply for all the early experimenters with negative policy rates: (1) foreign exchange rate has an important role in their monetary policy setting; (2) commercial banks react to negative rates asymmetrically, lending rates are more influenced by negative policy rates than the deposit rates; and (3) it seems important to partly isolate banks from the impact of the asymmetry by compensating part of their excess reserve holdings through remunerating average reserve holding at higher rates than the marginal rate would imply.

Tuomas Välimäki

Notwithstanding the experience of a number of central banks with negative rates, the ability to bring interest rates into the negative domain proved to be limited. This is shown indirectly by the fact that central banks, which used to consider 25 basis points the minimum worthwhile change of interest rates before the Great Recession, were very cautious about reducing rates below zero, moving in steps which were a fraction of the usual 25 basis points.

---

[7] The interest rate margin fell from 1.8 per cent at the beginning of 2008 to below 1.3 per cent at the beginning of 2015.

In addition, when maintained for a long time, negative interest rates proved to be problematic for banks' profitability. It proved practically impossible for banks to charge negative rates to depositors, especially retail ones. Hence, part of banks' funding costs no longer reflected changes in the central bank rate.

2.1.2 Central Bank Action and Communication

Central bank action during the Great Recession can be seen under two dimensions: first, the price, or interest rate, dimension; second, the quantity, or balance sheet, dimension. The two dimensions ceased, during the crisis, to be one the dual of the other. In fact, balance sheet management went well beyond regulating the amount of liquidity the central bank provided to the market to steer the interest rate in the desired position within the interest rate corridor. Balance sheet management still aimed at influencing interest rate conditions, but in a much more complex way than before the Great Recession. It became the tool through which central banks tried to regain control of the short-term rate, to bring order in the spreads between that rate and more macro-economically relevant interest rates and to further ease monetary policy even when the lower bound had been reached. In effect, balance sheet management, or balance sheet policy in Woodford's (2012a) terminology, was added during the crisis to the tools available to the central bank. Friedman and Kuttner (2011) even argue that balance sheet management will permanently remain an additional tool in the panoply of the central bank.

The use of the balance sheet as an additional instrument of monetary policy was not, however, a vindication of the quantitative Friedmanian approach as opposed to the Wicksellian one. The Wicksellian approach had to be made more complex, not abandoned. Monetary policy had to recognize that the control of the interest rate had become more difficult during the Great Recession, that the relationship between the rate controlled by the central bank and those more relevant for the macro-economy had become unstable, and that there was a lower limit below which it was not possible to push the nominal interest rate. But the idea that monetary policy is basically an interest rate story was confirmed during the Great Recession. This issue will be discussed again in Chapter 3.

The price and the quantity dimensions of central bank action will be illustrated in turn.

Two developments are characteristic of the interest rate dimension:

1. The very deep lowering of the interest rate corridor.
2. The eventual settling of the central bank interest rate on the bottom of the interest rate corridor.

Figure 1.14, in Section 1.2.4, clearly shows these two developments in the case of the ECB. The rate on the MRO, which before the Great Recession was the most important central bank rate, was brought down between 2008 and 2016 from 4.25 to 0 per cent, albeit with two, ex post, difficult to justify, increases in 2011. The overnight rate, EONIA, recorded an even larger decrease, from plus 460 down to minus 35 basis points, because it moved, given the large liquidity outstanding in the market, down to a level close to the deposit facility rate. This is consistent with the mechanism explained in Section 1.2.4. Of course, to the extent that excess liquidity brought the overnight rate close to the bottom of the corridor, it was just a tool to reduce the short-term interest rate within the corridor. During the crisis, however, as mentioned, and as illustrated later in this section, balance sheet management affected other dimensions of the interest rate, for example, by influencing longer-term and riskier interest rates.

The interest rate experience of the Fed presents a number of similarities with that of the ECB, but also significant differences. Just after the failure of Lehman Brothers and the AIG bailout, the Fed experienced a tension between the desire to continue controlling the FFR and the strong downward effect on this rate exercised by the large amount of reserves injected into the system to counter the stress affecting market functioning (Bech and Klee, 2009). The answer to this tension was the authorization from Congress to pay to banks, beginning in October 2008, interest on excess reserves (IOER). This action potentially created a corridor similar to that of the ECB, as represented in Figure 2.8.

This figure is designed to allow a better comparison with the ECB experience, but is not the usual representation of the Fed corridor. In Figure 2.8, the Effective Federal Funds Rate (EFFR) is reported within a corridor having the primary credit (aka discount) rate as a ceiling and the lower limit of the Fed's target range as a floor. Here one sees that the huge amount of outstanding liquidity kept the (EFFR) close to the bottom of the corridor.

Indeed, as seen in Figure 2.9, which is the more usual representation of the Fed corridor, the EFFR was even below the IOER and thus around the middle of the target interest rate range, which was kept within the 0–25 basis points range between December 2008 and December 2015. The IOER was not really a floor for the overnight rate, because important money market institutions did not have access to the Fed.

In Figure 2.9, the EFFR is reported within a corridor having the rate on RRP (Interest Rate on Reverse Repurchase Agreement Operations) as the floor and the IOER as the ceiling. The peculiarity of this corridor is that it is limited by two absorbing facilities rather than by a providing and an absorbing facility, as in the case of the ECB, and as represented in Figure 2.8. This peculiarity results from the fact that, in the calculation of the EFFR, trading between banks and some other important money market participants (including

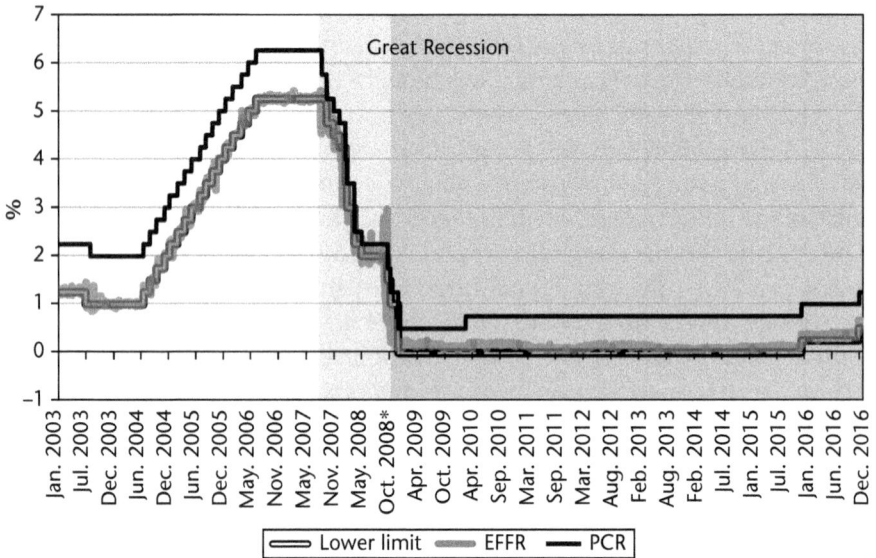

Figure 2.8 EFFR and Interest Rate Corridor in the USA (2003–2016)

Note: EFFR—Effective Federal Fund Rate, PCR—Primary Credit Rate. (*): Fed started paying interest on reserves in October 2008.

Source: FRED.

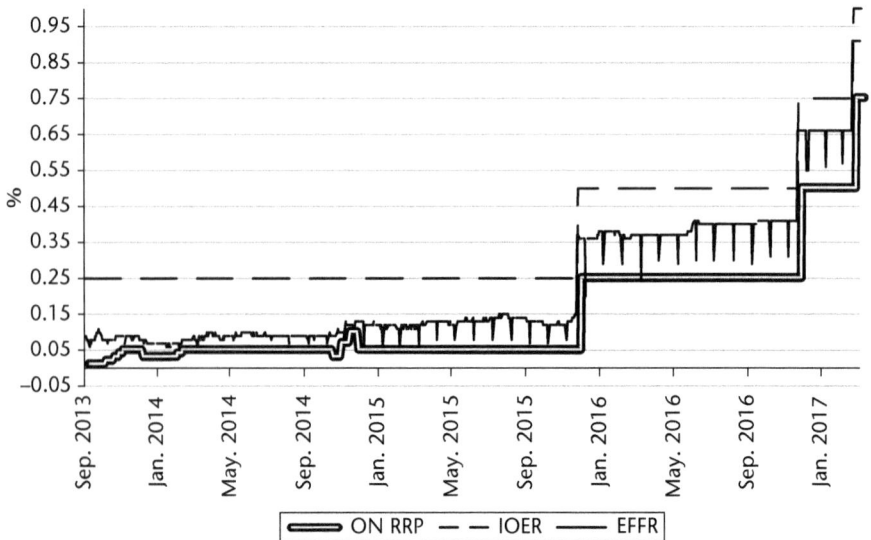

Figure 2.9 EFFR, IOER, and Interest Rate on ON RPP in the USA (2013–2017)

Note: IOER—Interest Rate on Excess Reserves, ON RRP—Interest Rate on Reverse Repurchase Agreement Operation, EFFR—Effective Federal Funds Rate.

Source: Datastream and Fed.

government-sponsored agencies) is taken into account. But ultimately it is only banks that have access to the deposits with the Fed, which are remunerated with the IOER. The other money market participants only have access to the lower remunerated RRP. This implies that it is the RRP rate rather than the IOER that establishes the lower limit of the Fed corridor.

In conclusion, with the huge amount of liquidity outstanding in the market, both for the ECB and the Fed, the rate at which the central bank absorbs liquidity became the de facto policy rate, that is, the rate relevant for the market pricing of reserves. As mentioned, a key difference between the two central banks is that there are two absorbing facilities in the case of the Fed but only one in the case of the ECB.

The quantity dimension of the action of the ECB and the Fed, which was the real novelty during the crisis, can obviously be seen in terms of both the assets and the liabilities on the central bank balance sheet. Figure 2.10 gives a summary indication of the total balance sheet size of these two central banks and, for comparison, that of the Bank of England. The sharp increase in the size of the balance sheet after the failure of Lehman Brothers is evident in all three central banks. The ECB experienced the smallest increase, still its balance sheet increased by 26 per cent just in the first quarter after the failure of Lehman Brothers, after having grown by 'only' 10 per cent on average in each year of the previous decade. In subsequent years, the balance sheet of the

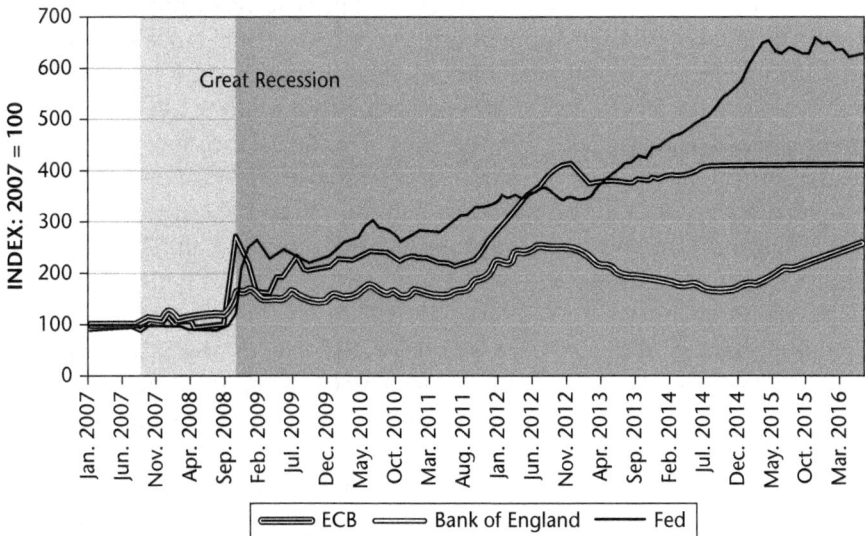

Figure 2.10 Total Assets for the ECB, the Fed, and the Bank of England, Index 2007=100 (2007–2016)

Source: ECB Statistical Data Warehouse, FRED, Bank of England.

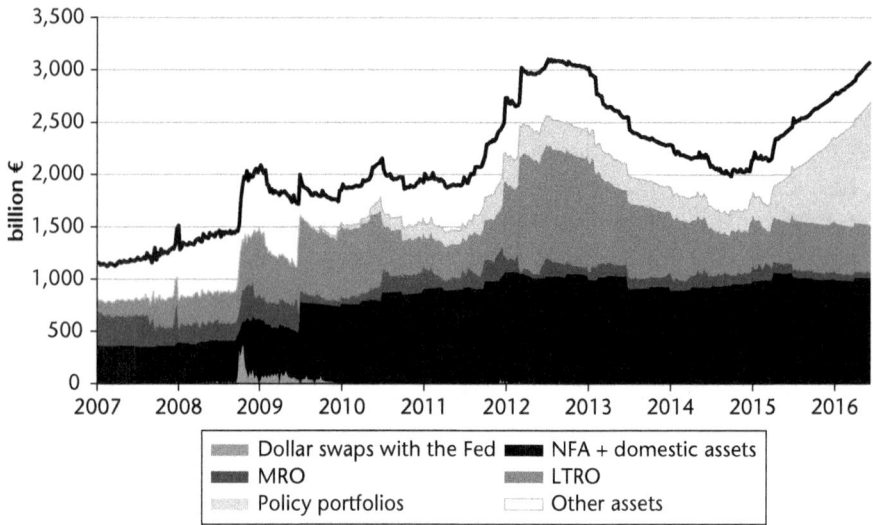

Figure 2.11 ECB Assets (2007–2016)

Note: NFA—Net Foreign Assets. MRO—Main Refinancing Operations. LTRO—Longer-Term Refinancing Operations.

Source: ECB Statistical Data Warehouse.

ECB grew less strongly than that of either the Fed or the Bank of England. Indeed, when the Fed balance sheet reached its peak at the beginning of 2015, it was 6.5 times larger than at the beginning of 2007, the balance sheet of the Bank of England was four times larger, whereas that of the ECB had increased merely by a factor of two. It was only subsequently, when the ECB started its own quantitative easing (QE) that the growth of the balance sheet of the ECB started approaching that of the two other central banks.[8]

A more detailed look at the assets and liabilities from 2007 until 2016 of the ECB (in Figures 2.11 and 2.12), and the Fed (in Figures 2.13 and 2.14), reveals some common features, but also some important differences between the two central banks.

An important common feature is that, on the *liability side* of the balance sheet, it was bank reserves (i.e. current accounts and deposit facility of banks in the case of the ECB; current accounts in the case of the Fed), which reflected the increase in the asset side.

Differences are more visible on the *asset side* of the two central banks' balance sheets. In the case of the ECB, the asset increase was dominated for

---

[8] The official name the ECB gave to what is commonly called QE is the Expanded Asset Purchase Programme (EAPP).

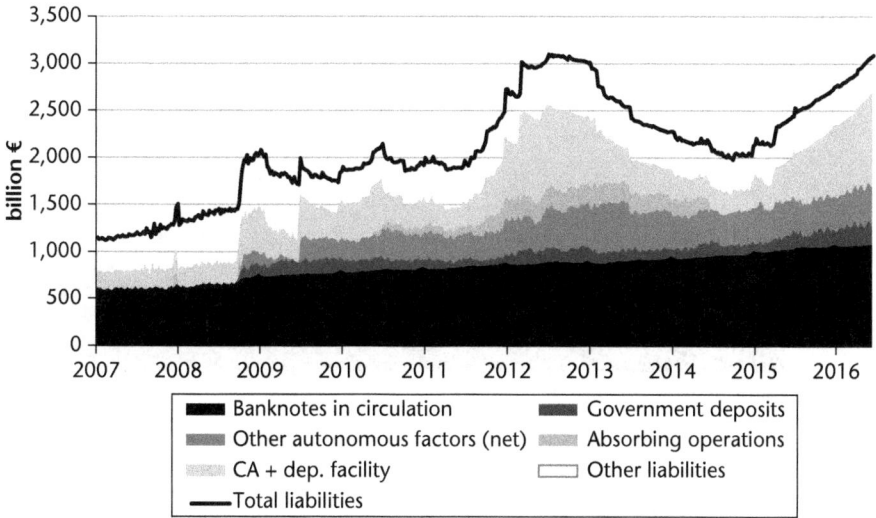

Figure 2.12 ECB Liabilities (2007–2016)
Note: CA—Current Accounts. Dep. Facility—Deposit Facility.
Source: ECB Statistical Data Warehouse.

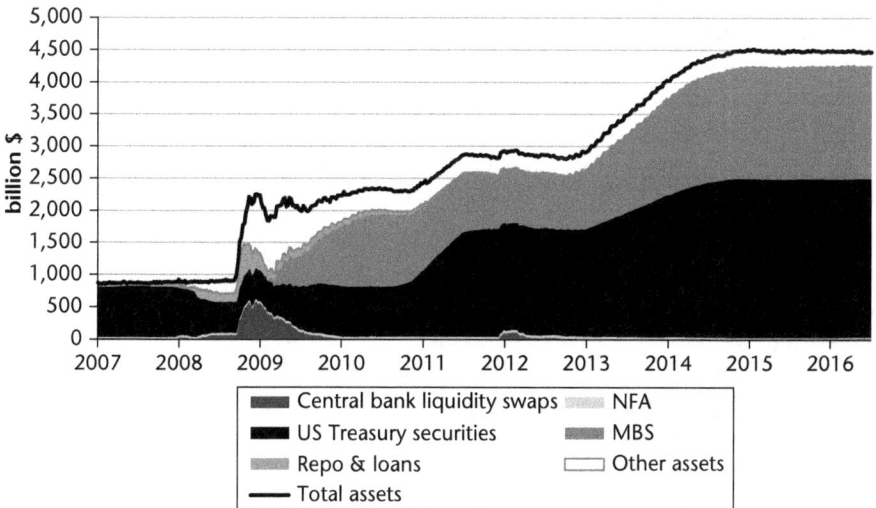

Figure 2.13 Federal Reserve Assets (2007–2016)
Note: NFA—Net Foreign Assets. MBS—Mortgage-Backed Securities.
Source: FRED.

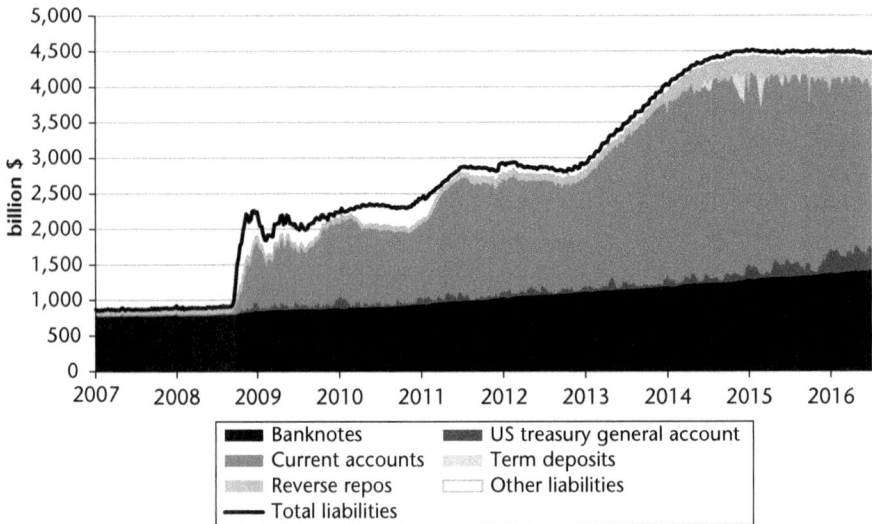

Figure 2.14 Federal Reserve Liabilities (2007–2016)
Source: FRED.

the first six years of the crisis by lending to banks on a repurchase, that is, temporary, basis, under extensions of longer-term refinancing operations (LTRO). The duration of the LTRO was increased, on an ad hoc basis, from the three-month maturity prevailing before the crisis to one year in June 2009, then to three years in December 2011, and finally to four years with the so-called targeted longer-term refinancing operations (TLTRO) in 2014 and 2016. Beginning in 2015, the ECB also started QE.

In the case of the Fed it was already at the turn between 2008 and 2009 that purchases of securities (mortgage-backed securities—MBS) and then treasury paper led to an increase of the asset side of the balance sheet. The official name of the Fed purchases was LSAP. However, as in the case of the ECB, the market term of QE, for quantitative easing, eventually prevailed.

QE replaced a number of temporary operations that the Fed had launched immediately following the failure of Lehman Brothers (see Box 13).

The different sources, on the asset side of the ECB's and the Fed's balance sheets, of the additional liquidity had implications for monetary policy over an extended period during the Great Recession. With its purchases, the Fed enacted an active balance sheet management, in the sense that it directly determined the size of its balance sheet and therefore the amount of liquidity to be injected into the money market. In effect, the major changes in the balance sheet of the Fed coincided with the various waves of QE. Instead, the

Box 13 FED AND ECB ACTIONS DURING THE GREAT RECESSION

The Fed and the ECB responded to the financial crisis through a number of tools designed to provide liquidity to financial institutions, support conditions in financial markets, and, in the later part of the crisis, further ease monetary conditions even when interest rates had approached zero.

A. The Fed

1) LIQUIDITY PROVISION TO FINANCIAL INSTITUTIONS
The first set of tools involved the provision of short-term liquidity to banks, depository institutions, and other financial institutions.

The TAF provided credit to depository institutions in generally sound financial conditions against adequate collateral through an auction mechanism, used to minimize stigma and encourage its use. The TAF was created in December 2007 and expired in March 2010, given the return to more normal conditions.

The PDCF was an overnight loan facility that provided funding to primary dealers as most of them, including major money market intermediaries similar to banks, had no access to Fed lending. The facility was set up in March 2008 and expired in February 2010, as there had been no borrowing since mid-May 2009, given the price of borrowing and the return to a fully functioning money market.

The TSLF was a loan of treasury securities to primary dealers for 28 days against eligible collateral in two types of auctions in order to free up the much-demanded risk-free US treasury securities from the growing Fed balance sheet and alleviate pressure on other forms of collateral. The facility was set up in March 2008 and expired in February 2010, as there had been no borrowing since August 2009 and the financing markets had returned to less stressed conditions.

The liquidity swap lines with foreign central banks allowed foreign central banks to offer liquidity to their domestic institutions in dollars and reciprocally allowed the Fed to provide liquidity, if needed, in foreign currency to US institutions. These swaps lines were created in December 2007 on a temporary basis and were converted to standing arrangements in 2013.

Lending to Specific Institutions
In March 2008 the FRBNY extended credit to a Delaware limited liability company, Maiden Lane LLC, to fund the purchase of a portfolio of mortgage-related securities, residential and commercial mortgage loans, and associated hedges from Bear Stearns Companies Inc.

In September 2008, the FRBNY extended an $85 billion credit line to AIG. In November 2008, this financial support was restructured and two new limited liability companies were created, Maiden Lane II LLC and Maiden Lane III LLC.

Loans made by the FRBNY to Maiden Lane LLC, Maiden Lane II LLC, and Maiden Lane III LLC were repaid in 2012.

2) LIQUIDITY PROVISION DIRECTLY TO BORROWERS AND INVESTORS
IN KEY CREDIT MARKETS
A second set of tools involved the provision of liquidity directly to borrowers and investors in key credit markets authorized under the exceptional lending provision of Section 13(3) of the Federal Reserve Act.

(continued)

Box 13 CONTINUED

The CPFF was a liquidity backstop to US issuers of commercial paper (CP) through a specially created limited liability company (LLC) called the CPFF LLC. The facility was set up in October 2008 and expired in February 2010, amid a return to a functioning CP market.

The AMLF financed the purchases of high-quality asset-backed commercial paper (ABCP) from money market mutual funds by US depository institutions and BHC. The facility was set up in September 2008 and expired in February 2010, as credit outstanding under the AMLF had been zero since October 2009.

Under the **Term Asset-Backed Securities Loan Facility (TALF)** the FRBNY extended credit up to five years to holders of eligible ABS. This facility was set up in November 2008 and was closed for new loan extensions against newly issued Commercial Mortgage-Backed Securities (CMBS) in June 2010, and for new loans against all other types of collateral in March 2010.

3) LSAP/ QE

As a third set of instruments, the Fed expanded its traditional OMO by purchasing longer-term securities for the System Open Market Account (SOMA) Portfolio. The goals of these operations were to provide further policy accommodation at a time when policy rates had reached the ZLB, to support the functioning of credit markets, and to put downward pressure on longer-term interest rates. From 2008 to 2014, the Fed conducted a series of LSAPs for a total of about $3.8 trillion. In 2011 and 2012, the Fed extended the average maturity of securities held in the SOMA by selling short-term securities and purchasing those with longer tenors.

Large-Scale Purchase Programme I (November 2008–March 2010)

The Fed purchased $1.25 trillion of agency MBS, $175 billion of agency debt, and $300 billion of longer-term treasury securities.

Large-Scale Purchase Programme II (November 2010—June 2011)

The Fed purchased a further $600 billion of longer-term treasury securities at a pace of about $75 billion per month.

Maturity Extension Programme (September 2011–December 2012)

The Fed purchased $667 billion of treasury securities with remaining maturities of six years to 30 years, selling an equal par amount of treasury securities with remaining maturities of three years or less.

Large-Scale Purchase Programme III (September 2012–October 2014)

Starting in October 2012, the Fed purchased agency MBS at a pace of $40 billion per month. Beginning in January 2013, the Fed purchased longer-term treasury securities at a pace of $45 billion per month, following the completion of its Maturity Extension Programme in December 2012. From January 2014, the FOMC reduced the pace of asset purchases by $10 billion per month, and concluded the purchases in October 2014. Under the LSAP III, the Fed purchased about $1.6 trillion of securities almost equally split between MBS and US treasuries.

Reinvestment policy

Since the summer of 2010, the Fed has reinvested principal payments from its holdings of agency debt and agency MBS in agency MBS and rolled-over maturing treasury securities at auction. The FOMC maintained this reinvestment policy until September.

Balance Sheet Normalization

In September 2017 the Fed decided to initiate its balance sheet normalization plan by reducing its reinvestment of maturing securities in accordance with the June 2017 Addendum to the FOMC's Policy Normalization Principles and Plans.

4) FORWARD GUIDANCE

After short-term interest rates had fallen close to zero in December 2008, the Fed began providing forward guidance about the future course of its monetary policy by announcing its intention to maintain policy rates lower for longer than otherwise might have been expected. In that context, forward guidance aimed at providing additional monetary policy accommodation by pushing lower longer-term borrowing rates.

The Fed implemented various types of forward guidance based on a precise calendar (August 2011–September 2012) or the achievement of thresholds for key economic indicators such as the unemployment rate and inflation (October 2012–December 2013).

After the first increase of the target range for the FFR in December 2015, the FOMC indicated that the timing and size of future adjustments would depend on 'realized and expected economic conditions relative to its objectives'.

5) CONTROL OF THE FFR

Prior to the financial crisis, the Fed's main tool consisted of OMO to manage the amount of banks' reserve balances so that the interest rate in the federal funds market would trade close to the target set by the FOMC. Changes in the FFR would then be transmitted to other short-term interest rates, affecting longer-term interest rates and overall financial conditions and hence inflation and economic activity.

During the Great Recession, the FOMC steadily lowered, between August 2007 and December 2008, its target for the FFR from 5.25 to a range of 0 to 0.25 per cent, and conducted liquidity provision and LSAPs. These programmes dramatically increased banks' reserve balances from $15 billion to $2.6 trillion, which pushed down the FFR below the FOMC's target. In response, the Fed used several tools to offset the effect of its liquidity operations on reserves and to regain control of short-term interest rates, the most effective being its ability to pay interest on banks' reserve balances, which was granted by the US Congress in October 2008.

As only depository institutions can earn the IOER rate, the Fed created supplementary tools, in particular the ON RRP facility, to put a more effective floor under short-term interest rates. The ON RRP facility is available to a variety of counterparties, including eligible money market funds, government-sponsored enterprises, broker-dealers, and depository institutions that may invest funds overnight with the Fed at a rate set by the FOMC.

Thanks to these new tools, the EFFR was set within the new target range also after its first increase from 0–0.25 to 0.25–0.5 per cent in December 2015, with the IOER rate equal to the top of the range and the rate on the ON RRP facility equal to the bottom of that range.

These developments are consistent with the monetary policy normalization principles that were first announced by the FOMC in June 2011 and amended in September 2014 and March 2015. After raising the FFR, in a second step the FOMC decided to reduce its securities holdings primarily by stopping reinvestments, but selling agency MBS is not

(continued)

Box 13 CONTINUED

---

envisaged. In the longer run, the Fed intends to come back to a SOMA portfolio composed primarily of treasury securities and of an amount of holdings necessary to implement monetary policy efficiently and effectively.

Sources:

- Federal Reserve—Monthly Reports on Credit and Liquidity Programmes and the Balance Sheet
- Federal Reserve—Quarterly Report on Federal Reserve Balance Sheet Developments <https://www. federalreserve.gov/monetarypolicy/quarterly-balance-sheet-developments- report.htm>
- Board of Governors of the Federal Reserve System—Policy tools <https://www.federalreserve.gov/ monetarypolicy/policytools.htm>
- Federal Reserve—Conducting of monetary policy <https://www.federalreserve.gov/pf/pdf/pf_3.pdf>
- Board of Governors of the Federal Reserve System—Policy normalization <https://www.federalreserve. gov/monetarypolicy/policy-normalization.htm>
- 'Monetary Policy 101: A Primer on the Fed's Changing Approach to Policy Implementation'—Jane E. Ihrig, Ellen E. Meade, and Gretchen C. Weinbach; Finance and Economics Discussion Series, Divisions of Research & Statistics and Monetary Affairs Federal Reserve Board, Washington, DC; 2015-047 <https://www.federalreserve.gov/econresdata/feds/2015/files/2015047pap.pdf>
- The Federal Reserve's Monetary Policy Toolkit: Past, Present, and Future—J Yellen; 26 August 2016 <https://www.federalreserve.gov/newsevents/speech/yellen20160826a.htm>

B. The ECB

1) LIQUIDITY PROVISION TO BANKS
Liquidity provision in euros

The ECB provided liquidity to the banking sector through existing and new refinancing operations, some of which embedded new features, with the aim to ease bank-funding conditions and improve bank lending to the euro-area economy.

On 9 August 2007, the ECB exceptionally allotted the full amount of bids received at an ad hoc fine-tuning operation to counter disorderly conditions in the euro money market.

From August 2007, the ECB launched supplementary liquidity-providing LTRO with a maturity of three months.

The ECB lengthened the maturity of its credit operations by offering liquidity provision at six months (from March 2008 until May 2010), one year (from June 2009 until October 2011), and three years with the option of early repayment after one year (in December 2011 and March 2012).

In June 2014, **the ECB introduced** TLTROs aimed at improving bank lending to the euro-area non-financial private sector, excluding loans to households for house purchase. The TLTRO-I programme included a series of eight operations between 2014 and 2016. TLTRO-II, with enhanced attractiveness, consisted of four operations, each with a maturity of four years, starting in June 2016 with the last one carried out in March 2017. Borrowing costs in the TLRO-II operations could be as low as the negative interest rate on the deposit facility.

From October 2008 (until at least early 2018), all liquidity-providing operations (except TLTROs for which banks' demand is subject to specific requirements) were conducted through a fixed-rate tender procedure (the rate prevailing for the MRO) and full allotment, under which banks could get their full bid amount against adequate collateral, whose eligibility set had been gradually broadened.

Liquidity provision in foreign currencies

From December 2007, the ECB conducted US dollar liquidity-providing operations, in connection with the US dollar TAF, against ECB-eligible collateral for various maturities.

In addition, from October 2008 to January 2009, the ECB offered US dollar liquidity through EUR/USD foreign exchange swaps. In both cases, the Fed provided US dollars to the ECB by means of temporary swap lines.

From November 2008 to January 2010, the ECB conducted EUR/Swiss franc (CHF) foreign exchange swap operations to support further improvements in the short-term Swiss franc funding markets. The SNB provided the Swiss francs to the ECB by means of a swap arrangement.

In 2013 these swaps lines were converted to standing arrangements.

ELA

A few euro-area credit institutions have received central bank credit exceptionally through ELA by Eurosystem NCBs, under the condition that they were solvent and faced temporary liquidity problems.

2) PURCHASE PROGRAMMES (JULY 2009–JUNE 2014)

CBPP1 (July 2009–June 2010)

From July 2009 to June 2010, the Eurosystem purchased €60 billion of euro-denominated covered bonds issued in the euro-area. The CBPP1 aimed at 'encouraging banks to maintain and expand their lending to clients, help improve market liquidity in this market segment, and easing funding conditions for banks and enterprises'.

SMP (May 2010–September 2012)

In May 2010, the Eurosystem started purchasing securities under the SMP, in order to address 'the severe tensions in certain market segments which had been hampering the monetary policy transmission mechanism'. The scope of the interventions was determined by the Governing Council, subject to its assessment of the commitments taken by some euro-area governments to accelerate fiscal consolidation and ensure the sustainability of their public finances. The SMP was terminated when the OMT programme was announced in October 2012.

The liquidity provided through the SMP was reabsorbed on a weekly basis until June 2014.

CBPP2 (November 2011–October 2012)

From November 2011 to October 2012, the Eurosystem purchased €16.4 billion of covered bonds.

OMT (August 2012)

In August 2012, the ECB announced the OMT in euro-area secondary sovereign bond markets 'to safeguard an appropriate monetary policy transmission and the singleness of the monetary policy'. A necessary condition for OMT was strict and effective conditionality attached to an appropriate European Financial Stability Facility (EFSF)/ESM Programme. Transactions targeted sovereign bonds with a maturity of between one and three years. No ex ante quantitative limits were set on the size of OMT and the intention was to fully sterilize the liquidity created through the OMT. The OMT was never activated.

3) APP (FROM OCTOBER 2014)

The APP aimed at 'addressing the risks of a too prolonged period of low inflation' by providing monetary stimulus to the euro-area economy in the context of policy interest rates being at their lower bound.

(continued)

Box 13 CONTINUED

Monthly purchases under the APP averaged €60 billion from March 2015 to March 2016, then €80 billion until March 2017, and then again €60 billion until December 2017. In October 2017, the amount to be purchased every month was further reduced to 30 billion, starting in January 2018.

The APP operations are intended to be carried out until the end of September 2018 and 'in any case until the Governing Council sees a sustained adjustment in the path of inflation that is consistent with its aim of achieving inflation rates below, but close to, 2 per cent over the medium term'.

The APP consisted of purchases of private- and public-sector securities under four programmes:
- **CBPP3** (from October 2014)

In October 2014 the Eurosystem started to buy covered bonds under the CBPP3 to 'help enhance the functioning of the monetary policy transmission mechanism, support financing conditions in the euro-area, facilitate credit provision to the real economy and generate positive spillovers to other markets'.
- **ABSPP** (from November 2014)

In November 2014 the Eurosystem started to buy ABS under the ABSPP. The ABSPP helped banks to diversify funding sources and stimulated the issuance of new securities.
- **PSPP** (from March 2015)

In March 2015 the Eurosystem started to buy public-sector securities under the PSPP. The securities include: (1) nominal and inflation-linked central government bonds; and (2) bonds issued by recognized agencies, regional and local governments, international organizations, and multilateral development banks located in the euro-area.
- **CSPP** (from June 2016)

In June 2016 the Eurosystem started to buy corporate sector bonds under the CSPP. The measure 'helped further strengthening the pass-through of the Eurosystem's asset purchases to financing conditions of the real economy'.

At the end of September 2017, the Eurosystem held about €2.1 trillion of securities under the APP of which €1.7 trillion were part of the PSPP.

Reinvestment policy

In December 2015, the ECB announced that principal payments of maturing APP holdings would be reinvested for as long as necessary.

4) FORWARD GUIDANCE

From October 2008 the ECB lowered its key policy rates while adjusting the size of the corridor for the rates on the ECB's deposit and marginal lending facilities, with the deposit facility rate being set at a negative level since June 2014. After short-term interest rates had fallen close to their ELB, the ECB started to purchase assets to control long-term rates, by influencing rate expectations and directly compressing the term premium.

In implementing these policies, the ECB introduced various types of forward guidance:

- Through the prevailing rate for the liquidity-provision operations, for example, the borrowing conditions for TLTRO-II are linked to the policy rates prevailing at time of allotment.

- Through a calendar for policy rate outlook, as the ECB communicated that policy rates would 'remain at present or lower levels for an extended period of time, and well past the horizon of our net asset purchases' (Press conference, 8 December 2016).

- Through a calendar and inflation objective for the APP, for example, 'our net asset purchases are intended to continue at a monthly pace of €60 billion until the end of December 2017, or beyond, if necessary, and in any case until the Governing Council sees a sustained adjustment in the path of inflation consistent with its inflation aim' (Press conference, 8 December 2016).

5) CONTROL OF THE EURO SHORT-TERM INTEREST RATE

Prior to the Great Recession, the ECB's main tools consisted of: (1) the minimum reserves requirements equal to a 2 per cent of banks' certain liabilities; (2) the calibration of liquidity by means of the MROs; and (3) a fine-tuning operation carried out on the last day of the reserve maintenance period to balance liquidity conditions over the period. These tools allowed short-term rates, in particular EONIA, to trade close to the minimum bid rate prevailing at the MRO.

This situation prevailed until October 2008, when the ECB introduced the full allotment policy. This new policy created an excess of liquidity in the banking sector and pushed down the short-term rates close the deposit facility rate. Moreover, from December 2011, fine-tuning operations at the end of reserve maintenance periods were discontinued to support money market activity. In January 2012 the reserve requirements ratio was lowered from 2 per cent to 1 per cent.

Sources:
- ECB—Operational Framework <https://www.ecb.europa.eu/mopo/implement/html/index.en.html>

Christophe Beuve

ECB, until January 2015, let the banks determine how much liquidity to take from its refinancing operations, since it moved, in October of 2008, from an auction modality with a fixed quantity and a variable rate to one with a fixed rate and a variable quantity. This approach also led to a large increase of the ECB's balance sheet, because the stress affecting banks led them to borrow well beyond the need deriving from autonomous factors and required reserves. As a result, the euro-area also experienced excess liquidity, as discussed in Chapter 1. In addition, the ECB created incentives for banks to borrow more from its operations by offering increasingly favourable conditions on its lending, such as longer maturities and lower costs. In 2016, the ECB went to the extreme of even paying banks to borrow from its TLTRO, as part of its move towards negative interest rates. Still, until the start of QE in 2015, it was banks that mostly influenced the outstanding amount of central bank operations, thus driving the ups and downs in the ECB balance sheet. In this light, the recurrent decreases of the ECB balance sheet size, documented in Figure 2.11, denote a lessening of tensions, leading banks to reduce their borrowing from the ECB. Overall, the development of the total balance sheet of the ECB, before it also entered into a QE programme, reflected two factors: first, the stress affecting the banking sector, thereby increasing the demand for liquidity;

second, the conditions, such as price and maturity, at which the ECB supplied liquidity to the banks.[9]

As indicated, in Section 2.1.1, the Great Recession jeopardized three critical, if unacknowledged, conditions that had previously underpinned monetary policy: (1) the ability to precisely control the central bank rate; (2) a stable relation between the policy rate and rates more relevant for the macro-economy; and (3) the ability to cut rates enough to achieve the central bank objective.

To understand the reaction of the Fed and the ECB to these three obstacles, one should concentrate primarily on the developments on the asset rather than the liability side of their balance sheets. Indeed, the increase of bank reserves was more a consequence of actions taken on the asset side than a policy aim per se. The ECB and the Fed bought assets whose purchases would help the conduct of monetary policy. The increase of bank reserves was, so to speak, the source of funding for their purchases. This is consistent with the breakdown of the money multiplier documented in Section 1.2.2, showing the disappearance of any link between bank reserves, or base money, and monetary aggregates.[10]

As mentioned, to regain the ability to control its interest rate, the ECB moved, in October of 2008, from an auction procedure based on offering to banks a fixed quantity of liquidity at a variable rate, to a procedure with a fixed rate and a variable quantity. Basically the ECB realized that it could no longer forecast with precision banks' demand for reserves, because this demand was no longer dictated by autonomous factors and required reserves. Indeed, demand for reserves was strongly influenced by the need to get liquidity from the central bank, because private sources of liquidity had dried up. The ECB thus decided to leave, week after week, the task of determining the amount of central bank liquidity outstanding in the market to the banking sector. Over time, this, together with the increasingly favourable conditions applied to refinancing operations, led, as mentioned, to an overwhelming amount of liquidity. The end result was to push, in a stable way, the overnight interest rate down to the bottom of the corridor. The move to QE at the beginning of 2015 reinforced this development.

The reaction of the two central banks to the explosion of the risk premia, including those between the uncollateralized interest rates (Euribor or Libor)

---

[9] The ECB (2015a), took the view that the demand for liquidity from banks was the dominating factor in the ups and downs in its balance sheet. Papadia (2016b), stressed, instead, that supply factors also led to changes.

[10] Woodford (2012a) gives a theoretical reason why bank reserves lose their power to affect macroeconomic conditions when their remuneration, as that of any other short-term asset, reaches the zero level. Basically, the argument is that changes of bank reserves produce macroeconomic effects because, or rather when, they cause changes in interest rates. But this effect is, obviously, muted, when interest rates are at the zero bound.

and the OIS rates that appeared after the failure of Lehman Brothers, was to bring onto their balance sheet part of the intermediation that banks were no longer able to carry out. In many ways, the two central banks acted as central counterparties, lending to those banks to which other banks were not willing to lend, and 'borrowing', in the form of huge bank reserves, from banks that were unwilling to lend to risky commercial counterparties. Cour-Thimann and Winkler (2016) note this same phenomenon, which they qualify as 'balance sheet of last resort'. They furthermore add the interesting, but hard to quantify, observation that the increase of the size of the central bank balance sheet is only a partial indication of its additional intermediation activity: 'contingent easing', of the kind enacted by the ECB with its Outright Monetary Transactions (OMT) Programme and the move to fixed-rate full allotment auction, should be added to get a comprehensive measure. Indeed, the commitment to increase liquidity had its effects even if it was not followed by an actual increase of liquidity.

The increased intermediation activity was particularly visible and persistent in the case of the ECB. In fact, between 2008 and 2011 the ECB remedied the reduced turnover in the uncollateralized euro money market by extending its balance sheet, as it can be seen in Table 2.1.

The turnover in the euro-area uncollateralized, or unsecured, interbank money market came down, between 2008 and 2011, by more than 300 billion euro. Over the same period, the turnover in the collateralized, or secure, money market increased by more than 200 billion euro, resulting in a net reduction of about 100 billion in overall money market turnover. However, the balance sheet of the ECB over the same period increased by a similar amount, indicating that part of the transactions that were carried out before the crisis on private banking market had moved onto the books of the ECB.

Another important instance in which the ECB had to fight the explosion of spreads by intermediating the funds that the private market was no longer capable of managing will be examined in Section 2.1.3: the swaps established between the Fed and the ECB allowed the ECB to provide to European banks the dollar funds they could no longer find on the private market. In relative

Table 2.1 Change in Euro Money Market Turnover and Increase in Eurosystem Balance Sheet (2008–2011)

Reduction in unsecured turnover (€ bn)	Increase in secured turnover (€ bn)	Net reduction of turnover (€ bn)	Increase in Eurosystem balance sheet (€ bn)	Substitution between Eurosystem and market intermediation (%)
(1)	(2)	(3) = (1)–(2)	(4)	(5) = (4)/(3)
327	212	115	113	98

Source: ECB Money Market Study and ECB Balance Sheet.

terms, this intermediation was on a small scale compared to the overall expansion of the ECB balance sheet. As seen in Figure 2.11, other items dwarf 'dollar swaps with the Fed'. This item, however, is qualitatively important as it signals that, as the central bank had to substitute private-sector intermediation, it had to move beyond its usual operations: lending short-term liquidity in its own currency to banks in its jurisdiction. The swaps with the Fed allowed, as illustrated in Section 2.1.3, the ECB to extend its actions from euro to dollar funding. Analogously, with the growing maturity of lending, caused by the substitution of weekly refinancing operations (MRO) with LTRO and by eventually moving from a three-month to a four-year maturity for these operations, the ECB also substituted faltering medium-term private-sector lending.

The sovereign debt crisis brought about yet another instance in which the ECB had to lend its balance sheet to an impaired market that was no longer able to generate reasonable spreads. As shown in Figure 2.6, during the European phase of the Great Recession, the spreads between the bonds of so-called peripheral and those of core countries escalated to disorderly high levels, albeit from levels that were too low before the crisis. The Securities Market Programme, first, and the announcement of the OMT programme, later, complemented dysfunctional markets that had moved from a 'good' to a 'bad' equilibrium, and brought the spreads between peripheral and core countries bonds down to levels more justifiable by economic fundamentals. The QE programme further extended the intermediation of the ECB on three dimensions. First, it increased the amounts bought by the ECB to unprecedented levels. Second, it extended the purchases to asset classes other than public and covered bonds: namely asset-backed securities (ABS) and corporate bonds. Third, it bought assets in both the periphery and the core countries.

The task of the Fed in fighting too high spreads affecting the transmission of monetary policy was much less extended over time than that of the ECB. In fact, as it will be examined in Section 2.2.3, USA banks returned to more stable conditions much more quickly than euro-area banks. Furthermore, in the USA there could not be, obviously, any problem analogous to that appearing between the core and the periphery of the euro-area. It was thus only in the first year after the bankruptcy of Lehman Brothers that the Fed, as illustrated in Box 13, actively sought to complement with its balance sheet the impaired functioning of particular markets. The Fed did so by employing a series of targeted temporary operations, after examining reserves and discount window lending flow through the banking system and financial markets.

Overall, the actions of the two central banks to regain control of short-term rates and counter disorderly spreads fit well into the paradigm of central banks reacting to the sudden move from a 'good' to a 'bad' equilibrium. On the quantity side, the taking onto their balance sheet the intermediation that the private sector was no longer capable of performing corresponded to the need to offset, at least partially, the macroeconomic damage resulting from the sudden need to deleverage that the shift from one equilibrium to the other imposed on private companies and households. On the price side, as seen in Box 14, the policy used by central banks during the Great Recession can be characterized as pricing the cost of their intermediation lower than the market prices prevailing in the 'bad' equilibrium but higher than those that had prevailed in the previous 'good' equilibrium. This pricing could be usefully called 'Diamond–Dybvig pricing', to clearly indicate its analytical underpinning. This issue is further analyzed in Box 15.

The lending by the central banks during the Great Recession is often assessed against Bagehot's prescription, according to which: 'to avert panic, central banks should lend early and freely (i.e. without limit), to solvent firms, against good collateral, and at "high rates"'[12] brought under the label of 'Lending of Last Resort'.

Some criticism has been levelled towards the actions of the ECB and the Fed as being inconsistent with Bagehot's prescription in two aspects: first, the collateral against which the central banks lent was 'not good', as it was affected by too high credit risk; second, the rates at which the Fed and the ECB lent were not 'high'. The conceptual scheme used in this book, based on the 'multiple equilibria' theory, leads to assessing, instead, consistency between central bank action and Bagehot's principle. The consistency is recovered, observing that collateral is 'good' in a 'good' equilibrium condition, even if it may be affected by significant credit risk in the 'bad' equilibrium. Analogously, as mentioned, Diamond–Dybvig pricing meant that rates applied by central banks to their facilities ranked 'high' with respect to their level in a 'good' equilibrium, while being lower than those prevailing in the 'bad' equilibrium. In a way, central banks adopted the long-standing practice of insurance companies to limit the moral hazard they create through the inclusion of deductibles in their contracts, thus granting only partial insurance. In addition, one may see in the same light the fact that central banks did not step in immediately to counter the effects of the switch from a 'good' to a 'bad' equilibrium, but let imprudent borrowers, banks, or sovereigns suffer the consequences of their actions for some time.

As far as defining what the ECB and the Fed did during the Great Recession as Lending of Last Resort, Papadia (2014) argues that this is possible but not very helpful, given the ambiguity of the term.[13] A strict interpretation of

---

[12] This is the summary of Bagehot's prescription in the words of Tucker (2009, p. 5): 'The repertoire of official sector interventions in the financial system: last resort lending, market-making, and capital.'

[13] See Goodhart (1999, pp. 339–40): 'There are few issues so subject to myth, sometimes unhelpful myths, that tend to obscure rather than illuminate real issues, as is the subject of whether the central bank (. . .) should act as a lender of last resort (LOLR).'

Lending of Last Resort refers to bilateral lending from the central bank to an individual bank that finds it difficult to fund itself in the market. Thus, this concept has more to do with financial stability than monetary policy. What the Fed and the ECB did was to lend vast amounts to the entire economy and not to individual banks. Papadia argues that what these central banks did during the Great Recession is better categorized by the clearly macroeconomic concept of 'elastic currency', as enunciated in the Federal Reserve Act: 'The System, then, was to provide [not only] an elastic currency—that is, a currency that would expand or shrink in amount as economic conditions warranted . . .'

The financial intermediation carried out by central banks during the Great Recession is an important, but not the only, aspect of a more general phenomenon: the substitution of public intermediation for private intermediation, in both the USA and the euro-area.[14]

In the USA, the substitution enacted by the Fed was concentrated in the period after the Lehmann Brothers collapse; the Fed worked alongside the Federal government, plugging the funding gap created by the crisis. In the euro-area, the most important manifestation of this phenomenon was the substitution of private with public funds towards the periphery.

The overall move of intermediation from the private to the public sector in both the USA and the euro-area is visible in Figure 2.15.

Gross public debt increased in both the USA and the euro-area during the Great Recession, as the governments in the two jurisdictions increased their intermediation, continuing an already prevailing trend in the case of the USA. The counterpart of this increased intermediation by the public sector was different between the USA and the euro-area. Households reduced their debt in the USA, but not in the euro-area. At the same time, financial and non-financial corporations increased their debt in the USA since the impact of the Lehman Brothers failure faded around 2011. In Europe, instead, households as well as financial and non-financial corporations kept their debt nearly constant, breaking the trend of steady increase that had prevailed in the years just before the beginning of the Great Recession. Overall, there has been no generalized deleveraging during the Great Recession, indeed debt has continued increasing, but with a substantial re-composition, mostly from the private to public sectors.

Two of the three negative consequences of the crisis for the conduct of monetary policy mentioned—namely the loss of precision in the control of the short-term interest rate and the disorderly spreads between that rate and those more relevant for the macro-economy—challenged the ECB more than

---

[14] Cour-Thimann and Winkler (2016) also stress this substitution.

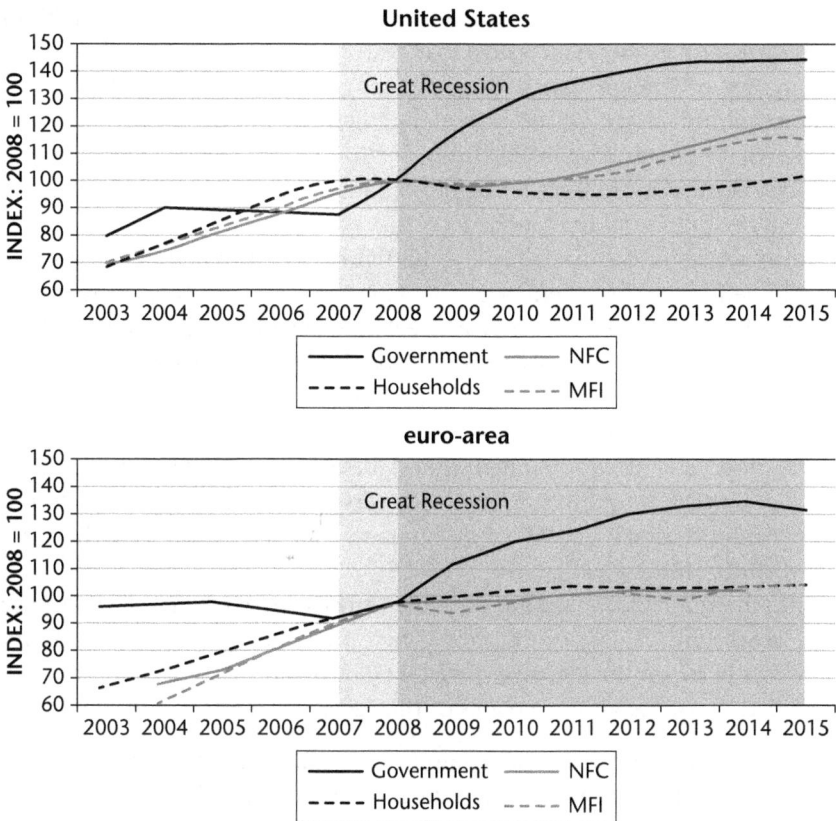

Figure 2.15 Trend in Indebtedness of Institutional Sectors in the USA and the Euro-Area, Debt to GDP ratio. Index 2008=100 (2003–2015)

Note: NFC—Non-Financial Corporations, MFI—Monetary and Financial Institutions.

Source: ECB Statistical Data Warehouse, FRED, OECD (2017), Main Economic Indicators (database).

the Fed. However, the third negative consequence, the difficulty of bringing interest rates low enough in the negative domain to respond to too low inflation and economic activity, affected equally the Fed and the ECB.

As the Taylor rule (depicted in Figure 2.7), and indeed any normative approach to the conduct of monetary policy, prescribed that rates should be brought further down in 2009, the Fed found itself in a difficult situation, as it had already lowered its rate as close to zero as it judged appropriate, when the target range for the FFR was fixed at 0–25 basis points in December 2008. The main answer to this difficulty was found in three waves of QE, as described in Box 13, which led to the purchase of a total of 3.8 trillion dollars of treasury-backed securities and MBS. The basic idea behind QE was that, in a Tobinian approach of imperfect asset substitution, the exchange of bonds in the portfolios of private investors with Fed reserves would have pushed yields on bonds lower and given an incentive to investors to move towards riskier assets, like equities or foreign assets, thus reducing their return as well. Forward guidance reinforced the QE effect by reducing the distribution of probabilities for the risk-free rate. Because of the generalized fall in returns, an easing of monetary conditions followed. The proximate cause of this was the reduction of the term premium that, added to the expectation of short-term rates, determines the yield curve. Thus, a flattening of the yield curve was the most immediate expected effect of QE. This causality link is consistent with the fact that the effect of balance sheet management was expected from changes on the asset side of the central bank balance sheet rather than on the liability side. In fact, if the Fed had bought very short-term paper, say treasury bills, the portfolio-balance effect would have been quasi-non-existent, because one asset (treasury bills) would have been substituted in private investors' portfolios by another asset with very similar characteristics: reserves held with the central bank. As a consequence, there would not have been the desired effect on the yield curve.

While the empirical assessment of the effectiveness of QE will be undertaken in Section 2.1.4, it can be noted here that there were similarities and differences between the Fed and the ECB QE programmes.

The distinguishing characteristics of the Fed's QE were:

1. The vast size, as one can see again in Figure 2.13, in which the purchases of treasury bonds and Mortgage Backed Securities are the dominant cause of the unprecedented increase of the asset side of the balance sheet of the Fed.

2. The concentration of the purchases on the largest, longest-term, and most efficient bond market segments: Treasury and Mortgage Backed Securities paper.

3. The immediate target of lowering the yield on the purchased bonds.

The outright purchases of securities by the ECB went through two different phases.

The first phase lasted between July 2009, when the ECB launched its first Covered Bond Purchase Programme (CBPP), and the beginning of 2015, when the Expanded Asset Purchase Programme (EAPP) was implemented. In this phase the ECB purchases had different characteristics than those of the Fed:

1. The amounts purchased by the ECB were relatively small, as confirmed by looking again at Figure 2.11. There it is shown that, until the beginning of 2015, it was the LTRO rather than the so-called 'policy portfolios' that dominated the increase of the balance sheet.

2. Purchases were targeted to market segments considered to be impaired and unable to generate reasonable prices, or, in the preferred conceptual approach of this book, most affected by the switch to a 'bad' equilibrium.

3. Spreads (e.g. between sovereign bonds of peripheral countries and German securities or between covered bonds and sovereign securities) rather than the yield of the German securities, which are the closest approximation in the euro-area to a risk-free bond, were targeted.

In the second phase, which started at the beginning of 2015 with the implementation of the EAPP, the ECB's QE moved closer to that carried out by the Fed. The ECB started making significantly larger purchases, primarily carried out on the largest bond segment in the euro-area, that is, the sovereign one. Furthermore, the ECB adopted a clear aggregate objective to ease monetary conditions beyond what could be achieved via the lowering of policy rates. Of course, the programme had to take into account the differences between the USA and the euro-area capital markets, particularly the absence of a federal bond in the euro-area. This partly explains why the ECB bought many assets in addition to sovereign paper (covered bonds, ABS, corporate bonds). Still, the EAPP moved much closer in design to the Fed's QE than previous programmes. The similarity is also seen in balance sheet developments: since the beginning of 2015, QE purchases (denoted in Figure 2.11 as policy portfolios) led the expansion of the balance sheet of the ECB, mirroring the experience of the Fed since 2009.

Through its action, the ECB offset the reduced private funding for banks in the periphery of the euro-area and the corresponding private capital inflows to the core of the euro-area. An important consequence of these actions was the enormous increase of so-called target balances, that is, of the credit and debit positions of national central banks (NCBs) towards the ECB, as explained in Box 14.

It is often maintained that facts speak louder than words. Mercier and Papadia (2011) advance the hypothesis that the contrary is true in central banking: often changes in monetary conditions immediately follow the announcement of measures (words) without waiting for their implementation (facts). The reason, they argue, is that the words are credible and markets know that facts will follow words and just anticipate their effects.

The importance of words in carrying out monetary policy was enhanced during the Great Recession in major central banks around the world. Indeed, communication became an even more important component of central bank policy. Under the name of 'forward guidance' it seemed even to have become an independent tool to remedy the impossibility of bringing interest rates lower than the 'lower bound'.[21] The question that arises to assess the effectiveness of

---

[21] The issue of forward guidance is further examined in Section 2.1.4.3.1.

Box 14 TARGET BALANCES

When countries enter a monetary union, they share a single currency, and this is like sharing a bank account. Some countries may spend more while others save more. This is not an issue if they switch roles from time to time. It becomes an issue if a pattern of persistent spenders and savers emerges. Trust that the spenders will eventually reimburse their debt can start to erode. Such is the story of the euro-area, and the target balances exemplify it.[22]

Target balances result from imbalances in cross-border payments within the euro-area. Essentially, target balances are positions in the balance sheets of the central banks of the euro-area. They used to be very small, but swelled after 2007, to become major liability positions in the NCBs of the most indebted countries that were also hit hardest by the crisis, and major asset positions in other NCBs. Why? As long as trust holds, a spender can easily finance its debt and the savers find there a profitable business. Thus, until 2007, the payment outflows of the spending euro-area countries (related to persistent current account deficits or large net investments abroad) were easily matched by payment inflows from the saving countries (notably related to investments and interbank loans).

When trust among banks tumbled during the financial crisis, especially with the debt crisis of some euro-area sovereigns, private outflows were no longer matched by private inflows and the internal cross-border euro-area payment flows became largely imbalanced. The 'target balances' record these payment imbalances in the balance sheets of the respective NCBs.

Target balances are named after the payment system of the euro-area, called 'TARGET', which channels, executes, and settles in central bank money the payments between banks.[23] The settlement of cross-border payment flows results in changes in the debit or credit position of the banks' respective NCBs in TARGET, that is, the target balances.[24] These balances are largely negative in the NCBs of so-called peripheral countries, that is, Greece, Ireland, Portugal, Italy, and Spain, and, conversely, largely positive in so-called core countries, that is, Germany, the Netherlands, and Luxembourg, and in Finland (Figure B.14.1). By design, all the target balances add up to zero.

The mechanics of target balances and central bank intermediation during the crisis

Banks that faced persistent net outflows, often aggravated by flight-to-safety effects, turned to their NCBs for funding. To contain the effects of the crisis on activity and inflation, the ECB decided to accommodate banks' demand for funds, allowing the net outflows to carry on. As a result, the NCBs of countries facing net outflows recorded increasing target liabilities, whose magnitude matched that of their refinancing activity. As for the NCBs whose banks were recipients of the corresponding net inflows, they recorded target claims. Their magnitude also matched the amount of excess deposits that banks parked at the central bank, as depositing at the central bank was preferred over continued lending to peripheral countries.

---

[22] For more details, see Cour-Thimann (2013) and Cour-Thimann and Winkler (2016).

[23] 'TARGET' stands for 'Trans-European Automated Real-Time Gross Settlement Express Transfer System'. In May 2008, the system built by linking national structures was fully replaced by the Eurosystem's centralized TARGET2 platform. For simplicity, both systems are referred to here as 'TARGET'.

[24] The bilateral flows are aggregated and netted out throughout the Eurosystem, leaving each NCB with a single net position vis-à-vis the ECB only.

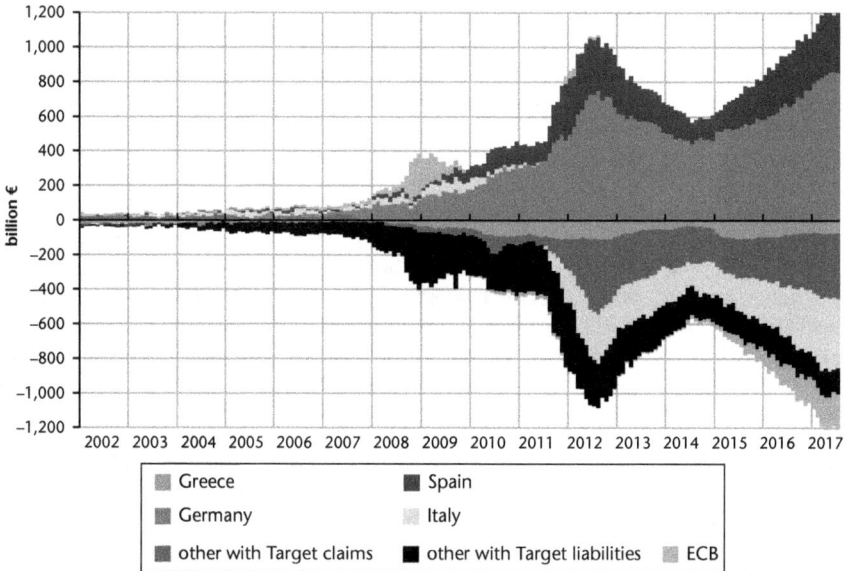

Figure B.14.1 Target Balances in the Euro-Area Central Bank Balance Sheets

Note: Last observations: end-October 2017. A positive (negative) sign reflects a net claim (liability) of the NCB or group of NCBs vis-à-vis the ECB in the TARGET2 payment system. The target balances are vis-à-vis the ECB and add up to zero. The item 'other with target claims' regroups the NCBs of Luxembourg, the Netherlands, Finland, and Estonia. The item 'other with target liabilities' regroups all other non-represented NCBs: they tend to have liabilities in peak crisis times, even if they have claims during certain periods (as in the case of Italy). The ECB's own target balance, which has changed sign, results from its involvement in certain monetary policy operations (such as foreign currency swaps and APPs).

Source: Updated from Cour-Thimann (2013).

In the process, the Eurosystem took a role of intermediation that the market could no longer fully fulfil; in doing so, it often accepted lower-quality assets as guarantees in the operations employed to refinance banks, which further fuelled the policy discussion around target balances. The investors from the saving countries could reduce their exposure to the crisis countries, and a shift in risk exposure took place in creditor countries, from private hands to the public, central banking sector.

The link between target imbalances, Trust in countries' financial health and ECB measures

Target balances depend essentially on two factors: first, trust in the countries' financial health, second, ECB measures affecting the availability of central bank liquidity. As regards the first factor, when banks in the debtor countries see renewed net payment inflows, they have to rely less on central bank funding, and target imbalances recede. This happens when concerns regarding the financial health of their banks and their sovereigns diminish, for example, when the countries undertake reforms, or receive

(continued)

Box 14 CONTINUED

foreign or IMF aid to enhance their fiscal sustainability and competitiveness. The opposite effect takes place when trust decreases. As regards the second factor, when the ECB takes measures to increase the availability of central bank liquidity, particularly in the peripheral countries, and the intermediation activity of the central bank increases, so do target balances.

Thus, the target imbalances receded after reaching a first peak of over 1 trillion euros (about 10 per cent of euro-area GDP, counting the sum of target claims, or equivalently, of liabilities) at the height of the euro-area sovereign debt crisis in July 2012. At that time, in addition to pledges for structural reforms by certain debtor countries, the ECB provided what one can interpret as a kind of insurance to the financial markets that it was ready to take part of the sovereign debt risk onto its balance sheet.[25] This reduced risk aversion and facilitated risk-taking on the part of private investors. Net cross-border payment flows reversed directions and target imbalances receded markedly until mid-2014.

Having seen signs of deflation risks, the ECB, at the beginning of 2015, took new, stronger measures, increasing the provision of central bank money to banks and the financial system, thereby causing target imbalances to swell again. These imbalances then reached new all-time highs.

Among the ECB measures, QE was akin to exercising the insurance option provided earlier in 2012 to the markets. Indeed, private investors altogether reduced their exposure to sovereign debt risk, by ordering their banks to sell bonds to the respective countries' central banks.[26]

Because of the shift in risk exposure involved in target balances, some have called for settling target liabilities against assets.[27] However, in such a case, the very expectation that the associated constraint could become binding might hinder the settlement of cross-border transactions in the euro-area's payment system, marking de facto the end of the single currency area. There is no getting round the fact that sharing a single currency is like sharing a bank account and the issue of target balances reminds us of this fundamental feature of monetary union. A durable reduction of the target imbalances requires the return of confidence in the financial health of euro-area individual economies.

Philippine Cour-Thimann

[25] The ECB President Mario Draghi stated at the Global Investment Conference in London on 26 July 2012: 'Within our mandate, the ECB is ready to do whatever it takes to preserve the euro. And believe me, it will be enough.' This statement was soon followed by the announcement of a monetary policy measure of 'OMT' whereby the Eurosystem would be ready to buy sovereign bonds in the secondary market from certain countries under the conditionality attached to an adjustment programme.

[26] Under the ECB programme, the NCBs purchase sovereign bonds bearing the signature of their own sovereign in secondary markets, which could be anywhere in the euro-area. For instance, banks operating from Germany for the account of non-euro-area investors can sell Italian government bonds to Banca d'Italia. This implies a recording of net payment flows from that NCB to those banks with a bank account at the Deutsche Bundesbank, and thus an increase in both the Target liability of Banca d'Italia and in the Target claim of the Deutsche Bundesbank. The investors can then choose whether or not to reinvest the proceeds of the sales in new Italian assets (doing so would imply a return of Target balances to the preceding level).

[27] See, for instance, Sinn (2014).

forward guidance is whether it conveys much more information than is provided by a final objective of price stability embedded in 'normal' communication. Conceptually, one can distinguish two types of forward guidance (Papadia, 2013b), if the central bank reaction function is formalized as:

$$r = f(x_0) \tag{2.1}$$

where r is the policy interest rate (or some other tool available to the central bank, e.g. the size of its balance sheet), f is the form of the reaction function, and x_0 is the vector of economic variables that enter the reaction function. Forward guidance can give information on either f or on the central bank reading of x_0. One would imagine that information on f, or changes in f, would have a stronger effect than information on x_0. In fact, the central bank obviously has better information than the market on its own reaction function. In addition, changes in the form of the reaction function are quite exceptional, whereas information about economic conditions is more routine. More generally, while forward guidance should be subsumed within the wider communication policy, it is plausible (and even logical) that communication becomes more important when the central bank has an important message to send. So, in conclusion, while forward guidance is not an independent tool and should be considered just as part of the tool of communication, communication can have important effects when it is the conduit of an important message at a specific point in time.

A case in point, not under the rubric of forward guidance, but still an example of extremely effective communication, was the speech of the ECB President Draghi in July 2012, when he said, 'Within our mandate, the ECB is ready to do whatever it takes to preserve the euro.' These words were followed a few weeks later by more precise words, in the guise of a decision by the ECB Governing Council to prepare the OMT programme to be effectively launched if and when needed. Words this time did not even have to be followed by facts: just the prospect of facts was sufficient to invert the tendency of the spread between peripheral and core countries' bonds from becoming even greater. Markets trusted that the ECB would literally do 'whatever it takes' to calm the markets and preserve the euro.

2.1.3 *Global Central Bank Collaboration*

It was seen in Chapter 1 that central banks provided liquidity before the Great Recession in carefully controlled quantities and only in national currency to national banks.[28]

---

[28] This section draws on Papadia (2013a).

During the Great Recession, central banks instead provided liquidity in unlimited amounts, and in foreign currency and to foreign banks. While central banks could provide, on their own, unlimited liquidity in national currency to national banks, as seen in Chapter 1, the provision of liquidity in foreign currency or to foreign banks could take place only through cooperation with other central banks. The form this cooperation took during the Great Recession was a swap network, through which central banks committed to lend to each other large, in some cases unlimited, amounts of their currency, which other central banks would then on-lend to their own banks. Thus monetary policy became potentially more complete for both the lending and the borrowing central bank: the former could reach foreign banks; the latter could provide foreign currencies. The swaps were the foreign component of the overall response to the crisis from central banks. In addition to the swaps, during the Great Recession central bank cooperation even led to a global monetary policy move, when the central banks of six advanced economies (the USA, Canada, the UK, euro-area, Switzerland, and Sweden) simultaneously reduced rates by 50 basis points in October 2008.

The exceptional level of central bank global action during the Great Recession can only be understood by taking into account both the extreme gravity of the crisis and the long history of central bank collaboration. These actions allowed central banks to unite to avoid a repeat of the Great Depression. Central bank cooperation thus contributed to global economic governance. As mentioned in Section 1.4.3, the globalization of the private sector of the economy contrasts with the basic maintenance of a national ambit in public policies, thus producing an imbalance between the two complementary elements of a thriving economy: the market and public action. As a consequence, global governance has been substantially undersupplied (Kindleberger, 1988). With their global action the Fed and the ECB, together with the other central banks participating in the swap network and the joint interest rate reduction, partially filled the void, providing an example of global governance.

Within the network, the swaps granted by the Fed were by far the most important.[29] In particular, beginning in October 2008 the Fed decided that the ECB, the Swiss National Bank (SNB), the Bank of England, and the Bank of Japan could draw an unlimited amount of dollars from the swaps, up to a three-month maturity. At the peak of the crisis, the swaps surpassed the half-trillion-dollar level, with most swaps being taken by the ECB (Figure 2.16). Additionally, another ten central banks could draw sizeable amounts of dollars from the Fed. However, it was not only the size and scope of the swaps that were exceptional; it was nearly unprecedented that the swaps took place in

---

[29] The pricing of the swaps is further examined in Box 14.

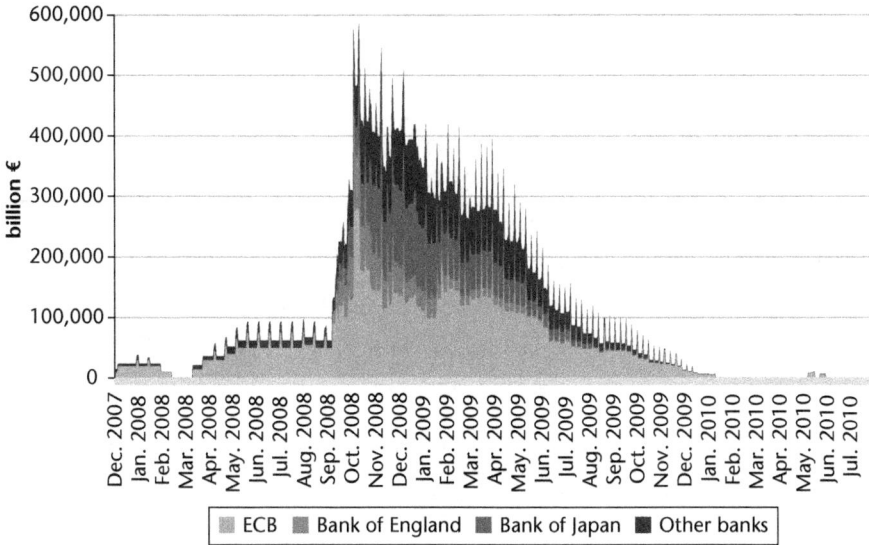

Figure 2.16 Central Bank Liquidity Swaps Provided by the Fed (2007–2010)

Note: Other banks include SNB, National Bank of Denmark, Bank of Sweden, Bank of Norway, and Bank of Mexico.

Source: FRED.

liquidity management and not in the traditional domain of exchange rate management.

Although the swaps granted by the Fed were the most prominent, other central banks also established swaps, thus making the network genuinely global. In addition, the swaps between the Fed, the ECB, the Bank of Japan, the Bank of England, the Bank of Canada, and the SNB were reciprocal, with each central bank making its currency potentially available to all other participating central banks.

The main reason for the swaps granted by the Fed was the unprecedented illiquidity in the foreign exchange swap market, combined with the substantial gap between lending and stable liabilities in dollars of non-US banks, in particular European ones. Until the failure of Lehman Brothers, non-US banks could fill much of this gap by exchanging their national currencies in the swap market against dollars. The price they paid for borrowing dollars indirectly through the foreign exchange swap market was very close to what they would pay when borrowing directly in the Libor market. Covered interest parity, whereby the interest rate differential between two currencies is equal to the forward discount or premium of one currency against the other, has been one of the more robust empirical regularities in international finance. However, with the crisis, this relationship broke down as the foreign exchange swap

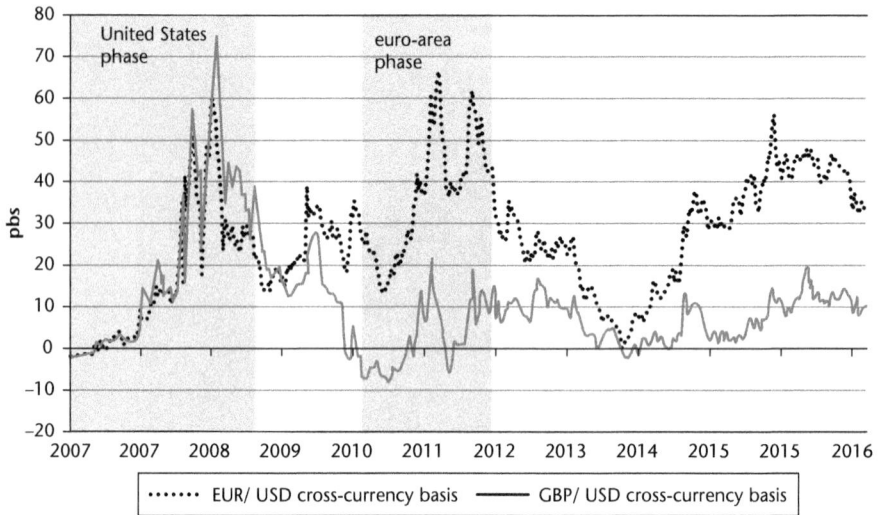

Figure 2.17 Five-Year Euro and Sterling against the US Dollar Cross-currency Basis (2007–2016)

Source: Bloomberg.

market dried up and borrowing dollars via that route became much more difficult. Figure 2.17 shows that the cost differential between the direct and the indirect borrowing of dollars moved from around zero to high peaks for the euro and the pound. This is another instance of a spread that was initially very limited but then exploded after the beginning of the Great Recession, with its two phases in the USA and the euro-area clearly visible.

Although lending among central banks has a long history, the swap network established in 2007 nevertheless represented a quantum leap in central bank cooperation. The unprecedented nature of the swaps also derived from the fact that they were mostly the international extension of domestic 'non-standard' monetary policy measures. Indeed, the swaps granted by the Fed extended the Term Auction Facility (TAF) beyond the borders of the USA (Baba and Packer, 2009).

Essentially, during the crisis the Fed, the ECB, the Bank of Japan, the Bank of England, and the SNB did something that is normally anathema: in principle, they gave up control over their balance sheets, via both domestic liquidity measures and the swaps. For those with a monetarist inclination, believing there is a constant or easy-to-forecast money multiplier and a stable money demand function, this heresy can be brought into sharper relief by noting that central banks no longer controlled the growth of the monetary base, which indeed grew dramatically. Of course, as illustrated in Box 15, the swaps, like other central bank facilities, were priced à la Diamond–Dybvig, so that they would not

---

Box 15 AN EXAMPLE OF DIAMOND–DYBVIG PRICING: CENTRAL
BANK SWAPS DURING THE GREAT RECESSION

This box concentrates on the swaps between the Fed and the ECB since December 2007, when the fixed-rate full allotment auction started for these operations. In particular, this box compares the cost of funding from central banks with the cost of borrowing dollars through the cross-currency swap market, before and during the crisis.

The pricing of the swaps agreed by central banks during the Great Recession is a clear example of what, in the text, is called Diamond–Dybvig pricing, that is, a pricing of the central bank facilities that is attractive for banks in a 'bad equilibrium' situation, but would be too expensive in a 'good equilibrium' situation. This kind of pricing, often called backstop pricing, is also consistent, as explained in the main text, with the Bagehot prescription to grant central bank's funding at punitive interest rate during crises.

Table B.15.1, drawn from an ECB (2014a) and a Fed (2011) publication,[30] gives the most important dates related to the swap agreements between the ECB and the Fed. It is worth remembering that this kind of agreement has also been undertaken with other central banks to provide liquidity in the market (see ECB (2014a), and Section 2.1.3).

To reduce the liquidity disruptions, after the establishment of a reciprocal currency swap agreement, the ECB and the Fed proceeded through different stages: first, enlarging the size of the lines in July 2008 and then agreeing swap arrangements with other central banks. Once the market dislocation became systemic, the Fed and the ECB started offering, from 13 October 2008, through the swaps and the connected repurchase operations of the ECB, unlimited amount of dollars to European banks at the cost of the relevant OIS plus 100 basis points. The spread on the OIS was reduced to 50 basis points in November 2011.

The background to the decision to establish swap lines is given in the main text in Section 2.1.3 and the quantity and the price aspects of the swaps are reported in Figures 2.16 and 2.17 respectively.

The basic problem related to the dollar liquidity needs of European banks was that the cost of borrowing dollars through the cross-currency swap market increased in 2007 and then literally exploded after the failure of Lehman Brothers in September 2007 because of the increase of the basis. The increase of the cross-currency basis swap can be seen in Figure B.15.1.

The 'basis' is defined as:
where:

$$Basis_t^{eur,\$} \equiv \frac{F_{t,t+s}}{S_t}(1 + r_t^{eurLibor}) - (1 + r_t^{\$Libor})$$

where:
S_t is the dollar/euro spot rate at time t,
$F_{t,t+s}$ is the dollar/euro forward rate contracted at time t for delivery at time $t+s$ and $r_t^{eurLibor}(r_t^{\$Libor})$ is the uncollateralized euro (dollar) interest rate from time t to time $t+s$.
The formula shows that the basis swap can also be defined as the deviation from the 'covered interest parity', according to which the forward premium or discount of a currency with respect to another is equal to the interest rate differential between the two currencies.

(continued)

---

[30] See ECB (2014a) and Goldberg, Kennedy, and Miu (2011).

155

Box 15 CONTINUED

Table B.15.1 Swap Agreement Operations between the ECB and the Fed (2007–2014)

Date		Description	Amount (billion $)
i) 2007	12 December	ECB establishes swap agreement with Fed	20
	17 December	ECB begins conducting 28-day US dollar repo operation with fixed rate	
ii) 2008	11 March	Fed enlarges swap line with ECB	30
	2 May	Fed enlarges swap line with ECB	55
	11 August	ECB begins conducting 84-day US dollar repo operation with fixed rate	
	18 September	Fed enlarges swap line with ECB	110
	26 September	Fed enlarges swap line with ECB	120
	29 September	Fed enlarges swap line with ECB	240
	13 October	Fed enlarges swap line with ECB	Unlimited
	15 October	ECB discontinues overnight US dollar repo operations	
	15 October	ECB begins conducting 7-day US dollar repo operation with fixed rate	
	21 October	ECB begins conducting 7-day and 28-day US dollar foreign exchange swap operations with fixed rate	
iii) 2009	3 February	Fed extends swap agreements until October 30 2009	Unlimited
	25 June	Fed extends swap agreements until February 2010	Unlimited
	28 July	ECB discontinues 28-day US dollar repo operation	
	6 October	ECB discontinues 84-day US dollar repo operation	
iv) 2010	1 February	Swap agreement with Fed expires	
	9 May	ECB re-establishes swap line with Fed	Unlimited
	11 May	ECB begins conducting 7-day US dollar repo operation with fixed rate	
v) 2011	12 October	ECB begins conducting 84-day US dollar repo operation with fixed rate	
	30 November	Pricing of swap reduced from USD OIS + 100 basis points to USD OIS + 50 basis points, bilateral network of swaps established with Fed	Unlimited
vi) 2013	31 October	Temporary swap agreements with Fed converted to standing bilateral swap lines	Unlimited
vii) 2014	231 April	ECB discontinues 84-day US dollar repo operations	

Source: Drawn from ECB (2014a) and Goldberg, Kennedy, and Miu (2011).

The covered interest parity is one of the most robust results in international finance, and therefore normally the 'basis', that is, the deviation from covered interest rate parity, is zero. Indeed, this was the situation prevailing before the Great Recession. Figure B.15.1 shows, instead, that the 'basis' moved sharply up from zero during the Great Recession, particularly during the American and the European phases of the crisis. This meant that

Figure B.15.1 Basis Swap between the Dollar and the Euro (2008–2016)
Note: Basis—three-month EUR/USD cross-currency basis.
Source: Bloomberg.

European banks had to pay much more than the Euribor interest rate to fund their positions in dollars. It is likely that the extreme level of the 'basis' was more an indication of a completely dysfunctional market, in which it was just impossible to borrow, than just evidence of a higher price. Further, between October 2008 and November 2008 the cost of borrowing dollar in the market for euro-area banks increased by about 200 basis points. A similar path was observed after July 2011, when obtaining US dollars in foreign exchange swap market rose by 150 basis points. In this phase, the cost of borrowing dollars through the market was pushed upward by the European sovereign debt problem (see Ando, 2012, for further details about the decomposition of swap-implied US dollar rates from 2007 to 2012).

Figure B.15.2 compares the cost at which euro-area banks could borrow dollars in the market, by first borrowing euros, thus paying the Euribor rate, and then swapping the proceeds for dollars, with the cost of the dollar liquidity-providing operations that the ECB could offer thanks to the swaps with the Fed, that is, the fixed-rate tender with full allotment, with a duration of seven days.

The comparison between the cost of funding in the market, given by the sum of the basis reported in Figure B.15.1 and the Euribor (three-month interest rate), and the cost of dollar funding from central banks is a very good example of Diamond–Dybvig pricing: the cost of central bank funding is 'punitive' with respect to a normal situation, in which the basis should be zero, but is quite a lot lower than the market price resulting from the switch to a 'bad equilibrium'. Figure B.15.2 indeed demonstrates that borrowing dollars in the swap market was costlier than the pricing of the dollar funding by the ECB only during the American and the European phases of the crisis (i.e. the 'bad equilibrium' situation), while in all other, less disturbed conditions, central bank funding was more

(continued)

Box 15 CONTINUED

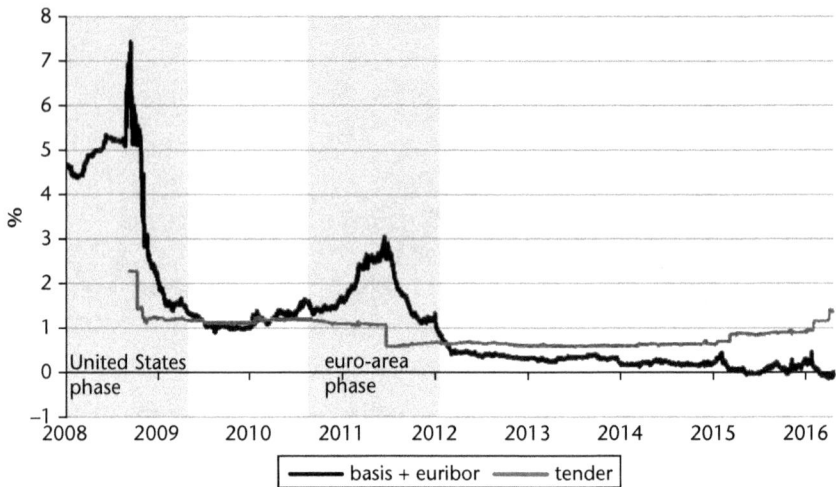

Figure B.15.2 Cost of Borrowing Dollars from Central Banks or in the Market through the Cross-Currency Swap Market

Note: Basis—three-month EUR/USD cross-currency basis; Euribor—three-month interest rate; Tender—fixed rate tender with full allotment with a duration of seven days.

Source: ECB Statistical Data Warehouse and Bloomberg.

expensive than market funding, which has approached zero since 2013. Basically, central bank funding cut the peaks in the cost of borrowing dollars in the most acute phases of the crisis. As mentioned in the main text, Diamond–Dybvig pricing reduces the moral hazard created by central bank interventions.

A finer comparison between the cost of central bank funding and funding in the market would require considering that, due to data availability, the duration of the two funding modalities is not the same, being three months for the market funding and seven days for the central bank funding. This raises somewhat the cost of market funding. In addition, one should take into account the cost of posting collateral that European banks had to bear to get dollar funding from the ECB, as well as the stigma effect, that created negative disincentives for banks to borrow from the central bank, lest they would be marked as being unable to borrow in the market. These are refinements carried out by the ECB (2014a) and Goldberg, Kennedy, and Miu (2011). In addition, one would have to consider that different banks were confronted with different borrowing conditions, mostly depending on their credit standing. An interesting analysis in his respect is in Goldberg, Kennedy, and Miu (2011). However, these refinements would not invalidate the main message derived from Figure B.15.2: both the Fed and the ECB used Diamond–Dybvig approach in pricing the swaps.

Alessandra Marcelletti

attract banks in normal circumstances (i.e. in a 'good' equilibrium), and thus would have an effect on central bank balance sheets only in crisis conditions (i.e. in a 'bad' equilibrium). Still, given the crisis, the pricing was convenient for banks, and banks did indeed draw very large amounts of liquidity from central banks.

As mentioned, the swaps were the international dimension of non-standard monetary moves. They extended the counterparties that the issuing central bank could access: in a way, the ECB acted as the thirteenth District Bank of the Fed.

Furthermore, the swap lines can be understood within the overall interpretation of the action of central banks during the Great Recession: with the swaps central banks complemented the impaired intermediation of the market by bringing part of it onto their books, to avoid even more extended damage to the economy. This implied moving from the provision of the net amount of liquidity necessary to keep interest rates at the desired level to carrying out proper financial intermediation. This meant, in turn, moving into medium-term and foreign currency lending, that is, areas normally outside the competence of central banks.

2.1.4 Assessment

In Section 2.1.1, we examined the breakdown of conditions that formed the basis of monetary policy before the Great Recession. While central banks globally rose to the ensuing challenges, they only managed to restore some of the earlier settings and stabilize conditions. The quest for a 'new normal' continues to this day.

We now assess the extent to which the pre-crisis setting was actually restored, identify where additional efforts may be appropriate in re-establishing pre-crisis conditions, and consider aspects of the new normal that are at odds with the pre-crisis model of monetary policymaking. The breakdown of the incumbent model before the Great Recession is marked by three features: loss of control over the interest rate as the operational target, instability of premia between policy target rates and rates more directly relevant to monetary policy transmission, and problems that emerge at or near the ELB for nominal interest rates.

2.1.4.1 DIVERGENT APPROACHES OF THE FED AND ECB IN REGAINING CONTROL OF SHORT-TERM RATES

In line with the consensus view prior to the Great Recession, short-term interest rates had become the operating target for all major central banks. While central banks applied a variety of monetary policy instruments and operating procedures, all revised their frameworks to move towards 'a symmetric corridor approach with open market operation volume determined by the central bank'.[31] With the dramatic shift in central banks' assessment of the liquidity supply in the early phases of the crisis, there was a renewed need to adjust operating procedures in all major currency areas. As the ability of central banks to steer the operational target deteriorated, bold action was necessary to regain control at the starting point of the risk-free yield curve. Under the prevailing view, smooth functioning of the transmission mechanism required that the central bank tightly control the overnight rate, and subsequently let the rest of the risk-free maturity structure be driven by expectations about future central bank actions.

In the euro-area, the prevailing pre-crisis thinking assumed that the inability of banks to coordinate their bids in liquidity-providing operations would result in increased volatility in the aggregate demand for liquidity. Hence, the ECB scaled back aggregate bank bids in its liquidity tender operations, which were intended to supply the market with what the ECB considered sufficient for banks to meet their reserve requirements and autonomous liquidity factors, and thereby achieve neutral liquidity conditions. This combination of a smoothly functioning interbank market and averaging system applied to reserve requirements provided enough leeway for banks, so that the interest rate elasticity of the demand for liquidity was low (flat demand curve around neutral liquidity in Figure 2.18(a)). Hence, exogenous shocks to the aggregate liquidity resulted in small changes in the overnight rate. Volatility of the overnight rate was contained and the central bank had tight control over its operational target. This approach succeeded as long as banks could rely on access to a smooth-functioning interbank market.

Unfortunately, equilibrium conditions changed as the functioning of the secondary market deteriorated. Following the Lehman Brothers collapse, the ability of banks to deal with large fluctuations in their liquidity conditions diminished, resulting in a preference for hoarding liquidity and increased interest rate elasticity of demand (steeper demand curve in Figure 2.18(b)). Under these circumstances, changes in the aggregate demand for liquidity, instead of volatility in the supply factors, started to drive volatility. The ECB could no longer accurately estimate the liquidity conditions at which the market rate would settle at the level of the policy rate. Figure 2.18(c) highlights the sharp increase in volatility of the short-term rate in this situation. Unforeseen changes in liquidity preference also shifted the demand curve, resulting in changes in the primary market price for liquidity, that is, the allotment price in variable-rate tenders. In the euro-area, this phenomenon was aggravated by crisis conditions that drove market participants to diminish their

---

[31] See e.g. Papadia and Välimäki (2011).

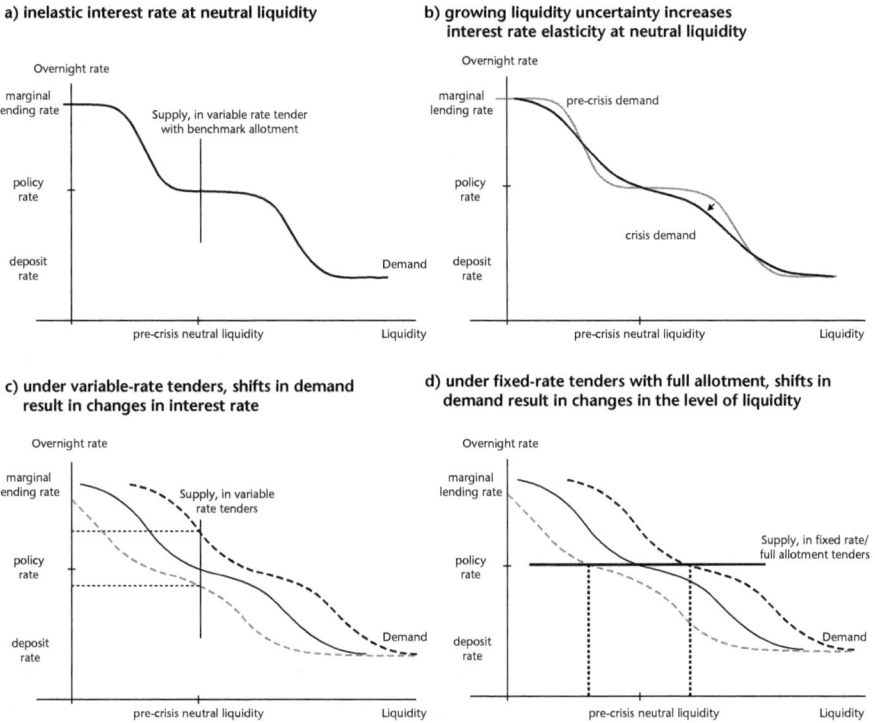

Figure 2.18 Changes to the Market for Central Bank Reserves during the Great Recession

Source: Bank of Finland calculations.

reliance on the interbank market in securing their liquidity positions. Bid rates for variable-rate tenders rose to levels close to the marginal lending rate. The ECB adjusted its operating procedures to deal with the dramatic tightening in liquidity conditions and the spike in short-term market rates.[32]

Figure 2.18(d) illustrates the impact of the switch of the tender procedure from variable-rate to fixed-rate tenders with full allotment. Under the full allotment procedure, the ECB regained perfect control over the primary market price for central bank reserves by fixing the price at which it was ready to satisfy the demand of banks in full. It also meant that the ECB accepted the loss of its direct influence over the level of money market liquidity.

Even if the central bank could set the primary market price for liquidity with a fixed-rate full allotment procedure, this did not necessarily imply tight control of the operational target for the secondary market price of liquidity,

---

[32] In this sense, tension peaked on 8 October 2008, when the average rate of the accepted bids in the MRO hit 4.99 per cent and the key policy rate stood at 4.25 per cent.

that is, the short-term money market rate. Indeed, as policy operations were conducted only once a week, banks felt compelled to secure additional liquidity directly from the central bank above and beyond what they needed to meet their reserve requirements. This excess of liquidity resulted in the EONIA falling significantly below the fixed rate applied in the ECB's MRO.

After switching to the fixed rate with full allotment procedure in weekly operations, the ECB extended the use of the new procedure to the LTRO. Providing banks with reserves at different maturities at the same price increased the incentive for banks to bid for more liquidity than what was strictly needed to comply with their reserve requirements. The situation was made worse by the fact that the interbank market was not functioning properly. Banks that had to pay large risk premia in the money market wanted to guarantee their liquidity positions with longer central bank operations, and the banks that were receiving the excess liquidity from the market were not willing or able to lend it. Hence, aggregate liquidity was abundant and the overnight rate was pushed close to the floor provided by the deposit facility rate. The deposit rate became the focal point of short-term money markets and the de facto monetary policy rate.

Figure 2.19 shows three distinct states of interest rate elasticity to changes in liquidity. In the first state, which existed before the market turmoil of August 2007, the corridor framework with reserves averaging worked well. The EONIA spread (difference between EONIA and the minimum bid rate in the MRO) was extremely stable and it was nearly impossible to detect *any* liquidity effect (top right chart in Figure 2.19). In the second state, which followed the emergence of the Great Recession, changes in liquidity uncertainty and preferences for excess liquidity resulted in higher excess liquidity and a shift in the equilibrium to the steeper part of the demand curve (lower left-hand chart in Figure 2.19). In the third state, there was a disproportionate rise in demand for excess liquidity as the ECB started to provide the market with one-year financing at a fixed rate below the prevailing market rate (lower right-hand chart in Figure 2.19).

As long as the banking system continued to operate with a significant excess of central bank reserves, the deposit facility rate remained the key policy rate for steering short-term money market rates and the volatility of the overnight rate stayed contained. In practice, however, the ECB switched to a floor system for steering the shortest-term money market rates and moved away from the system with a symmetric interest rate corridor that prevailed before the crisis. This meant that the monetary policy stance was adjusted by changing the remuneration of excess reserves, that is, the deposit rate. The return to the symmetric corridor system with the main refinancing rate anchoring short-term market rates would have called for a significant tightening of liquidity conditions. Without active selling of the monetary policy assets bought under

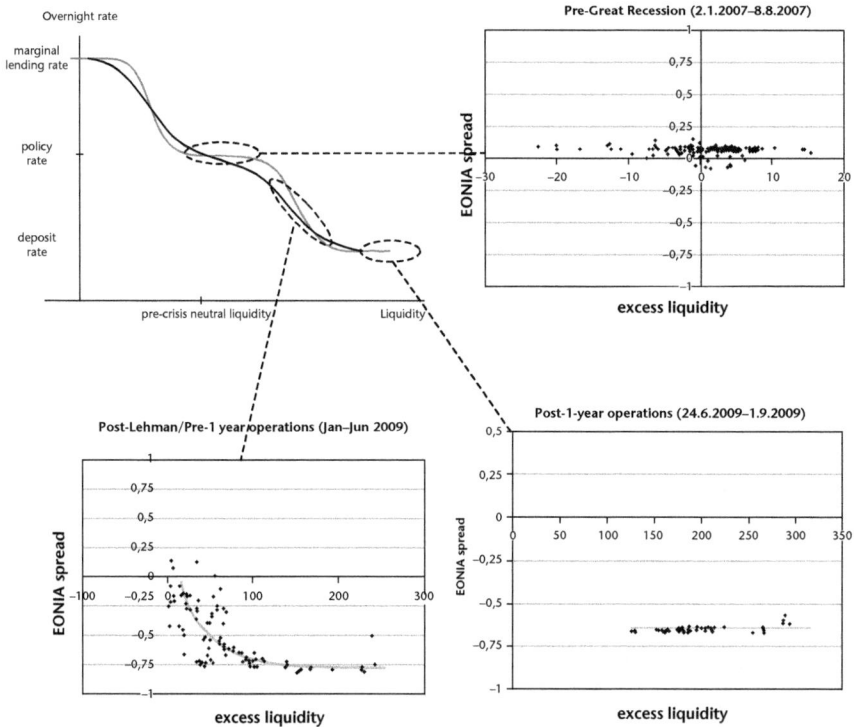

Figure 2.19 Elasticity of EONIA before and during the US Phase of the Great Recession (January 2007–September 2009)

Source: Bank of Finland calculations.

the purchase programmes, such a shift would take years to materialize after net purchases and reinvestments were discontinued.[33]

The ECB's loss of control over its monetary policy operational target was mirrored on the other side of the Atlantic. With increasing preference for liquidity, the previously stable relationship between quantities and prices started to crumble. The new liquidity facilities and asset purchases described in Section 2.1.2, resulted in huge excess of reserves (bank reserve balances skyrocketed from $15 billion to a high of $2.6 trillion). Under such circumstances, the volatility of the EFFR shot up. The annual standard deviation of the spread between the EFFR and the target was only few basis points in the years preceding the Great Recession. Even in 2008, it was still close to ten basis

---

[33] This is due to the long average maturity of the monetary policy bond holdings. Even if the asset purchases are part of the hold-to-maturity portfolios of the NCBs, the Eurosystem can sell its bond holdings if there is a legitimate monetary policy basis for doing so. Current estimates suggest that a return to neutral liquidity conditions is unlikely to occur before the latter half of the 2020s (see Section 3.2).

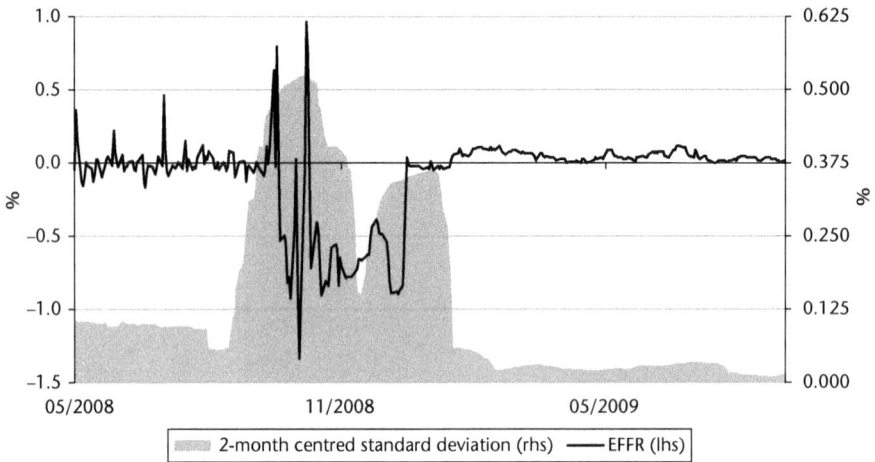

Figure 2.20 Off-Target Deviations of the EFFR together with the Volatility of the Spread (2008–2009)

Source: Bloomberg and Bank of Finland calculations.

points. Figure 2.20 shows the spread trend from January 2008, together with a centred standard deviation of the spread.

With unforeseen levels of excess liquidity, the asymmetric operational framework applied by the Fed needed updating. Whereas the upward spikes in the money market rate could be contained by the discount window (overnight credit facility), the downside swings were limited only by zero (as excess reserves were not remunerated). This issue was quickly addressed after the Lehman Brothers failure. In early October 2008, the US Congress passed the Emergency Economic Stabilization Act, granting the Fed the possibility of paying interest on bank reserve balances. This innovation reshaped the Fed's operational framework to make it more like the ECB's corridor approach before the crisis. In addition, the Fed's Board began to set an IOER rate to create a floor for depository institutions with Fed accounts that were willing to lend their reserves.

The EFFR calculation includes interbank trading deposits from institutions without Fed accounts. Due to the spottiness of the commitment of banks to remunerate with IOER deposits from cash-rich institutions, such as government-sponsored enterprises, the EFFR lacked any binding floor. Thus, the Fed started to express its new policy target as a range for preferred effective FFRs. Figure 2.20 depicts the spread between the EFFR and the mid-point of the target range. The EFFR typically traded very close to the mid-point after early 2009, that is, well below the floor set by the IOER. This difference between the IOER and the EFFR was a concern for the Fed as it was impossible to anticipate what would happen with this difference after the 'lift-off' from zero interest policy (Williams, 2016).

Given the vastness of excess reserves, it was unclear whether the effective FFR would increase in tandem with the IOER. The Fed addressed this problem with a two-tiered floor system. Whereas IOER sets the floor for interbank deposit rates, other money market institutions may take advantage of lower overnight reverse repurchase agreements (ON RRPs). As with holding reserves in a Fed account, financial institutions essentially lend money to the Fed in ON RRP transactions. The ON RRP facility differs from reserves in that the Fed provides each counterparty with collateral (Williams, 2016). As evidenced by EFFR behaviour after the first three rate hikes, the Fed was able to control its target effectively with the new system with two de facto floors.

Overall, the unforeseen liquidity drought and the impairment of the interbank money market that followed the failure of Lehman Brothers (widely considered by market participants as too big to fail), significantly affected the ability of the Fed and the ECB to control their respective operational targets. The ECB's first response was to switch from controlling the level of liquidity it supplied to the market to fixing the primary market price for liquidity. The Fed instead devised several new liquidity-providing facilities that resulted in a vast excess of liquidity. In both cases, the setting of the monetary policy stance shifted from the quantitative to the price side, that is, from the provision of central bank reserves to the remuneration of excess reserves.

Using different approaches, the Fed and ECB each managed to stabilize money markets and regain control of their operational targets. But for how long? The ECB must rethink its operational procedures when the excess liquidity matures and the volatility of short-term interest rates increases. This will likely happen when the focus of market pricing switches back from the deposit facility rate to the main refinancing rate. Similarly, the Fed has moved ahead with raising the FFR target even with vast amounts of excess liquidity in the banking sector. Despite the scepticism over the Fed's ability to control short-term rates while exiting a zero-interest rate policy with banks holding a massive amount of excess reserves, the two-tier floor system applied since late 2015 seems to have done the trick. The spread between the IOER and the EFFR has held stable as the target was increased.

2.1.4.2 REMEDYING IMPAIRED MARKETS AND REPAIRING THE TRANSMISSION MECHANISM

The loss of control over short-term interest rates was a consequence of changes in the demand for liquidity. As discussed in Section 2.1.4.1, the Fed and the ECB both eventually regained control of their operational targets by adjusting their operational frameworks. Unfortunately, the increased uncertainty did not just affect liquidity in the narrow sense (central bank reserves), but market liquidity in several important segments of the money and capital markets as well. Furthermore, the Great Recession (and the sovereign debt crisis in the euro-area in particular) affected the transmission of monetary policy impulses from short-term interest rates further along the yield curve and eventually to the lending rates banks were asking for new loans to the business sector and households.

2.1.4.2.1 ECB Efforts to Restore the Monetary Policy Transmission Mechanism
As long as the central bank implements monetary policy by controlling the very short-term rate (i.e. the one-day interbank EONIA rate in the euro-area), the OIS curve derived from the expected values for future EONIA rates signals market expectations about the future monetary policy stance. A key element of an effective monetary policy transmission is that the yields of other debt instruments move in tandem with the OIS curve, reflecting changes in the current and expected policy. The upper chart in Figure 2.21 shows the

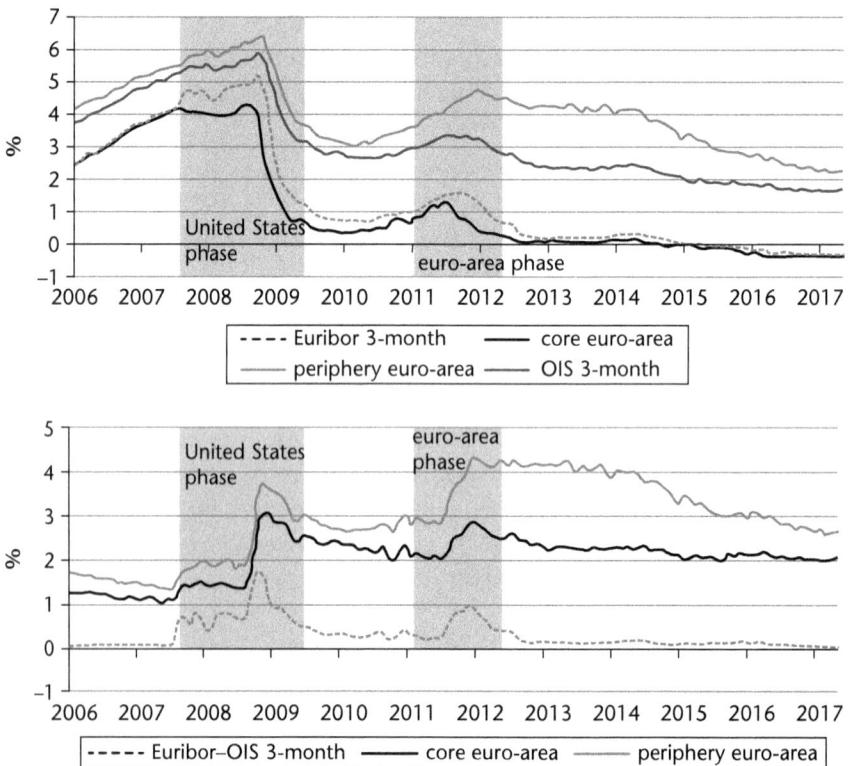

Figure 2.21 Euro-Area Reference and Bank Lending Rates to Non-Financial Corporates (2006–2017)

Note: Periphery includes: Greece, Ireland, Italy, Portugal, and Spain. Core includes: Austria, Belgium, Netherlands, Finland, France, and Germany.

Sources: ECB, Macrobond, and author's calculations.

three-month OIS together with the three-month Euribor and the average bank lending rates of new loans to non-financial corporations in the core and the periphery of the euro-area. It is easy to see that the standard monetary policy tool, that is, the policy rate, is the main driver behind the cost of bank lending.

However, unfortunately, the transmission from OIS to the other rates experienced three sudden alterations during the Great Recession. These changes are best seen in the lower panel, which gives the same market rates as differences to the expected policy rate (i.e. the OIS). In August 2007, we see the first increase, with liquidity uncertainty driving up the unsecured inter-bank rates and thus causing a significant widening in the Euribor–OIS spread. The second increase occurs right after the Lehman Brothers failure and affects bank lending rates more directly. Specifically, the difference between the average lending rate of new loans to non-financial corporates and the expected policy rates doubled within a brief period. The third transmission deviation materialized during the European phase of the crisis. Here, the sovereign debt crisis resulted in increases in the bank lending rates, especially in the European periphery, and, consequently, financing conditions tightened significantly, despite ECB efforts to ease conditions.

The impact of rising uncertainty was confined mainly to money market rates for several months after the US subprime crisis hit European financial markets. To address increases in the Euribor–OIS spread, the ECB relaxed the timing of its liquidity provision within the reserve maintenance periods, and increased the average maturity of liquidity provision by shifting volumes from weekly MROs to three-month LTROs. The ECB treated this disturbance as a phenomenon hindering the smooth functioning of the money and financial markets rather than as an issue affecting the whole economy. Indeed, even if the timing of the liquidity provision was relaxed, the volumes provided over the reserve maintenance periods were kept neutral. Moreover, the policy rates were initially kept constant during the money market turmoil—and even increased in July 2008, just two months before meltdown started. This is a clear illustration of the separation principle,[34] whereby those responsible for setting the monetary policy stance tended to focus on Harmonised Index of Consumer Prices (HICP) inflation, which was still stubbornly high at the time.

Of course, a sudden increase in the spread between market rates and the policy rate does not need to hamper monetary policy transmission as long as the market rates after the jump hold stable. As long as the policy rate is sufficiently distant from the lower bound, the impact of a larger premium can be addressed by a rate cut. When the crisis began to unfold in the euro-area, the

---

[34] Under the separation principle applied by the ECB before the Great Recession, the determination of the monetary policy stance was to be kept separate from its implementation through liquidity operations.

ECB, in the first phase of the crisis, applied a clear separation between determination of the monetary policy stance through the setting of the interest rate and policy implementation with liquidity operations (Trichet, 2008). With the benefit of hindsight, it may be worthwhile asking whether the separation principle had been interpreted too rigidly by the ECB in the early phases of the Great Recession. Even if the ECB was successful in bringing the average EONIA to the level of the policy rate, its volatility increased and the risk premia in the longer money market segments persisted at elevated levels. Eventually, the persistence of these spreads started to push bank-financing costs up gradually and drive up bank lending rates faster than the policy rate.

In the months after the Lehman Brothers collapse, the euro-area economy went through its own hard landing, and the financial market's ability to intermediate funding to the real sector deteriorated significantly. The macro-economic situation became dire. The inflation rate decreased from 4.1 per cent in July 2008 to –0.7 per cent in July 2009. In the euro-area, gross domestic product (GDP) fell by close to 5 per cent. In the most acute phase of the Great Recession, fear of deflation entered the picture. The ECB, like other major central banks, faced a conundrum. Should it make a pre-emptive move and cut policy rates quickly to their lower bound to avoid falling into the liquidity trap, or should it keep its powder dry by not totally exhausting the conventional policy tool before the deflationary spiral materialized (Bini-Smaghi, 2008)?

The ECB went for a sharp easing of the monetary policy stance by cutting the policy rate and facilitating liquidity provision. The main refinancing rate was cut over seven months from 4.25 per cent to 1 per cent. The idea that 1 per cent was the true lower bound for policy rates, a hotly debated topic in the first part of 2008, became largely irrelevant after short-term interbank rates plunged well below the policy rate after the ECB provided several hundreds of billions of euros in liquidity through its one-year lending operations (Figure 2.22).[35] The separation principle was then dead.

Gerlach and Lewis (2010) analyse the ECB's rate-setting behaviour during the American phase of the Great Recession. They find that the ECB's reaction function changed after the collapse of Lehman Brothers. The cutting of the rates was much more intense than the pre-crisis regime would have suggested as a response to deteriorating GDP and inflation figures. They conclude that the ECB's behaviour comports with the theoretical literature on optimal

---

[35] In the first of three 12-month lending operations, banks bid for €442 billion. This resulted in excess liquidity increasing from some €20 billion to levels well above €200 billion. As the excess was provided with one-year operations, it not only pushed the overnight rate close to the deposit rate, but carried over to longer money market maturities.

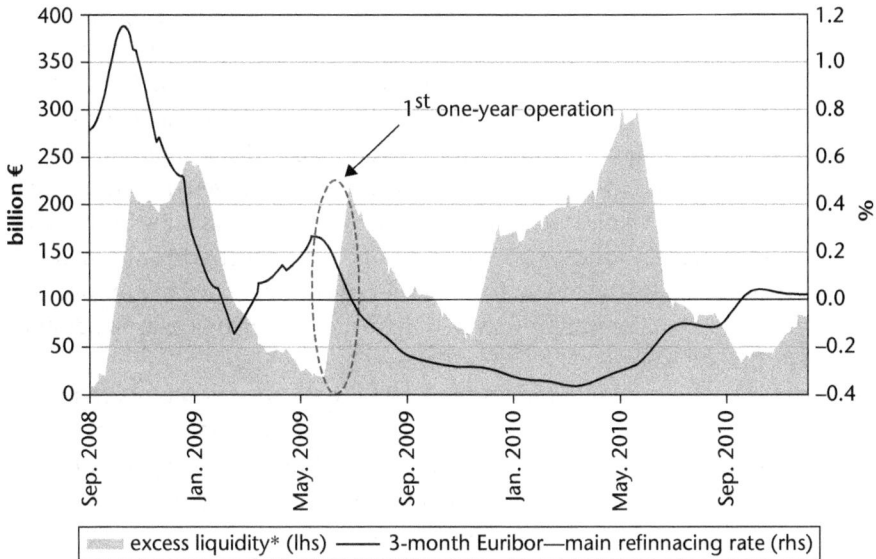

Figure 2.22 Spread between MRO Rate and Three-Month Euribor, Excess Liquidity (September 2008–December 2010)

Note: Both series as one-month moving average. *Current account holdings –reserve requirements + net use of standing facilities.

Source: Macrobond and Bank of Finland.

monetary policy in the presence of a ZLB: if the central bank foresees the ZLB approaching, it should cut interest rates more aggressively than its regular reaction function would suggest.

Besides conducting extraordinary liquidity operations and cutting rates, the ECB launched its first Asset Purchase Programme (APP, in the specific form of a Covered Bond Purchase Program, CBPP) in May 2009. The purpose of the programme was to encourage banks to maintain and even expand their lending to firms and households, as well as improve market liquidity in the covered bond market segment. This covered bond market was (and still is) a key funding market for European banks, and one of the most important segments in euro-area financial markets. By the end of 2008, the size of this market size exceeded €2.4 trillion. After the intensification of the Great Recession in mid-September 2008, the primary market issuance of covered bonds stalled and the secondary market liquidity deteriorated (Beirne et al., 2011). As the crisis progressed, market liquidity dried up, resulting in increased concerns over the liquidity risk facing banks, and even the possibility of insolvency. Amidst these fears, the ECB launched the CBPP.

The CBPP served two important purposes. First, the announcement of the programme in itself provided a positive signal to the market. Markets gridlocked since the collapse of Lehman Brothers began to function again. With cash-rich investors waiting on the sidelines for secure investment opportunities, and potential issuers afraid of being the first to test the waters, the Eurosystem announced that it was entering the market with a new programme that encouraged investors and issuers to return to the market. The gridlock vanished. Beirne et al. (2011) point out, however, that the revival of the covered bond market facilitated by central bank intervention was driven by banks substituting the issuance of unsecured bonds with covered bonds. Together with the surge in primary market supply, the monetary policy intervention helped to improve the market liquidity by narrowing the secondary market covered bond spreads and tightening bid-ask spreads.

The second benefit from launching an APP in the euro-area was operational. Setting up the facilities to intervene in the capital markets simultaneously by 16 central bank trading rooms was not a trivial task. The preparations for the information technology (IT) systems and the governance structures for a new style of decentralized intervention took several weeks, but once the set-up was created, it could easily be extended to other types of purchase programmes. The Eurosystem benefited from this experience, especially when new programmes had, later on, to be established, sometimes within a couple of days.

The crisis mood started to wane later in 2010 and early 2011, as GDP, and international trade in particular, started to recover from their sharp declines. Although there was still considerable slack in the euro-area economy and the pressures on headline inflation were coming mainly from the rebound in the oil price, there was eagerness to start normalizing the interest rates before their low level started to affect financial stability. Consequently, the monetary policy stance started to tighten because banks bid for declining amounts of excess liquidity in the full allotment operations and because of expectations of ECB rate hikes in the coming months. Unfortunately, the 'European phase' of the crisis was already at the ECB's doorstep. Bank funding costs started to vary from one bank to another, resulting in bank lending rates increasing more sharply in the periphery.

Indeed, the impact of the Great Recession was hardest on peripheral economies, as many had put themselves in quite vulnerable situations over the years. These developments turned the spotlight on their fiscal positions and the health of their banking sectors (see Section 2.2).

The third jump in the spread between the market rates and the monetary policy rate emerged with the intensification of the 'euro-area phase' of the Great Recession. Whereas the ECB had been successful in stabilizing the Euribor–OIS spread as well as the difference between the bank lending rates and the policy rate in core economies by the end of 2013, lending rates in periphery countries persisted much longer at elevated levels. The singleness of the common monetary policy was tested severely, especially by the inter-action between sovereign and bank risk.[36]

In the euro-area, banks operate mainly within one jurisdiction. Hence, the financial performance of banks tends to correlate with the economic perform-ance of their home country. The economic performance is also a key deter-minant behind the fiscal developments in that country. This results in a natural correlation between sovereign risk and the risk of banks located in the same country. During the European phase of the crisis, this correlation morphed into a 'diabolic loop', in which banks were holding large amounts of sovereign debt on their balance sheets for risk management and regulatory purposes, and, simultaneously, the sovereigns were seen to be providing a fiscal backstop to the systemically important banks located in their jurisdic-tions. Under these conditions, a sovereign default would have resulted in banks in the same jurisdiction defaulting, as well as a failure of the financial system (or a systemically important bank), thus resulting in major fiscal difficulties for the home sovereign. Hence, the sovereign and bank risk became almost perfectly correlated.

Analysing the sovereign and bank risk measured by five-year credit default swaps (CDSs), one observes that in Italy, for example, these measures had increased hand in hand from summer 2009 to July 2012, when ECB President Mario Draghi gave his famous 'whatever it takes' speech in London (see Figure 2.41 for an illustration of this phenomenon). In the Spanish case, the price of sovereign risk increased to higher levels than even that of the largest banks.[37] The risks were magnified in the summer of 2011 and again in 2012 when first talks appeared over a potential debt restructure in Greece. Eventu-ally the recourse to private-sector involvement made it evident that even the sovereign debt of developed countries cannot be seen always and everywhere as a safe asset. The ghost of Deauville had started to play a leading role on the European stage.

In October 2010, German Chancellor Angela Merkel and French President Nicolas Sarkozy agreed that sovereign bailouts from the European Stability Mechanism (ESM) would require private creditors to carry the risks related to their euro-area sovereign bond holdings from 2013 onwards. From time to time, this agreement has been blamed for increases in sovereign spreads in late 2010 and early 2011. Brunnermeier et al. (2016) describe Deauville as a watershed moment in the European Monetary Union (EMU)'s evolution.

---

[36] For more on the sovereign bank nexus see e.g. <http://bruegel.org/wp-content/uploads/imported/publications/201204_Hazardous_Tango_RSF.pdf>.
[37] Two of the largest Spanish banking groups had major businesses in Latin America. This reduced the dependence of these banks on Spanish economic developments.

The first major effort by the ECB to recover the singleness of monetary policy by facilitating banks' longer-term funding was to launch two three-year operations with favourable interest rates. The operations, announced in December 2011, eased pressure on banks to sell their liquid assets at depressed prices and helped prevent an excessively rapid deleveraging of bank balance sheets. In terms of volume, the two three-year operations were a success. The first operation involved 523 banks; the second, 800 banks. In all, these banks obtained slightly more than €1 trillion in funding. When maturing operations are taken into account, the net liquidity increase stemming from the two operations amounted to €465 billion, the excess liquidity in the banking sector rose to €800 billion, and the Eurosystem balance sheet grew to €3 trillion.

Darracq-Paries and De Santis (2013) assess the macroeconomic implications of these operations, assuming that their main transmission channel works through the mitigation of liquidity and funding risks in the euro-area banking system. They find that, in the presence of acute tensions, exceptional central bank liquidity measures can help support bank lending to the real economy and avoid an abrupt drying up of credit supply. The three-month Euribor–OIS spread declined from 1 percentage point on the day of the announcement to 40 basis points at the end of March 2012.

The elevated yields in the periphery resulted in banks adjusting their balance sheets from lending to sovereign bond holdings. This further reduced lending to the real economy. On one hand, the three-year central bank operations facilitated the functioning of the sovereign bond market by providing to banks in the periphery funds to invest in domestic sovereign debt. On the other hand, the increased portfolios of domestic sovereign securities exacerbated the bank–sovereign nexus. Furthermore, the heterogeneity in borrowing costs for firms and households across the euro-area persisted at an elevated level. Ultimately, it took the 'whatever it takes' speech from the ECB President, its operationalization by the ECB's Governing Council as the OMT programme, and the decision to build a euro-area-wide banking union to break the negative spiral pushing up the sovereign and bank bonds risk premia of the periphery relative to their German counterparts.

In the first half of 2012, when the risk of a break-up of the euro-area emerged, the single currency area had started to turn into something that resembled a system with fixed exchange rates. A 'peso problem' entered the scene.[38] Sovereign bond yields in the periphery were affected by a redenomination risk. For example, the slopes of the Spanish and Italian term structures had inverted, a phenomenon that could be seen as a sign of imminent default expectations or

---

[38] Peso problem refers to a phenomenon in which the possibility of a rare event has a significant impact on asset prices.

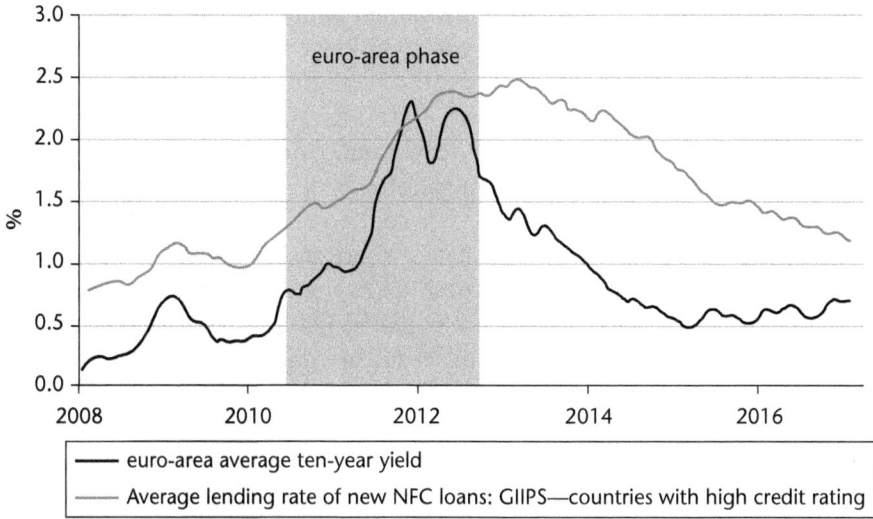

Figure 2.23 Distribution of Sovereign Yields and the Difference in Bank Lending Rates between Periphery and Core (2008–2017)
Source: Macrobond and author's calculations.

break-up of the euro-area. When bank and sovereign risks are closely correlated, changes in sovereign yields also signal changes in the banks' funding costs.

Figure 2.23 illustrates the distribution of the euro-area sovereign yields, measured as the difference between euro-area weighted average and the yield on the German ten-year bund. The explosion in the spread could not be justified by developments in the fiscal or economic fundamentals in euro-area countries. This measure of sovereign risk increased by close to 2 percentage points over 2010–2011, with an almost matching 1.5 percentage-point surge in the difference of the average lending rates of new loans to non-financial corporates in core countries compared to those of the periphery.

The reduction in the sovereign spreads following the introduction of the OMT programme was impressive. The difference between euro-area average and German ten-year yield was halved by the end of 2013 and returned to pre-sovereign crisis levels by the end of 2014 without any purchases under the OMT. Similarly, the CDS spreads for Italy and Spain came down from over 6 per cent to well below 3 per cent by the end of 2012.

How did the OMT programme bring down the risk premia without any actual purchases? The promise to do 'whatever it takes' to preserve the euro was a credible threat for those speculating against euro-area sovereign bonds. It removed the tail risk of a euro-area break-up and the risk of a sovereign default due to market impairment. The conditionality applied in the programme meant that the Eurosystem would not buy bonds from sovereign issuers who neglected the sustainability of their public finances.[39] Thus, while a sovereign issuer could rely on the ECB ensuring the functioning of the market, it could not substitute central bank financing for reforms. The prerequisite for the activation of the OMT was an ESM programme with International Monetary Fund (IMF) involvement. Furthermore, the announcement of the OMT programme brought back the two-sided risk of price developments in sovereign bond markets in the periphery. Before the OMT pledge, it seemed to be a profitable strategy to have a short position in the bonds of the periphery as a counterpart to a long position in the core countries. When the ECB intervention changed the trend in euro-area bond prices, investors had to start covering their positions, resulting in further price increases. The vicious circle became a virtuous circle.

In line with the developments in the sovereign bond markets, bank funding rates and corporate bond rates also declined across jurisdictions. These developments further facilitated banks' return to an unsecured market, and the funding conditions of banks eased, in the periphery in particular. The fact that bank lending rates continued to persist at somewhat elevated levels in the periphery relative to the core mostly reflected the higher risks underlying lending to the corporate sector in countries with lower economic performance.

The macroeconomic impact of the OMT has been studied, for example, by Altavilla, Giannone, and Lenza (2014). Using a multi-country macroeconomic model, they find statistically significant and economically relevant effects on credit and economic growth in Italy and Spain, while spill-overs to France and Germany are found to be limited.[40] Fratzscher, Lo Duca, and Straub (2014) show that the equity indexes in Italy and Spain increased by 9 per cent, and that banks' equity went up by 14 per cent due to the OMT's announcement effect.

Even if the switch to the full allotment procedure in the liquidity provision, the major lengthening of the maturity of central bank lending, and the OMT programme can all be seen as having achieved their goals, this positive assessment cannot be extended to all interventions the ECB entered into during the Great Recession. The second Covered Bond Purchase Programme (CBPP2), launched in October 2011, aimed at easing funding pressures of the euro-area banks, thus facilitating their lending possibilities. However, the announcement of a series of three-year LTROs, immediately after the CBPP2

---

[39] A prerequisite for OMT is the conditionality attached to an appropriate EFSF/ESM programme. In addition, the IMF's involvement was expected in the design of a country-specific conditionality for monitoring such a programme.

[40] GDP in Italy and Spain was estimated to be 1.5–2 per cent higher at the end of a three-year projection period with the OMT announcement, compared to a counterfactual scenario without such an announcement.

had been launched, crowded out the need for the new purchase programme. Eventually, the ECB bought only €16.4 billion-worth of covered bonds, instead of the intended €40 billion. The fact that the operation failed to reach the originally intended size should not be taken as a signal of a wider-reaching failure, however. The purpose of this intervention was simply fulfilled by another, more effective, intervention.

The Securities Markets Programme (SMP) can also be said to have only partially met its objectives. The SMP was aimed at ensuring depth and liquidity in market segments that were relevant for monetary policy transmission. Originally, it was announced to cover public and private securities markets, but eventually only sovereign bonds were bought from five jurisdictions.

To emphasize the role of this intervention as a means of restoring dysfunctional markets and not generally easing funding conditions, the liquidity impact from these purchases was sterilized by collecting deposits from the monetary policy counterparties. De Pooter et al. (2015) find significant announcement effects from the SMP, but only limited effectiveness for actual purchases. They conclude that the SMP influenced yields through the confidence channel rather than through any direct purchase. Eser and Schwaab (2013) also document clear announcement effects from the SMP interventions. Moreover, they find tentative evidence for longer-term effects on sovereign bond yields, which they estimate to make up three-quarters of the immediate impact. Even if a positive yield impact from the SMP could be identified, it is clear that this intervention failed to prevent the sovereign bond yields in the periphery from rising to levels that made the fiscal positions of some periphery countries unsustainable.

What were the key differences in the design of the SMP and OMT that may have affected the difference in their effectiveness? First, the OMTs lacked ex ante defined limits, while the SMP was repeatedly announced to be limited in its size and duration. Stressing the limitations of the intervention most likely reduced the effectiveness of the SMP.[41] Indeed, by demonstrating that the central bank is willing to go 'all in', the credibility of the intervention may increase to levels at which no purchases need be conducted. Second, SMP purchases, unlike OMTs, carried no formal conditionality. This lack of conditionality was likely a reason the ECB found itself stressing the limitations of the intervention. Furthermore, without additional measures to secure the fiscal position of sovereign issuers, some investors may have seen the central

---

[41] Analogously, a central bank that is trying to prevent the external value of its domestic currency from depreciating is always in a worse position than a central bank trying to depress the value of its currency. This arises from the fact that foreign reserves needed to defend a currency are always more limited than the domestic reserves the central bank can create itself. This influences the credibility of the intervention, and credibility is the main driver behind the success of an intervention.

bank purchases more as a chance to get rid of their holdings of securities of peripheral countries at fair prices instead of an action to improve the sustainability of their sovereign debt.

The central bank's signals over the limited nature of the purchases in time and volume may occasionally have resulted in a run for exit. This feature probably got worse after the private-sector involvement in Greek bonds took place without affecting the Eurosystem holdings of Greek sovereign debt. With the exclusion of central bank holdings from debt restructuring, the remaining investors are likely to take more severe cuts in the value of their bonds. In such a case, central bank purchases may increase the price an investor gets from selling her bond, but at the same time it may also increase the expected loss, in case of an issuer default, to those investors that stay in the market may (as the share of bonds owned by the central bank grows). In its OMT specifications, the ECB states that it accepts its purchases are to be treated similarly to those of other investors *pari passu* in case of a default. This should have further alleviated the urge among private investors to run for the exit.

2.1.4.2.2 *Fed Efforts to Restore Impaired Monetary Policy Transmission*

In the American phase of the Great Recession, the Fed launched a number of programmes to support the financial institutions and functioning of financial markets.[42] Before the Great Recession, the Fed had operated successfully within a narrow monetary policy implementation framework with low levels for required reserves, a small number of counterparties with access to refinancing operations, and a collateral framework composed of just a few classes of securities. During the crisis, however, it was acknowledged that operating with a wider coverage of financial market participants as counterparties and against a wider selection of collateral allowed the central bank to assume the tasks of improving the function of the financial markets and bolstering the access of businesses and households to credit.

A wide range of measures was used to fine-tune the monetary policy stance. The Fed aggressively brought its interest rate target down from 5.25 per cent to close to zero in just over a year. As the Fed was the first out of the gate in tackling the impacts of the Great Recession, it was eager to cut interest rates forcefully when it foresaw that the ZLB could become binding, precisely in line with the theoretical literature on optimal monetary policy in the presence of a lower bound. Furthermore, the Fed influenced longer rates by starting to communicate the Federal Open Market Committee (FOMC)'s expectations of the future path of interest rates. This feature, *forward guidance*, will be dealt with in Section 2.1.4.3.1.

---

[42] See Box 13 in Section 2.1.2 for a review of the individual measures taken.

176

The actions outside the interest rate policy can be divided in three groups according to their functions (Bernanke, 2009a): lending to financial institutions, providing liquidity to key credit markets, and the purchase of longer-term securities.

The first of these sets of actions comes closest to the traditional lender-of-last-resort function, that is, providing central bank reserves to financially sound financial institutions. The Fed started to reduce the penalty for discount window borrowing in August 2007.[43] It also increased the term over which these loans were granted from overnight to 90 days. Yet it was not immediately clear how greatly these actions would facilitate banks' situation, as, even before the crisis, discount window borrowing had carried a stigma. According to former Fed Chairman, Bernanke, banks tried to avoid going to the window as 'banks were reluctant to rely on discount window credit to address their funding needs. The banks' concern was that their recourse to the discount window, if it somehow became known, would lead market participants to infer weakness—the so-called stigma problem' (Bernanke, 2009b). The costs related to the stigma may materialize, for example, via banks resorting to expensive substitutes, such as selling assets at fire-sales prices, for discount window borrowing. Banks may also start reducing lending to the real economy to insure themselves against a need to resort to the discount window. According to Armantier et al. (2015), banks were willing to pay a premium of around 44 basis points to avoid borrowing from the discount window during 2007–2008.[44] In the aftermath of the bankruptcy of Lehman Brothers, the premium stood as high as 1.25 per cent. These levels confirm that a stigma may indeed become an economically relevant issue that the central bank needs to swiftly address.

During the crisis, the Fed tried to attenuate stigma by moral suasion, as well as creating a new facility, the TAF, to encourage term borrowing. The immediate success of the TAF emphasizes the impact of stigma on discount window borrowing. Although the bid rates in TAF auctions exceeded the discount window rate, bid volumes grew many times compared to discount window borrowing. At the peak of the programme, the outstanding TAF volume stood at USD 493 billion, whereas discount window borrowing mostly remained at a double-digit number of billions. However, even if the TAF was able to overcome stigma, Taylor and Williams (2008) argue that it did not influence the spread between the Libor rate and the OIS rate, which was one of the aims for the new measure.[45] Taylor and Williams relate the inability of the TAF to

---

[43] The spread between the discount window borrowing above the federal funds target rate was reduced in two steps, from 100 to 25 basis points.

[44] The average discount window stigma premium was estimated to stand at 44, 42, and 46 basis points against TAF, ABCP, and repo rates respectively.

[45] According to Bernanke, the Fed introduced the term auction facility to relieve the pressures in the market for interbank lending. Board of Governors of the Federal Reserve (2008).

influence the money market risk premia to the fact that neither total liquidity, expectations of future overnight rates, nor counterparty risk were affected by the measure.[46] Yet, the claim by Taylor and Williams is contrasted by the evidence presented in McAndrews, Sarkar, and Wang (2017), which indicates the efficacy of the TAF in helping the interbank market to relieve liquidity strains.

As only depository institutions were eligible for discount window borrowing, the Primary Dealer Credit Facility (PDCF) was created, to extend the access to the Fed to major market intermediaries that were not depository institutions. Primary dealers serve as the trading counterparties for the Federal Reserve's open market operations (OMO). Their role as liquidity providers in the market for US treasury securities is essential. The PDCF imitated the Federal Reserve's discount window by providing an overnight loan facility for primary dealers. As explained by Weinberg (2015), PDCF credit was fully collateralized, and eligible collateral was restricted initially to investment-grade securities. In the acute phases of the crisis, in September 2008, the set of eligible collateral was expanded to all types of instruments that can be pledged in the triparty repo. The PDCF ran between March 2008 and February 2010. The programme reached its peak volume of USD 130 billion in the aftermath of the failure of Lehman Brothers in September 2008.

As the Fed's balance sheet grew, the American central bank started to also lend its US treasury securities against less liquid debt instruments to free up these high-demand risk-free assets. Financing markets play a key role in the efficient allocation of capital, and in early 2008 these markets had become severely impaired, as lenders had reduced the amount they were willing to lend against a given amount of collateral, demanded greater compensation for lending against riskier collateral, and halted lending against certain types of collateral altogether (Flemming et al., 2010). To address this disruption, the Term Securities Lending Facility (TSLF) was established in March 2008 for the benefit of primary dealers. Unlike the TAF or the PDCF, the TSFL did not provide counterparties with central bank reserves, instead it auctioned securities in exchange for securities. Hence, the aim of the TSFL was indeed to promote liquidity in the market for the treasury and to foster the functioning of financial markets more generally. Flemming, Hrung, and Keane (2010) assess the effectiveness of the TSLF and argue that it precipitated a significant narrowing of repo spreads between treasury collateral and less liquid collateral. Their evidence suggests that the provision of treasury collateral through the TSLF mitigated a more general shortage of liquid collateral.

---

[46] Increases in liquidity stemming from banks borrowing from the Fed by the TAF were offset by sales of securities by the Fed (Taylor and Williams, 2008).

Finally, as shown by Armantier et al. (2015), foreign banks were particularly likely to experience discount window stigma. According to Benmelech (2012), foreign banks accounted for almost 60 per cent of TAF lending. Furthermore, the impaired access of foreign banks (primarily European banks) to dollar funding was tackled by creating swap lines between the Fed and foreign central banks. The European central banks created TAF-like auctions to allocate the funding to their domestic banks (see Section 2.1.3).

One way to assess the impact of these measures is to look at the liquidity premia in the money market and the covered interest rate differentials between currencies. The tensions in the dollar-funding market for foreign banks eased rapidly in the first quarter of 2008 (see Figure 2.17), thanks largely to internationally coordinated central bank actions. The dollar intermediation of central banks to euro-area banks continued at significant levels even after 2009, when swap lines were no longer heavily drawn upon. Their mere existence alleviated pressure on these market segments.

The money market risk premium, measured by the Libor–T-bill spread, which had exploded in the aftermath of the Lehman Brothers collapse, was halved in a few months thanks to the new measures and provision of large amounts of excess liquidity. Even so, it stayed at a level three times higher than the pre-crisis level. The elevated premium was no longer generated by liquidity risk, but mostly by increased credit risk related to banks (see Section 2.2.1). The liquidity safety-net provided by the Fed's new actions eased the funding pressures of financial institutions, helping such institutions to avoid fire sales that would have further worsened market conditions.

The second set of policy measures involved the provision of liquidity directly to investors and borrowers in key credit markets. Lending to financial institutions does not necessarily help against market instability or declining availability of funds in markets for commercial paper or ABS. At the height of the crisis one money market fund had fallen to 97 cents to the dollar after writing off debts issued by Lehman Brothers. This created a fear that money market funds would 'break the buck'. The fact that investors could lose part of their capital underlined the riskiness of money market funds, which investors considered as equivalent to an insured bank deposit. This resulted in an unprecedented flight to quality, from high-yielding to treasury-only money market funds. These broad investor flows within the money market sector severely disrupted the ability of commercial paper issuers to roll over their short-term liabilities (Adrian et al., 2011). These kinds of market disruptions were seen as potentially limiting the activities of the commercial paper issuers and in particular their capacity to meet the credit needs of households and businesses.

To resist a bank run-type panic, the Fed agreed to make non-recourse loans to banks that purchased asset-backed commercial paper (ABCP) from the money market funds.[47] Thus, banks were by-passed by such measures as the Asset-Backed Commercial Paper Money Market Mutual Fund Liquidity Facility (AMLF), which supported the orderly liquidation of prime money market fund positions.

In addition to AMFL, US issuers of commercial paper were provided with a liquidity backstop, the Commercial Paper Funding Facility (CPFF), which reduced the repayment risk to encourage investors to return to the term market. This facility effectively broadened the access to the discount window further to issuers of commercial paper. One can see the CPFF as central bank liquidity provision in a market-based financial system, where maturity transformation occurs outside of the commercial banking sector in a quantitatively and economically important magnitude (Adrian et al., 2011). Concerning future policy options, the CPFF can be seen as a model for a market-based lender-of-last-resort liquidity backstop in future crisis situations.

With these facilities geared to a larger set of institutions than the traditional banks, the Fed could effectively channel liquidity to non-bank institutions and prevent such institutions from having to sell assets at fire-sale prices. As the functioning of the commercial paper market was quickly restored in 2009, interest rates and spreads came down. Moreover, after having fallen sharply for several months, average issuance maturities started to rise.

The third group of actions by which the Fed supported credit markets involved purchases of long-term assets. These purchases will be assessed in Section 2.1.4.3.2 as part of the LSAP that the Fed used to address problems stemming from the ELB for short-term nominal interest rates.

2.1.4.3 EASING MONETARY POLICY BELOW THE LOWER BOUND

With the Great Recession, central banks moved from theory to practice in addressing the lower bound for interest rates, that is, the infamous 'liquidity trap'. A confluence of three areas of monetary policy response pushed interest rate policy towards this lower bound. First, forward guidance from the Fed and the ECB pushed down longer-term interest rates by influencing market expectations of economic trends and inflation, as well as their reaction functions. Second, through provision of low-cost, long-term funding to banks and the capital markets via asset purchases, central banks lowered financing costs and secured the flow of credit to the real economy. Third, by lowering the policy rate into negative territory, the ECB evidenced that the true ELB clearly lay below zero. Even if some of these measures are standard parts of central bank monetary toolkits, they were unconventional both in the

---

[47] A non-recourse loan refers to loan agreements where the collateral underlying the loan is the ultimate means of payment.

sense that they had rarely been used and that their calibration during the Great Recession was extreme.

As central banks moved into uncharted waters by relying on odd tools and wild calibration, uncertainty, related to the scale and the scope of the impact of their actions, soared. While elevated uncertainty is hardly an excuse for inaction or a limp policy response, it does influence the choice of instrument used. Williams (2013) suggests that the optimal strategy in the presence of high uncertainty is to rely on the particular instrument associated with the least uncertainty and use alternative, more uncertain instruments only when the least uncertain instrument has been employed to its fullest extent.

2.1.4.3.1 Forward Guidance

Forward guidance on interest rates can be seen as central bankers revealing their own views on future economic development, and thereby influencing market expectations on the path of policy action. It may also be seen, however, as a means by which the central bank discloses information directly about its reaction function.[48]

Campbell et al. (2012) distinguish between two forms of forward guidance. 'Delphic' forward guidance is when a central bank indicates its policy course through forecasts and elaborations of macroeconomic fundamentals and outcomes. In other words, Delphic forward guidance states expectations without promises. In contrast, 'Odyssean' forward guidance comes from central banker statements that bind banks to a particular course of action. When the lower bound for policy rates has been reached, the central bank may ease financing conditions in the real economy by promising to keep the rates low beyond the period at which the lower bound is strictly binding (Woodford, 2012b).

Of course, a 'lower for longer' path for policy actions is likely to be suboptimal once the lower bound no longer applies, so Odyssean forward guidance should be seen as a commitment device to address a time inconsistency problem, as laid out in Kydland and Prescott (1977).[49]

Odyssean forward guidance has a stronger economic impact than its Delphic counterpart for two reasons. First, we can reasonably assume that a central bank possesses more private information on its own reaction function than on the forthcoming economic outlook, so releasing information intended for internal consumption is likely to have a bigger effect on market and public expectations than a regular forecast. Second, even if forward guidance can rarely (if ever) be seen as an unconditional commitment by

---

[48] The recourse to forward guidance is also covered in Section 2.1.2, both in the main text and in Box 13, as well as in Section 2.1.4.3.1.

[49] As an extreme example, one could revert temporarily to price-level targeting as a way to signal an intention to hold interests rate low for a longer period. See Chapter 3, Section 3.3, for more on price-level targeting.

central bank to an action plan for several quarters or years ahead, disclosing its intentions may limit the central bank's incentives to deviate from the announced path. In contrast, a Delphic revelation via forecast is likely to change each time relevant new data are released.

When the Fed hit the lower bound for its policy rate in December 2008, explicit forward guidance became one of its main policy tools. In its December 2008 FOMC statement, the Fed said, 'the Committee anticipates that weak economic conditions are likely to warrant exceptionally low levels of the federal funds rate for some time'. In March 2009, the term 'some time' was replaced with the slightly longer-term expectation of an 'extended period', that is:

> The Committee will maintain the target range for the federal funds rate at 0 to 1/4 percent and anticipates that economic conditions are likely to warrant exceptionally low levels of the federal funds rate for an extended period.

Reference to the anticipation of economic conditions that would keep the policy rates at low level for a rather vaguely defined timeframe falls under the Delphic form of forward guidance. In August 2011, the Fed reinforced its forward guidance by adopting a calendar-based element:

> The Committee currently anticipates that economic conditions—including low rates of resource utilization and a subdued outlook for inflation over the medium run—are likely to warrant exceptionally low levels for the federal funds rate at least through mid-2013.

This message was reinforced in January 2012 by extending the calendar-based guidance on low rates to prevail until 'at least through late 2014'. Even if the guidance was still formulated as an anticipation, the fact that it was supplemented with the reference to a precise date may be seen as Odyssean forward guidance, as it expressed the intentions of policymakers rather than pure expectations. In September 2012, the FOMC offered the clarification that its guidance should be understood as both its expectation for future economic developments and as a clarification on its reaction function:

> The Committee expects that a highly accommodative stance of monetary policy will remain appropriate for a considerable time after the economic recovery strengthens.

The calendar-based leg of the guidance was simultaneously extended to mid-2015. In December 2012, the FOMC went further, spelling out that its forward guidance was *more about its reaction function* than about its economic forecast:

> [T]he Committee [. . .] currently anticipates that this exceptionally low range for the federal funds rate will be appropriate at least as long as the unemployment rate remains above 6–1/2 percent, inflation between one and two years ahead is projected to be no more than a half percentage point above the Committee's 2 percent longer-run goal, and longer-term inflation expectations continue to be well anchored.

With this statement, the Fed signalled its shift from calendar-based forward guidance to a state-dependent format.

Campbell et al. (2012) find evidence, extending the earlier finding by Gürkaynak, Sack, and Swanson (2005), on the impact of the Fed statements on longer-term yield in the first years of the Great Recession. In both studies, the 'path' factor in guidance accounts for most of the variation in the expected FFR four to six quarters out.[50] Thus, the Fed could influence, through expectations, the forecasted path of its policy rate.

Campbell et al. (2012) present somewhat puzzling evidence that an unexpected tightening of future FFR *lowers* unemployment expectations. When a tightening of monetary policy is associated with a better-than-expected outcome for employment, observers seem to focus on the policy change as a reaction to better-than-expected economic conditions, instead of as a shift to tighter policy for given economic conditions.

Campbell et al. (2012) attribute this to the Delphic nature of the forward guidance used by the Fed until 2011. In a later paper, Campbell et al. (2016) assess whether the change from Delphic to Odyssean forward guidance after the American phase of the Great Recession improved economic performance under the Fed's guidance. They conclude that a pure rule-based approach (à la Taylor) would have delivered a shallower recession and kept inflation closer to the target in the first years of the crisis than the guidance actually applied. They also find, however, that, starting in 2011, interest rate futures suggested that the Fed's monetary policy accommodation would last considerably longer, and consequently the FOMC's Odyssean forward guidance boosted the real activity and brought inflation closer to the target.

According to Williams (2016), the introduction of the calendar-based forward guidance was effective in delaying private-sector forecasts of the lift-off date, that is, when the Fed would raise its rates for the first time. He likens the bluntness of calendar-based forward guidance to sledgehammer blows, relative to the gentle taps provided by the previous forms of verbal guidance in shifting public expectations on future policy.

Wu and Xia (2016) estimate market expectations of the lift-off date. They show that the expected lift-off date kept on extending until early 2013, when the zero-interest rate policy was believed to continue until 2016. In mid-2013, when a slowdown of the purchases was mentioned for the first time, the market revised its expectation of the lift-off to 2015.

---

[50] Gürkaynak, Sack, and Swanson use principle component analysis to obtain the two most important factors (the 'target' and the 'path') explaining the expected FFRs. The first of the orthogonalized factors is changes in the current FFR. The path factor involves no change in the current rate, but rather forecasts of future rates.

Boneva, Harrison, and Waldron (2015) study the properties of a threshold-based forward guidance, in which the policymaker is able to commit to holding rates longer than it would do under the optimal discretionary policy rule. In their structure, the state-contingent commitment acts as a hedge against asymmetric policies resulting from the ZLB. Incoming negative shocks delay the lift-off date, that is, the moment when the zero interest rate policy is to be abandoned. Their findings show that thresholds must be calibrated to generate an 'overshoot' of goal variables to realize the full benefits. Furthermore, whereas Feroli et al. (2015) subscribe to the view that the Odyssean calendar-based forward guidance exercised by the Fed during 2011–2013 had a powerful impact, they strongly encourage moving to a state-contingent form of guidance—at least as the time for lift-off approaches.

Selecting the appropriate threshold values to be used as trigger points for lift-off or tapering off of purchases is a non-trivial problem. To be effective in shaping expectations of market participants and the general public over the future path for monetary policy, the variables for which the thresholds are set should have stable relations to the ultimate goal. Otherwise, the central bank's reaction function will be ambiguous, and thus not communicable. The problem with the unemployment rate, which was used as a trigger variable both by the Fed and the Bank of England in 2013, is the unstable relation between unemployment and employment, brought about by changes in labour force participation when the economy is recovering and while the output gap is still clearly negative.

Moreover, how should the trigger point be quantified? The threshold should be ambitious enough to make a difference for market expectations, but if it is too ambitious, it may not be credible, as it could be seen to be in strong contradiction to the discretionary (time-consistent) behaviour of the central bank.

One option in overcoming the selection problem might be to use the ultimate goal—the inflation target—as the contingency. The target is normally set to the inflation outlook rather than to ex post values. If the central bank's own inflation forecast were to be used as a trigger, the forward guidance would risk becoming just another expression of its already-stated monetary policy strategy (i.e. inflation targeting). Using market expectations instead as a threshold creates an endogeneity problem. Market forecasts (or pricing) of inflation depend on expectations about monetary policy accommodation, which depends in turn on the market expectations (or pricing) of inflation.

Forward guidance should also not be seen in isolation from other unconventional measures taken during a crisis. For example, Chen, Cúrdia, and Ferrero (2012) find that combining the Fed's large-scale APPs with a commitment to keep interest rates low allowed these programmes to double their effects in boosting GDP growth and inflation. Moreover, Krishnamurthy and

Vissing-Jorgensen (2011) find that the Fed's LSAP affected bond yields via expectation channels, which can be interpreted as these purchase programmes incorporating forward-guidance-type signals. Perhaps forward guidance, a sort of Open Mouth Operation, would be strengthened by the central bank putting its money where its mouth is.

Another communicational aspect relates to a situation that arises after having been on the lower bound for interest rates for a long time. Large volumes of excess reserves push rates to the floor of the interest rate corridor, thereby cutting interest rate volatility to minimal levels. Here, forward guidance can reduce uncertainty related to the interest rate path. The developments in May 2013, when then FOMC Chairman Ben Bernanke (Bernanke, 2013) first hinted at a possible slowdown of the Fed's purchase volumes, that is, a turn in the monetary policy accommodation cycle, are relevant in this respect. This resulted in a sharp reaction by the markets. At the 19 June 2013 FOMC press conference, economic conditions were described positively, with the chairman suggesting: 'the Committee currently anticipates that it would be appropriate to moderate the monthly pace of purchases later this year'. As a result, the prices of fixed income securities fell significantly during the press conference and the US dollar appreciated sharply (Neely, 2015). This episode is often referred to as 'taper tantrum'.

Several other 'taper tantrums' followed in the summer of 2013. These developments made it clear to all central banks that the market needs to be gradually acquainted with a turn in the cycle, well in advance of the actual movement of the policy parameters. Moreover, the calibration of policy needs to be responsive to market reactions. Setting the monetary policy stance clearly derives from an interplay between the central bank and the markets.

The ECB moved to explicit forward guidance on rates in July 2013.[51] This slower response may relate to the fact that the lower rate had not previously become strictly binding for the ECB. Figure 2.7 on Taylor rules illustrates that the ZLB constrained the Fed from moving down to optimal levels for the policy rate much earlier than the ECB. The optimal policy rate suggested by the Taylor rule fell substantially below zero only in the euro-area phase of the Great Recession. Moreover, the ECB was still able to ease financing conditions in the euro-area during 2011–2013, with measures that addressed impairments in the transmission of monetary policy. The ECB Governing Council had earlier stated frequently that it never pre-commits. This may have had a

---

[51] The ECB exercised various types of forward guidance throughout most of the Great Recession. For example, on the provision of liquidity, the ECB has pre-committed to using the full allotment procedure for several quarters or even years ever since 2008. Similarly, Draghi's 'whatever it takes' speech and the subsequent OMT programme roll-out in 2012 were seen as a strong commitment from the ECB towards preserving the euro.

negative impact on the ECB's willingness to adopt active forward guidance as an easing measure. It may also have influenced the formulation of the guidance eventually taken:

> Looking ahead, our monetary policy stance will remain accommodative for as long as necessary. The Governing Council expects the key ECB interest rates to remain at present or lower levels for an extended period of time. This expectation is based on the overall subdued outlook for inflation extending into the medium term, given the broad-based weakness in the real economy and subdued monetary dynamics.   (Introductory statement to ECB press conference, 4 July 2013)

This formulation clearly framed forward guidance as an *expectation* that was dependent on available data, rather than as an *intention* to keep rates low longer than the normal reaction function suggested. ECB President Mario Draghi further elaborated this issue at the following month's press conference by explaining:

> However, our formulation of forward guidance is in line with our strategic framework, which is anchored in our assessment of the medium-term outlook for inflation, or price stability. And this outlook depends on economic activity and on money and credit developments.
> (Introductory statement to ECB press conference, 2 August 2013)

In the terminology advanced by Campbell et al. (2012), the newly applied guidance was clearly intended as a Delphic clarification of the ECB's outlook rather than an Odyssean commitment or a disclosure of changes in the ECB's reaction function. Furthermore, the timing of the introduction of forward guidance by the ECB was rather telling. After the tapering talks by the Fed, the interest rate cycle seemed to have started turning globally. The euro-area economy, however, was still not ready for tighter financial conditions and the outlook for prices was yet to normalize. Hence, the forward guidance initiated by the ECB needs to be understood as a measure to detach the evolution of European interest rates from those of the USA. Figure 2.24 illustrates the developments of German ten-year bunds and US treasury bonds. The spread widens by some 20 basis points after the ECB explicitly reveals its interest rate expectation for the first time.

In October 2014, President Draghi started giving forward guidance on the trend in the size of the ECB's balance sheet. As banks started repaying their three-year loans back to the ECB, the central bank balance sheet started to shrink. To resist this tightening bias in financial conditions, the ECB switched to referring to the peak size of the balance sheet prevailing in early 2012 as the target towards which it would steer the balance sheet. In January 2015, the ECB announced an EAPP in which monthly volumes (€60 billion per month) and duration (end September) were announced.

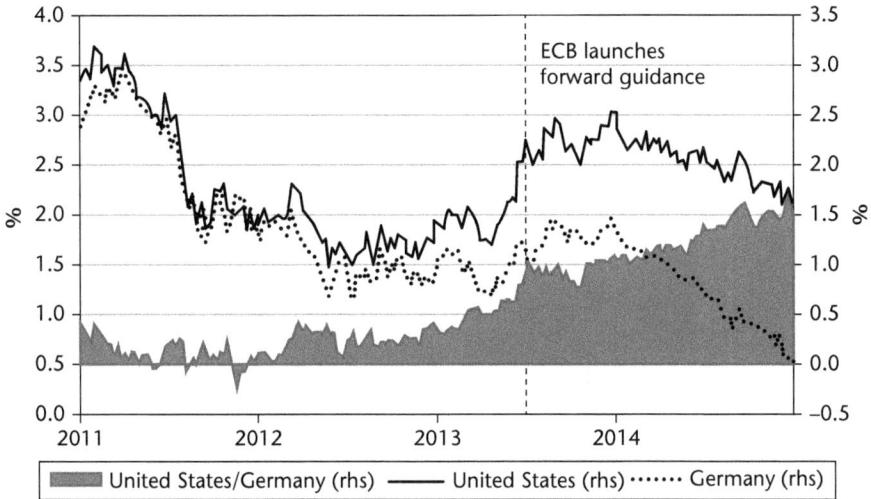

Figure 2.24 Germany and USA Ten-Year Sovereign Yields (2011–2014)
Source: Macrobond and author's calculations.

To stress that the purchase intention was not an unconditional commitment, the announcement explained that the purchases will 'in any case be continued until we see a sustained adjustment in the path of inflation which is consistent with our aim of achieving inflation rates below, but close to 2 per cent over the medium term'.

In December 2015, the duration of the purchase programme was first lengthened. In January 2016, the monthly volumes were increased. In March 2016, the ECB started to exercise calendar-based forward guidance on interest rates. Guidance was formulated as an expectation and was made indirectly by sequencing the unwinding of different measures taken in the crisis:

> Finally, looking ahead, taking into account the current outlook for price stability, the Governing Council expects the key ECB interest rates to remain at present or lower levels for an extended period of time, and well past the horizon of our net asset purchases.   (ECB statement issued after policy meeting, 10 March 2016)

When expressed as an expectation, which depends on the outlook for price stability, this guidance has obvious Delphic elements. However, the downward bias (current or lower) on rate developments, together with dating the lift-off well past the calendar date included in the purchase guidance, give it a strong Odyssean flavour. Applying the methodology used by Wu and Xia (2016), Figure 2.25 presents the timing when the market expected EONIA to return to positive values. Where the dots lie above the dashed line, EONIA was

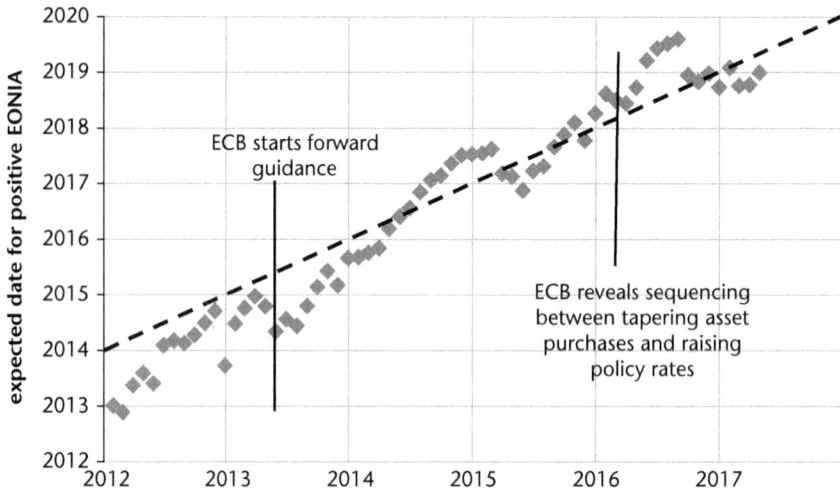

Figure 2.25 Market Expectations of the Time EONIA Exceeds Zero (2012–2017)
Source: Macrobond and Bank of Finland calculations.

expected to stay in the negative territory for more than two years. Based on the figure, both the first instance when explicit forward guidance was given and the moment when the sequencing between tapering and lift-off were introduced increased market expectations about the length of the period over which low rates would prevail.

The ECB forward guidance in late 2016 and early 2017 with sequencing has to be seen as a combination of calendar-based and state-contingent forward guidance. In March 2017, for example, the calendar-based leg for asset purchases stated that 'our net asset purchases are intended to continue at a monthly pace of €60 billion until the end of December 2017'. The state-contingent leg added a caveat: 'or beyond, if necessary, and in any case until the Governing Council sees a sustained adjustment in the path of inflation consistent with its inflation aim'. With the contingency set on the 'sustained adjustment path of inflation', the meaning of this sustained adjustment in the path of inflation (SAPI) concept became a focal point for the markets.

Due to the tight link between ECB's forward guidance, long-term funding to banks, and asset purchases, a quantitative analysis that effectively distinguishes the roles of the individual tools applied to ease monetary policy is almost impossible in practice. Hence, the quantitative assessment about the effects on the real economy and inflation of ECB's forward guidance is dealt with in Section 2.1.4.3.2, together with an assessment of LSAP.

2.1.4.3.2 *Quantitative Easing and Negative Interest Rates*

> The problem with QE is that it works in practice but it doesn't work in theory.
>
> (Bernanke, 2014b)

Standard monetary policy influences economic activity and eventually prices by altering the financing costs in the economy. Under normal conditions, the central bank steers the risk-free short-term market rate of interest to a level consistent with its objective. The monetary policy stance is more or less completely described by the current and expected future levels of the policy rate. The quotation by the Fed's former Chair Bernanke refers to a view according to which a central bank that finances its government debt purchases by issuing excess reserves can be seen as merely exchanging one safe asset for another.

There is no obvious reason why such transactions should significantly change interest rates or have a material impact on the rest of the economy. Yet there is a multiplicity of channels through which QE may influence (and has been shown to have influenced) the economy.

First, asset purchases may affect the market and public's expectations about the future stance of monetary policy. The large-scale purchases by the central bank may push back the expected lift-off date, pulling down the expected future risk-free rates, especially in medium-term maturities.[52] The central bank uses this 'signalling channel' to complement its forward guidance with asset purchases.

Second, the impact of asset purchases on the valuation of future returns from the assets, the prices of the instruments being bought, as well as their spill-overs to other financial instruments needs to be considered when assessing monetary policy transmission. This is the portfolio (re)balancing channel.

Third, QE may influence the real economy by, for example, depressing the exchange rate, inducing wealth effects, and facilitating re-anchoring of displaced expectations after a long period of off-target inflation.

As discussed, central banks resorted to influencing expectations by forward guidance when the short-term risk-free rate fell to its lower bound. Eventually, most major central banks engaged in affecting the prices of financial assets directly by purchasing debt instruments on a large scale from the capital markets, that is, QE. Long-term asset acquisition reflects the central bank's willingness to push long-term yields lower. This simultaneously raises the

---

[52] The impact can be assumed to manifest itself most significantly in the medium-term maturities. The downward movement of the short end of the risk-free yield curve is limited by the lower bound, while the length of the signal is likely to be limited in duration. The longer-term yields may also shift upward if the intervention is effective in raising the inflation expectations or the outlook for growth.

prices of the assets being bought. The worry that such transactions would result in (expected) losses for the central bank is assuaged by a view that the prevailing yield curve is higher and prices lower than the yields and prices consistent with its own expectations. Similarly, the purchases would generate losses if the ex post path for the interest rates would materialize at a much higher level than implied in the purchase prices. As it is logical to assume that the central bank does not deliberately enter into loss-making transactions, QE is a coherent strategy as long as markets interpret the large-scale purchases of long-term assets as an indication of the central bank's readiness to stick with lower rates for longer than it has announced. Of course, no central bank has explicitly stated that its asset purchases limit its leeway to set the future monetary policy stance to levels deemed appropriate for the future outlook for inflation and growth. Profit maximization is hardly a high priority in the setting of the monetary policy stance, even for central banks exercising QE. Still, the potential for asset purchases producing significant effects through the signalling channel is a common feature of empirical studies on QE.

Beside this signalling effect via the risk-free yield curve, purchases may lower the term premium by reducing uncertainty related to future rates. LSAP may also have a more direct effect on financial market prices and, consequently, economic developments. Asset purchases may change the marginal investor's valuation of future returns of the assets. When the central bank buys longer-term assets or assets that carry credit risk premia, it may remove interest rate, liquidity, and credit risk from the market, thereby reducing these premia. On one hand, liquidity conditions are likely to improve when a new major buyer enters the market. On the other hand, after major purchases, some assets may become so scarce that the market-making function is significantly impaired. When the purchases concentrate on public-sector assets, they compress the returns from these assets, which may incentivize investors to switch to assets with higher risk-adjusted returns. Bernanke (2010) described the importance of this portfolio-balance channel as follows:

> [P]urchases work primarily through the so-called portfolio balance channel, which holds that once short-term interest rates have reached zero, the Federal Reserve's purchases of longer-term securities affect financial conditions by changing the quantity and mix of financial assets held by the public. Specifically, the Fed's strategy relies on the presumption that different financial assets are not perfect substitutes in investors' portfolios, so that changes in the net supply of an asset available to investors affect its yield and those of broadly similar assets.

This portfolio (re)balancing channel is sometimes divided further into several subcomponents. The typology varies in the literature, but term premia, capital constraints, scarcity, and (re)anchoring channels appear in many studies on the effects of QE. The increase in asset prices works in the same manner as capital injections to banks with large holdings of the involved assets. This may facilitate lending by capital-constrained institutions.

The re-anchoring channel could play a role if the lower bound had been reached and the central bank's ability to boost economic developments and inflation were in doubt, resulting in private inflation expectations falling off the anchor provided by central bank's target. Under such circumstances, the launch of a QE programme could boost confidence in the central bank's willingness and ability to return to the target sooner rather than later. In a liquidity trap, forceful countervailing policy measures such as QE may be needed to re-anchor inflation expectations after persistent downward off-target deviations (see Gürkaynak, Sack, and Swansson, 2005).

Many of the major central banks started QE at some point in the Great Recession, buying large quantities of debt instruments issued or guaranteed by the public sector. In some cases, however, private-sector securities were included in the set of assets eligible for purchases.

While the Bank of Japan was by far the front-runner in QE, most recent empirical studies on QE policies concentrate on the Fed's actions. Again, the identification and quantification of the impact of the measures taken on the real economy and prices is no trivial task. Hence, many studies take the straightforward approach and analyse the effects on financial markets after policy announcements. These studies tend to confirm a sizable impact on longer-term interest rates, in particular those involving LSAP.

Andrade et al. (2016) compare the estimated effects of different QE programmes in the euro-area, the USA, the UK, and Japan, based on 36 studies. When standardizing the purchase volumes to 10 per cent of the relevant GDP, the median impact on the relevant ten-year government bond yield slightly exceeds 50 basis points, ranging between 30–60 basis points in the euro-area, 30–175 basis points in the USA, 35–100 in the UK, and 10–25 in Japan.[53]

The impact of LSAP probably depends on the economic situation in which the central bank enters into QE, as well as the scale and the scope of its QE purchases. If the lower bound has already been reached and the primary aim of the purchases is to push monetary policy accommodation further along the yield curve, the combination of the purchase programme with forward guidance should start as soon as possible, that is, before the yield curve goes flat. If, however, a general reduction in the financing conditions is not considered the

---

[53] The programmes covered in these studies cover the two large-scale asset purchase programmes as well as the monetary extension programme in the USA, asset purchase programme in the euro-area, asset purchase facility in the UK, and comprehensive monetary easing, as well as the qualitative easing programmes in Japan.

main channel of asset purchases, the allocation of purchases among various asset classes is central. In the USA, the main parameter in this regard was the allocation of purchases between MBS and treasury bonds. In the euro-area, the first choice was on the relative shares for private- and public-sector issuers, followed by allocation of purchases among governments carrying highly diverse credit-risk premia.

Quantitative easing in the USA The Fed carried out three large-scale APPs and a Maturity Extension Programme between 2008 and 2014.[54] The cumulative (net) amount purchased in these programmes was $3.8 trillion, with MBS slightly outweighing treasuries. Agency debt played only a minor role. The quantities in the first episode (LSAP1) consisted of $1.25 trillion in MBS, $175 billion in agency debt, and $300 billion in longer-term treasury security purchases. In the second programme, the Fed purchased $600 billion in longer-term treasury securities. In the third programme, it bought $1.6 trillion-worth of securities almost equally split between MBS and treasuries. Under the Maturity Extension Programme, the Fed purchased cumulatively $667 billion in treasury securities with remaining maturities of six to thirty years. This programme differed from the LSAPs in that its purchases were funded by sales of an equal amount of treasuries with remaining maturities of three years or less.

The standardized effect of the purchases on the ten-year treasury yields reported by Andrade et al. (2016) varies in each episode between 0.3 and 1.75 percentage points. The estimates seem to depend more on the method used in the analysis than the specifics of the intervention episode in question.

Using the rule of thumb suggested, for example, by Chung, Herbst, and Kiley (2015), a 25 basis-point change in the 10-year treasury-bond rate is associated, on average, with roughly 1 percentage-point change in the FFR. From a monetary policy standpoint, the estimates by, for example, D'Amico et al. (2012), imply that Fed's first and second LSAP programmes, respectively, were comparable to 140 and 180 basis-point reductions in the federal funds target rate.

One way to illustrate the monetary policy stance when the policy rate has reached the lower bound and the central bank has started to add accommodation with non-standard monetary policy measures is to estimate the shadow rate, revealing the impact of the non-standard policy measures on the policy rate. Shadow rate models capture information on the monetary policy stance that is embedded in the yield curve by providing a shadow yield curve that is not restricted by the lower bound (Kortela, 2016). In recent years, researchers have

---

[54] See also Box 13.

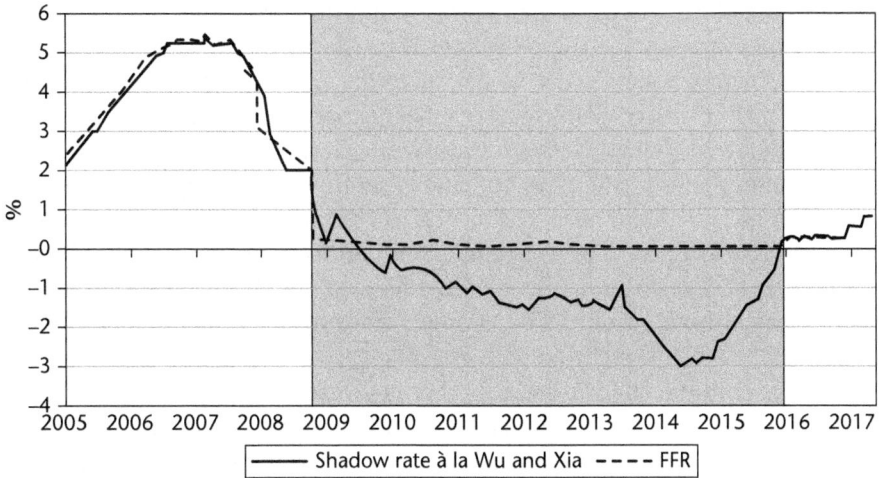

Figure 2.26 US Monetary Policy Stance as a Shadow Rate (2005–2017)
Source: Macrobond and FRED.

even used shadow rates to quantify the monetary policy stance.[55] While shadow rate estimates vary considerably, they provide a neat, intuitive illustration of the stance that is not directly observable from a central bank's policy rate.

The shadow rate estimated by Wu and Xia (2016) is provided in Figure 2.26 to exemplify these measures.[56] Based on the Wu and Xia estimate, the shadow rate for the Fed was considerably below the FFR target band between 2009 and late 2015. The low point for the shadow rate, –3 per cent, was reached by May 2014. By this measure, the stance indicated by the shadow rate started to tighten rapidly in November 2014 after LSAP3 purchases ended.

Krishnamurthy and Vissing-Jorgensen (2013) exploit variation in the mix of securities purchased under the four episodes to study separately the effects of treasury purchases and MBS purchases. In line with the evidence found in many other studies, they find that signalling was the key channel by which the purchases affected longer-term yields. They also emphasize the importance of additional effects from other channels. Even if the Fed has alluded to a broad-based effect of large-scale purchases on all longer-term fixed income assets, they find little evidence for a duration channel.

Similarly, Christensen and Rudebusch (2016) analyse the declines in government bond yields that followed the QE announcements by the Federal

[55] These include Bullard (2012), Christensen and Rudebusch (2016), Krippner (2015), Kortela (2016), Lemke and Vladu (2016), and Wu and Xia (2016).

[56] The Wu and Xia shadow rate uses the maximum of the model-based shadow rate when the US policy target rate is below 25 basis points. It uses the effective federal funds rate when the target rate is 25 basis points or more.

Reserve and the Bank of England. With empirical dynamic-term structure models, they decompose these declines into changes in expectations about future monetary policy and changes in term premiums. In their analysis, declines in US treasury yields mainly reflect expectations of more accommodative monetary policy in the future, while declines in UK yields reflect reduced term premiums.[57] They conclude that the relative importance of the signalling and portfolio-balance channels of QE may depend on market institutional structures and central bank communications policies. Similarly, Andrade et al. (2016) find that in the euro-area the fall in yields after the programme announcements was stronger the longer the maturity of bonds purchased.

Notwithstanding their duration channel discussion, the evidence of Krishnamurthy and Vissing-Jorgensen (2013) is more consistent with narrower portfolio-balancing channels, where asset purchases have a greater impact on prices of purchased assets. In their estimates, when cumulating the changes in interest rates across the eight QE announcements, the ten-year treasury yield, ten-year agency debt yield, and the current-coupon agency MBS yield declined by 91, 156, and 113 basis points, respectively (Gagnon et al., 2011).

In the American phase of the Great Recession, the capital constraints limited the arbitrage possibilities for participants in the MBS market. The Fed dealt with this issue by making massive purchases of MBS as part of its large-scale APPs (Khrisnamurthy and Vissing-Jorgensen, 2013). Whereas releasing the capital constraint played a major role in reducing the MBS yields (especially in 2008–2009 when many market participants found it difficult to access capital), the scarcity channel only peaked during 2012–2013.[58] In that case, banks had an incentive to make new mortgage loans to ease the shortage of MBSs (Krishnamurthy and Vissing-Jorgensen, 2013). The fall in MBS yields was supposed to lower interest rates on new mortgage loans, thus facilitating the developments in the housing sector. Hancock and Passmore (2011) note that the Fed's LSAP1 lowered risk premia embedded in mortgage and swap markets. Their pricing models suggest that the mere announcement of the programme reduced mortgage rates by about 85 basis points, which meant that strong and credible government backing for mortgage markets specifically and the financial system generally had a large impact even before actual

---

[57] Bauer and Rudebusch (2013) also present evidence that signalling is the most important channel through which quantitative easing operates. Others, most notably Gagnon et al. (2011), find that reduction in the term premium has greater impact than the signalling effect.

[58] Scarcity is a narrow channel that operates via limited spill-overs from the class of assets purchased by the rest of the financial market. Within this channel, e.g. MBS purchases in the USA would influence only the MBS price, underlying instruments, and assets with similar liquidity characteristics.

MBS purchases commenced. Once the purchases started, Hancock and Passmore estimate that the abnormal risk premia embedded in mortgage rates decreased by roughly 50 basis points. Many studies on the impact of the Fed's asset purchases conclude that the influence of the targeted purchases is stronger in crisis time, when term and risk premia are higher. Thus, the impact of the first LSAP by the Fed has generally been found to exceed those of subsequent programmes.[59]

Unlike the scarcity effects from the MBS purchases, the welfare benefits from the scarcity channel of large-scale treasury purchases are ambiguous. Treasuries are used as safe assets, especially by investors that cannot hold liquidity directly at the Fed. The reduced supply of these convenience-services-offering instruments due to the large-scale purchases by the Fed may have decreased welfare benefits (Krishnamurthy and Vissing-Jorgensen, 2013). This effect might, however, have been mitigated if there had been enough high-rated private-sector bonds to benefit from the demand for safe assets spilling over from the treasury market.

Movements in the foreign exchange rate provide a route for the portfolio-balancing channel to influence the economy. When domestic and foreign debt instruments are not seen as perfect substitutes by investors, bond purchases by the domestic central bank lead to a reduction of domestic bonds held by the private sector and a decline in their yields (Deutsche Bundesbank, 2017). This, as well as the lower yields via the signalling and duration effects, could motivate investors to increase their foreign bonds holdings. This shift generates a net outflow of capital that causes the domestic currency to depreciate against other currencies. There may also be a negative feedback loop from the foreign exchange channel if the appreciation of trading partner currencies causes the rest of the world to ease their monetary policies, and thereby depreciate their currencies against the domestic currency. Thus, QE measures are sometimes seen as applications of beggar-thy-neighbour policies that increase the likelihood of currency wars between large currency areas.

Using a simple portfolio-balance model under the assumption of long-run purchasing power parity, Neely (2015) demonstrates that the observed asset price behaviour in the USA is consistent with the expected effects of asset purchases, and that the quantitatively significant effects identified are consistent with the data. The responses in the foreign exchange market were also consistent with past estimates of the effects of similar conventional monetary policy shocks for the exchange rate of the euro, the British pound, and the yen against the dollar. There is no evidence that the Fed would have placed more importance on the foreign exchange rate as a channel for bringing

---

[59] See e.g. Krishnamurthy and Vissing-Jorgensen (2011, 2013), D'Amico and King (2013), and Meaning and Zhu (2011).

accommodation when deciding on QE measures than when it was making standard monetary policy decisions.

The final leg of monetary policy transmission, that is, the impact of QE on the real economy and inflation, is not at all straightforward to quantify. Lower long-term interest rates, higher stock prices, and a lower foreign exchange rate all provide stimulus to real activity over time. For example, Chung et al. (2012) estimate that the first large-scale asset purchase increased the level of real US GDP by almost 2 per cent above the baseline by early 2012, and that the full programme raised the level of real GDP by almost 3 per cent by the second half of 2012. Furthermore, their model simulations suggest that 2012 unemployment would have been 0.75 percentage point higher and the inflation rates 1 percentage point lower had the Fed never engaged in QE. If their simulations are correct, the USA appears to have avoided deflation thanks to LSAP.

Engen, Laubach, and Reifschneider (2015) estimate the peak contributions from QE to have been considerably lower than those simulated by Chung et al. (2012), arguing that it took time for private-sector forecasters to perceive that the Fed had switched to a significantly more accommodative policy than had been anticipated at the start of the crisis. Accordingly, they estimate that the change in public perceptions exerted considerable downward pressure on real long-term interest rates over time, which, together with the downward pressure on term premiums associated with asset purchases, gradually gave considerable support to the economic recovery. Notably, their analysis also reveals that the gradual nature of the changes in policy expectations and term premium effects, together with a persistent belief that the pace of recovery would be fast, may have limited the net stimulus to real activity and inflation. According to the estimates in Chung et al. (2012), the peak effect lowered the unemployment rate by 1.2 percentage points from a counterfactual in the absence of the unconventional policy actions, and would have added 0.5 percentage points to the inflation rate by early 2016.

While the estimates of the impact of QE on the real economy and inflation are still uncertain, this does not imply that the central bank should not act to address the issue at hand. According to Williams (2013), the optimal policy responds strongly to shocks, especially when the lower bound for nominal interest rates approaches.

Quantitative easing and negative interest rates in the euro-area The ECB started LSAP in the euro-area in January 2015. Given that the impact of the Great Recession on economic developments was not smaller on the European side of the Atlantic, the ECB's late start appears to be at odds with the US monetary policy. However, the differences in the initial monetary policy responses may be justified by differences in financial market structures and the structure of the currency area in particular. The ECB's initial policy reactions consisted mostly of measures designed to work their way through the bank-lending channel. This reflected the fact that the role of banks in channelling funds to the rest of the economy is much more important in the euro-area than in the USA, where capital markets have a larger role in the financial transmission.

Furthermore, the fact that government bonds in the euro-area are not credit-risk-free assets in the traditional sense raises political economy considerations that do not exist when there is a single jurisdiction and a single fiscal authority acting as counterparty to the monetary policymaker. This feature created limitations to the LSAP not encountered in other jurisdictions. To facilitate the broadest-based easing possible, ECB purchases were allocated to different sovereign issuers according to the ECB's 'capital key'. To avoid excessive exposure and facilitate market function, issuer and issue limits were applied to ECB portfolios. As the stock of purchases grew, the combination of strict limit requirements and the desire to comply with the capital key increased the likelihood of a severe scarcity of assets to be bought.

Following a declining trend in inflation expectations and the loss of economic growth momentum, the ECB engaged in two Private-Sector Purchase Programmes in September 2014. The monthly volumes in its Asset-Backed Securities Purchase Programme (ABSPP) and a third Covered Bond Purchase Programme (CBPP3) were limited in scope and only reached a peak amount of €13.6 billion. Indeed, already in June the ECB had lowered its deposit rate to negative territory (–0.10 per cent) to add monetary stimulus. In combination with the announcement of two Credit-Easing Programmes, the ECB lowered the rate further to –0.20 per cent. Despite these efforts, inflation expectations continued to decline. By the end of 2014, market-price-based probabilities for the Eurosystem entering in a deflationary cycle started to flag disanchored price expectations.

Under these circumstances, the ECB launched the EAPP that, in addition to the ABSPP and the CBPP3, included a Public-Sector Purchase Programme (PSPP). Corporate-sector bond purchases (CSPP) were added to the APP in March 2016.

The APP was initially scheduled to run from March 2015 to September 2016 with an announced monthly volume of €60 billion. The duration was extended three times, first to March 2017, then to the end of 2017 and finally to September 2018. The monthly volume was raised to €80 billion in March 2016 and returned to the original volume of €60 billion in April 2017 to be further brought down to 30 billion in January of 2018. Hikes in the total purchase amount lifted the initial purchasing target of €1.14 trillion to €2.28 trillion and then to €2.55 trillion. In addition to calendar-based guidance, the ECB also stated its willingness to continue with the purchases until euro-area inflation would return on a sustainable path to the target. In June 2017, over three quarters of the purchases had been made under the PSPP, leaving the private-sector asset purchases with slightly more than 20 per cent. In December 2015 and March 2016, the announcements of the increases in asset purchase total volumes were accompanied by reductions in the deposit rate, first to –0.30 and then to –0.40 per cent.

The ECB's wide-ranging package also included TLTROs. These were designed to provide banks with cheap funding while they extended credit to the real sector. The TLTROs were initiated in two waves. In the first wave, the allocation of limits to banks depended on bank size and willingness to lend to non-financial corporates and households (not including housing loans). The banks had to pay back in advance the liquidity borrowed from the central bank if they failed to meet the set balance sheet targets.[60] In the second wave, banks no longer faced the threat of early repayment, but the interest rate for the loans was tied to credit trends. The original borrowing rate for the bank was fixed to the main refinancing rate prevailing when the operation took place, but if the bank extended sufficient credit to the real sector, the cost of the operation would drop to the deposit rate. Thus, the funding cost for the banks varied between 0 per cent and –0.4 per cent depending on lending performance.

Praet (2016) reports that the ECB saw these non-standard measures as part of a broad-based effort to reduce funding costs for the real sector. With the negative deposit rate, the ECB sought to discourage liquidity hoarding by those selling assets. With the TLTROs and ABSPP, the ECB aimed at supporting direct bank lending to non-financial corporates.

In their survey of the empirical studies of the effects of the QE programmes, Andrade et al. (2016) put the estimated impact of purchases with size standardized to 10 per cent of GDP in a range of 27 to 64 basis points. The median of the estimates for the ECB, at 43 basis points, is slightly lower than that of episodes in all jurisdictions (53 basis points). Andrade et al. (2016) attribute this finding to the calmer market conditions in which the ECB implemented its QE compared to those surrounding LSAP1 in the USA. The signalling effect may also have been dampened somewhat in the euro-area as the lower bound was effective for longer maturities than in the USA and the long-end of the yield curve was at a lower level compared to that in the USA at the start of QE. Andrade et al. (2016) find that the signalling effects persisted for several months in the euro-area and had magnitudes similar to those stemming from standard monetary policy announcements. One of the still prevailing open issues on the impact of the LSAP on the risk-free yield curve relates to the potential influence of stock of bonds being bought relative to the impact of

---

[60] For most banks, the trigger point was when loans extended to non-financial corporates and households (excluding housing loans) began to increase during the intervention period. Banks meeting their balance sheet objectives, however, were granted a lower trigger point (see ECB press release, 5 June 2014).

the flow of new purchases. Intuitively, the impact of a given purchase volume on the prices of the assets should be inversely related to the volume available in the market. The evidence backing signalling as a key channel of QE, together with the persistence of the effect, indicates that, when the share of sovereign bonds held by the central bank increases, a smaller flow of purchases would be needed to maintain the same level of monetary policy accommodation.

According to Altavilla, Giacomo, and Motto (2015), the non-standard measures have exerted significant signalling effects on inflation expectations. They show, for instance, that the APP announcement in January 2015 raised inflation expectations in all maturities. Expectations derived from five-year inflation-linked swaps, for example, indicate a 10–25 basis-point increase. Furthermore, the model-based study by Andrade et al. (2016) indicates that re-anchoring of the displaced private-sector expectations could account for a third of the APP's overall impact on inflation.

This is relevant because increases in deflationary probabilities and fear of the disanchoring of expectations were among the main factors that led to the APP in the first place. Figure 2.27 presents the risk-neutral probabilities of average five-year break-even inflation derived from inflation options. The probability that average inflation would be negative over the following five years based on market prices jumped to almost one-third at the end of 2014. The launch of

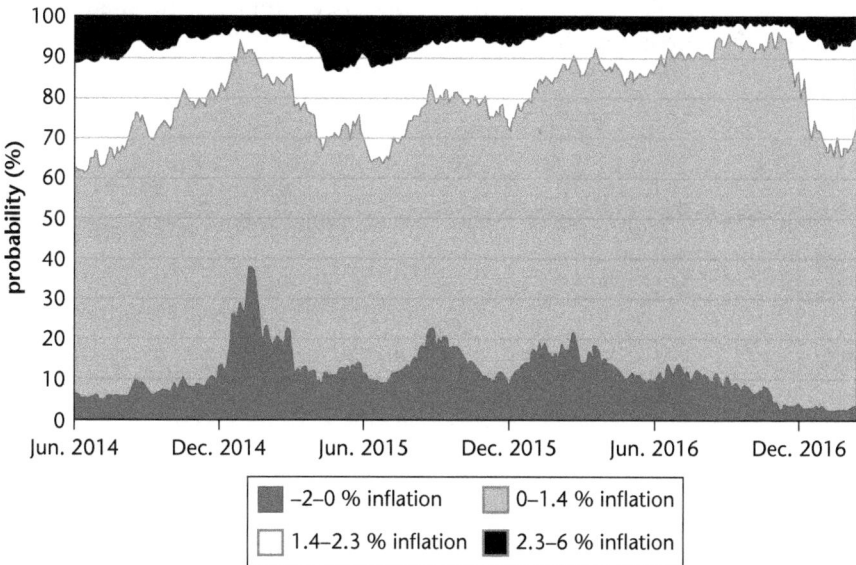

Figure 2.27 Evolution of Inflation Expectation based on Inflation Options: Probability Distribution for Five-Year Inflation Expectations, Three Observations Moving Average (2014–2016)

Source: Bloomberg and the Bank of Finland calculations.

the APP seems to have rapidly abated or even eliminated the fear of a deflationary cycle. However, according to this measure, it took until late 2016
before the probability that the average inflation would reach levels anywhere
close to the target would gain significant ground.

As asset purchases by the central bank increase the central bank reserve
holdings of banks, the negative remuneration for excess reserves applied by
the ECB could potentially intensify the channels through which monetary
policy is transmitted. This effect can be illustrated by shadow rates, which,
along with other non-standard measures, incorporate the negativity of policy
rates in the euro-area. The shadow rate model for the euro-area is similar to
that for the USA. However, lacking a constant lower bound for the policy rate
similar to the zero applying to the Fed (range of 0–25 basis points), the
estimated shadow rate for the euro-area is sensitive to the choice of the
lower bound (see Christensen and Rudebusch, 2016). The monetary policy
stance in the euro-area was determined by the deposit rate during the crisis, so
the lower bound for rates has varied over the years since the deposit rate
entered negative territory. To deal with this issue, Kortela (2016) suggests
using a shadow rate model with a time-varying lower bound for the euro-
area (see also Lemke and Vladu, 2016). He incorporates a time-varying lower
bound into the earlier three-factor shadow rate model of Krippner (2015), and
demonstrates that the changes in the lower bound significantly affect longer-
term yields as well. Figure 2.28 shows the co-evolution of the shadow rate
estimated by Kortela together with the EONIA rate. While the EONIA reflects

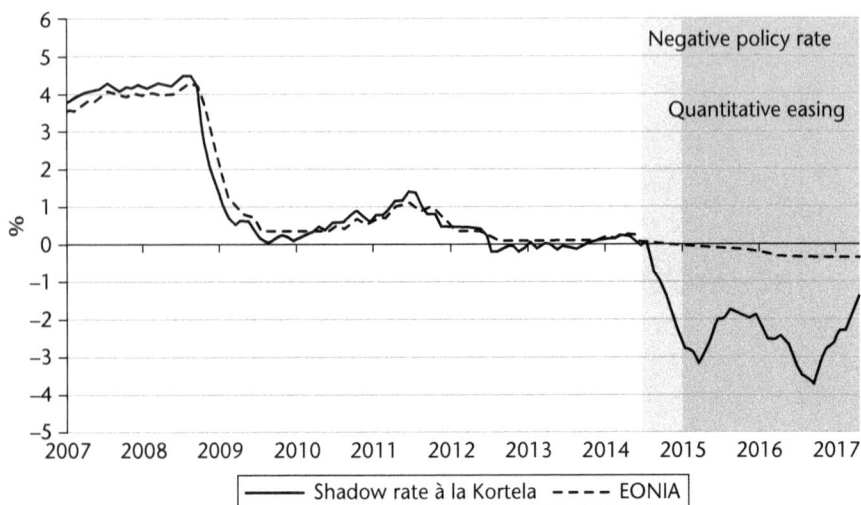

Figure 2.28 Shadow Rate with a Time-Varying Lower Bound for the ECB (2007–2017)
Source: Bank of Finland calculations.

the monetary policy stance in normal times, the shadow rate reflects the stance consistent with the term structure of interest rates if there was no ELB for interest rates. When the lower bound for interest is not constraining, the shadow rate follows the EONIA rate.

The difference between the EONIA rate and the shadow rate highlights the stimulus impact provided by non-standard measures when the lower bound is binding. The lowest level for the deposit rate has been –0.4 per cent. The shadow rate for the euro estimated by Kortela fell to –3 per cent when the PSPP was launched in early 2015, and reached a low point of –3.75 per cent in September 2016. These estimates demonstrate the significance of the impact the non-standard measures may have had on the monetary policy stance. Naturally, they should be interpreted with care. Even if the literature on shadow rates is expanding rapidly, the estimates have wide confidence bands and vary considerably depending on the model specifications. For example, the width of the 95 per cent confidence band for the time-varying shadow rate estimated by Kortela is 2 percentage points.

As for the other transmission channels, several studies validate the duration and credit risk channels.[61] Long-term sovereign yields react to the ECB asset purchases significantly more than the signalling effect would suggest across euro-area jurisdictions. This indicates a substantial duration risk effect. Yet, as the finding is mostly related to sovereign market segments, it may also implicate a scarcity or demand for safety effect (Altavilla et al., 2015).

LSAP have compressed sovereign spreads in the euro-area. As mentioned, the purchases are allocated to debt instruments issued by various jurisdictions according to their shares of ECB capital. This means, for example, that Italian government bonds are underweighted relative to market capitalization while German bonds are overweighed.[62] Consequently, the compression of sovereign spreads must be attributable to factors other than direct purchases. As seen in CDSs, the reduction in the default risk of periphery countries may relate to the expected improvements in the economic conditions, as well as increases in the expected future inflation due to the non-standard measures. Spreads, however, came down more than predicted by market pricing based on default risk alone (Altavilla et al., 2015). One reason may be that the lower bound was binding for a wide range of maturities in core countries, but non-binding or applicable only to the very short end of the yield curve in periphery countries. Hence, the signalling effect has had a bigger impact on jurisdictions less constrained by the lower bound.

---

[61] See e.g. Altavilla et al. (2015) and Andrade et al. (2016).

[62] As the capital key is derived from the GDP and the population of each country, countries with high debt-to-GDP ratios are under-bought relative to their share of overall euro-area government debt.

As to the foreign exchange channel, Deutsche Bundesbank calculations (2017) show the euro's daily loss against the USD following the announcement was the second largest ever—despite the fact that the January 2015 initial APP decisions were well anticipated by the markets. Furthermore, the depreciation of the euro on the APP announcements was broad based. Out of the six biggest daily depreciations of the euro effective exchange rate (measured against 38 largest trading partners), three involved APP announcements.

Easing announcements are often well anticipated by the markets and this should mitigate the impact of signalling effects. To account for that, a longer (more than one or two days) window needs to be included in the analysis to understand the full impact of the policy move on the foreign exchange rate. For example, between the initiation of the credit-easing measures in mid-2014 and the January announcement, the euro depreciated by 18 per cent against the dollar. Again, the effect was rather broad based. In the half-year run-up to the launch of QE, the euro depreciated by slightly more than 10 per cent against the euro-area's 19 largest trading partners. The Deutsche Bundesbank (2017) estimates that the impact of all ECB APP announcements and releases of APP-related information accounted for a 4.7 per cent drop in the euro's nominal effective exchange rate and 6.5 per cent against the dollar. The same study finds no further significant effects stemming from actual purchases.

As the bank-lending channel is more important in the transmission of monetary policy to the real economy in the euro-area than in the USA, the effect of central bank asset purchases on the capital positions of banks may have played a significant role with banks facing funding constraints.[63] This effect could have materialized via several routes. First, replacing riskier assets with central bank money in banks' balance sheets reduces the riskiness of their assets, allowing banks to increase their provision of riskier loans. Similarly, the increased valuation of assets on bank balance sheets relieves pressure on value-at-risk limits and capital constraints, providing the banks with the possibility of increasing lending. Third, lower yields of marketable debt instruments give banks greater incentive to lend rather than invest in domestic sovereign bonds. Finally, generally lax financing conditions influence the funding costs of banks, allowing them to lend at lower rates.

Following the examples by the Danmarks Nationalbank (also known as National Bank of Denmark), the ECB was the first major central bank to cut its policy rate to negative territory in June 2014. The rate was subsequently cut three times more, reaching –0.4 per cent in March 2016. Furthermore, with TLTRO2, the ECB not only remunerated excess reserves at negative rate,

---

[63] See Gertler and Karadi (2011) for details on the underpinnings of this valuation mechanism.

but also provided banks with funding at a negative nominal rate. After three years of negative rates, there are no indications of substitution to cash. The narrow monetary aggregate M1, sum of currency in circulation and overnight deposits, has been growing at an annual rate of 8–12 per cent during the 2015–2017 period.

However, the negative interest rate policy may also affect bank profitability, which consequently may set a lower bound for the policy rate if the bank-lending channel is an important part of the monetary policy transmission. Cœuré (2016) reports that 60 per cent of euro-area bank income is generated from net interest rate income. Thus, net interest rate plays a considerable role in bank profitability. If the negativity of the policy rate transmits itself directly to the reference rates widely used in bank lending, but a considerable part of funding (i.e. retail deposits) has an ELB at zero, bank profitability is hurt by negative policy rates.

The impact of negative short-term rates on bank profitability varies signifi-cantly among banks. The negative policy rate tends to hurt more if the bank gets a larger share of bank profits from net interest rate income, if a larger share of its funding comes via short-term retail deposits, or if the bank's assets are more sensitive to the trend of short-term interest rates. Moreover, the negative impact of the negative policy rate only kicks in over time. The positive impact stemming from increased valuation following the reductions in the interest rate materializes almost immediately, but the negative net interest rates creeps in slowly, especially for the banks whose lending is based on long maturities and rate-setting periods. Between June 2014 and May 2016, the average deposit rate in the euro-area dropped by 0.2 per cent, while the average loan rate decreased by 0.8 per cent (Cœuré, 2016).

Even if a negative policy rate reduces the interest rate margins, lower rates combined with increased demand stemming from improved economic con-ditions (due to accommodative monetary policy) increase lending volumes and reduce the level of non-performing loans (NPLs) (both conditions improve bank profitability). Thus, when applying a negative policy rate, the central bank needs to be aware of the risk of banks compensating for the reduced interest rate margins by reducing lending volumes or by increasing the margins they apply to loans. Up to 2017, the bank lending survey indi-cated improving loan supply conditions in the euro-area. This evidence is corroborated by data that show rising bank lending volumes.

The TLTROs has eased borrowing conditions for firms and households in the euro-area. The ECB (2017) reports that banks in peripheral countries that participated in TLTROs reduced their bank lending rates considerably more than those that did not. There is no similar impact for banks in the core countries. This applies to both waves of the ECB's targeted longer-term funding, indicating that TLTROs have been particularly effective in easing bank-lending conditions in the jurisdictions where bank funding was more expensive and the need for monetary stimulus most pronounced. Granular data show that the median lending rate for firms in peripheral countries was 20 basis points higher than in the core countries after the TLTRO, whereas the difference had stood at 120 basis points in June 2014 just before the ECB launched its credit easing (Draghi, 2017).

As regards the effects on the real economy and inflation, Wieladek and Pascual (2016) find that the euro-area GDP would have been 1.3 per cent lower in case of a counterfactual where the first round (January 2015) of QE had not been initiated. Similarly, they estimate the positive impact of QE on the euro-area inflation to be 0.9 per cent. They claim that the estimated effect on GDP is one third lower than those estimated for the USA or UK. With a cross-country study on the effects of the policies, they relate the lower impact to differences in structural and banking sector reforms taken by the countries. The healthier the banking sector and the better functioning the labour market are in a country, the larger the pass-through of non-standard policies to GDP. Their results suggest that Spanish GDP benefits four times more than Italian GDP from QE measures. As for inflation, the impact estimated for Germany is largest and for Spain the lowest, which is consistent with the impression that the impact of the QE measures on inflation falls with the amount of slack in the economy.

ECB calculations (Praet, 2016; Constâncio, 2016) indicate that the monetary policy accommodation provided through ECB non-standard measures since June 2014 increased GDP cumulative growth by over 1.5 per cent in the period 2015–2018. Annual euro-area inflation is also estimated to be 0.5 per cent higher in 2016–2018, resulting in the price level exceeding the counterfactual by 1.5 per cent at the end of the estimation period.

2.2 Financial Stability

2.2.1 Consequences of the Great Recession

In Section 1.3, the point was stressed that financial stability was the neglected field among the responsibilities of central banks before the Great Recession. In a way, there was no explicit room for it in the neat central bank model then prevailing. However, the problem of financial instability came back with a vengeance during the Great Recession; it started to be visible after August 2007, but showed all its destructive potential after the failure of Lehman Brothers in September 2008.

The negative consequences of the Great Recession for financial stability are highly complex and multifaceted; there is no pretence of providing a complete description here. An exhaustive description can be found in the semi-annual Financial Stability Reviews (FSR) of the ECB, in the Global Financial Stability Reports (GFSR) of the IMF, which have the same periodicity, as well as in the Annual Reports (AR) of the US Financial Stability Oversight Council (FSOC).

It is interesting to note, just to give a synthetic impression of the increased importance of the issue, that the summary of the IMF GFSR for October 2014 was 311 words long, while the one for April 2007, that is, the last one before the crisis (IMF, 2007), was just 83 words long. But even a fourfold increase seems to be an underestimate of how much financial stability issues grew in importance within central banks because of the Great Recession.

The salient phenomena that emerged in the financial stability field during the Great Recession, albeit appearing with different guises and timing in the USA and in the euro-area and evolving throughout the crisis, are the following:

1. Limited size of the trigger of the crisis (the subprime segment of the financial market in the case of the USA, Greece in the case of the euro-area).

2. Explosion of financial stress.

3. Evaporation of market and funding liquidity, as well as liquidity hoarding by banks.

4. Four waves of losses affecting the balance between banks' increased risk and depleted capital, each followed by capital reconstitution.

5. Low profitability of banks making the reconstitution of capital by banks more difficult.

6. Sustained disintermediation by banks, particularly across borders.

7. Increased importance of shadow banking.

8. Significant increase in interest rate spreads, brought about by dysfunctional markets.

9. Instability of short-term interest rates.

These phenomena were mutually overlapping and carried consequences for both price and financial stability. Indeed, most of the issues analysed in the FSR of the ECB, in the AR of the FSOC as well as in the IMF GFSR are also relevant for monetary policy. Consistently, most of the policy measures relevant when analysing financial stability are 'dual-purpose', or possibly 'double-edged' measures,[64] influencing, not necessarily always in the desired way, both price and financial stability. In contrast, macro-prudential measures, precisely

---

[64] This is explicit in the following quotation: 'Timely ECB action to address risks to euro-area price stability has been critical in not only ensuring price stability but also in easing financial stress which had at times reached extreme levels' (ECB FSR, December 2012, p. 10).

targeted at financial stability, were quite rare. Indeed, the term macro-prudential appears for the first time in 2011 in the Executive Summary of the IMF GFSR. In the GFSR of October 2014, some seven years after the beginning of the crisis, the emphasis on macro-prudential measures is clearly visible, but mostly to underline the difficulty in using them:

> The conduct of macroprudential policy is far from easy. Implementation is still in its infancy, and its effectiveness is not yet necessarily well understood. But in a world in which financial stability risks are likely to continue to build if left unaddressed, MPTs [macro-prudential tools] should prove to be invaluable complements to conventional policy tools in building the resilience of the financial system. (p. 44)

The May 2014 issue of the ECB FSR confirms the limited contribution of macro-prudential measures to the management of the Great Recession, reporting in a table the unsystematic use in the euro-area of macro-prudential measures addressing housing market imbalances and (excessive) lending in foreign currency.[65] Therefore, the crisis, especially in its most acute phase, had to be managed practically with the same tools used for monetary policy, with little help from macro-prudential measures. Meanwhile, traditional supervisory tools were deemed of limited use in a systemic crisis. Possible, controversial yet important, exceptions to this conclusion are the stress test, led by the Fed at the beginning of 2009, and the Asset Quality Review (AQR), led by the ECB at the end of 2014. These complex and demanding actions, which will be described in Section 2.2.2.2, are not generally regarded as part of macro-prudential measures. However, if one looks at their comprehensiveness, at their emphasis on linkages between institutions, at their macroeconomic framework, their macro-prudential nature emerges quite strongly.

One encompassing way to look at the nine consequences of the Great Recession for financial stability listed at the beginning of this section is to understand them, consistently with the overriding paradigm used in this book, as consequences of the sudden shift from a 'good' to a 'bad' equilibrium as described by Diamond–Dybvig (Diamond, 2007). This view is explicitly recognized in the IMF GFSR of April 2012: 'The Sovereign Debt Crisis: Shifting from a Bad to a Good Equilibrium'. Thus the report acknowledges that there was an opposite move previously. The report furthermore states:

> These developments dramatically highlighted the risk of adverse, self-fulfilling shifts in market sentiment that could rapidly push fragile sovereigns into a bad equilibrium of rising yields, a funding squeeze for domestic banks, and a worsening economy. (p. 1)

---

[65] Table A.1.

Of course, the adjective 'good' applied to the equilibrium prevailing before the crisis should not be understood literally. In the interpretative framework à la Kindleberger and Aliber (2005), Minsky (1986), and Reinhart and Rogoff (2009), presented and empirically illustrated in Chapter 1, the equilibrium prevailing before the crisis was carrying the hidden seeds of its own demise. In this sense, the pre-crisis equilibrium was not truly a good one. It is interesting, along this line of thinking, that, in its FSR, the ECB sets risks to the financial system in two different categories: *exogenous* (sources of risk and vulnerability outside the euro-area financial system) and *endogenous* (sources of risk and vulnerability within the euro-area financial system). This line of analysis is a sort of Minsky approach, in which instability can originate within the financial system and not just as a reaction to external shocks. The brewing of instabilities during the so-called 'good' equilibrium period preceding the Great Recession is well described in the following quotation from the IMF FSR of September 2007 (IMF, 2007):

> The benign economic and financial conditions of recent years weakened incentives to conduct due diligence on borrowers and counterparties. . . . Leverage has played a key role in amplifying the disturbances. The ease with which some banks and other investment vehicles, including hedge funds, were able to borrow against difficult-to-price collateral traded in illiquid markets severely aggravated conditions when market liquidity evaporated, resulting in a process of forced deleveraging at 'fire sale' prices and the failure of some funds. Institutions that have suffered the most have had strategies that were based on high levels of leverage and had assumed continued liquidity in secondary markets.   (p. x)

This quotation shows one characteristic of the financial system that was obviously not 'good' before the Great Recession: excessive leverage, corresponding to an excessive level of debt, or credit seen from the other side of the balance sheet.[66] The liquidity mismatch, with assets having a longer maturity than liabilities, added to the vulnerability. Also, the FSOC AR of 2011 has a quotation that is pure Minsky: 'Aspects of the financial system that appear to make markets more liquid and financial institutions more prosperous in normal times may be the same ones that make the world more dangerous in crisis' (p. ii). Consistently with the assessment that the situation before the Great Recession was not 'good' in a full sense of the word, policy actions to deal with the crisis had to find a balance between engendering more favourable expectations while not returning to the situation prevailing before the crisis.

Two of the nine phenomena listed at the beginning of this section, namely the sharp increase in interest rate spreads caused by dysfunctional markets as

---

[66] IMF GFSR, April 2008: 'There was a collective failure to appreciate the extent of leverage taken on by a wide range of institutions—banks, monoline insurers, government-sponsored entities, hedge funds—and the associated risks of a disorderly unwinding' (p. ix).

well as the instability of short-term rates, which characterized, from a financial stability perspective, the Great Recession, have already been amply illustrated in Section 2.1.1, which dealt with the consequences for monetary policy. The other seven phenomena are documented one after the other in what follows, distinguishing, when needed, the USA from the euro-area experience as well as showing how the different phenomena evolved during the Great Recession.

2.2.1.1 THE VERY LIMITED SIZE OF THE TRIGGER OF THE CRISIS

During the first months of the crisis in 2007, the argument was often put forward that it was only 2005, 2006, and 2007 vintages of subprime lending that recorded large losses, and that the subprime market itself was a very small segment of the real-estate-linked financial market, which was in turn only a part of the large US financial market.[67]

According to available estimates, only about 13 per cent of outstanding mortgages were subprime,[68] and total outstanding mortgages were only about one third of the total loans outstanding in the USA. Therefore, subprime lending was about 3 per cent of total lending. Still, this small, indeed even tiny, market segment, showed its destructive potential:

> The turbulence that had hit the US banking markets . . . spilled over to the European banking markets in late September, triggered first by US Congress' initial rejection of the Troubled Assets Relief Program (TARP) and then amplified by the revelation of counterparty losses on exposures to Lehman Brothers.
>
> (ECB FSR, December 2008, p. 83)

Somewhat analogously, between the autumn of 2009 and the spring of 2010, financial markets started to be roiled by the revelations about Greece's misreporting of public finance data. At the time, the argument was made that Greek GDP was less than 2 per cent of the aggregate GDP of the euro-area and therefore its importance should not be exaggerated. The error made in both cases was not looking at the issue from the multiple equilibria perspective, in which there is no need for proportionality between cause and effect. The error is very honestly acknowledged by Bernanke (2015a, ch. 7) in his memoirs:

> Housing, as I told the Joint Economic Committee in March 2007, has entered a substantial correction. What was the bottom line? I offered committee members my tentative conclusion: At this juncture, the impact on the broader economy and financial markets of the problems in the subprime market seems likely to be contained.

---

[67] See figure 1.8, p. 12, of GFSR Oct. 2008.   [68] Bernanke (2015a, ch. 7).

He made the point in even more general terms in chapter 5:

> Toward the end of my tenure as chairman, I was asked what had surprised me the most about the financial crisis. 'The crisis' I said. I did not mean we missed entirely what was going on. We saw, albeit often imperfectly most of the pieces of the puzzle. But we failed to understand—'failed to imagine' might be a better phrase—how those pieces would fit together to produce a financial crisis that compared to, and arguably surpassed, the financial crisis that ushered in the Great Depression.

If the author of this chapter would have written his memoirs he could not have claimed more foresight than the Chairman of the Fed.

The error was only widely recognized after the fact, with hindsight. In addition, the breakdown of proportionality between cause and effect in multiple equilibria models means many small events could take place without causing significant damage. Therefore, it is very difficult to identify those developments that would instead produce disproportionate crises.

The possibility of multiple equilibria creates a double risk: on one hand, as happened with the Great Recession, the relatively small size of the trigger may lead to an underestimation of the potential damage; on the other hand, one may ring the alarm bell too often, causing unnecessary panic. In statistical terms, the first risk could be assimilated to a Type 1 error, rejecting the hypothesis when it is true, whereas the second risk could be assimilated to a Type 2 error, retaining the hypothesis when it is false. The discriminating factor should be an assessment of the vulnerability of the actual economic conditions to a shift in expectations. This is referred to as 'tipping point' in Box 11. Such assessment, however, is very difficult to make. In fact, as reported in Section 1.4.4, 'false beliefs' masked the unsustainability of the situation before the Great Recession, proving that this kind of assessment is hard to reach. The fact that Cassandras will often incur Type 2 errors is, of course, one of the important sources of difficulty.

2.2.1.2 AN EXPLOSION OF FINANCIAL STRESS

During the Great Recession, financial stress literally exploded. In the euro-area, the two acute phases of the crisis (the American phase after the failure of Lehman Brothers and the European one after the revelations by the Greek Prime Minister about the misreported budget deficit) are clearly visible in Figure 2.29.

The figure, reporting a composite indicator of systemic stress (CISS) for the euro-area, drawn from the FSR of the ECB,[69] shows that the measurement of

---

[69] A number of figures are drawn with data published in the ECB FSR, kindly provided by the Financial Stability Directorate of the ECB.

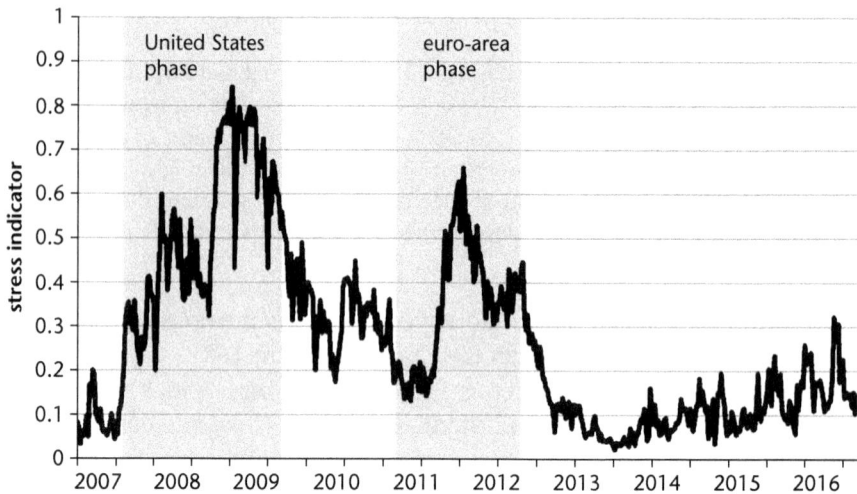

Figure 2.29 CISS in the Euro-Area (2007–2016)

Note: The CISS index has a minimum value of 0 and a maximum value of 1. The construction of the index is explained in: Hollo, Kremer, Lo Duca (2012).

Source: ECB.

stress was close to 0, its theoretical minimum, in the euro-area at the beginning of 2007. The first peak exceeded 0.8, that is, not far from the theoretical maximum of 1, after the failure of Lehman Brothers in the autumn of 2008. Then, in late 2011/early 2012, another peak was reached, higher than 0.6, before irregularly coming down. To better assess the degree of stress during the Great Recession, it is useful to look at the longer time series of CISS, starting in 1987, published by Holló, Kremer, and Lo Duca (2012). The time series includes the 1987 stock market crash, the 1992 ERM crisis, the LTCM failure, and the 9/11 terrorist attacks. Yet none of these events caused the CISS indicator to exceed 0.3. Based on the CISS metric, the failure of Lehman Brothers caused a financial stress nearly three times as large as the most stressful crisis episode since 1987, while the Greek crisis was more than twice as stressful as any other major event occurring in the two decades before the Great Recession.

Figure 2.30 shows a market-based systemic risk measure in the USA shortly before and during the Great Recession. Drawn from the World Bank's Global Financial Development Database (GFDD), it depicts a sharp increase of the probability of default at the start of the Great Recession but then an equal sharp recovery in the following two years, showing that the crisis in the USA was acute but not protracted. It is interesting to observe that there is no repeat of the increased probability of default on the occasion of the euro-area phase of the crisis.

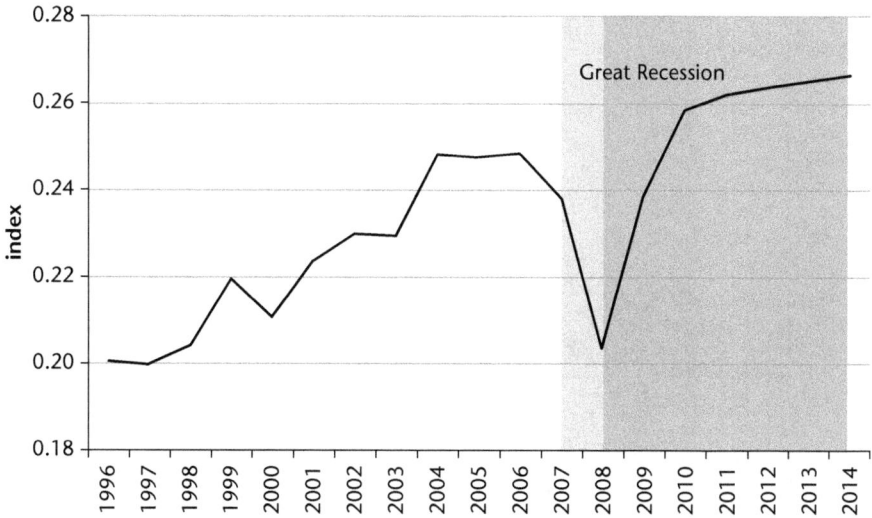

Figure 2.30 Market-Based Systemic Risk Measures in the USA (1996–2014)

Note: Z-score index ranges between 0 (high probability of insolvency) and 1 (low probability of insolvency). The z-score is defined as $z \equiv (k+\mu)/\sigma$ where k is equity capital, μ is return, and σ is standard deviation of return.

Source: GFDD, World Bank.

2.2.1.3 EVAPORATION OF BOTH MARKET AND FUNDING LIQUIDITY AS WELL AS LIQUIDITY HOARDING BY BANKS

These phenomena can be seen from two different perspectives. One perspective, which is quantitative, consists in measuring the stress by looking at the liquidity that commercial banks took from the Fed and the ECB during the Great Recession, in order to substitute evaporating market liquidity. This was seen in the extraordinary increase of the balance sheet of the two central banks (as examined in Section 2.1.2), when they had to carry out the amount of intermediation that the market was no longer capable of delivering.

Another perspective to assess liquidity risk and hoarding is taken by Papadia and Välimäki (2011). Their approach (reporting analyses from Eisenschmitt and Tapking, 2009) is to decompose the total spread between the remuneration of a contract affected by credit risk (like Euribor or Libor) and a contract practically free from credit risk (like a repurchase operation or, in the case of the USA, a treasury bill) into two components: liquidity and credit risk. The figure (reproduced here as Figure 2.31) displays the liquidity premium in the euro-area during the most acute phase of the crisis, between May 2007 and the end of 2009. Figure 2.31 reports, in particular, the total spread as well as the CDS of the bank participating in the Euribor panel with the lowest credit

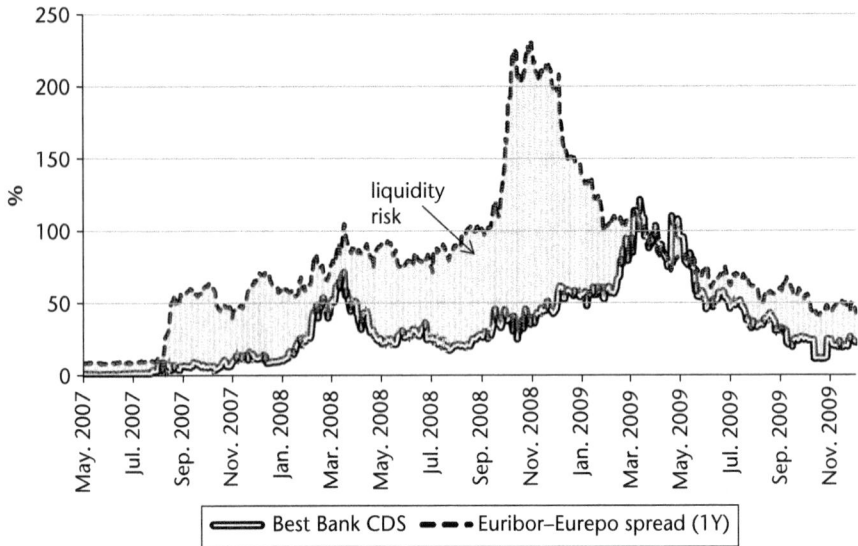

Figure 2.31 Liquidity Premium in the Euro-Area (2007–2009)
Source: Papadia and Välimäki (2011, p. 302).

risk, representing the credit risk component in the Euribor interest rate. The shaded difference between the two lines is interpreted as liquidity premium.[70]

Figure 2.31 shows that the spread had an obvious credit risk component, as the CDS of even the bank with the lowest credit risk increased substantially. Indeed, stressed financial conditions made the creditworthiness of all banks, even the most creditworthy, doubtful. The spread was also affected, however, by liquidity risk, because the fear of not disposing of the needed liquidity in the future led to liquidity hoarding, independently of the creditworthiness of counterparties. A seemingly counterintuitive phenomenon happened: banks reduced their lending because of a deterioration of their own credit rating, not because of a deterioration of the credit rating of their counterparties. The chart also shows that liquidity risk started to increase in the euro-area in the summer of 2007, but then exploded at the end of 2008, remaining around this very high peak for a few months, explaining over 80 per cent of the total spread in that period. Then spreads came down, yet remained clearly higher than before the crisis.

A similar figure, Figure 2.32, is provided for the USA, again showing that there was both liquidity and credit risk contributing to the spread between a

---

[70] The measure of liquidity risk reported in Figures 2.31 and 2.32 should be taken, as always with this kind of measures, *cum grano salis*. Indeed, in the case of the euro-area for a short period in 2009, the total spread is lower than just the credit risk component, which would imply a nonsensical negative liquidity risk.

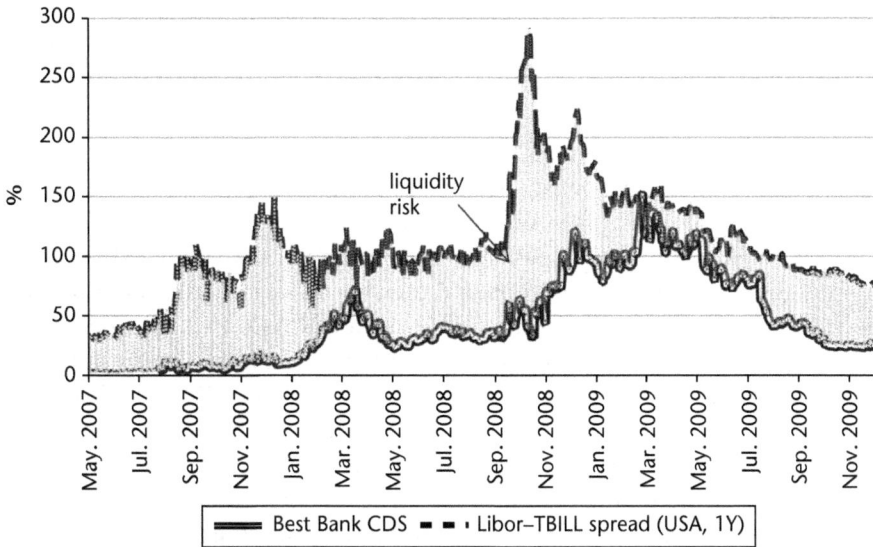

Figure 2.32 Liquidity Premium in the USA (2007–2009)
Source: Papadia and Välimäki (2011, p. 304).

rate affected by credit risk, that is, the Libor rate, and the yield on US treasury bills, taken as a short-term risk-free rate in the USA.

The pattern in the 2007 to 2009 period in the USA is similar to that observed in the euro-area: liquidity risk increased in the summer of 2007 and then recorded a paroxysmal jump at the turn between 2008 and 2009, followed by a decrease, but not quite to the level prevailing before the crisis. Also in the case of the USA, the CDS of the bank with the lowest level of credit risk increased substantially between 2007 and 2009.

2.2.1.4 FOUR WAVES OF LOSSES AFFECTED THE BALANCE BETWEEN BANKS' INCREASED RISK AND DEPLETED CAPITAL, EACH FOLLOWED BY CAPITAL RECONSTITUTION

The four waves can summarily be described as follows. A first, sudden, and violent wave of losses, directly due to the subprime crisis, hit mostly American financial institutions and banks from the core of the euro-area, especially from Germany, Belgium, and France. Indeed, some European banks that had invested in US subprime assets suffered major losses in the initial phases of the crisis. The losses were so large that either they led those banks to fail or the banks required substantial government support to prevent failure. Instead, more prudent, or just less international, banks in the euro-area periphery initially suffered less. The three subsequent waves of losses hit mostly euro-area banks. The second wave struck mostly banks in the euro-area periphery, due to the repercussions of the Greek revelations about fiscal misreporting. The third wave was the result of the unwinding of the real estate bubble in Spain and Ireland, creating large NPLs. The fourth wave built up over time in Italy, Portugal, and, in an extreme fashion, in Greece, mostly driven by the very large increase of bad loans, which durably affected banks located there. Large NPLs were, in turn, mostly led by the economic recession.

The subprime-related losses during the first wave of stress, as estimated by the IMF GFSR, show a time pattern clearly consistent with a sudden move from a 'good' to a 'bad' equilibrium and then a gradual and partial normalization: on impact, prices dropped to 'fire-sale' levels, followed by a period of re-normalization. The first estimate of losses for non-prime (subprime and alt-A) mortgages was given in the IMF GFSR of September 2007 (see box 1.1, page 12, of that report) for American institutions and was calculated to be around 200 billion dollars. In the subsequent issue of the GFSR, in April 2008, the estimate of the subprime-related losses was revised and extended, broadening the perimeter of the affected institutions and the considered assets. As a consequence, the estimate of the losses grew to close to 1 trillion dollars (p. x). In October of 2008, the estimate was further increased to 1.4 trillion (p. xiii). In April 2009, the estimate of losses reached a peak of about 2.5 trillion for banks and 4 trillion in total. Consequently, estimates were progressively enlarged: they began with non-prime assets for the USA in September 2007 and progressed to a global approach on all assets in April 2009, by which time estimated losses grew twentyfold. Beginning with the October 2009 issue of the GSFR, the estimate of the total losses started to be reduced, first to 3.4 trillion, then further down to 2.3 trillion in the issue of April 2010 (p. xi), and finally down to 2.2 trillion in the issue of October of the same year (p. x), the last GFSR to report an estimate of global losses.

The ECB FSR, on its side, estimated in June 2010 the total write-downs for the euro-area banking system from the first wave of stress to be over half a trillion euros, showing the potency of the move from a 'good' to a 'bad' equilibrium.[71]

The losses on the lending business deriving from the second, third, and fourth waves of stress can be easily seen in the growth of NPLs of banks in the periphery of the euro-area. This phenomenon is visible in the impaired loan ratios in Figure 2.33.

In Figure 2.33 it can be seen that the quality of bank portfolios in the periphery progressively deteriorated between 2007 and 2015, with the share of impaired loans growing from 2 to 12 per cent. Conversely, in the core, after an initial worsening from 2 to 4 per cent, there was a gradual improvement, such that, by 2015, the share of impaired loans was close to its level in 2007.

---

[71] ECB FSR, June 2010, box 11, p. 87.

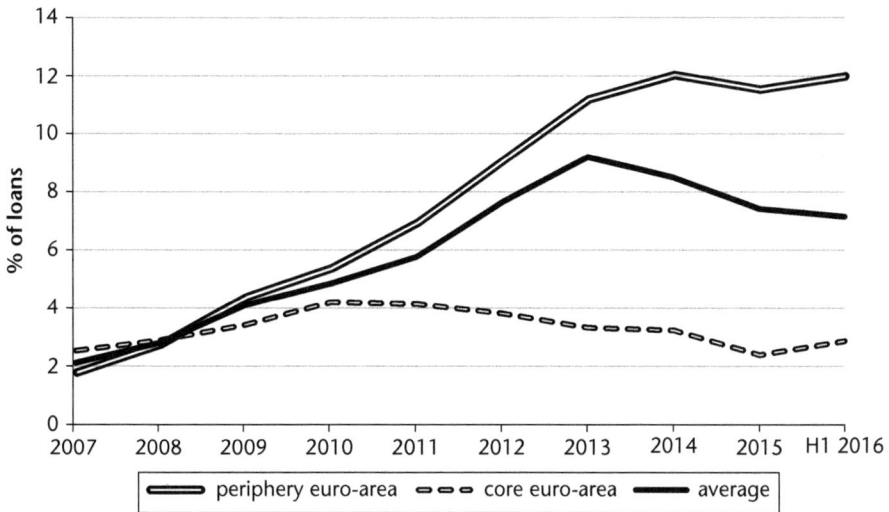

Figure 2.33 Impaired Loan Ratios of Significant Banking Groups in the Euro-Area (2007–2016)

Source: Drawn from the ECB Financial Stability Report. Bloomberg and ECB calculations.

In the periphery, another source of losses for banks derived from the depreciation in the marking-to- market value of the sovereign bonds of peripheral countries that they held in their portfolios.

The gradual and persistent increase of NPLs in the euro-area, in particularly in its periphery, contrasts with the experience in the USA. As displayed in Figure 2.34, NPLs in the United States worsened abruptly during the first two years of the Great Recession but then came down consistently from the beginning of 2010, eventually getting close, by 2016, to their level before the crisis.

As the Great Recession brought about too low a capital endowment for banks in relation to their risk-weighted assets, banks engaged in an effort to reconstitute their capital. A striking difference appeared, however, in the recapitalization process between the USA and the euro-area. In the euro-area, as seen in Figure 2.35, there was a gradual increase in capital ratios of significant banking groups from about 8.5 per cent in 2010 to slightly above 12 per cent in 2015, a total increase of nearly 4 percentage points. The numerator in the ratio (capital) started to increase since 2010, as a first wave or recapitalizations were carried out to prepare for the first stress test, but there was an attempt to avoid a decrease of balance sheet size. In Ireland and Spain, Asset Relief Programmes were carried out and the correction was faster, but there was no quick and coordinated action at the euro-area level using public funds that would lead to a quick balance sheet cleaning.

The adjustment in the USA, instead, was much quicker than in the euro-area, as it can be seen in Figure 2.36.

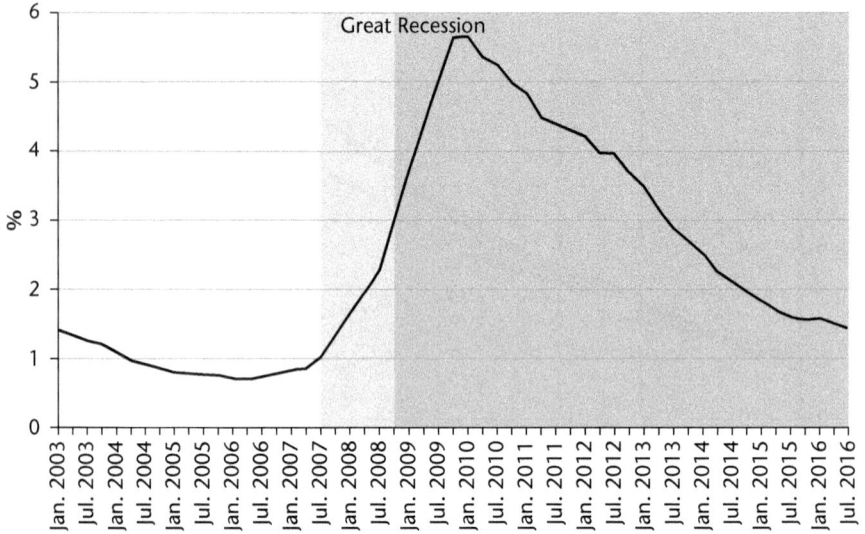

Figure 2.34 Non-Performing Total Loans to Total Loans in the USA (2003–2016)

Source: FRED, Federal Financial Institutions Examination Council (US), NPL (past due 90+ days plus non-accrual) to Total Loans.

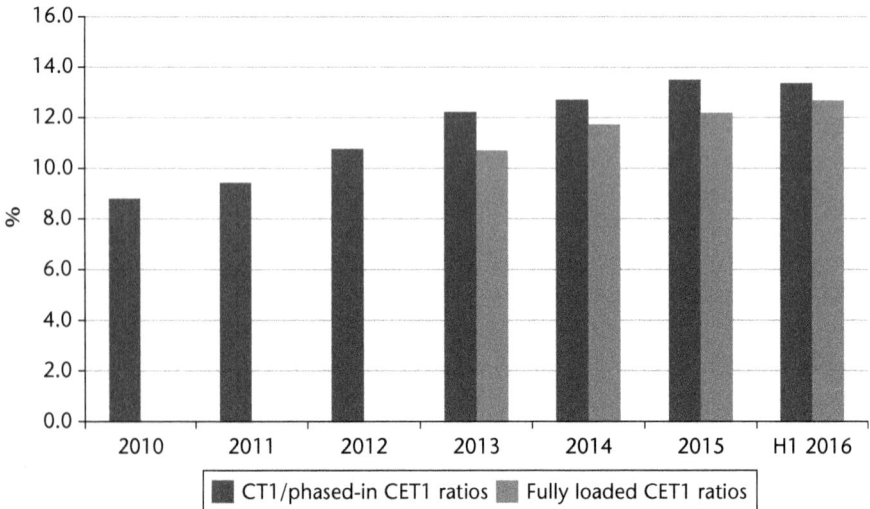

Figure 2.35 Core Tier 1/Common Equity Tier 1 Capital Ratios of Significant Banking Groups in the Euro-Area (2010–2016)

Source: Drawn from the ECB Financial Stability Report. SNL Financial and ECB calculations.

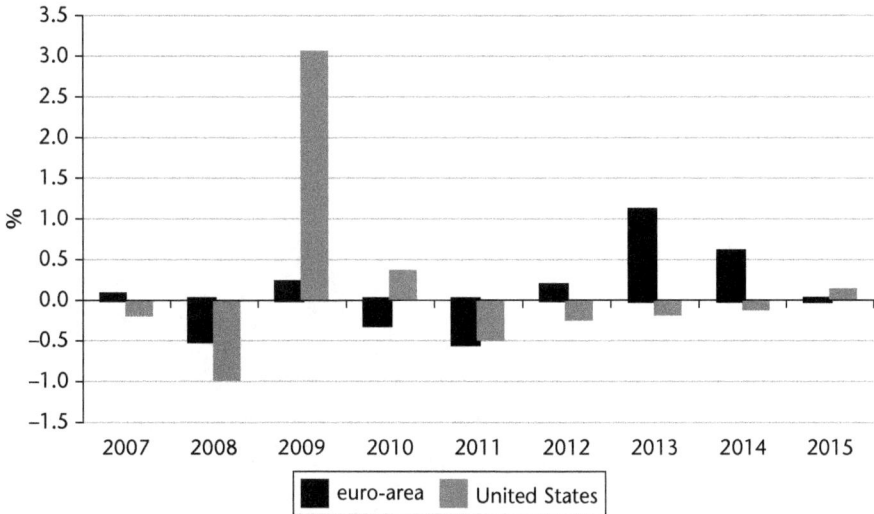

Figure 2.36 Percentage Change in Bank Capital-to-Assets Ratio in the USA and the Euro-Area (2007–2015)

Source: IMF–Global Financial Stability Report.

Recapitalization in the USA was concentrated in 2009, just after the Lehman failure, as American banks increased, by a staggering 3 per cent, their capital-to-asset ratios. This occurred because the forceful action of public authorities obliged banks to increase their capital endowment, if necessary through public funds provided by the Supervisory Capital Assessment Programme (SCAP) and TARP approved a few weeks after the bankruptcy of Lehman Brothers, as it will be seen in Section 2.2.2.2, and a large programme of transfer of troubled assets to Fannie and Freddie.

2.2.1.5 LOW PROFITABILITY MADE THE RECONSTITUTION OF CAPITAL BY BANKS MORE DIFFICULT

The ability of banks to reconstitute their capital was affected by their low profitability after the inception of the Great Recession. This difficulty was more prolonged in the European Union (EU), and in particular in the euro-area, than in the USA (Figure 2.37). In fact, in the USA there was a deep dent in the return on bank assets in 2008, but this recovered quite quickly in the following years, returning nearly to the level that prevailed before the Great Recession, itself higher than the one prevailing in Europe. In Europe, instead, there was barely a recovery during the Great Recession. In particular, in the euro-area the return on assets dipped into negative territory in 2011 and then remained close to zero for a number of years.

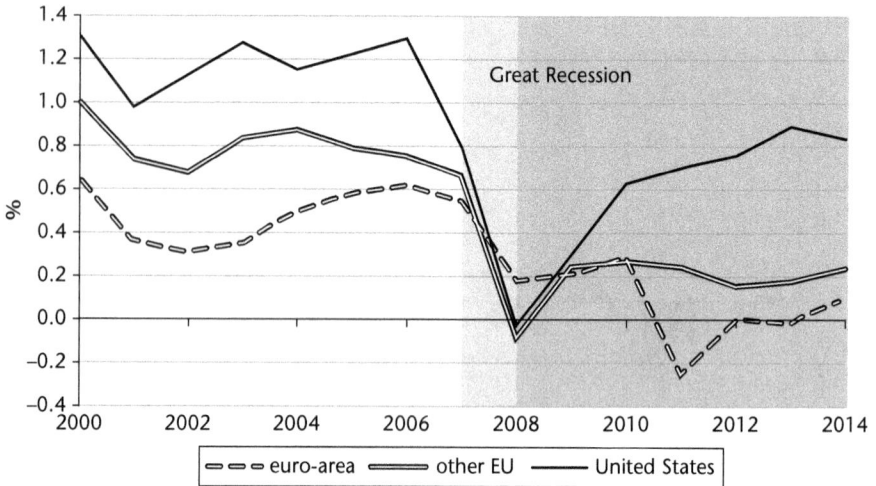

Figure 2.37 Return on Assets for Euro-Area, Other EU Countries, and the USA (2000–2014)

Note: Weighted averages (%) for a fixed sample of euro area, non-euro area, and US banks.

Source: Drawn from the ECB Financial Stability Report. Bloomberg and ECB calculations.

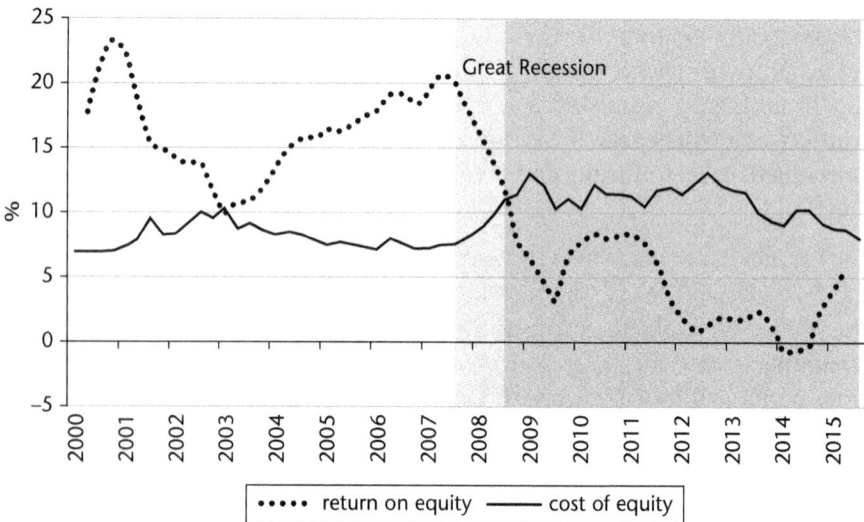

Figure 2.38 Return on Equity and Cost of Equity for Euro-Area Banks (2000–2015)

Source: Drawn from the ECB Financial Stability Report. Bloomberg, Datastream, Consensus, Economics, ECB calculations.

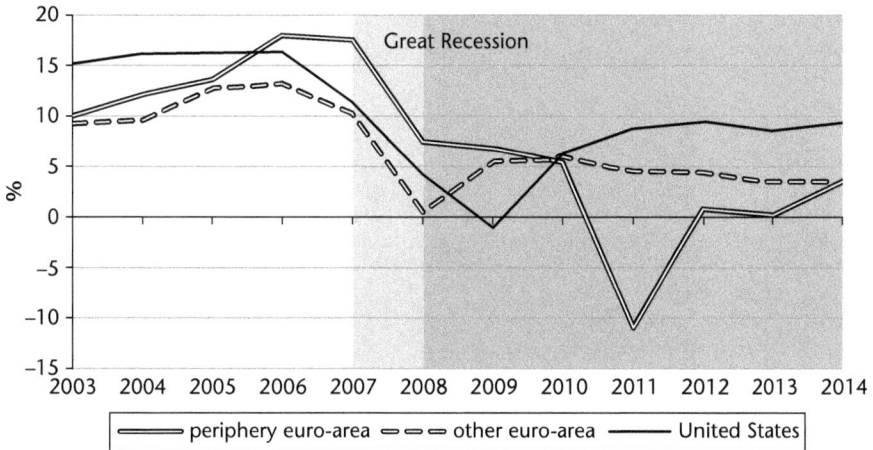

Figure 2.39 Return on Equity of Banks in Periphery and Core Euro-Area Countries and the USA (2003–2014)

Note: Periphery euro-area countries include: Cyprus, Ireland, Italy, Portugal, Slovenia, and Spain. Other euro-area countries include: Austria, Belgium, Finland, France, and Germany.

Source: Drawn from the ECB Financial Stability Report. Bloomberg and ECB calculations.

The sharp deterioration in the profitability of euro-area banks is also shown by the fact that the return on their equity moved from well above to well below the cost of equity after the onset of the Great Recession, as it is visible in Figure 2.38. In the same Figure one sees that the gap lasted for the following seven years, and only narrowed considerably in 2015.

In Figure 2.39 one sees another perspective on the striking difference between the profitability of American versus euro-area banks, as measured by the return on equity. In the US banks recovered reasonably well after faltering in 2009. Non-periphery euro-area banks faltered in 2008, but partially recovered in subsequent years. In Figure 2.39 the dismal performance of euro-area banks since the beginning of the Great Recession is particularly visible for banks in the euro-area periphery, as they moved, in the European phase of the Great Recession, from being more profitable to being less profitable than banks in the USA and in the core of the euro-area, then remained persistently in this situation for a number of years. However, periphery and other euro-banks returned to a similar level of profitability by 2014, albeit a significantly lower one than before the Great Recession.

The quick and the quasi-full recovery in the USA of the return on equity compared to the cost of equity is also visible in Figure 2.40.

The worse profitability of banks in the periphery of the euro-area was, as mentioned, largely due to the progressive deterioration of their loan portfolio

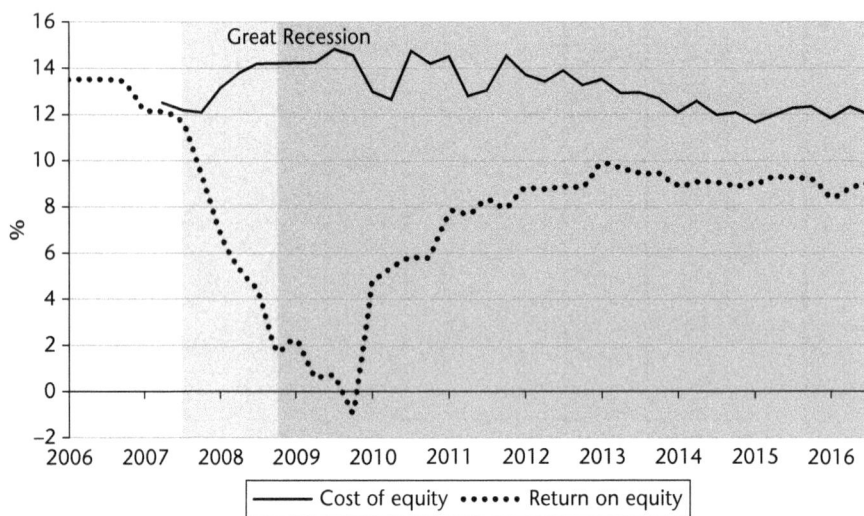

Figure 2.40 Average Return on Equity and Cost of Capital in the USA (2006–2016)

Note: The cost of equity is derived using the Capital Asset Pricing Model (CAPM). Data used to compute it began after 2007.

Sources: Federal Reserve Economic Data, and the author's calculations with Bloomberg LP data.

and to the losses on sovereign paper of peripheral countries, caused in turn to a large extent by contagion. During the European phase of the crisis, a critical interaction appeared in the euro-area between the credit risk of banks and that of their relevant sovereign. This interaction is shown in Figure 2.41, which displays on the vertical axis the average CDS of a number of euro-area and global banks in two different periods, grouped by country of incorporation, and in the horizontal axis the CDS spread of their sovereign.

As it can be seen, the points for the euro-area banks and sovereign CDS spreads are mostly aligned along a 45-degree straight line, showing a one-to-one linkage between the two creditworthiness indicators. However, the scatter diagram for the global banks shows a much lower coefficient between the CDS of banks and that of their sovereign, indicating a weaker link between the financial soundness of the two.

As is often the case, correlation is not necessarily causation. Indeed, the strong link between sovereign and bank creditworthiness in the euro-area probably reflects different causal relationships. In the core, particularly in Germany, the low CDSs of the banks are influenced by the high creditworthiness of the German government. Indeed, as mentioned, some German banks suffered large losses in the first phase of the Great Recession, but the awareness of the market that the solid financial position of the Federal government ultimately stood behind them limited the effects of the losses on their creditworthiness.

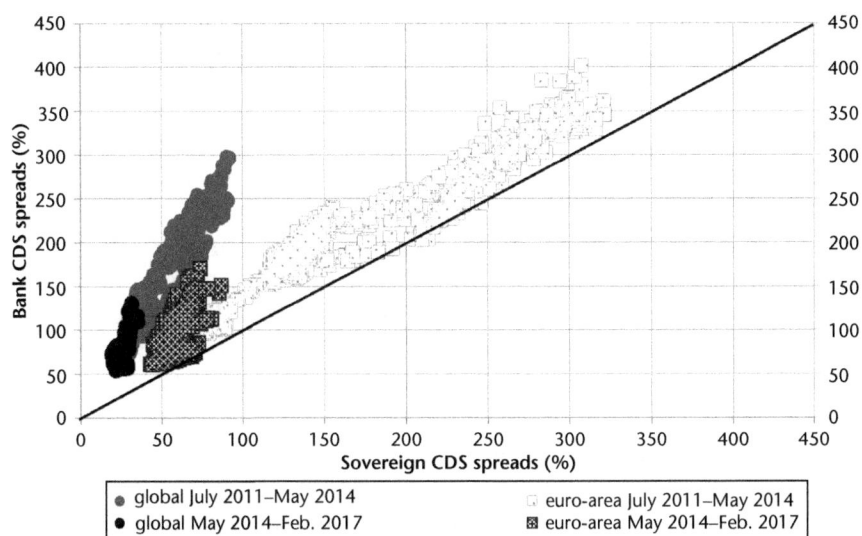

Figure 2.41 Sovereign and Bank Credit Default Spreads (July 2011–May 2014 and May 2014–February 2017)

Note: Average CDS spread for the euro area and global large and complex banking groups (LCBGs) versus the average sovereign CDS spread where the LCBGs are headquartered (France, Germany, Italy, Spain, and the Netherlands for euro-area LCBGs, and the USA, the UK, Switzerland, Denmark, Sweden, and Japan for LCBGs).

Source: Drawn from the ECB Financial Stability Report. Bloomberg, ECB and ECB calculations.

In the periphery there were, in turn, very different stories between Spain and Ireland, on one hand, and Greece, Portugal, and Italy, on the other. In the case of Spain and Ireland, as documented in Section 1.4.2, it was the imprudent expansion of bank credit to the real estate sector that brought the government, which had impeccable deficit and debt conditions, into a stressed situation when it had to massively intervene to bail out banks. In the case of Greece, instead, and, to a much lower extent, Portugal and Italy, it was the persistent effect of the recession on NPLs that affected the creditworthiness of banks. An additional pressure was created by the precarious situation of their respective governments, which affected the valuation of government bonds held by national banks. In Greece, in particular, the so-called private-sector involvement, whereby a heavy cut was applied to the value of government securities in March 2012, further contributed to the weakening of banks. Whatever the specific causes, in all peripheral countries a 'diabolic loop' (Brunnermeier et al., 2016) prevailed for a long period during the Great Recession, whereby a negative spiral was established between the creditworthiness of banks and that of their sovereign.

Overall, in the euro-area, particularly within its periphery, during the crisis, poor profitability persistently weakened balance sheets. The recapitalization process and the recognition of NPLs were slow and late. As a consequence, euro-area banks remained for much longer than American banks in impaired conditions, affecting their ability to fund economic growth.

2.2.1.6 THE REDUCTION IN BANK INTERMEDIATION WAS PART OF THE PROCESS OF RE-EQUILIBRATING BALANCE SHEET RISK AND CAPITAL

The disintermediation process in the euro-area during the Great Recession has already been discussed in Section 1.4.2, looking at the loans-to-deposit ratio in Figure 1.36. There it was seen that the ratio had already increased in the period preceding the Great Moderation but, in the euro-area, the increase was particularly strong during the Great Moderation. Then the ratio started its decline with the beginning of the Great Recession. Here the same phenomenon is looked at concentrating on the development during the Great Recession.

Figure 2.42 shows that the reduction of the ratio of bank credit to deposits during the Great Recession was a phenomenon extended to both the euro-area and the USA. However, the pattern over time was different, as the reduction in the USA was concentrated in the first few years of the Great Recession, whereas in the euro-area it manifested itself just after the beginning of the crisis and then again, with more intensity, after 2012.

A more detailed view of the euro-area is displayed in Figure 2.43, which shows the total asset of banks during the Great Recession.

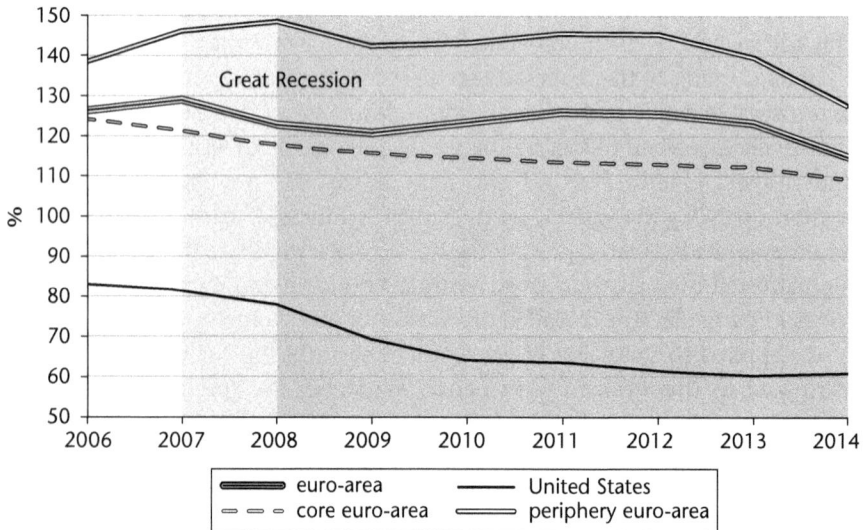

Figure 2.42 Bank Credit to Bank Deposits for the Euro-Area and the USA (2006–2014)
Source: GFDD, World Bank.

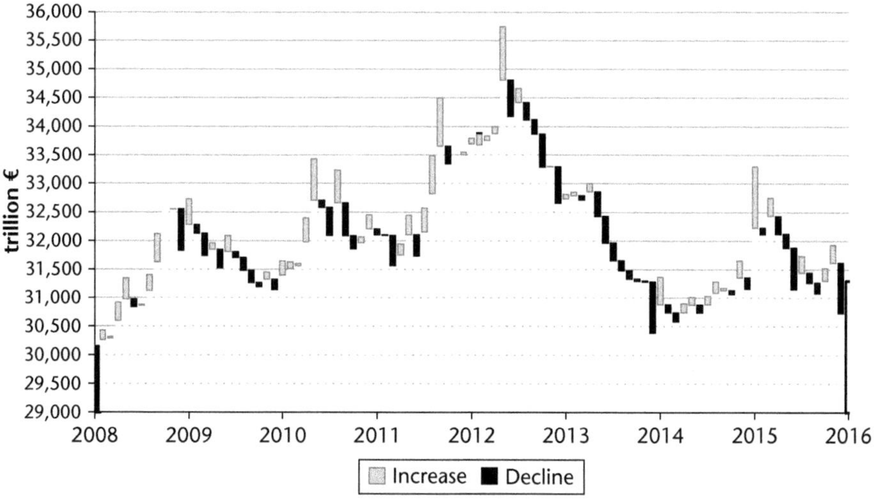

Figure 2.43 Bank Deleveraging in the Euro-Area (2008–2016)
Source: ECB and author's calculations with ECB Statistical Data Warehouse.

The figure shows that, after having grown between 2008 and 2012, total bank assets came down from nearly 36 trillion to less than 32 trillion euro, that is, close to a 10 per cent decrease, between the spring of 2012 and the end of 2015. Significant deleveraging in the euro-area was therefore quite a late development during the Great Recession, unlike in the USA.

The reduction of euro-area bank balance sheets in the late phase of the Great Recession reflects the fact that it was difficult for banks, especially those in the periphery with the most pressing recapitalization needs, to raise equity capital, given the low profitability. Therefore, deleveraging was, eventually, acknowledged as the way to re-establish an appropriate proportion between the risk-weighted balance sheet and capital.

The disintermediation process was more intense for cross-border lending by American and, particularly, euro-area banks. Indeed, as seen in Figure 2.44, while banks in the USA and the euro-area had increased their cross-border lending until 2007, they inverted (sharply in the case of euro-area banks) this tendency after the beginning of the Great Recession.

The retrenching of banks within their borders partly overlaps with a more general phenomenon of financial fragmentation that took place in the euro-area during the Great Recession. This is illustrated in Figure 2.45, which reports the Financial Integration Composites (FINTECs) Index elaborated by the ECB.[72] The price-based indicator showed a sustained increase in integration between 1995 and 2007, followed by a strong fragmentation in the following

---

[72] An explanation of the composite indicator is in ECB (2015).

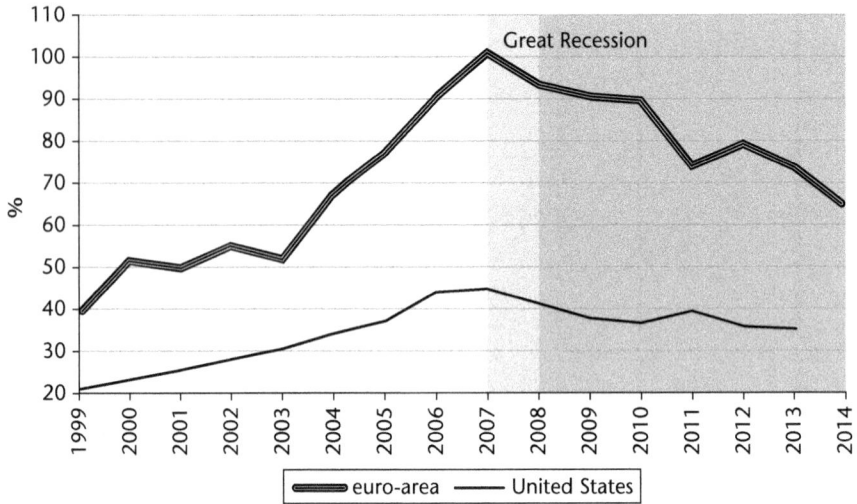

Figure 2.44 Foreign Claims of Home Country Banks in the Euro-Area and the USA (1999–2014)

Source: GFDD, World Bank.

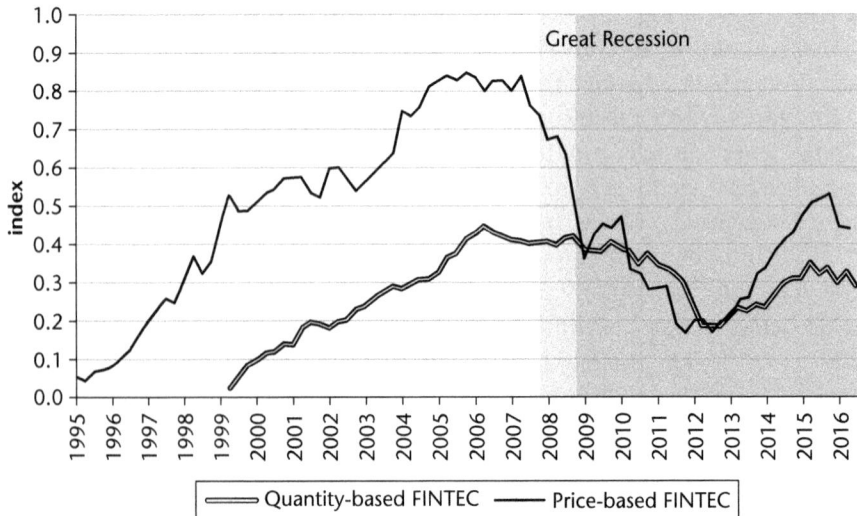

Figure 2.45 Price-Based and Quantity-Based FINTEC Indices in the Euro-Area (1995–2016)

Note: The price-based FINTEC aggregates ten indicators and the quantity-based FINTEC aggregates five indicators. The FINTEC is bounded between zero (full fragmentation) and one (full integration).

Source: ECB and ECB calculations.

five years, and only a partial recovery since then. The quantity-based indicator, only available since 1999, also showed a trend of increasing integration until 2006, a relatively flat trend over the subsequent few years, followed by a steady decrease between early 2010 and mid-2011 and a partial recovery since then.

2.2.1.7 WHILE BANKS WERE REDUCING THEIR ROLE, THE SHADOW-BANKING SECTOR INCREASED ITS INTERMEDIATION, PARTICULARLY IN THE EURO-AREA

This is seen in Figure 2.46, which documents that, in the euro-area, shadow-bank intermediation increased by nearly 50 per cent between 2008 and 2014. This trend was due to the explosive growth of investment and hedge funds, while bank intermediation stagnated.

The reduced role of banks relative to shadow banking is just one aspect of the more general phenomenon that, contrary to expectations, it was banks and related markets (such as the unsecured money market) that suffered during the Great Recession more than other intermediaries, such as hedge funds. This is true even though in the USA many of the problems arose in the non-bank sector, in particular because of the debacle of many ABS having real estate as underlying assets and because of the difference in regulation among different types of financial institutions. The concentration of problems in the banking sector during the Great Recession was due to the fact that banks are at the core of the financial system, where the tensions eventually end. This also explains

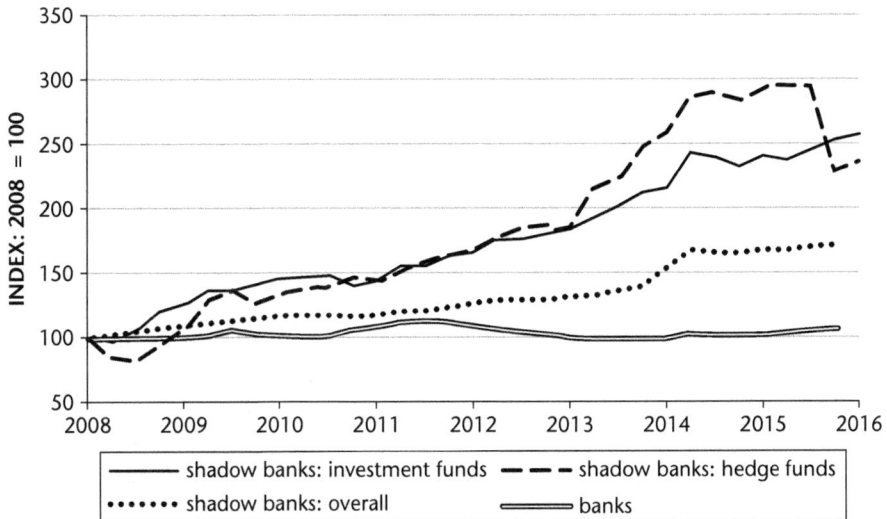

Figure 2.46 Increase in Shadow Banking in the Euro-Area, Index 2008=100 (2008–2016)
Note: Investment funds are calculated excluding money market funds.
Source: Drawn from the ECB Financial Stability Report. ECB and ECB calculations.

why, in the end, it was to a large extent central banks that had to counter the effects of the crisis, given their special relationships with and responsibilities for banks.[73] Ultimately, the holistic approach that central banks bring to financial stability is determined by their particularly intense relationship with banks that occupy a central position within the financial system.

2.2.2 Central Bank Action and Communication

Responsibility for financial stability fell back on central banks during the Great Recession because of their ability to provide liquidity quickly, without physical limitations, and due to their holistic view of the financial system, as well as of the economy.

In addition, the Fed, unlike the ECB until the Banking Union was established in 2014, had specific supervisory responsibility for most banks, which made it even more central in the effort to regain financial stability.

Actions of the two central banks in the financial stability domain can be classified in two main categories:

1. Actions affecting both price and financial stability, what one could call 'dual-purpose' actions.
2. Actions specifically targeted at financial stability, falling either in the micro or macro dimension.

The two types of measures are examined in turn, stressing their most salient characteristics rather than providing an exhaustive account.

2.2.2.1 'DUAL-PURPOSE' MEASURES

'Dual-purpose' actions were so numerous and so incisive that they inevitably influenced both price and financial stability. This is confirmed by looking, for instance, at chapter 3 of the IMF GFSR of October 2009, which dealt with the aftermath of the Lehman Brothers bankruptcy: most of the central bank measures there analysed were in the 'dual-purpose' category, addressing both monetary policy and financial stability issues. The fortunate coincidence during the Great Recession was that, at least in its initial phase (i.e. in the first few years after the bankruptcy of Lehman Brothers), the targets of price and financial stability largely coincided. The coincidence of actions needed to pursue both the price and the financial stability objectives under the impact of the crisis is not surprising, because the origin of the disturbances for both is to be found, as

---

[73] The sense that responsibility for financial stability fell, because of something similar to a gravity phenomenon, upon central banks is clearly visible in the account of the crisis by Bernanke (2015a, location 7175). In chapter 21 he writes: 'The reality was that the Fed was the only game in town. It was up to us to do what we could, imperfect as our tools might be.'

argued in Section 1.4.2, in a common phenomenon: the move from a 'good' to a 'bad' equilibrium. This put both the USA and the euro-area in quadrant IV of Figure 1.18, reported in Section 1.3, where no dilemma appears, as both too low risk appetite and too low inflation require monetary expansion. Thus, what the two central banks did to contrast the consequences of this move had a beneficial effect on both objectives, until the very low level of interest rates started to create risks for financial stability, as it will be explored in Chapter 3.

Consistently with the considerations above about 'dual-purpose' measures, many of the monetary central bank actions examined in Section 2.1.2 can be looked at here from a financial stability perspective.

Central banks could address, but not fully resolve, with their dual-purpose measures, the following three financial stability consequences of the Great Recession, among those mentioned in Section 2.2.1:

1. Evaporation of both market and funding liquidity, as well as liquidity hoarding by banks.

2. Repeated episodes of disproportion between banks' increased risk and depleted capital, because of large losses, followed by long periods of capital reconstitution.

3. Huge increase in interest rate spreads brought about by dysfunctional markets.

Specifically, the price stability-oriented actions illustrated in Section 2.1.2 to deal with the evaporation of liquidity and liquidity hoarding also attenuated the effects of these developments on financial stability. In fact, if central banks, in their provision of an 'elastic currency' had not financed the gap that had appeared in bank balance sheets, a wave of bank failures would have materialized, with systemic instability consequences. Again, the way to visualize this action is that central banks brought onto their balance sheet the intermediation that the private sector was no longer able to perform at a cost the economy could afford. As mentioned, this intermediation was carried out, according to Diamond–Dybvig pricing, at rates that were penalty rates (as required by Bagehot, 1873) compared with 'good' equilibrium prices, but cheaper than the prices that the market generated during the 'bad' equilibrium. This pricing pattern not only reduced moral hazard, it also reduced the risk of financial losses for central banks: if, also thanks to their actions, the market moved back towards 'good' equilibrium prices, the assets bought by central banks would recover their value, bringing banks gains rather than losses.

Of course, as already recalled, a very serious practical difficulty emerged in providing banks with huge amounts of liquidity during the Great Recession. In crisis conditions, the actual distinction between insolvent and illiquid institutions becomes much more difficult to discern. Conceptually, the prescription is clear: the central bank should provide liquidity only to banks that would be solvent in normal, non-crisis, conditions, but risk failing because of the move from the 'good' to the 'bad' equilibrium. However, the translation of this concept into practice is plagued by the need to make all sorts of assessments and even judgements, with a high degree of subjectivity, which an analytical approach can reduce, but not eliminate. In addition, to assess whether a bank would be sound in a 'good' equilibrium, the central bank has to move from the single institution to the entire financial system, as spill-overs and linkages are no longer an important part of the story, but are basically the entire story.

A partial solution to the problem of lending to banks whose solvency was not beyond doubt was provided by the fact that part of the liquidity was supplied by the central bank under the form of Lending of Last Resort narrowly defined. It was argued previously, in Section 2.1.2, that the concept of Lending of Last Resort has two variants, a macro and a micro variant. The macro variant would be better called provision of an 'elastic currency', leaving the use of the term Lending of Last Resort only for the micro variant. In the ECB terminology, the micro variant of Lending of Last Resort is denominated Emergency Liquidity Assistance (ELA). At the Fed, the same activity normally goes under the name of discount window,[74] which is extended against good collateral. However, to deal with the impact of the failure of Lehman Brothers, the Fed also lent under the exceptional window, covered under Section 13(3) of the Federal Reserve Act, allowing emergency lending.

At both central banks, Lending of Last Resort, in the micro variant, was qualitatively critical, because it addressed the problems of specific financial institutions, yet remained contained as a share of the total liquidity provision. In a way, Lending of Last Resort to individual institutions can be seen as something intermediate between dual-purpose measures, addressing both price and financial stability, and actions specifically targeted at financial stability.

Dual-purpose measures also helped deal with the second financial stability consequence of the Great Recession mentioned earlier in this section, namely the disproportion between banks' increased risk and depleted capital, because of large losses.

---

[74] From the website of the Federal Reserve Board, <https://www.federalreserve.gov/monetarypolicy/discountrate.htm>: 'The Federal Reserve Banks offer three discount window programs to depository institutions: primary credit, secondary credit, and seasonal credit, each with its own interest rate. . . . Under the primary credit program, loans are extended for a very short-term (usually overnight) to depository institutions in generally sound financial condition. Depository institutions that are not eligible for primary credit may apply for secondary credit to meet short-term liquidity needs or to resolve severe financial difficulties. . . . The discount rate charged for primary credit (the primary credit rate) is set above the usual level of short-term market interest rates. (Because primary credit is the Federal Reserve's main discount window program, the Federal Reserve at times uses the term "discount rate" to mean the primary credit rate.)'

Central banks, of course, could not provide capital to banks. They did, however, help them move towards a better equilibrium between capital and the risk-weighted balance sheet through their QE purchases, which increased the price of assets held by banks.

In addition, they helped forestall fire sales that would have bankrupted banks. Indeed, Bindseil et al. (2016) convincingly make the point that fire sales by stressed banks and recourse to central bank funding are substitutes as emergency liquidity sources. By providing liquidity to banks, central banks granted them time to re-establish a more adequate balance between asset size and capital; they were also able to sell assets at prices closer to the 'good' equilibrium. The partial substitutability between liquidity provision by central banks and fire sales is obvious, accepting Bindseil et al.'s (2016) measurement of liquidity as 'as the fire sale discounts to be accepted in case a certain quantity has to be sold in the shortest possible period of time'. Of course, by providing liquidity, central banks ran the risk that the needed recapitalization process would be unduly slowed down. This indeed happened in the euro-area, partly because the pressure on banks to recapitalize was delayed in this jurisdiction.

Dual-purpose actions also helped to address the third financial stability consequence of the Great Recession mentioned earlier in this section, that is, the huge increase in interest rate spreads brought about by dysfunctional markets. This made it necessary the partial transfer of the intermediation function from the private sector to the central bank. This transfer was most visible in the substitution of the unsecured interbank market with the ECB balance sheet, illustrated in Section 2.1.2, but is equally visible in the foreign exchange swaps between central banks, presented in Section 2.1.3, and in the provision by the Fed, in the first phase of the crisis, of lending facilities extended to various sectors of the private financial market (as illustrated in Box 13). The transfer of intermediation activity from the private sector to the central bank can also be recognized in the purchase of government securities by the ECB during the European phase of the crisis. Some sovereign borrowers in the euro-area periphery were charged such a high cost for their debt that they would have become insolvent. Given the link between banks and their sovereign, the insolvency of the latter would have brought about the insolvency of the former as well as systemic instability. At the same time, the private sector greatly increased its demand for ECB liabilities, under the guise of bank reserves. Thus, the ECB de facto intermediated funds between lenders, which were only willing to lend sizable amounts to it, and sovereign borrowers in the periphery, which could not find the funding they needed at prices they could afford and that were not distorted by the shift to a 'bad' equilibrium.

2.2.2.2 MICRO- AND MACRO-PRUDENTIAL MEASURES

As mentioned, the action of the two central banks aimed at regaining financial stability was not limited to 'dual-purpose' measures; their actions also extended to micro- and macro-prudential measures. The action in the prudential field was significantly more extended for the Fed than for the ECB. This derived from the fact that the Fed had traditionally carried out supervisory functions, whereas these functions could only be exercised by the ECB at the beginning of November of 2014, when the crisis was already seven years old.

Central banks, in their micro- and macro-supervisory function had a four-fold responsibility:

1. Draw lessons from the crisis and adapt regulation accordingly.
2. Dissipate the veil of opacity that was affecting banks, thus making it more difficult to assess their different degrees of financial solidity.
3. Help banks regain the ability to adequately fund the economy.
4. Make sure that banks would carry out the necessary corrections in their strategies and operations.

Although the illustration of the regulatory changes enacted during the Great Recession requires a treatment of its own and, in any case, was an activity in which central banks did not have a dominant role, it is useful to consider here the most important, sort of emblematic, actions of the Fed and the ECB under the three other supervisory responsibilities mentioned above. An illustration of these supervisory activities will put into relief the vast dimension of the financial stability task loaded onto central banks, and its impact on the central bank model that prevailed before the Great Recession.

Among the many actions of the Fed in the financial stability domain during the Great Recession, the one requiring the most intense effort and producing the most important results was the so-called stress test.[75] This stress test built on the supervisory experience of the Fed, but went well beyond any exercise carried out before the crisis. US Treasury Secretary Geithner announced the stress test on 10 February 2009, but it was the Fed, as the most important supervisor, that led it. From February to May 2009 the exercise went on, covering the 19 largest American-owned banks (BHC—bank holding companies), representing two thirds of the assets of the US banking system. The stress test was a fully integrated macro/micro exercise, with economists and bank examiners working together.

---

[75] As it often happens, the clumsier official name—SCAP—was soon forgotten and only the shorter one recalled in the text was maintained. The exercise is described in two Fed publications: Fed (2009a; 2009b). The SCAP gave way in subsequent years to a yearly, broader CCAR—Comprehensive Capital Analysis and Review.

More than 150 examiners, supervisors and economists from the Federal Reserve, Office of the Comptroller of the Currency, and Federal Deposit Insurance Corporation participated in this supervisory process.

(Press release of Fed, 24 April 2009)

[The resulting capital need] estimates benefit from the input of extremely detailed information collected from each of the 19 BHCs, the extensive review and analysis of that information by the SCAP teams and the judgment of supervisors and other experts. The breadth and depth of the resources brought to bear in formulating these estimates are unparalleled.... the SCAP is considerably more comprehensive than stress tests that focus on individual business lines, because it simultaneously incorporates all of the major assets and the revenue sources of each of the firms.

By ensuring that these large BHCs have a capital buffer now that is robust to a range of economic outcomes, this exercise counters the risk that uncertainty itself exerts contractionary pressures on the banking system and the economy.

(Overview of results, May 2009, pp. 1–2)

As mentioned in Section 2.2.2, the Fed's Stress test is not generally considered as belonging to macro-prudential measures. Tools typically considered to be micro-prudential were used in this activity, like a granular review of the loan book, and onsite examinations as well as off-site reviews. However, its extension, its emphasis on the system rather than on individual institutions, and its clear macroeconomic framework also gave it a definite macro-prudential character.[76]

In terms of objectives, it is clear that the stress test aimed at discharging three of the responsibilities mentioned above, namely: dissipating the veil of opacity which was affecting banks, re-establishing their ability to fund the economy, and ensuring banks would carry out the necessary corrections in their strategies and operations.

The 2009 stress test brings into sharp relief three considerations crucial to evaluating the impact that the renewed responsibility for financial stability imparted on the Fed, and more generally on central banks.

The first consideration is that, as one could expect, the Fed acted as a part of the US administration. The very fact that the stress test began with an announcement of the Treasury Secretary, could end, if necessary, with a recourse to treasury money, but that it was led by the Fed proves that the central bank was not isolated but participated in a collective effort with the US government to deal with the crisis. Of course, this was facilitated by the fact

---

[76] This point is also made by Constâncio (2015): 'The macroprudential policy function has added a new dimension to stress testing going well beyond the examination of individual bank results. Enhancements in the macro stress testing framework are underway . . . Furthermore, efforts are being made in the direction of going beyond banks and integrating, to the extent possible, the shadow banking sector in the broader framework. These steps are necessary to provide the macro dimension to stress testing exercises and make them fit for macroprudential policy use.'

that the new Treasury Secretary of the Obama administration was Timothy Geithner, the former President of the Federal Reserve Bank of New York (FRBNY). The collaboration between the Fed and the administration seems obvious when considered in itself, but it is less obvious when comparing it to the experience of the ECB, which did not entertain collaboration with governments, at least until very late into the crisis, if at all. Furthermore, it is not clear that the embedment of the Fed within the administration would have been consistent with some extreme interpretations of central bank independence prevailing in Europe, according to which a weak government is welcome as it contributes to central bank independence.

The second consideration, adjacent to, but distinct from the previous one, is that the Fed did not enact the stress test using private law contracts but rather statutory tools. The Fed did not provide incentives to banks, by means of appropriate financial contracts like refinancing agreements, to behave in the desired way: it imposed the desired behaviour. The words of Bernanke (2015a, ch. 18, location 5820) are very explicit in this respect:

> [W]e told the banks that they had six months to raise enough capital to allow them to remain viable and continue to lend normally, even in the adverse scenario. If they were unable to raise the required capital from private markets within six months, they would have to take capital from the TARP under conditions imposed by the Treasury.

The third consideration is that in the stress test, and more generally in its action during the Great Recession, the Fed closely followed the so-called 'Brave Plan'. This was not necessarily the case because its leaders had been leafing through the pages of Bagehot's 1873 book, in which the brave plan was exposed, but because of a dispassionate reading of the financial system. Bindseil (2014, p. 236) presents the 'Brave Plan' as follows:

> Risk Endogeneity. Bagehot also provides a further different perspective on liquidity support and central bank risk taking by arguing that supportive liquidity provision would be necessary to minimize the central bank's eventual own financial risks because such measures would be the only way to prevent a financial meltdown and any accompanying massive losses for the central bank. Bagehot explicitly writes: '(M)aking no loans as we have seen will ruin it (Bank of England); making large loans and stopping, as we have also seen, will ruin it. The only safe plan for the Bank (of England) is the brave plan, to lend in a panic on every kind of current security, or every sort on which money is ordinarily and usually lent. This policy may not save the Bank; but if it does not, nothing will save it.' In other words, the riskiness of exposures would itself be endogenous to the central bank measures, and hence more liberal central bank policies could imply lower financial risk taking than more conservative policies. This insight opens a very different perspective on central bank risk taking in times of financial crisis.

The Fed was fully aware that the equilibrium in the market depended on its actions. The paradigm of 'exogenous risk factors' that a private financial institution takes in managing risk, analogous to the 'small country assumption' in international economics whereby international prices are exogenous to the action of the 'small country', was totally inadequate for the central bank. Prices in the financial market clearly depended on the action of the central bank. In particular, if the central bank could move, through its action, the economy back to a 'good' equilibrium, it would not incur losses but rather profits on its monetary policy operations.

Bernanke (2015a) in his memoirs stresses that the back-up capital offered by TARP was critical in the stress test exercise. It provided a backstop in case of need, but also avoided the credibility gap that could result from the fear that bank capital holes would not be exposed in the stress test just because there would be no way to fill them if private sources were insufficient.

In the case of the ECB, the emblematic action in the financial stability domain was the AQR,[77] conducted in 2014, before the central bank took on the task of supervising the euro-area banking sector. Centralization of banking supervision in the ECB was, in turn, the only fully fledged component of, so-called, Banking Union, as illustrated in Box 16. No agreement to fully implement its two other components, that is, a single resolution mechanism (SRM) and a single deposit guarantee system, could be reached.

The AQR has some similarities, but also some important differences, with the American stress test.

An important similarity between the ECB AQR and the Fed stress test is the enormous size of the effort and the breadth of the exercise. The ECB reported that the AQR, which lasted 12 months and was concluded in the autumn of 2014, covered 130 euro-area banking groups, representing about 82 per cent of the total assets of the euro-area banking system, and involved approximately 6,000 experts from 26 national supervisors.[78] The ECB described AQR as follows:

> The execution of the comprehensive assessment required extraordinary efforts and the mobilization of substantial resources by all parties involved, including the national competent authorities of the participating Member States, the European Banking Authority, the ECB and the participating banks.   (ECB 2014b, p. 1)

Another important similarity is that, like the American stress test, the ECB AQR aimed at clarifying the financial health of banks and at putting them in conditions of appropriately funding the economy going forward. Indeed, in terms of transparency, the ECB exercise was arguably superior to that of the Fed.

---

[77] The official name of the ECB exercise was 'Comprehensive Assessment', and it included an AQR together with a stress test. Veron (2014) stresses the importance of this exercise in the euro-area context.

[78] ECB (2014b).

Box 16 THE EUROPEAN BANKING UNION

The Banking Union was created in response to the Great Recession, in particular when it morphed into the sovereign debt crisis in Europe. As described by Véron (2014), the 'trigger' for establishing the Banking Union was the 'deterioration of market conditions for euro-area sovereign debt that started in 2010 and accelerated in mid-2011, with the contagion then extending to large countries such as Spain and Italy' (pp. 1–2). What came to be known as a 'vicious circle' or 'doom loop' between the banking sector and the public finances of their sovereigns was driving further instability throughout the monetary union, even spilling over into EU countries not in the euro-area (see Shambaugh, 2012). As a result of this serious financial instability throughout the system, there was speculation about the future of the euro and even whether it would survive the crisis. In April 2012, during a hearing at the Committee on Economic and Monetary Affairs of the European Parliament, ECB President Mario Draghi addressed key issues concerning the financial crisis and its broader impact on the economy in Europe. In order to regain financial stability throughout the system, he called for strengthening banking supervision and the resolution of failed banks at the European level. At that time it had become increasingly apparent that banking supervision conducted on a national level, with varying standards, was no longer sustainable in a monetary union.

While the 'mismatch' between deeper integration and a fragmented supervision became evident as the crisis unfolded (Constâncio, 2013), already back in 1999, Executive Board Member (ECB) Padoa-Schioppa predicted that it would be necessary to provide 'the banking industry with a true and effective collective euro-area supervisor' (Padoa-Schioppa, 1999). The absence of a euro-area supervisor and financial backstop for banks helped create a situation in which many European banks were in a vulnerable position going into the crisis. According to Véron (2014), the weakened position of some banks was 'caused by uncontrolled balance sheet expansion and risk accumulation by European banks in the decade preceding the crisis, itself enabled by weak supervision'. Moreover, national supervisors 'lacked the instruments to contain private capital flows' (Constâncio, 2013). Therefore, over a decade after the euro was launched and several years into the crisis, it was no longer possible to postpone joint banking supervision at the European level.

A month after President Draghi's call for system-wide banking supervision, the European Commission formally declared the need for a European Banking Union to address threats to financial stability. By June 2012, the European Council decided to assign the task of banking supervision to the ECB, within a single supervisory mechanism (SSM); however, the relevant regulation was approved only in October 2013. The ECB, as mentioned in the main text of the book, was the only institution that realistically could quickly take on this responsibility. Still, it took nearly two and a half years between the decision to attribute supervision to the ECB and the time the SSM became fully operational, and more than three and a half years before the SRM would be put in place.

As noted by Véron (2014), the 'highly ambitious' transfer of banking supervision from the national to the European level is 'changing the structures of the European financial system' and 'has wide-ranging political implications'.

In October 2013, the ECB began a 12-month Comprehensive Assessment uniformly conducted on about 130 significant euro-area banks (see ECB Banking Supervision website). The assessment was viewed as a key step to prepare for the ECB to take up the role of the SSM; the assessment's purpose was to make bank balance sheets more transparent and to establish more consistent supervisory practices throughout the system. As explained on the ECB website, its main goals were:

transparency—to enhance the quality of information available on the condition of banks; *repair*—to identify and implement necessary corrective actions, if and where needed; and *confidence building*—to assure all stakeholders that banks are fundamentally sound and trustworthy.

ECB President Draghi declared: 'Transparency will be its primary objective. We expect that this assessment will strengthen private sector confidence in the soundness of euro-area banks and in the quality of their balance sheets.'

Market participants needed to be convinced about the soundness of the Comprehensive Assessment. Previous EU-wide stress tests of banks—conducted in 2009 and 2010 by the CEBS and another one in 2011 by the EBA—lacked not only the financial backstop but also the resources and authority necessary to perform thorough tests. Thus, they relied heavily on reports from national supervisory authorities, which were found, in many cases, to be neither sufficiently robust nor consistent across countries. The ECB had a hard time convincing market participants that this time, under the SSM, more rigorous procedures and standards were in place, as well as sufficient staff dedicated to the task. A year later, in October 2014, the results of the Comprehensive Assessment were published by the ECB (see ECB website). Eighty-two per cent of the euro-area banking system was covered, including significant credit institutions, financial holding companies, or mixed financial holding companies. Conducting the Comprehensive Assessment was a massive undertaking, involving approximately 6,000 individuals from the ECB, the EBA, and 26 national supervisory authorities. The banks assessed were located in 19 countries (the 18 countries using the euro at the time, plus Lithuania, which was expected to adopt the euro in January 2015). The assessment had two main components:

(1) **AQR** intended to enhance the transparency of bank exposures, such as the adequacy of assets and collateral valuation.

(2) **Stress test** to evaluate the resilience of banks' balance sheets, jointly conducted with the EBA. The test sought to analyse how a bank's capital position was likely to develop over three years, under both baseline and adverse scenarios.

Results from the AQR and the stress test were then integrated into a 'join-up', the first time such an exercise was implemented in Europe. Findings from the AQR were incorporated into the stress tests of each bank by adjusting their initial balance sheet positions. A key aim was to ensure that each bank had a sufficient capital and liquidity buffer in the event of a crisis. Joining and reinforcing the 'point-in-time AQR' with the 'forward-looking stress test', was an attempt to strengthen the entire assessment (see ECB website).

Ultimately, the Comprehensive Assessment provided an aggregate disclosure of the outcomes, both at a country and at a bank level, along with possible recommendations for supervisory measures. In general, the process of banking supervision is an ongoing cycle of regulatory and supervisory policies intended to guide the development of various methodologies and standards for supervising banks across the euro-area. A Comprehensive Assessment (often referred to as an AQR) is now produced annually on selected euro-area banks (see ECB website for further details), and lessons learned throughout the process are intended to continuously improve banking supervision, thereby fostering greater financial stability throughout the whole system.

The Banking Union was launched with two basic components:

(*continued*)

Box 16 CONTINUED

-**SSM** to supervise all banks in the euro-area, including:

'significant' *banks* (approximately 130 banks, mainly the largest euro-area banks, but also several smaller 'high-priority' banks considered at-risk) are directly supervised by the ECB, accounting for over 80 per cent of euro-area banking assets; and

all other 'less significant' banks (approximately 3,500 in total), supervised by national supervisory authorities—often the national central bank, but sometimes the task is shared with another authority which can also take a leadership role, depending on the country; see ECB website for details—under the oversight of the SSM.

- **SRM** to resolve any failing euro-area banks.

A third component could not yet be implemented, namely a **European Deposit Insurance Scheme (EDIS)** to protect depositors. Similar to the Federal Deposit Insurance Corporation (FDIC) in the US, EDIS, if enacted, would insure at euro-area level the retail deposits (up to an established amount, e.g., 100,000 euros) of individual account holders. It might also be possible for EDIS to reinsure national schemes. Provision of sufficient funding for such scheme is critical, and the difficulty of achieving this is holding back the enactment of this third component of a fully fledged banking union.

The SSM became fully operational in November 2014, at which time the ECB assumed full supervisory responsibility for all participating euro-area banks. Any EU countries outside the euro-area not participating in the SSM, which would like to, may enter a memorandum of understanding with the ECB to establish how their relevant national supervisors will cooperate with the ECB on banking supervision.

Concerning the decision-making process, the SSM has a Supervisory Board comprised of: a representative from each National Supervisory Authority (NSA)—if he or she is not from the NCB, a NCB representative may accompany the NSA representative on the Board, yet together they have only one vote—plus a chair, a vice-chair, and four additional ECB representatives. In order to ensure an operational link between the SSM and the rest of the ECB, the Vice-Chair of the SSM is also an ECB Executive Board Member.

The SRM regulation came into force in August 2014, thereby establishing uniform rules and procedures for resolving any bank failures, supported by the Single Resolution Fund (SRF). In December 2014, the EU Council appointed members of the Single Resolution Board (SRB) and adopted a methodology for bank contributions to the SRF. About a year later, in January 2016, the SRB became fully operational, determining whether and when to place a bank into resolution. At the same time, a framework was established for using resolution tools and the SRF. However, there are serious concerns about the sufficiency of the SRF to fund potential future bank failures (Véron, 2017).

Progress in the creation of the '**Single Rulebook**' (a term coined in 2009) was critical to achieving a banking union. In order to more efficiently regulate, supervise, and govern the financial sector in all 28 EU countries, the European Council established the Single Rulebook, which is primarily administered by the EBA. It aims to provide a 'single set of harmonised prudential rules on capital requirements, recovery, and resolution processes as well as a system of harmonised national Deposit Guarantee Schemes' (see EBA website). Harmonization, obviously, takes time and is complex when so many different countries are involved. Thus far, much progress has been made; nevertheless, a critical issue is that some countries must continue to amend their laws to make further progress on this front.

Current issues and future challenges

In a press conference on the ECB's 2016 AR on supervisory activities (see ECB website) **NPLs** were the headline feature. Nouy and Lautenschläger (2017) reported:

NPLs in the euro-area declined by €54 billion to a level of €921 billion between the third quarters of 2015 and 2016. As a result, the ratio of NPLs shrank from 7.3 % to 6.5%. Still, in some Member States, NPLs remain a big issue.

As noted in the main text of the book, NPLs are concentrated in peripheral countries, particularly Greece and Cyprus, but also Portugal, Ireland, Italy, and Slovenia (Angeloni, 2017). To address this serious issue, the ECB has issued guidance to banks and has asked them to devise and submit a strategy for reducing their NPLs. In some countries further regulatory and judicial changes are needed; these changes are obviously beyond the scope of the ECB, but continue to be advocated in order to improve harmonization across the euro-area. The ECB, through the SSM, is continuing to work with banks to refine their internal models for calculating the risk levels of their assets in order to make those models more accurate, consistent with international standards, and comparable across the euro-area. Higher capital ratios have also been called for (see ECB Banking Supervision press release website).

Another key issue, also documented in the main text of the book, is that **bank profitability** in the euro-area has been falling since the Great Recession, but unevenly across banks, according to Angeloni (2017).

The ECB has publicly advocated the **consolidation of the banking industry** across euro-area borders as well as within individual countries (see Nouy and Lautenschläger, 2017). The argument is that cross-border mergers could offer customers a wide range of services throughout the euro-area at banks that now have stringent and consistent standards. Banks, in turn, it is argued, would benefit from economies of scale in a larger market thus making them potentially more profitable. Some critics have questioned, however, whether it is the ECB's job to promote such consolidation and whether it would lead to less competition among banks and therefore actually be less advantageous for consumers; these are matters for further discussion and debate.

As noted by Véron (2017), with the creation of the Banking Union, there has been a 'tentative' shift away from the assumption of a public bail-out of creditors of failed banks towards burden-sharing (or bail-in) by private stakeholders and a 'partial' centralization of bank resolution decisions through the SRB and SRF.

To further advance banking supervision in the euro-area, Véron (2017) recommends a number of **future actions**:

- bank insolvency laws should be further harmonized and additional legislative reforms are necessary to make the bail-in framework more consistent across countries;
- regulations should be enacted to limit bank exposures to sovereign debt portfolios;
- risk-sharing is needed to prevent local bank failures form triggering a sovereign default, especially in smaller countries;
- enacting a deposit insurance scheme (such as EDIS);
- creating a financial backstop from the ESM for the SRB and EDIS;
- establishing the ability of the ESM to intervene when needed in 'precautionary bank recapitalizations'; and

(continued)

Box 16 CONTINUED

- ensuring smaller banks, only indirectly supervised by the ECB, are 'subject to consistently high prudential and supervisory standards without burdening them with unnecessary administrative requirements'.

Efforts to shore up several banks are underway. Once these cases are resolved, it would, according to observers such as Véron (2017), add credibility to the ECB's supervisory effectiveness, and signal 'the euro-area banking sector is still in need of considerable restructuring but no longer in a situation of systemic fragility (even though smaller banks in Italy and elsewhere remain a concern)'.

BANKING UNION TIMELINE (SEE ECB WEBSITE FOR FULL DETAILS
INCLUDING PRESS RELEASES)

April 2012	ECB President Mario Draghi, before the Committee on Economic and Monetary Affairs of the European Parliament, advocated strengthening banking supervision and resolution at the European level.
May 2012	European Commission called for a Banking Union and began making legislative proposals over the next several months.
June 2012	European Council (euro-area Heads of State or Government) decided to assign supervisory tasks to the ECB within an SSM. However, there were many steps over the course of more than a year before these tasks were formalized.
Sept. 2013	European Parliament formally approved the European Commission's legislative proposals regarding the SSM.
Oct. 2013	EU Council formally adopted the SSM Regulation. ECB, together with national supervisors, began a Comprehensive Assessment of the financial health of 130 banks.
May 2014	SSM Framework Regulation came into force, detailing the legal structure for cooperation between the ECB and national supervisory authorities within the SSM.
Aug. 2014	SRM regulation came into force, establishing uniform rules and procedures for resolving failed banks under the SRM.
Sept. 2014	ECB published a list of 120 'significant' banks it will directly supervise.
Oct. 2014	Results of the Comprehensive Assessment are published.
Nov. 2014	SSM became operational.
Dec. 2014	EU Council appointed members of the SRB and adopted a methodology for bank contributions to the SRF.
Jan. 2015	Lithuania became the 19th euro-area country, thereby automatically joining the SSM. The ECB began supervising three of its largest banks.
Jan. 2016	SRB became operational. A framework was established for using resolution tools and the SRF.

Ariana Gilbert-Mongelli

There were, however, two critical differences that affected the ECB exercise with respect to that conducted by the Fed.

The first difference relates to timing: the Fed exercise was started and terminated a few months after the failure of Lehman Brothers. The ECB exercise took place six years later, after three previous attempts had failed to convince the market that the banking system should be put on a definitively sounder basis. The Committee of European Banking Supervisors (CEBS) in 2009 and 2010 and its successor, the European Banking Authority (EBA), in 2011, carried out these early exercises. However, notwithstanding the important measures these two bodies took, such as the prescription to price-to-market sovereign exposures during the sovereign debt crisis, the market did not consider their stress tests fully credible for three reasons. First, the two bodies tasked to carry them out were given neither the legal authority nor the practical tools that were needed. Second, national bodies often acted more as champions of their banks than as credible supervisors, thus hampering the action of, first, the CEBS and then the EBA. Third, as it will be mentioned later in this section, the absence of a solid backstop affected the credibility of the exercises.

The delay in the decisive action to rehabilitate the euro-area banking system is reduced to five years if one counts the delay from the spark that started the European phase of the crisis, that is, the revelation of the true Greek deficit in the autumn of 2009. Still, it was far too long. Of course, one can explain the delay. The ECB was the only institution that could realistically take on the responsibility to supervise the euro-area banking system and effectively carry out the necessary cleaning work before taking this responsibility. But the Council of the EU decided to give to the ECB the task of supervising the euro-area banking system by launching a Banking Union only in the summer of 2012, and the decision was only formalized in the autumn of 2013. Then the ECB had to carry out, in the following 12 months, an extraordinary amount of work to prepare itself for the new task, including hiring hundreds of new employees and establishing the supervisory machinery. Explaining the delay in launching a decisive action to put the banking system on a sounder footing is not tantamount to saying that it did not have serious negative consequences, as will be seen in Section 2.2.3.

The second difference is that the ECB exercise, unlike the American one, had no solid backstop. This second difference is not independent from the first one, about timing. In the initial phase of the crisis, when TARP was decided, the policy, both in the USA and in Europe, leaned towards 'bailing-out', meaning using public funds when necessary to save banks from the risk of bankruptcy. This is what was indeed done in the initial phase of the crisis, mostly with national funds, except for countries under so-called Adjustment Programmes. In the later phase of the crisis, when the AQR took place, the pendulum had clearly moved towards 'bailing-in', meaning that not only equity holders but also lenders to banks should take the brunt of bank difficulties. The fact remains that the Fed stress test had a stronger backstop than the ECB AQR: the only mention of a backstop in the 'Aggregate Report on the Comprehensive Assessment' (ECB 2014b) aimed at reducing the role of public funds in any needed bank recapitalization.[79] In addition, there was no hint of possible European funds as a backstop, putting any possible burden on national treasuries, which, especially in the periphery, obviously had limited capacity to act as backstops.[80] The reluctance of the ECB to mention a euro-area backstop can be understood observing how extreme are 'the circumstances in which the ESM can also directly recapitalise sound banks'.[81] Five hurdles would have to be surpassed to get to this direct recapitalization: (1) no private source of capital should be available; (2) the bailing-in of 8 per cent of the liabilities of the bank, according to the Banking Resolution and Recovery Directive, should be insufficient to achieve the needed recapitalization; (3) the relevant national government could not recapitalize the bank; (4) the non-recapitalization of the bank would jeopardize the financial stability of the euro-area as a whole and of its member states; and (5) the decision to grant the direct recapitalization would have to be taken unanimously within the ESM. The contrast with the US situation could not be starker: in the US stress test banks were forced to take public funds if they could not recapitalize themselves in the market, whereas in the euro-area direct recapitalization could only take place in extreme circumstances. Market participants could not find reassurance about the existence of a European backstop given the hurdles just recalled. In addition, the absence of a European backstop

---

[79] 'In line with the November 2013 ECOFIN statement, capital shortfalls should in a first instance be covered by private sources. If this is revealed not to be sufficient or in the absence of access to sources of market financing, appropriate arrangements for recapitalising banks will be mobilised, including where appropriate resolution mechanisms and, if needed, through the provision of public funds (backstops). Any public support provided will be subject to the EU state aid rules. These rules ensure that the recourse to public backstops is significantly reduced through appropriate burden sharing arrangements.'

[80] With the coming into force, at the beginning of 2015, of the Bank Resolution and Recovery Directive in the EU, the ability of national government to support their banks was further limited, because the 'bailing-in' policy was given a strong legal basis.

[81] Strauch (2016) 'At the moment, the ESM provides a financial backstop for countries, should they suddenly need to inject money into the SRM. In extreme circumstances, the ESM can also directly recapitalise sound banks. At a later stage, we will need a common financial backstop. This could be a future role for the ESM.' The ESM can carry out so-called indirect recapitalization, as it did in the case of Spain, by lending funds to the sovereign, which can then on-lend them to the banks in need. Indirect recapitalization is, however, much weaker than direct recapitalization because the financial burden of the support remains with the national governments.

maintained the negative loop between the credit risk of a bank and that of its sovereign, documented in Section 2.2.1.

The absence of a solid European backstop can, of course, be explained: such a solution would have meant that the problems of banks in some countries, especially in the periphery, could unfairly burden governments, and ultimately tax-payers, in the core of the euro-area. More generally, the absence of a euro-area federal government that could take a decision similar to the one leading to the American TARP is the reason why there was no solid backstop behind the ECB action.

Explaining the absence of a solid backstop does not eliminate, however, the potential damage that this brought to the stress testing exercise. Markets had to be convinced that the ECB would not try to minimize capital needs because they could exceed the ability of national governments to provide a backstop. The overall credibility of exercises such as the American stress test or the ECB AQR depend both on the thoroughness of the exercise and on the availability of a solid backstop. The absence of the latter put an additional burden on the ECB to prove the former. Indeed, one sees the fear of the ECB that its exercise would not be viewed as credible transpiring from the numerous documents it published on this topic.

2.2.3 *Assessment*

An assessment of central bank action in the financial stability domain would require building a counterfactual of what would have happened if central banks had not done what they did. Such an assessment should be conducted both on the 'dual-purpose measures' and on the specific financial stability measures, including the two illustrated in Section 2.2.2.2. In addition, another counterfactual would be needed to determine what would have happened if central banks had done even more, or different things, from what they did. This endeavour is not attempted here and is probably close to impossible anyway. Still this section will try and shed some light on the assessment of central bank action in the financial stability domain. The tactics used will be to analyse the recovery of the American and euro-area banking system after the Great Recession hit them. In particular, what happened to indicators of bank soundness (i.e. profits, non-performing loans, capitalization, and ratings) will be assessed, but also, more importantly, what happened to the supply of credit during the Great Recession. Basically the question asked is: Over which time horizon and to what degree did banks reabsorb the consequences of the Great Recession (as illustrated in Section 2.2.1) and were again able to appropriately fund the real economy? Two standards of comparison, one across time and the other across jurisdictions, will be used to give a better perspective on the evidence offered:

1. How did banks perform in the USA and euro-area after they were hit by the Great Recession, compared to their performance before the onset of the financial crisis?

2. How different was the performance, after the onset of the Great Recession, between the euro-area and the US banking systems in terms of funding the real economy?

There are several obvious and important limitations in interpreting the exercise carried out on the basis of the tactics just presented as an assessment of the action of central banks in the financial stability domain. One limitation is that the ability of banks to recover from the Great Recession did not depend only on the financial stability actions of central banks: the actions of governments and banks themselves were also crucial. Furthermore, central bank actions in the monetary policy domain also had a strong effect on the rehabilitation of the banking sector:[82] in fact, as argued in Section 2.2.2.1, the 'dual-purpose' measures had an effect on both price and financial stability. Another factor is that the economic environment in which banks operated also had a critical importance for their ability to surpass the shock imparted by the Great Recession. Moreover, the role of banks is significantly more important in the euro-area than in the USA. A final limitation is that, specifically for the ECB, the task of supervising banks, an explicit financial stability responsibility, started to be exercised only at the end of 2014, seven years after the beginning of the Great Recession.

Still, what central banks did in the financial stability domain is important enough to take the timing and intensity of the rehabilitation of the banking sector as circumstantial evidence for the assessment of central banks in this area, even though the mentioned strong limitations have to be kept in mind.

Evidence about what happened to profits, non-performing loans, and capitalization with the appearance of the Great Recession has already been presented in Section 2.2.1. However, the perspective there was mostly a comparison between the periods before and after the beginning of the Great Recession. The perspective adopted here rather concentrates on what happened during the Great Recession: Basically, how fast and how completely did banks in the USA and in Europe recover from the hit suffered between August 2007 and September 2008?

In Figure 2.37 in Section 2.2.1.5 one sees that the return on assets of banks in the USA, in the euro-area, and in the rest of Europe worsened dramatically

---

[82] This is evident comparing the analysis carried out here with that of Cukierman (2016). Cukierman compares the recovery in bank credit in the United States with that in the euro-area, and attributes the slower pace of the latter to different modalities of liquidity provisions from the ECB with respect to the Fed.

in 2008. However, the profitability of American banks recovered quite robustly in subsequent years, whereas profitability in the euro-area worsened further and in the rest of Europe merely stabilized slightly above the lower level reached in 2008. In terms of profits it is seen in Figure 2.38, again in section 2.2.1.5, that, precipitously, at the onset of the Great Recession, the return on equity of euro-area banks moved from well above to well below banks' cost of equity. This phenomenon lasted for the subsequent seven years.

Figure 2.33, in Section 2.2.1.4, illustrated the persistent increase of NPLs in the euro-area, essentially due to the very grave deterioration in the periphery. In fact, in the periphery, NPLs increased from 2 per cent in 2007 to nearly 12 per cent by 2013, with limited improvement since. In the USA, instead, Figure 2.34 showed that the sharp deterioration at the beginning of the Great Recession was followed by a sustained recovery, eventually bringing the incidence of NPLs close to the level prevailing before the Great Recession.

The evidence about rating, presented in Figure 2.47, shows that banks in the USA and in Europe were progressively downgraded after the beginning of the Great Recession, but the deterioration was stronger and more persistent for European banks, particularly those from the euro-area periphery.

The overall evidence is that euro-area banks, especially those in the periphery, suffered a hit to their profitability and financial strength in the immediate

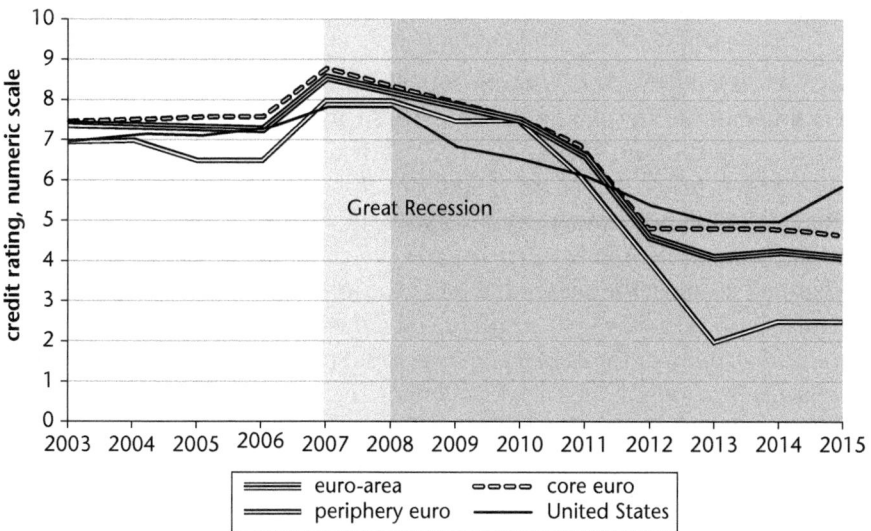

Figure 2.47 Ratings of Banks in the USA and in the Core and Periphery of the Euro-Area (2003–2015)

Note: The sample consists of the top ten banks within the USA and euro-area. The scale used to convert Moody's rating in numeric value is: 10 = Aaa, 9 = Aa1, 8 = Aa2, 7 = Aa3, 6 = A1, 5 = A2, 4 = A3, 3 = Baa1, 2 = Baa1, 1 = Baa3.

Source: Author's calculations with Bloomberg.

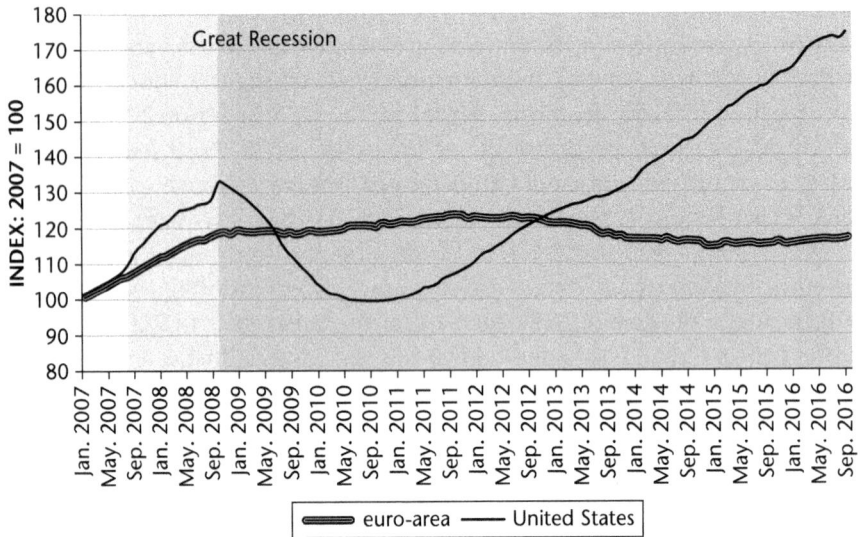

Figure 2.48 Stock of Bank Lending in the USA and in the Euro-Area, Index 2007=100 (2007–2016)

Source: ECB Statistical Data Warehouse and FRED, Federal Reserve Bank of St Louis.

aftermath of the failure of Lehman Brothers that was analogous to that of American banks; however, they recovered from it much more slowly and less completely.

Given this evidence, it is not surprising that bank credit developments have been different in the euro-area from those in the USA. As illustrated in Figure 2.48, in the euro-area there was a nearly decade-long stagnation. In the United States, instead, after the failure of Lehman Brothers there was a deep decline, followed, however, since the middle of 2010, by a sustained recovery.

It was seen in Section 1.4.2 that excessive credit growth before the Great Recession was one of the factors that led to the financial crisis. However, it is also true that financial instability hampers credit growth, which is an important indicator of the ability of the banking system to support the real economy with its intermediation. Indeed, the ECB definition of financial stability, fully reported in Section 1.3, says, *inter alia*: 'The financial system can be said to be stable if it is 'able to efficiently and smoothly transfer resources from savers to investors ...'.

Thus excessive credit growth can lead to instability, but meagre credit growth is also an indicator of financial instability. The optimality of the rate of growth of credit thus follows an inverted U, with either too low or too high growth being undesirable. Although credit growth is obviously the result of demand and supply changes, one would want to concentrate attention on the supply of bank credit as a more precise indication of the ability of banks to intermediate funds. The way to identify the separate effects of supply and

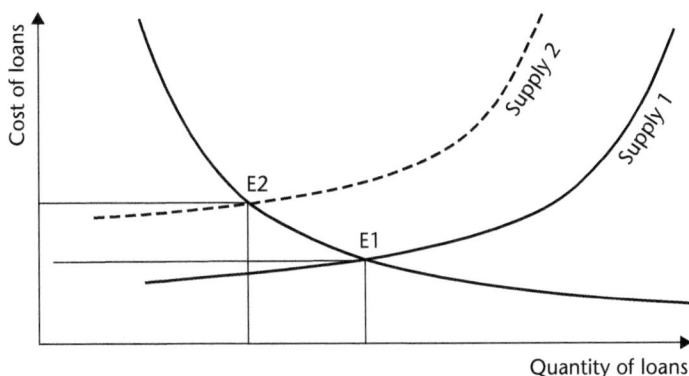

Figure 2.49 Schematic Identification of Lending Supply Shifts

demand is to consider the developments of the cost of bank intermediation jointly with its quantity.

Figure 2.49 clarifies this point. The identification of demand and supply shifts is facilitated when quantities go down and at the same time the price goes up, as in the move from equilibrium point E_1 to point E_2 in Figure 2.49. The only factor that can produce this joint change is a net shift of the supply curve, as in the move from Supply$_1$ to Supply$_2$.

Figure 2.50 translates the theoretical argument presented in Figure 2.49 into its empirical counterpart, presenting the cost of bank credit in the euro-area as measured by the interest rate margin, that is, the spread between the cost of loans and the remuneration of deposits.

Figure 2.50 shows that the cost of bank credit during the Great Recession was particularly unstable as it came down unevenly between 2007 and the end of 2012, but jerked up subsequently during the most acute phase of the crisis in Europe.

The phenomenon is particularly evident comparing the situation in a core country of the euro-area, such as Germany, to that in a peripheral country, such as Spain, as reported in Figure 2.51.

The cost of bank credit was significantly lower in Spain than in Germany before the Great Recession, but then, in the most acute phase of the crisis in Europe, the cost of bank credit in Spain more than doubled, while remaining practically unchanged in Germany. It was seen in Section 1.4.2 that real rates of interest were lower in the periphery of the euro-area than in the core in the first years of monetary union, due to the introduction of the euro and to the asymmetric reaction of the real and the financial side of the economy. The evidence of Figure 2.51 shows that lower bank margins also contributed to cheaper bank credit in the periphery until the European phase of the Great Recession, when margins rose dramatically.

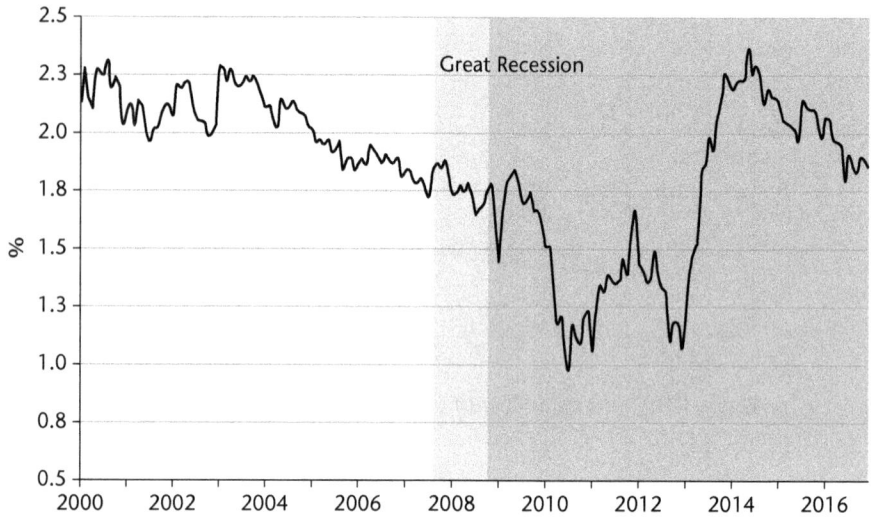

Figure 2.50 Spread between Lending and Deposit Rate in the Euro-Area (2000–2016)
Source: ECB Statistical Data Warehouse.

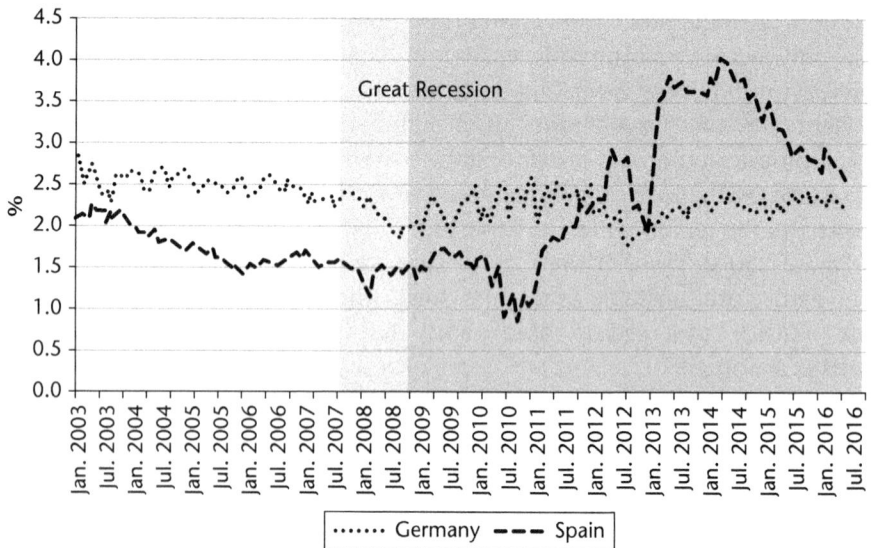

Figure 2.51 Spread between the Bank Lending and Deposit Rate in Germany and Spain (2003–2016)
Source: ECB Statistical Data Warehouse.

Overall, the evidence shows that the impairment of bank intermediation in the euro-area lasted for at least eight years after the start of the Great Recession. In the USA, instead, recovery was already taking place in 2010. Thus, both standards of comparison mentioned at the beginning of this chapter—the temporal one between what happened during the Great Recession and the previous situation, and the geographical one, between the USA and the euro-area—show that the recovery of financial stability in Europe, as indicated by the ability of the banking system to intermediate an adequate amount of funds at reasonable prices, was far from satisfactory for a long period of time, unlike in the USA.

While, on the face of this conclusion, the assessment would be much more favourable for the Fed than for the ECB, the fact should be recognized that the euro-area was subject, much more than the USA, to two waves of stress: first Lehman, then Greece. In addition, the five limitations about the exercise carried out in this section have to be recalled. One seems particularly important: the ECB was given the responsibility to use specific, statutory-based, financial stability-oriented tools only some seven years after the beginning of the crisis. Until then the responsibility was on national supervisors, which were jealous of their powers and, as mentioned, often defended their champions instead of forcing their banks to adjust. This fact has to be seen in conjunction with the consideration that was stressed when discussing the SCAP stress test carried out by the Fed: unlike the ECB, the Fed acted as a component of the government and its action was clearly coordinated with that of other branches of the executive, in particular the Treasury Department and other regulatory-supervisory institutions.

The responsibility for the delayed and incomplete recovery of the euro-area banking system is therefore to be found in the double whammy hitting it (Lehman first and Greece second) and in the incomplete design of monetary union in Europe. Until deemed not further acceptable due to the Great Recession, as mentioned in Section 1.4.3, the responsibility for banking supervision and whatever financial stability policies existed were left at national level. Thus, while on the face of it, the record of the ECB in the financial stability domain is clearly less satisfactory than that of the Fed, the responsibility for this should be found, rather than in the actual behaviour of the ECB, in the fact that the effects of the Greek-induced crisis hit banks already weakened by the consequences of the Lehman failure and in the limitations of the institutional design of the EMU. One way to summarize this latter point is that Banking Union in the euro-area was both late and incomplete: of the three components of Banking Union, namely single supervision, single resolution, and single deposit guarantee only the first one has been completely achieved, but even that was only seven years after the Great Recession had started. In addition, the ECB had not gone through financial crises before, nor had it had the opportunity to think through these types of issues as deeply as the Fed had had over time.

3

Central Banking after the Great Recession

3.1 Hits to the Pre-Crisis Central Bank Model

Bernanke (2015a)[1] expressed the overall shared conclusion that:

> the view is increasingly gaining acceptance that without the forceful policy response that stabilized the financial system in 2008 and early 2009, we could have had a much worse outcome in the economy.   (p. 87)

However, 'the forceful policy' carried out by central banks also delivered six hits to the pre-crisis central bank model. The six 'hits' are illustrated below.

The first hit impacting that model was the renewed responsibilities of central banks in the area of financial stability. The main reason for this conclusion is that it was no longer possible to maintain the same cavalier attitude towards financial stability that was prevailing before the Great Recession. Bernanke (2015a) vividly expressed this concept when he wrote:

> Central banks, not just in the USA but around the world, have been through a very difficult and dramatic period, which has required a lot of rethinking about how we manage policy and how we manage our responsibilities with respect to the financial system. In particular, during much of the [post-]Second World War period, because things were relatively stable, because financial crises were things that happened in emerging markets and not in developed countries, many central banks began to view financial stability policy as a junior partner to monetary policy. It was not considered as important. It was something to which they paid attention, but it was not something to which they devoted many resources. Obviously, based on what happened during the crisis and the effects we are still feeling, it is now clear that maintaining financial stability is just important a responsibility as maintaining monetary and economic stability.   (pp. 121–2)

---

[1] A similar point was made by Rajan (2013).

The attribution of heavier responsibility to central banks in the financial stability domain created inconsistencies with the pre-Great Recession central bank model in two areas. The first inconsistency was that the central bank could no longer carry out its functions nearly exclusively by means of market tools. Instead, statutory tools were required. Indeed the only, or at least the most important, obligation imposed by the central bank on private agents, specifically banks, for monetary policy purposes was the holding of a certain amount of compulsory reserves. Furthermore, as the example of the Bank of England showed, this obligation could be easily transformed into a voluntary agreement between the central bank and individual banks. The tools to pursue financial stability, instead, are mostly of a statutory nature. For example, constraints on bank lending in terms of loan-to-value or loan-to-income ratios or dynamic capital charges are based on legal obligations, unlike repurchase agreements and sales and purchases of securities (the most important tools of monetary policy operations) that are based on private contracts. The exercise of statutory tools is intrinsically dependent on the authority of the state and does not fit easily with the model of an independent central bank used to influence the behaviour of agents through economic incentives rather than mandating a given course of action.

The second inconsistency is even more serious. As was seen in Section 1.3, two conditions should be fulfilled to avoid dilemmas in which a central bank may have to make the political choice between pursuing financial or price stability: (1) the two targets should be independent of each other and (2) there should be two different tools assigned to them. Neither of these conditions is fulfilled. As regards the first, the IMF as well as Brunnermeier and Sannikov (2014) convincingly argue that price stability and financial stability are intertwined (see Box 9). It is true, as argued by Lamfalussy (2010),[2] that price stability and financial stability objectives are not necessarily inconsistent. Indeed, often there is a positive interaction between them and the pursuit of price stability then coincides with the pursuit of financial stability. This is the situation that prevailed in the first years of the Great Recession, as argued in Section 2.2.2.1. The same conclusion can be reached about the relationship between the price stability and the growth/employment objectives, because it is often the case that the pursuit of one is consistent with the pursuit of the other. It is sufficient, however, to have occasional cases of inconsistency to necessitate arbitraging between the two objectives. Such arbitrage requires

---

[2] 'The key question on which I shall focus my remarks is whether the active involvement of central banks in crisis management puts at risk the two main achievements of the pre-crisis years: the priority given to stability-oriented monetary policy, and independence of the central banks.... The first is to disagree with the argument that by necessity, or at least frequently, there is likely to be a conflict between the pursuit of the objective of price stability and the central bank's crisis prevention, or crisis management, macroprudential duties' (pp. 7–9).

a policy decision that a technical, independent institution, such as a central bank, is not in the best position to make.

An ingenious attempt to overcome this dilemma is proposed by Borio (2014a). He argues that any possible conflict between the price stability and the financial stability objectives disappears if one takes a long enough horizon. He argues, consistently, that there is no need to alter the price stability objective of the central bank. In Borio's view, however, this does not mean that monetary policy should not be adjusted to take financial stability concerns systematically into account.

> The key concept is that of sustainable price stability. In crude terms this means extending the time horizon over which you target price stability from the medium to the medium-long run. Before exploring in more detail the risks of failing to adjust monetary policy frameworks along the lines suggested, it is worth asking an obvious question: do the adjustments call for a change in mandates? I would say 'definitely no'. No need to include explicitly a financial stability objective. (p. 15)

Of course, the same kind of argument can be made about the possible inconsistency between price stability and growth. But the problem is that the longer the time horizon over which the central bank has to achieve its objectives, the more difficult it is for the principal for which it acts, namely the entire constituency, to check whether the central bank is indeed complying with its remit. Just for the sake of argument, with a long run horizon of something like 10 years during which price stability has to be respected, the accountability of the central bank would become very soft: there could be persistent deviations from stability for a long period of time, thus making it difficult to ascertain whether in fact the central bank is complying with its mandate. Furthermore, once it appeared that the central bank was not complying, it would probably be too late.

As regards the second condition to avoid the central bank being confronted with dilemmas, the problem is that interest rate changes and macro-prudential tools affect both macroeconomic and financial stability conditions, as shown by the BIS in its 2015 Annual Report. In a way, it is not possible to separate the effects of changes in interest rate and the effects of macro-prudential tools on inflation from those on financial stability. In the assessment of the BIS, both monetary policy, identified with interest rate changes, and macro-prudential measures change the cost of financial intermediation and, through this channel, consumption and investment. The 'separation principle' whereby macroprudential policies should be the first line of defense against financial imbalances while monetary policy should simply be a backstop, responding to financial stability concerns only after macroprudential policies have done all they can is not convincing, according to this analysis. Indeed, the BIS argues: 'Experience suggests that the two sets of tools are most effective when used as complements, leveraging each other's strengths' (p. 75).

A possible inconsistency between price stability and financial stability objectives emerged in the late phases of the Great Recession. The argument was put forward that the maintenance of central bank interest rates at very low levels, reinforced by large increases in the balance sheet of central banks, mostly because of QE, risked creating the same financial stability risk that incubated the Great Recession.

No conclusive evidence relating to asset prices and credit developments has confirmed that indeed the insistence of central banks in easing monetary policy, until their inflation objective was reached, engendered financial stability risks. Neither was it possible to conclude, however, that no financial stability risk was brewing. In the face of more evident financial stability risks, the restrictive impact of macro-prudential measures on financial intermediation and thus on the recovery of price stability from a situation of too low inflation would have clearly created a dilemma for the central bank. In such a case, the central bank would be forced into an unnatural arbitrage between price and financial stability.

The second most important hit to the pre-crisis central bank model during the Great Recession was the blurring of the border between monetary and fiscal policy. The Fed and the ECB acted as they did during the Great Recession in compliance with their monetary policy mandate. Nevertheless, it is obvious that the dividing line between fiscal and monetary became more tenuous. Although inevitably, under all circumstances, monetary policy has some influence on the funding of the budget deficit, with the Fed and the ECB holding around 20 per cent or more of the outstanding public debt in their respective jurisdictions, this effect has taken a new dimension in the two areas.

It was seen in Section 1.1 that during the Great Recession the increase in the ratio between the size of the balance sheet of central banks and GDP resembled the ratio prevailing on the occasion of the two world wars. However, the situation has been very different in terms of inflationary consequences, which were acute during the two world wars but non-existent during the Great Recession. This difference is consistent with what was seen in Section 1.2.2 regarding the breakdown of the Friedmanian chain-link between the monetary base, monetary aggregates, and inflation. Moreover, the exceptional expansion of central bank balance sheets, largely caused by the purchase of government securities, obviously was not put in place with the intention of favouring the funding of government deficits, but rather in the pursuit of price and financial stability. Still, central bank action de facto significantly helped the funding of the public deficit. Indeed, the clearest channel through which QE affected the real economy was the so-called portfolio balance effect. By reducing the yield on the securities bought under the QE programmes,[3] investors were pushed to purchase riskier as well as foreign securities, thus providing cheaper finance to riskier sectors of the economy and pushing the exchange rate down. In a way, central banks have become too important players on the market for government securities in the USA and the euro-area, but also in the UK and Japan, to maintain that there is strict separation between fiscal and monetary policy.

One way to confirm this conclusion is to note that national treasuries could have done something close to what central banks did with their QE. This was an important change with respect to the past, in which there was only very limited substitutability between central bank and treasury action. As argued in Sections 2.1.2 and 2.1.4.3.2, QE worked by substituting bonds, and particularly sovereign bonds, in the portfolios of investors, with a much shorter duration asset, namely liabilities of the central bank in the form of bank reserves. It was also argued that if treasury bills instead of bonds had been bought under QE, very little effect would have been generated because their characteristics are very similar to those of bank reserves. Symmetrically, the treasuries could have substituted bonds with treasury bills in their funding, engendering a 'portfolio balance effect' similar to that of QE. If treasuries in their funding policies could do what central banks did under QE, it is clear that the neat separation between monetary and fiscal policy was blurred.

Reinhart and Sbrancia (2011) have forcefully made an additional point: financial repression has historically been an important factor in reducing excessive debt, particularly government debt. While no obvious measures, other than those in Greece, were visible during the Great Recession to deal with debt that would fall in the Sbrancia and Reinhart categorization of financial repression, there is one development as well as a risk that raise worries in this area.

The development, visible in the euro-area periphery, was that the abundant liquidity provision from central banks led banks to purchase large amounts of securities issued by their own sovereign. While there is no definitive evidence that this was forced on banks, the phenomenon was just too large not to be noticed, as about 10 per cent of total banking assets in Italy and Spain in 2015 (Affinito, Albareto, and Santioni, 2016) was invested in public sector debt.

---

[3] See Section 2.1.4.3.2. The effect of the Fed QE between 2008 and 2012 was estimated by Kaminska and Zinna in 140 basis points for ten-year Treasury bonds. In the euro-area, according to the estimates of R. A. De Santis, the effect of ECB policy was to reduce the GDP-weighted ten-year euro-area sovereign yields up to October 2015 by 63 basis points, with the vulnerable periphery countries benefiting most. Most of the impact in the euro-area occurred between September 2014 and February 2015. A more thorough examination of the effects of QE is in Section 2.1.4.3.2.

The risk is that, although no situation of fiscal dominance has been created as yet, whereby monetary policy is subjugated to the funding needs of the government, governments may try to resist a reduction of the involvement of central banks in the sovereign bond market. The risk may come particularly at a time when the central banks would want to reduce their holdings of government securities accumulated during QE, as the need to maintain an exceptionally easy monetary policy recedes. At a time when the yield on government securities would recover towards higher levels, the request by governments to central banks not to aggravate the move by reducing their holding of sovereign bonds could become particularly pressing.

The third hit to the pre-crisis central bank model during the Great Recession—applying to both the Fed and the ECB, but to the ECB with particular force—was the risk of engendering moral hazard. As discussed in Section 2.1.2, central banks had to step in to attenuate the grave consequences that a shift from a 'good' to a 'bad' equilibrium would have brought about, directly for banks and indirectly for the economy, in both the USA and the euro-area, and for sovereigns in the latter case. Still, it was clear that these interventions were made necessary by the fact that some banks as well as some sovereigns had put themselves into a dangerous zone. They made themselves prone to the risk of an equilibrium shift. By fighting the consequences of the equilibrium shift, central banks risked condoning imprudent behaviour. In so doing, as already seen in Section 2.1.2, central banks went well beyond the traditional Lending of Last Resort function and furnished 'an elastic currency', as stated in the Federal Reserve Act. The action of central banks in this area was further complicated by the fact that, in crisis conditions, it becomes much more difficult to distinguish between insolvent and illiquid banks. It requires judging whether a bank would be solvent in normal, non-crisis, conditions, that is, if the 'good' equilibrium was still prevailing. This complex exercise helps explain why central banks had to take on more financial stability responsibilities during the crisis and started to be given so-called macro-prudential duties.

In the euro-area, the shift to a 'bad' equilibrium also affected sovereigns that had run imprudent policies, in either the fiscal or the banking domain, leading to the fourth hit to the pre-crisis central bank model. The ECB also had to fight the consequences of this shift, which risked leading to the demise of the entire euro construction. The pressure on the ECB to act was made more acute by the fact that, in the design of the Maastricht Treaty leading to monetary union, there was really nothing that could substitute the no longer available exchange rate as a tool to deal with idiosyncratic shocks. In fact, the burden of providing a mutual insurance mechanism fell inexorably on the shoulders of the ECB, particularly at the beginning of the European phase of the crisis, before the temporary European Financial Stability Facility and then the permanent European Stability Mechanism were created. The Outright Monetary Transaction programme, announced in August 2012, was the tool to address the risk of a demise of the euro and the absence of an explicit mutual insurance mechanism. The obvious need to target this tool specifically to the countries in the periphery of the euro-area that had run imprudent, fiscal or supervisory, policies, however, raised further moral hazard problems.

Two factors attenuated the moral hazard consequences for banks and sovereigns. In the case of banks, central banks followed the Bagehot remit to lend freely but at 'high' rates, in the sense that they lent at rates higher than those that would have prevailed if the shift to a 'bad' equilibrium had not occurred, but lower than the market rates actually prevailing in the 'bad' equilibrium. This was called Diamond–Dybvig pricing in Section 2.1.2 and was illustrated in Box 15. For the ECB this was even more strongly the case when it lent through the so-called Emergency Lending Assistance facility, which carried an overcharge with respect to normal operations. In the case of the Fed, a clear example of lending at rates that were lower than market rates but higher than 'good' equilibrium levels was with the swaps provided to other central banks, as examined in Section 2.1.3 and illustrated in Box 13. Papadia (2013a) presents the pricing of the swaps as follows:

> Of course, the swaps were priced so that they would not attract banks in normal circumstances, and thus would have an effect on central bank balance sheets only in crisis conditions. Still, given the crisis, the pricing was convenient for banks, which indeed drew very large amounts of liquidity from central banks.

The proof that facilities were expensive under normal conditions is that the drawing from them ceased when the crisis situation eased.

Also in the case of sovereigns in the euro-area, Diamond–Dybvig pricing was applied to the purchases of sovereign bonds from peripheral countries. In fact the market price of these bonds was raised by the sheer prior communication that the ECB would buy these bonds, still this price was clearly lower than it would have been in a 'good' equilibrium.

The most important factor attenuating moral hazard in the case of sovereigns, however, was so-called macroeconomic conditionality. Accordingly, a country requiring special assistance through purchase of its bonds in the so-called Outright Monetary Transactions programme had to agree a macroeconomic adjustment programme with the relevant European and international institutions. This was done through the European Commission and the ECB, but also with the IMF. The three institutions came to be known as the 'troika', until the opprobrium connected to this term in some programme countries obliged the use of a blander name: the 'institutions'.

The fifth hit to the pre-crisis central bank model referred specifically to the ECB and consisted exactly in its participation to the so-called troika.[4] Initially this was necessary, but it carried its problems. In fact, the ECB found itself in the difficult position of being both the central bank of the country needing support and a member of the creditor institutions team. This also led the ECB to give its opinion on issues, such as fiscal or structural policies, well beyond its area of responsibility, thus moving beyond its technical expertise and wading into a fully political arena.

Overall, the blurred lines between fiscal and monetary policy, the extended Lending Of Last Resort, or better 'elastic currency' liquidity provision, and, in the euro-area, participation in the troika during the Great Recession led to the phenomenon, repeatedly occurring throughout history during crises, that central banks move much closer to the government. The neat separation between the political responsibilities of the government and the technical responsibilities of the central bank becomes more tenuous.

The closeness of the central bank to the government was, in some circumstances, a positive factor. For example, as was noted in Section 2.2.2.2, during the US stress test, the Fed acted as a part of the US administration, and this had a positive effect on the overall recovery of the American banking system. In the euro-area, instead, the stress tests that were conducted could not count on a back-stop (such as the one the Treasury offered in the USA), and as a result their effectiveness was affected.

The sixth and last hit on the pre-crisis central bank model during the Great Recession was the need for the ECB, and even more forcefully for the Fed, to take better into account the repercussions of their actions on the global economy. As discussed in Section 2.1.3, to effectively deal with the dislocations caused by the crisis, the Fed and the ECB, but also the central banks of some other advanced economies, had to reach beyond their normal sphere of action, namely lending national currency to national banks, to also lend foreign currencies or to foreign banks.

A summary way of expressing what has happened during the Great Recession is that central banks have been overburdened, in the USA and even more so in the euro-area, with tasks well exceeding their technical remit of ensuring price stability. Orphanides (2013) put the issue as follows:

Following the experience of the global financial crisis, central banks have been asked to undertake unprecedented responsibilities. Governments and the public appear to have high expectations that monetary policy can provide solutions to problems that do not necessarily fit in the realm of traditional monetary policy....

---

[4] Gros (2015) supports the view that the participation of the ECB to the troika raised problems.

Overburdening monetary policy may eventually diminish and compromise the independence and credibility of the central bank, thereby reducing its effectiveness in maintaining price stability and contributing to crisis management.   (p. 3)

3.2 Was the Pre-Great Recession Central Banking Model Jeopardized?

The question in the title of this section is the most crucial in this book. The model of central bank prevailing before the crisis was the result of a century-long quest for a monetary technology that would achieve two important objectives: on the one hand, be more efficient than the gold standard and avoid the sustained, even if not secular, inflation and deflation periods that affected that monetary technology; and, on the other hand, avoid the prolonged, and at times acute, price instability that had characterized the period after the gold standard was abandoned, around the First World War.

As discussed in Section 1.1, central banks have had shifting mandates in their multi-secular lives with the most pressing problem forcing itself to the top position in their hierarchy of objectives. Price instability was the most persistent problem for the decades following the First World War, and thus the control of inflation took precedence with respect to the other objectives to which central bank action was dedicated in the past, namely, financial stability, real growth, and the funding of the public deficit.

Practical experience, especially that of the Deutsche Bundesbank since the Second World War, as well as decades of economic analyses, have illustrated the advantages of an independent central bank pursuing the dominant objective of price stability, as seen in Box 2. In Europe, the search for monetary stability at the continental level gradually found its basis in the common control of inflation rather than in actions directly targeting exchange rate stability. The creation of the ECB, modeled on the Deutsche Bundesbank, marked the apex of that process, achieving the double objective of the monetary unification of Europe and the enshrinement at the constitutional level of an independent central bank, responsible for price stability. In the USA, the break of inflation, obtained with the forceful policy enacted by the then Fed Chairman Volcker between 1979 and 1982, once again established price stability as the main responsibility of the Fed, even without any institutional innovation.

From an institutional perspective, the technical and non-political task of identifying the best tools to achieve price stability fits well with the attribution, within a democratic set-up, of this task to an independent agency. The inflation targeting strategy, complemented by the interest rate based, Wicksellian approach to monetary policy, was further specified by the Taylor rule. Interest rates were controlled by means of an interest rate corridor, beautifully completing on the operational side the model that served advanced economies for decades before the Great Recession.

However, as argued in the previous section, the Great Recession delivered six hits to that model. The most serious hit came from the experience during the Great Recession that, contrary to what was hoped, advanced economies had not graduated from financial, and especially banking, instability and that price stability did not, by itself, assure financial stability. As a result, the objective of financial stability climbed again in the ranking of central banks' objectives, thereby creating potential dilemmas. Crockett (2011) was explicit in recognizing the difficulties of this development for the central banking model prevailing before the crisis:

> The adoption of financial stability as a major, and perhaps co-equal, responsibility of central banks significantly complicates the governance model, and for several reasons. First, there is no single, quantifiable, objective of financial stability that is as clear and understandable as that of price stability. Second, the related responsibilities are multifaceted. Maintaining independence for central banks will accordingly come under greater challenge once responsibility for financial stability assumes a more prominent role.

Furthermore, the need to fight the potentially disastrous economic consequences of the Great Recession, with its shift from a 'good' to a 'bad' equilibrium, forced central banks to look for a complementary tool, beyond the control of a short interest rate. The result was a huge increase in the size of the balance sheet of the central banks, which brought them very close to fiscal policy and to actions that raised moral hazard problems, with banks and, in the euro-area, with sovereigns.

In the euro-area a specific problem was the incomplete macroeconomic set-up designed in the Maastricht Treaty, which forced the ECB to take on the task to assure the survival of the euro and move into policy areas far from its specialized role and expertise.

Furthermore, central banks had to raise their sight from the national to the global economy.

Overall, both the Fed and the ECB, but also some other advanced economies' central banks, moved much closer to governments, in a way that was not fully in line with their independence, especially if that was interpreted in the rigid way more common in Europe.

As a consequence of these developments, the question now is whether the long history of central banks is at another critical juncture in which their ability to take 'shifting mandates' is again put to the test. In other words, has another epoch in central banking started?

This question can also be seen as part of a broader question, namely whether the general approach of market economies in a global system, organized around liberal principles, which seemed to be winning at the end of the last century, is at risk.

Although this book cannot answer this broader question, it should be noted that if the answer were positive, then the specific issue about the central bank model would become just a detail in a much wider epochal change: the destiny of central banks would be overwhelmed by much broader changes with vast and deep political implications. Implicitly, the arguments developed in this book, which ends up not proposing a radical change in the central banking model prevailing before the crisis, assume that we are not about to see an abandonment of the general approach that affirmed itself in the decades after the Second World War and brought economic and political progress to a large part of the world. Populist forces, it is assumed, will ultimately not prevail.

A significant hurdle has to be overcome before answering positively to the specific question raised in the title of this section, namely whether the central banking model that prevailed before the crisis has been jeopardized. Inflation had been exercising its nefarious effects well beyond the economic sphere, in Europe more than in the USA, for decades before a monetary technology to deal with it was invented that did not have the serious drawbacks of a commodity currency like the gold standard. The invention and then the diffusion of that technology was a long and difficult affair that seemed to finally have been completed at the end of the last century. The risk is that if the component in that technology of an independent central bank devoted to price stability is removed, the inflation evil that one might, wrongly, have thought definitely defeated might return. The negative experience of a number of emerging economies, still suffering from too high inflation, shows that price instability is always looming and has to be kept in check by an appropriate monetary policy.

The question in the title of this section does not apply only to the institutional set-up of the central bank; it also extends to strategic and operational issues: is the concentration on the interest rate when conducting monetary policy still appropriate? Should the inflation targeting approach be revised? Does the corridor approach to interest rate control remain the best operational set-up? Will this approach work as it did before the crisis?

Strategic and operational issues are easier to deal with than institutional ones. Indeed, the question about the continuing validity of the pre-crisis model based on an independent central bank devoted to price stability is the most difficult one. One can deal with it better by splitting it into two sub-questions. The first is whether what has happened during the Great Recession represents a permanent change or whether there will be, eventually, a return to the comfortable situation prevailing before the crisis. The second sub-question is whether one can devise adaptations of the model, without radically altering it, which would be enough to deal with the issues that arose during the Great

Recession. As long as the changes during the Great Recession are not permanent and as long as one can devise changes that adapt, as opposed to radically change, the model prevailing before the crisis, one can avoid the great cost of jettisoning it.

These two sub-questions will be dealt with in turn after considering strategic and operational issues in the next section.

3.3 Strategic and Operational Issues

As illustrated in Section 1.2.2, the evidence generated during the Great Recession has further weakened the empirical basis of the Friedmanian approach to monetary policy, while reinforcing the view that it is the interest rate that dominates monetary conditions. Indeed, the balance sheet tool was also used during the Great Recession to influence interest rate conditions, not in a revival of a quantitative approach to monetary policy. In fact central banks managed their balance sheet either to regain control of the short-term rate, or to re-establish an orderly relationship between the short-term rate used as an operational target by the central bank and longer/riskier rates that are more important for the macroeconomy, or to further ease monetary conditions when the lower bound was reached. There is thus no question of returning to a 'base money–monetary aggregate-inflation' approach à la Friedman. Wicksell's approach, albeit with the important complications that turned out to be necessary during the Great Recession, will remain the analytical framework for conducting monetary policy.

Similar considerations can be made for the Taylor rule: the basic idea that the interest rate targeted by the central bank should be changed as a function of the inflation and the activity gaps will continue to inform the conduct of monetary policy. However, the need to complement the Taylor rule with additional considerations, leading to a more comprehensive approach, has been confirmed during the Great Recession. In sum, the hope of reducing monetary policy to a simple, constant rule is no more valid now, given the experience of the Great Recession, than it was before it began.

Instead the Great Recession has inspired some adaptations to another component of the pre-crisis central bank model, namely inflation targeting. Basically two proposals have been put forward to change inflation targeting to take into account the experience during the crisis. As already mentioned in Box 4, a first set of proposals[5] would raise the targeted rate of inflation to something

---

[5] This proposal was made by Ball (2014) and also considered by Blanchard, Dell'Ariccia, and Mauro (2010) and taken up by many other economists.

like 4 per cent, instead of 2 per cent, which is the level prevailing in most advanced economies, among which are the United States and the euro-area.

According to a second set of proposals, the central bank should no longer target a rate of inflation but rather the price level or, in another variant, nominal GDP. The two proposals are examined in turn.

The rationale of the proposal to raise the target for the rate of inflation from 2 per cent to something like 4 per cent is straightforward. Ball (2014) puts it in the following words:

> The primary reason to raise inflation targets is to ease the zero-bound problem, the constraint on monetary policy arising from the fact that nominal interest rates cannot be negative. A higher inflation target raises the long-run levels of nominal rates, allowing larger decreases in rates before the zero bound becomes binding. This flexibility makes it easier for a central bank to restore full employment when an economic slump occurs.   (p. 1)

In arguing for this change, Ball goes quite a bit further than Blanchard, Dell'Ariccia, and Mauro (2010), who had put the issue more as a question than as a firm proposal, even if these latter authors were clearly leaning in favour of the change. They supported a careful cost–benefit analysis of the possible increase in the inflation target. In fact their list of costs very much overlaps with the one provided in Section 1.2, while the benefit would, again, essentially be the wider margin of manoeuvre to reduce rates in case of a recession.

To be conclusive, the cost–benefit analysis that Blanchard and others propose would have to be very precise, indeed arguably more precise than our empirical knowledge allows. It is easy to conclude that, qualitatively, a rate of inflation of 4 per cent carries more costs than one of 2 per cent, but precisely estimating these costs and comparing them with the benefit of more room to reduce rates in case of a crisis does not seem realistic. This is the same kind of message that was drawn from Figure 1.9, which showed that the rate of inflation at which per capita growth in advanced economies is maximized is between 0 and 5 per cent. However, it is nearly impossible to be more precise than this and say, for example, that 2 per cent is definitely better than 4 per cent, or vice versa.

However, a consideration that neither Ball nor Blanchard, Dell'Ariccia, and Mauro took into account arguably pushes the conclusion towards maintaining the current 2 per cent target. A back-of-the-envelope estimation shows that about a billion people in advanced economies have adapted to the convention that their central banks target a rate of inflation of 2 per cent, which central banks argue is the empirical equivalent of genuine price stability. Price stability is now a fundamental parameter around which economic and financial decisions are taken in advanced economies. The convergence of consumers' and firms' expectations onto this number took decades, and the determination of central banks to stick to this objective—even when the problem was not too high but rather too low inflation—is aimed at preserving this convergence, which has remarkable macroeconomic benefits. The flattening of Phillips curves in advanced economies at around 2 per cent, as documented in Box 3 is a sign of this convergence.

The attempt to shift expectations from 2 to 4 per cent would probably require a very long time, with the additional difficulty that the communication device of equating genuine price stability with a measured inflation rate of 2 per cent would no longer be available. The transition cost from one to the other target would likely be large. In addition, it may be difficult to convince economic agents that the change from one to another target level would not be followed by yet another change, with the risk that expectations would be persistently unhinged.

One way to summarize the argument is that the target at 2 per cent is, to some extent, a convention: the optimality of this level as opposed to a contiguous level cannot be demonstrated in a categorical way. But this is not to say that conventions, when they become widespread and firmly held, are irrelevant.

Finally, moving the target from 2 to 4 per cent at a time when central banks find it difficult to achieve 2 per cent may lack credibility. This argument may have persistent validity in light of the discussion about the low level of the natural rate of interest going forward, developed in Section 3.5. If the natural interest rate remains very low, a central bank may have difficulties achieving a rate of inflation of 4 per cent because it cannot push the nominal rate low enough due to the lower bound. Further easing by means of the balance sheet tool could, in turn, be insufficient.

Overall, the advantages of raising the inflation target from 2 to 4 per cent are not obvious. This conclusion may change in the future and the inflation target could be raised without changing the institutional set-up of the central bank. New arguments and new evidence, in addition to that generated by the Great Recession, will, however, be needed to make a compelling case for raising the inflation target.

Another proposal that received renewed attention as a consequence of the Great Recession was to substitute the inflation target with a price level target (Eggertson and Woodford, 2003; Deutsche Bundesbank, 2010).

The main reason to revive this proposal is the argument that a price level target would help in dealing with the lower bound on interest rates.

The reasoning here is straightforward: if the central bank stabilizes the price level rather than inflation, any downward deviation in inflation today, which cannot be avoided by lower interest rates because they are already at the lower bound, must mean an upward, compensating deviation in inflation tomorrow, and vice versa. With a price level target there should therefore be opposing changes in actual and expected inflation, as the former are negative, the latter should be positive, and vice versa. But then a lower inflation today would mean a lower real interest rate going forward, which would, in turn, exert a monetary policy easing. In addition, the need to have higher inflation tomorrow to compensate for too low inflation today means that interest rates should be lower in the future than if the central bank had targeted the rate of inflation.

Eggertson and Woodford (2003) put the issue as follows:

> the management of expectations is the key to successful monetary policy at all times, not just in those relatively unusual circumstances when the zero bound is reached…. What actually matters is the private sector's anticipation of the future path of short-term rates, because this determines equilibrium long-term interest rates as well as equilibrium exchange rates and other asset prices…. How short-term rates are managed matters because of the signals that such management gives about how the private sector can expect them to be managed in the future. (p. 165)

A price level target sends the signal about the future conduct of monetary policy that offsets, at least partially, the inability to reduce current rates because of the lower bound.

With inflation targeting, the central bank forgets about past misses on inflation and only looks to the future. With price level targeting, the central bank keeps a memory of its own success, or failure, in achieving the desired rate of inflation and modulates its interest rate accordingly.

Two crucial assumptions[6] are needed for the price level target to deliver the desired favourable effects: first, that the central bank is credible in committing to keep a memory of past inflation misses; and second, that agents form expectations in a rational way and incorporate into their behaviour today what the economy is going to generate tomorrow.

With these two conditions, the traditional criticism against price level targeting (Fischer, 1995) was overcome: without forward-looking expectations, the need to compensate past misses on inflation would bring short-term volatility of inflation and of the variables connected to it, first and foremost economic activity. For instance, the memory of a negative deviation of inflation in the past would have to be compensated by easier monetary policy today, such that the economy would be subject to two shocks, in opposite directions. The long-term stability, that is, stationarity, of the price level might engender short-term instability.

---

[6] The Deutsche Bundesbank (2010) lists other critical characteristics for the price level target to generate the desired results.

Table 3.1. Correlation coefficient between actual and one year ahead expected inflation (c.1986–2017).

	Spain*	Germany	Italy	France	Euro-area**
Correlation	0.65	0.60	0.83	0.45	0.26

Note: data availability from January 1986 to January 2017; *data starts only in June 1987; **data starts only in January 1998.
Source: Author's calculations based on Eurostat and survey-based inflation expectations (see Appendix 1).

Overall, the translation into actual policymaking of the idea that price level targeting can have stabilizing effects, particularly when the central bank is confronted with the zero lower bound, requires settling a number of issues positively.

First, as mentioned above, it requires establishing beyond doubt that indeed economic agents form inflationary expectations in a rational, forward manner.[7] This is an issue that goes well beyond the scope of this book, but the use of the inflationary expectations estimated in Appendix 2 can shed some light on the issue. As mentioned above, the combination of a credible price level target and forward-looking expectations would require actual and expected inflation to be negatively correlated. Table 3.1 shows, instead, that, currently, actual inflation and expected inflation, as estimated in Appendix 2, are clearly positively correlated. Of course, this result is generated by economies in which central banks do not follow a price level target, so a necessary condition for the negative correlation is not present. In addition, the used estimates of inflationary expectations are really just a transformation of the prevailing rate of inflation. Still, the evidence in the table indicates how strong the change generated by the adoption of a price level target would have to be in order to move from a positive to a negative correlation between current and expected inflation.

Another issue to be dealt with favourably before moving to a price level target is how credible the commitment of the central bank could be in this respect. The credibility of such a commitment is in all likelihood connected to the relative ease with which economic agents can grasp the 'price level' as opposed to the 'inflation' concept. This is also an issue going beyond the ambitions of this book. There is, however, some empirical evidence that can help in dealing with the issue. A search for the terms 'inflation' and 'price level' in Google shows (Figure 3.1) that the word inflation is about four times as popular as the joint popularity of four terms one can use to denote the price level. A move to targeting the price level instead of the rate of inflation would

---

[7] Papadia (1983) reached mixed conclusions on this issue. Subsequent empirical investigations did not really reach more definite conclusions (Forsells and Kenny, 2002; Paquet, 1992; Dias, Duarte, and Rua, 2008; Andolfatto, Hendry, and Moran, 2008).

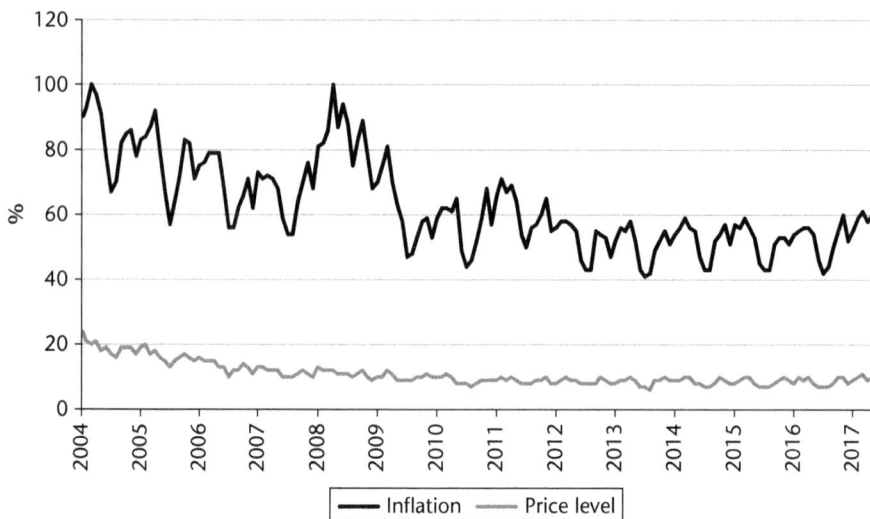

Figure 3.1 Relative Frequency of Searches of the Terms 'Inflation' and 'Price Level' (2004–2017)

Note: Price level also includes CPI level, CPI index, and CPI. In the vertical axis, the frequency is reported of Google searched relative to the maximum frequency, reported as 100. A value of 50 indicates that the frequency is a half of the maximum. A score of 0 means that the relative frequency was less than 1 per cent.

Source: Google trends.

be complicated by the fact that the former concept is much less well known by the general public.

A further issue, raised by Goodhart, Baker, and Ashworth (2013) for the case of GDP targeting, considered below, but also applying to price level targeting, has to do with the arbitrariness of the choice of the date from which the central bank should start 'keeping memory' of inflation misses. This arbitrariness may show up, in particular, in the awareness that the chosen date may appear, in hindsight, not appropriate. In this case the central bank should 'forget' the misses with respect to an initial price level target that turned out to be wrong, thus ultimately jeopardizing the shift from inflation to price level targeting.

The final issue with the suggestion to target the price level was previously raised when discussing the proposal to increase the inflation targets, namely that the behaviour of economic agents in practically all advanced economies has adapted to the 'convention' of a 2 per cent inflation target. Changing this would be very costly.

Overall, the opportunity of moving from inflation targeting to price level targeting is not clearly established; more evidence and stronger analytical underpinnings would be needed to carry out this costly change. Of course, this conclusion does not exclude the possibility that a milder version of the opportunity to maintain a memory of past inflation misses might prevail. According to this milder version, fully compatible with medium term oriented inflation targeting, the central bank would recognize, after a period in which inflation has been below target, that limited upward deviations in inflation from the target do not require forceful action. Economic agents could take into account in their expectations this kind of central bank behaviour and expect that inflation would be somewhat higher in the future. This effect would of course be substantially weaker than assumed in the analysis of Eggertsson and Woodford (2003), but the conditions for this to come into effect as well as the possible drawbacks would be less important.

A close relative of price level targeting is GDP targeting. According to this proposal, the central bank should stabilize the level of nominal GDP along a preset path.

The critical issues mentioned above for the adoption of price level targeting also apply to a target in terms of GDP. There are, however, two additional objections standing in the way of such change to the central bank strategy. The first is that targeting a variable that results from the addition of price and volume changes unnecessarily complicates the task of the central bank, since it would have to stabilize a variable influenced by a component, real growth, on which it has no long-term and limited short-term influence. The second objection, of a very practical but substantive nature, is that not only GDP figures come with long delays with respect to price figures but, as documented by Goodhart, Baker, and Ashworth (2013), they are substantially revised, so that the central bank would be uncertain even about past levels of its target.

The operational framework to steer interest rates will probably be different after the Great Recession from how it was before the crisis. Indeed, it has been seen in Section 2.1.1 that during the Great Recession the very abundant provision of liquidity pushed the interest rate from the middle to the bottom of the interest rate corridor and the modality of interest rate control moved to a so-called floor approach.

In Section 3.5 it will be argued that it would be imprudent to assume that the central banks will no longer need to use their balance sheet as a tool complementing interest rate changes. In addition, the conclusion of Papadia (2016a) is that excess liquidity will remain a feature in both the USA and the euro-area for years after the end of the Great Recession, as a consequence of the forceful QE implemented by the two central banks. The floor approach to interest rate control will persist in any case for quite some time as a legacy of the Great Recession.

The question, however, remains whether a situation of large central bank balance sheets and excess liquidity should merely be tolerated or instead actively sought as a permanent feature. Here different opinions seem to emerge on the two sides of the Atlantic.

For the euro-area, Bindseil (2016) thinks a return to a normal balance sheet should eventually be pursued. He does not really give an indication of the time horizon over which this result should be achieved, leaving open the possibility that this should only happen in the long run. However, the principle of 'parsimony' in designing the central bank balance sheet that he invokes would require going back to a central bank balance sheet as 'short' as possible. This would allow, in turn, a return to a symmetric approach, in which the short-term rate is kept in the middle of the corridor by appropriate liquidity provision, possibly through standing facilities instead of monetary policy operations.[8]

Conversely, Potter (2016) for the Fed does not see a strong need to return to a balance sheet that would resemble, in its basic pattern, the one prevailing before the crisis. In any case, he does not regard that prospect as realistic, given the long-lasting legacy of QE and the risk that the central bank may need to purchases large amounts of securities to fight the next recession, before the balance sheet would have shrunk back towards its pre-crisis configuration.

The difference of opinions between the ECB and the Fed on the optimal size of the central bank balance sheet going forward is somewhat ironic, noting that, before the crisis, the ECB had, as argued in Section 1.2.4, a broad approach to monetary policy implementation, whereas the Fed had a narrow one: in effect the total size of the balance sheet of the ECB was much larger pre-crisis than that of the Fed, relative to the number of banknotes outstanding, which defines its minimum size.

The most important differences between an implementation approach with or without excess liquidity are the following:

1. When excess liquidity prevails, the most important policy rate is the one at which the central bank absorbs such liquidity, namely the Interest on Excess Reserves in the USA and the rate on the deposit facility in the euro-area, not the rate at which liquidity is provided by the central bank.

2. The short-term inter-bank money market tends to be crowded out when excess liquidity prevails, since the need for banks to exchange scarce liquidity among themselves is severely limited.

3. Any worry the central bank may have about the availability of liquidity for the functioning of the payment system is obviously eliminated.

The weighing of these three characteristics to conclude about the optimality of one or the other approach is not obvious. The first characteristic has no clear welfare implications. The second has more of a negative connotation, if, as it is plausible, there is a benefit in having a functioning market. Views can,

---

[8] Bindseil (2011) defines this approach as TARALAC.

however, differ on how important the advantages of a short-term money market are, and whether there may be a thriving market also with limited bank participation. The third characteristic can be considered as positive, because it favours a smoothly functioning payment system.

All factors considered, the tentative conclusion can be reached that returning to a balanced liquidity approach seems preferable. First, it is not obvious that, in normal conditions, the payment system requires for its functioning excess liquidity. Indeed, it functioned smoothly without excess liquidity in both the USA and the euro-area before the Great Recession. Second, as a general principle, the central bank should only do what it can do better than the private sector and it is far from obvious that the short-term money market is better substituted, in normal conditions, by the central bank providing excess liquidity.

In any case the choice between one or other approach to the implementation of monetary policy will only have to be made a number of years after the legacy of the Great Recession, consisting of very large central bank balance sheets, has been overcome. Indeed, if the balance sheet tool has to be used in the future, as hypothesized below, the situation of large excess liquidity may last even longer. During the years in which excess liquidity will prevail, both new evidence and more analytical considerations will accumulate, advising for one or the other choice. In addition, neither choice will require an institutional change to the central banking model that was prevailing before the crisis, unlike the issues covered in the following two sections.

3.4 Central Banks in a New Regulatory and Supervisory Landscape

One long-term consequence of the Great Recession crisis was the change in banking and financial market regulations.

The change in the regulatory set-up post-Great Recession is multifaceted. It includes innovations in micro-supervision, the move from a bailing-out to a bailing-in approach to banking crises as well as structural modifications, such as the Volcker, the Liikanen and the Vickers changes in the USA, the euro-area and the UK respectively.[9] The net result of all these changes on the prospects for

---

[9] The Volcker Rule is a part of the Dodd–Frank Wall Street Reform and Consumer Protection Act, approved in 2010 and adopted in December 2013, based on a proposal made by the former Federal Reserve Chairman Paul Volcker in 2008. The Vickers Report contains the recommendations of the UK's Independent Commission established in the 2010 on banking implemented by the Financial Services (Banking Reform) Act of 2013. In October 2012 a group of experts led by Liikanen approved the 'Report of the European Commission's High-level Expert Group on Bank Structural Reform', the so-called Liikanen Report.

financial stability comes from opposing effects. On the one hand, it will be much more difficult to deploy public funds in case of crisis because of the move to bailing in, and this will make crisis management more complex (Scott, 2016). On the other hand, bailing in will have positive effects because it will reduce moral hazard. Better-capitalized banks will clearly be stronger in cases of crisis. In general, the more that is done with micro-prudential measures (such as concentration limits on lending), the less that needs to be done with other tools. This is not surprising given the complex relationship between financial stability, micro-supervision and macro-prudential policy documented in Box 9.

For the scope of this book, the basic question is whether in the new regulatory landscape the risk of dilemmas for central banks is obviated or not. Various measures such as micro-prudential measures, structural measures and the move from bailing out to bailing in should, on the whole, help reduce potential dilemmas.[10] However, these measures alone cannot eliminate the risk of financial instability in a comprehensive way. Among the regulatory changes enacted as a consequence of the Great Recession, the most promising ones in terms of freeing central banks from dilemmas between price and financial stability fall under the umbrella term of 'macro-prudential measures'. Notwithstanding the substantial work dedicated to developing these macro-prudential measures from a theoretical and an empirical point of view, they are far from constituting a well-defined set of measures whose application is uncontroversial and leading to reasonably certain results. This is somewhat surprising given that, as recalled in Section 1.3, the concept of macro-prudential policy was introduced in the late 1970s. Two explanations can be given for this extra-long incubation period: either macro-prudential policy is extremely complicated, requiring decades to be developed, or its development was delayed by strong bureaucratic inertia, particularly in central banks, which could only be overcome under the pressure of the crisis. Both explanations are probably relevant.

The papers analysing macro-prudential tools and trying to measure their effectiveness (e.g. Akinci and Olmstead-Rumsey, 2015; Lim et al., 2011; Kuttner and Shim, 2013; Cerutti, Claessens, and Laeven, 2015; Dell'Ariccia et al., 2012) generally start with a complex definition of what these tools are, often providing different, even if overlapping, definitions. The difficulty is not surprising, taking into account that macro-prudential tools are not intrinsically different from micro-prudential ones and even overlap to some extent with what, back in the 1970s and 1980s, were called direct measures, such as limits on bank credit.[11]

---

[10] The IMF GFSR of October 2014 concluded: 'Regulatory reform have [sic] strengthened the global banking system.'
[11] An example in Italy was the 'Vincolo di Portafoglio' and the 'Massimale sul credito'. In the UK an analogous measure was called 'The Corset'.

The common end result of such definitions is a 'macro-prudential index', resulting from the summation of different measures prevailing at a certain point of time in a given country. This approach cannot distinguish the intensity of the different measures and not even whether they are actually binding. To better comprehend the inevitable limitations of this kind of exercise, one may compare the 'macro-prudential stance' that these indexes attempt to gauge with the simplicity of the monetary policy stance as measured by the rate of interest.

Both in the euro-area and in the USA the institutional set-up of macro-prudential policies does not yet appear to have reached a fully settled situation, consistently leading to effective policies.

In the euro-area, macro-prudential policy, instead of clearly being allocated to a European level, is shared between national authorities, the European Systemic Risk Board (ESRB) and the ECB. National authorities have the most important operational responsibilities, because they can impose as well as lift macro-prudential measures. The ECB has only an asymmetric power of 'topping up' national measures, meaning that it can add to, but not subtract from, national measures. Against the reality of national authorities imposing very different macro-prudential measures in their jurisdictions, the topping up power of the ECB is difficult to use. The ESRB, on its side, only has the power to issue warnings and recommend macro-prudential measures. The General Board of the ESRB, including national authorities, which would be the main subjects of its recommendations, however, must agree with these. This approach de facto limits the effectiveness of this tool because decisions have to be taken on a qualified majority basis when a consensus cannot be reached. Overall, the effectiveness of the ESRB, created in 2010 on the basis of a recommendation of the 2009 De Larosière report and chaired by the ECB President, is far from having been clearly established.

In the USA the regulatory set-up is complex and liable to lead to some confusion. In addition, US regulatory reform is overwhelmingly focused on dealing with the too-big-to-fail problem, thus on Systemically Important Financial Institutions (SIFIs), and less on other potential sources of financial instability. A summary description of the American situation is that the Fed has, in principle, reasonably comprehensive macro-prudential tools for a small part of the American financial system, but fewer tools (and some potential gaps) for the rest. Indeed the Dodd–Frank reform gave a responsibility of overall oversight to the Fed, including its power, in principle, to override other regulators in the use of micro-prudential tools for macro-prudential purposes. The Fed has, in particular, a number of, potentially macro-prudential, tools it can use with banks and bank holding companies (conglomerates), such as setting minimum credit standards for consumer lending, mortgages, and so on. In addition, the Fed can apply countercyclical capital buffers to SIFIs, be they banks or non-banks, but not to non-SIFIs. The designation of a financial entity as a SIFI is a responsibility of the Financial Stability Oversight Council (FSOC). In practice, however, the designation of non-banks as SIFIs has turned out to be very difficult: General Electric reacted to this designation by disposing of its financial activities. When the insurance company Metlife was designated as a non-bank SIFI, it sued the federal government (and FSOC in particular) saying that the standards were illegal, and it won, at least the first degree of judgment. Overall, the practical ability of the Fed to impose macro-prudential constraints on banks is limited by a general difficulty in the use of macro-prudential tools, as will be emphasized below, namely the incentive for intermediation to move to non-banks or the foreign sector.

The FSOC, like the ESRB, has the ability to issue recommendations to regulators to apply macro-prudential measures to the institutions under their supervision. As in the case of the ESRB, however, the practical ability to do this, in a 14-member committee comprising individual supervisors who are protective of their own mandates, is extremely difficult. In conclusion, the somewhat trenchant assessment of Fischer (2015) about 'the relative unavailability of macroprudential tools in the United States' looks justified.

As shown above, both in the USA and in the euro-area, formally, the central bank is assigned an important, even dominant, role in the setting of macro-prudential policies. This feature, however, is not relevant in answering the fundamental question asked at the beginning of this section, namely whether, in the new regulatory landscape, the risk of dilemmas for the central bank is eliminated. The answer to this question does not depend on whether macro-prudential measures are decided by the central bank or by any other institution: the critical question is whether macro-prudential measures can assure financial stability on their own and thus avoid putting the central bank in a dilemma in the use of its monetary policy tools.

The evidence for the effectiveness of macro-prudential measures is gradually accumulating. The results achieved so far can be summarized as follows:

- Macro-prudential measures influence the rate of growth of bank credit.
- The effect is more significant on bank lending connected to house purchases.
- However, the evidence of an effect on house prices is less conclusive.
- The recourse to macro-prudential measures is much more frequent in emerging than in advanced economies, and only after the beginning of the Great Recession did the usage of such measures increase in advanced economies.
- The effect of macro-prudential measures is asymmetric, being stronger in booms than in busts.

- Macro-prudential measures, like direct measures in the 1970s, are liable to elusion and circumvention. In particular there is evidence of a shift of intermediation from the banking sector, the sector most impacted by these measures, towards the non-bank sector and towards foreign intermediation.

- Finally, macro-prudential tools mostly tend to be used in association with other tools (monetary and fiscal). Moreover their effectiveness is increased by this joint use, thus they appear more as complements than as substitutes for other measures.

The question of whether macro-prudential tools can assure, on their own, financial stability and thus relieve the central bank from potential dilemmas is addressed, together with other issues, in the next section.

3.5 How Wide Will the Scope of Responsibilities of Central Banks Be?

Section 3.1 illustrated the six hits to the pre-crisis central bank model, while Section 3.2 addressed the question of whether the central bank model that had affirmed itself before the Great Recession has been jeopardized by developments in its course. In this section, the crucial question is asked whether these developments are expected to remain a persistent feature of the economic environment within which central banks, particularly the Fed and the ECB, will have to operate, or whether they will fade away with the complete surpassing of the Great Recession. This question can be broken down into the following sub-questions, ranked in terms of importance and echoing the six hits delivered from the Great Recession to the pre-crisis central bank model:

- Will the new regulatory set-up, including macro-prudential policies, effectively deal with financial stability issues, thus freeing monetary policy from responsibilities in this area and avoiding dilemmas in which central banks will have to choose whether to assign their tools to either the price or the financial stability objective?

- Will a clear separation be re-established between fiscal and monetary policy, as central banks will no longer need to forcefully use their balance sheet as a monetary policy tool supplementing the interest rate?

- Will the moral hazard inevitably created during the Great Recession push banks and sovereigns towards the same kind of risky behaviour that created the preconditions of the crisis?

- Will the ECB have to step in again as implicit shock mutualizer in the euro-area, given insufficient government action in this respect?

- Will the ECB risk being involved further in 'troika like' activities?
- Will the Fed and the ECB have problems in taking a more global approach in exercising their responsibilities?

An attempt to provide an answer to these six sub-questions is provided below.

The answer to the first sub-question can only be given in probabilistic terms. It is indeed likely that the new regulatory set-up, and in particular the use of macro-prudential tools, will reduce the frequency and/or the depth of financial instability episodes. One may even hope that the intense, ongoing work to further develop the macro-prudential weaponry will reinforce its effectiveness to the point where it will be able to conclusively deal with financial instability risks. Hope, however, is not enough and one should therefore agree with Borio (2015):

> The experience so far indicates that it would be imprudent to rely exclusively on these [macro-prudential] frameworks, or even prudential regulation and supervision more generally, when seeking to tame the financial booms and busts that have caused such huge economic costs. Financial cycles are simply too powerful.... other policies, not least monetary and fiscal, should also play a role. (p. 6)

There are two main reasons for this conclusion. The first has to do with some intrinsic limitations of macro-prudential tools while the second has to do with some fundamental characteristics of central banks. The problem with macro-prudential tools is that they have a sectorial rather than a general effectiveness and can therefore quite easily be circumvented. In addition, the fact that they work better as complements, rather than substitutes, of general economic policy moves does not allow a clear objective-tool assignment. The second point is that central banks are exposed to dilemmas because they have two characteristics essential for the pursuit of financial stability, namely, a holistic approach to the entire financial system, which no other institution has, as well as the ability to move the interest rate, a tool that 'gets in all the cracks', which is exactly what macro-tools cannot do.

A return by central banks to the insouciant pre-2007 attitude as regards financial stability is not possible. The institutional set-up of central banks will have to be modified to deal with the risk of these dilemmas.[12]

The answer to the second sub-question listed above, namely whether the central banks will be able to return to the exclusive use of the interest rate as the dominant monetary policy instrument, is wide open. Friedman and Kuttner (2011) have clearly expressed the view that this will not be the case and that balance sheet management should remain a permanent feature in the panoply of central bank tools. Taylor (1993), however, reached the opposite conclusion. The question can be usefully addressed looking back at the

---

[12] This point was made for the first time to me by Ian Plenderleith in a private conversation back in 2012.

main reasons why the Fed and the ECB 'invented' the new balance sheet tool during the Great Recession, or at least developed it from the previous experience of the Bank of Japan at the beginning of the 2000s. One reason, prevalent during the first phase of the crisis, was to 'lend' the central bank balance sheet to complement the impaired intermediation capacity of the private sector. Another reason was to ease monetary policy even when the lower bound on interest rates had already been reached.

The degree of dislocation of the financial market reached during the Great Recession, documented in Sections 2.1.1 and 2.2.1, which required part of intermediation to move to the central bank balance sheet, was extreme and thus should be rare going forward. While no regularity should be expected here, the probability of having to deal with a similar situation in the foreseeable future is low. If that was the only reason for having recourse to the balance sheet instrument, the probability of this usage should be small. However, the second reason mentioned above, namely the need to ease monetary policy even when rates are at the lower bound, cannot be easily discarded. The issue here is germane to the question of whether or not advanced economies are confronting a 'secular stagnation'. In fact the prevalence of a secular stagnation would imply that interest rates, as well as inflation and real growth, would remain very low going forward, increasing the risk of bumping into the lower bound on interest rates and thus once again forcing central banks to complement interest rate reductions with balance sheet increases.[13] This issue has been considered from two different, but consistent, perspectives. One perspective is to figure out what are likely to be the general macroeconomic conditions of, mostly, advanced economies in the future. The other perspective is to look specifically at current estimates and prospects of the Wicksellian 'natural rate'. The two perspectives are examined in turn.

As presented by Papadia (2016c), there are at least five different variants that can be brought under a broad definition of 'Secular Stagnation'. First, there is the 'original' Hansen (1939)–Summers (2016) version. The second and third variants are the milder, in terms of persistence, versions of Bernanke (2005) and Rogoff (2016), going under the names of 'Savings Glut' and 'Debt Super-cycle', respectively. The fourth version is the 'Demographic Reversion' of Goodhart, Pradhan, and Pardeshi (2015), while the final variant is the 'Technology led stagnation' of Gordon (2016), which is the most pessimistic of all

---

[13] The former Chair and the Deputy Chair of the Fed clearly showed awareness of this risk. Yellen (2016a) and Fischer (2016). Fischer, in particular, said: 'Whatever the cause, other things being equal, a lower level of the long-run equilibrium real rate suggests that the frequency and duration of future episodes in which monetary policy is constrained by the Zero Lower Bonds will be higher than in the past. Prior to the crisis, some research suggested that such episodes were likely to be relatively infrequent and generally short lived. The past several years certainly require us to reconsider that basic assumption . . . . The answer to the question "Will r* remain at today's low levels permanently" is that we do not know' (pp. 3–4).

about the prospective rate of growth of advanced economies. More recently Borio (2017) has added a sixth variant, the 'Financial Cycle Drag', in which very low interest rates are heavily influenced by central bank policies on top of the lengthy consequences of a recovery from a particularly serious downturn in the financial cycle.

For the purpose of trying to assess the risk that central banks will be forced to continue using their balance sheet as a supplemental policy tool, the most important characteristic of the different variants of 'Secular Stagnation' is their implications for the future level of interest rates.

On this issue, Goodhart, Pradhan, and Pardeshi (2015) and Gordon (2016) send a relatively sanguine message. In the 'Demographic Reversion' approach of Goodhart, interest rates are expected to move away from the very low level prevailing in the mid-2010s, thus reducing the risk that the central banks will have to continue using the balance sheet tool. In Gordon's version, where supply factors dominate, there is no special reason to assume that nominal interest rates will remain very low for an extended period of time. Indeed, in his 'real economy' approach there is just no role for interest rates and the term does not even appear in the index of the book.

Instead, in the 'Savings Glut', the 'Debt Supercycle' and the 'Financial Cycle Drag' versions, which can be conflated into a 'Headwinds Hypothesis', as well as in the fully fledged 'Secular Stagnation', the nominal interest rates are supposed to remain compressed for a while longer going forward. The difference between the 'Headwinds Hypothesis' and the fully fledged 'Secular Stagnation' is the time horizon over which this low level should prevail: medium term for the 'Headwinds Hypothesis', long term or even very long term for the proper 'Secular Stagnation'.

Papadia (2016c) concluded his piece by mentioning that he started the analysis with a prior in favour of the 'Headwinds Hypothesis', but moved, on the basis of evidence, towards the longer lasting 'Secular Stagnation' variant. His argument is basically that the low level of interest rates prevailing around the second half of the 2010s is too exceptional an event from a historical perspective to be considered just a cyclical phenomenon that should gradually dissipate.

This conclusion is consistent with the results reached by Laubach and Williams (2015), who look at the second perspective mentioned above, which concentrates directly on estimates and forecasts of the natural rate of interest, often referred to as r*. These two authors build their estimates on the basic premise that the joint behaviour of inflation and activity, especially during the Great Recession, can only be reconciled with the extremely and persistently low level of the market interest rate if one assumes that the natural rate has substantially come down to around zero during the Great Recession. While noting that it is very difficult to ascertain whether the very low level of the interest rate is a permanent phenomenon, this is the conclusion that the two authors find more consistent with their data.

Overall, the conclusion that interest rates will remain very low going forward is not a categorical one. However, for the purpose of answering the second sub-question in this section, that is, whether central banks will have to continue using their balance sheet as a monetary policy instrument, one does not need a definitive view about the prospect for interest rates to remain around the depressed levels prevailing around the second half of the 2010s. Ascertaining that there is a significant risk that this will be the case is sufficient. Central banks may have to purchase large amounts of sovereign bonds swelling their balance sheets even when the Great Recession will definitely be in the rear window. The risk of a persistent confusion between monetary and fiscal policy thus remains.

In any case, even just the mechanical extrapolation of the balance sheets of the Fed and the ECB shows that they will need a number of years to get back to what one could broadly define as normality. Papadia (2016a) estimated that the ECB would need until sometime around 2030 and the Fed an estimated five years less. The Fed Reserve Bank of New York (2017) projected normalization in a time window between 2020 and 2023, with the median projection in 2021. Therefore the prospect of regaining a neat demarcation between monetary and fiscal policy is at least not imminent. This conclusion is reinforced by noting that the confusion between fiscal and monetary policy will also prevail when central banks will actively reduce the size of their balance sheet: not only purchases but also sales of government bonds can blur the borders between the two policies. The specific form that the blurring may take when central banks would wish to reduce the size of their balance sheet could take the form of 'financial repression' a la Reinhart and Sbrancia (2011). Furthermore, the probability of another recession within a time span in which the Fed or the ECB will not have regained a level of interest rates that would allow them to respond only by this tool makes more likely the risk of continued use of the balance sheet as a monetary policy instrument.

The third sub-question mentioned above is about moral hazard and the perverse incentive this may give to banks and sovereigns to repeat the imprudent behaviour that created the preconditions of the Great Recession. It was mentioned in Sections 2.1.2 and 3.1 that the Fed and the ECB took some measures to contain the moral hazard implicit in their lending huge amounts of money to banks and sovereigns that had put themselves in dangerous conditions, making them liable to a sudden shift in expectations from a 'good' to a 'bad' equilibrium. The instruments to reduce the moral hazard consequences were, for banks, the Diamond–Dybvig pricing of central bank facilities, at prices higher than those that would have prevailed in the 'good' equilibrium, but lower than those that actually emerged in the 'bad' equilibrium. For sovereigns,

Diamond–Dybvig pricing also helped, but the most important tool was the conditionality of macroeconomic programmes. Still, the fact that both banks and sovereigns did not bear the full brunt of their imprudence could lead to recurrent risky behaviour.

It is difficult to have a definitive view on how grave this risk is. However, both banks and sovereigns have arguably gone through a sufficiently painful time to avoid putting themselves in the same dangerous situation they were in before the Great Recession. It should be recognized, however, that this conclusion is based more on reasoning than on firm evidence.

The fourth sub-question mentioned above is whether there is a risk that the ECB will be called again to offset idiosyncratic shocks affecting one or other of the euro-area countries. The establishment of the European Stability Mechanism (ESM) has partially remedied the limitation of the Maastricht Treaty that had eliminated the exchange rate as a mechanism to deal with idiosyncratic shocks, but did not provide a substitute mechanism. The ESM, and before it the European Financial Stability Fund (EFSF), did indeed help in dealing with the funding difficulties of Greece, Spain, Ireland, Portugal, and Cyprus, but quantitatively their loans were a small fraction of the funding provided by the ECB to peripheral countries. This is obvious when comparing the Target balances reported in Box 14, which exceeded €1 trillion at their peaks, with the actual funding provided by the ESM, at €264 billion, but also with the amount of €373 billion of its remaining lending capacity. The credit extended to peripheral countries by the ECB was thus about four times the actual funding from the ESM and one-and-a-half times its potential maximum. The partiality of the solution offered by the ESM can also be ascertained noting that its potential funding would probably be insufficient if it had to be used for a large euro-area country such as Italy.

The fifth sub-question mentioned above concerns the ECB's participation in so-called troika activities. This participation created both potential conflicts of interest and the pressure for the ECB to move well beyond its area of responsibilities. As argued in Section 3.1, the participation of the ECB in the troika was not an institutionally well-founded activity but rather an answer to an emergency. ECB participation to the troika activity has caused sufficient confusion and stress to expect that the experience will not be repeated. Indeed, gradually the ECB has reduced its role in the troika and the risk that it should again be involved seems limited.[14]

The final sub-question is whether both the Fed and the ECB will have to take a more global approach in their actions. The answer is definitely positive

---

[14] An issue here is that the role of the ECB in the troika is prescribed in the Treaty Establishing the European Stability Mechanism, even if in a mild form, as the tasks are mainly attributed to the European Commission, only 'in liaison with the ECB'.

(Eichengreen et al., 2011). In the pursuit of both price and financial stability, the two central banks will have to better incorporate in their decision making the global repercussions of their actions. The issue is not that they have to pursue global objectives even if they are inconsistent with the interests of their jurisdictions: the two institutions are first and foremost responsible to their constituencies and must act accordingly. However, they should also recognize that global conditions, which are so important for the success of their policies, are far from being exogenous to their actions: the small country assumption decidedly does not apply to such large economies as the USA and the euro-area, and thus to the actions of their central banks.

Nevertheless, the adoption of a more global approach does not require, by itself, any institutional innovation, as it is more an issue of implementation than principle. The Fed and the ECB actively pursued a more global approach during the Great Recession, particularly by cooperating intensely to fight its negative consequences. Future operations would benefit from continuing to integrate this global approach when deemed beneficial, given the nature of the increasingly interconnected global economy.

The overall answer to the question about the scope of central bank activities addressed in the title of this section is an open one. In some aspects, there is a high risk that the scope of action of the Fed and the ECB will have to remain well beyond what it was before the Great Recession. In some other aspects, instead, the risk is minimal. Even an open answer, however, is enough to conclude that it would be most imprudent to assume that the two central banks, as well as the central banks of other advanced economies, could simply return to the model prevailing before 2007. Only if the answer to each of the six sub-questions was favourable could one safely assume a return to the pre-Great Recession model. This is tantamount to assuming that all the hits to the pre-crisis central bank model illustrated in Sections 3.1 and 3.5 would not repeat themselves. But the probability of this joint event is small, since it depends on the multiplication of the probability of each event. Unfortunately, however strongly we may desire it, a return to the status quo ante of a narrow central bank model is impossible. The question is not whether we need a change but rather what kind of change we need.

3.6 Possible Adaptations to the Central Banking Model

The reflection on possible adaptations of the central banking model utilized by most advanced economies before the Great Recession has just started. There have been many calls to innovate that model but we are still far from an emerging consensus. Some authors seem to think a radical change may be needed. Prominent among these is Goodhart (2010), who identified three epochs in central banking, with in-between confused periods searching for a new model. These are:

1. Victorian era (1840–1914)
2. Government control (1930–end of 1960s)
3. Triumph of markets (1980–2007).

Following the financial crisis, C[entral]B[anks] are now probably on the verge of a further fourth epoch, though the achievement of a new consensus on their appropriate behaviour and operations may well be as messy and confused as in the two previous interregnums (p. 2).

A similar sense of radical change is in the repeated use of the term 'Cross-road' to represent where central banks are since the Great Recession (Bordo et al., 2016). Borio (2014b) thinks that 'Central banking will never be quite the same after the global financial crisis' (p. 191). Yet, in response to the question of whether the events during the Great Recession require a change in the mandates of central banks, Borio's answer is definitely no. 'No need to include explicitly a financial stability objective' (p. 15), without this in any way implying that they can take lightly their responsibilities in this area.

Buiter (2016) shares the view that the model of an independent central bank devoted to price stability has been severely tested during the Great Recession. Indeed, he takes an even stronger position on this issue than the one reached in this book:

> There are several reasons for this likely weakening of central bank independence. This paper focuses on three: (1) the explosive growth of central bank powers and responsibilities since the GFC [Global Financial Crisis], without any matching increase in accountability; (2) the intrusion of many leading central bankers in political matters far beyond their mandates and competence; and (3) manifest errors in the design and implementation of monetary policy. But there are other forces driving AE [Advanced Economies] central banks to return to the status of being just the liquid windows of their national Treasuries . . . . Independent central banking is under threat in the advanced economies. The only way to preserve operational central bank independence where it makes sense, in the design and implementation of monetary policy, narrowly defined, is a return to 'narrow central banking'.

The conclusion reached in the previous section is that it is not prudent to assume that the responsibilities of central banks going forward will be so restricted that they could return to 'narrow central banking'. This outcome would be desirable, but its probability is too low to take is as basis for the future configuration of central banks, especially of the Fed and the ECB.

Another radical approach to central banking after the Great Recession is simply to go back to the Government Control Epoch, mentioned by Goodhart, and once again make central banks merely a government department. However, this approach would go against historical experience as well as economic analysis: the model of dependent central banks managing a fiat currency was tested and failed; returning to it would engender the same drawbacks that were painfully experienced while it prevailed. The progress achieved on price stability, after decades of instability, thanks to the monetary technology built into an independent central bank with the predominant objective of price stability, is too important to be put at risk. Great caution is therefore required in moving away from that model.

The attempt to identify the necessary adaptations is very much work in progress.

Eichengreen et al. (2011) recommend that central banks 'should go beyond their traditional emphasis on low inflation to adopt an explicit goal of financial stability'. Moreover, they propose this because they argue that the 'framework underpinning modern central banking must be rethought.... the conventional framework for central banking is inadequate'.

Bayoumi et al. (2014) take a less radical approach, asking for financial, as well as external, stability to be added to the central bank mandate, while simultaneously maintaining the prevalence of price stability. At the same time, to reflect a more complex mandate as well as the need to take into account the uncertainty about the relation between the objectives and the tools available to the central bank, they foresee less reliance on formal models and more serendipity.

Reinhart and Rogoff (2013) do not see the need for drastic changes in central bank mandates as they just mention that

> [n]ow, possibly, the pendulum is swinging back to place a greater weight on its initial mandate of financial stability, which policymakers and financial markets had come to take for granted during the post-war era. (p. 2)

The difficulty of coming to a consensus about the required changes is not surprising given that, over the centuries of their existence, central banks have tended to react in a pragmatic way to changing circumstances, rather than implement a set design. As recalled in Chapter 1, the very model described there took decades to fully develop and affirm itself in the advanced economies: from the First World War to the end of the twentieth century.

It should also be openly recognized that changing the still prevailing central banking model inevitably meets some psychological resistance from insiders, like the author of this chapter, whose professional experience coincided with the prevalence of that model. The hope is that the expertise and experience of insiders is suggesting the right approach. However, one cannot exclude the possibility that an element of nostalgia may affect the reasoning and the conclusions about which adaptations are needed.

Yet, insisting on a rigid defence of the model, also when objective changes in the environment require innovations, would run the risk of jettisoning a model that could be rescued by relatively modest changes. Central banks have emerged from the crisis with greater powers and broader responsibilities, which do not match a technocratic, independent institution. The view of central banks, run by central bankers, as philosopher kings exercising their power for the good of society, is tempting but utterly wrong: right governance can only be based on a proper institutional framework, not on the goodwill and competence of individuals.

What follows is an admittedly incremental rather than radical revision of the model, inevitably leading to a less elegant and less easy-to-manage version of central banking.

On the strategic and operational side, as discussed in Section 3.3, the only change that will definitely prevail with respect to the pre-crisis model is the persistence of a 'floor' approach to the fixation of the short-term interest rate within the corridor. However, at this stage it is unclear whether this situation should survive a possible normalization of the balance sheet of the Fed and the ECB. If, as hypothesized in Section 3.5, the Fed and the ECB will need to continue using their balance sheet for monetary policy purposes, the return to a pre-crisis pattern for their balance sheet would be a very distant prospect. Thus there would be plenty of time to further discuss whether to continue with a floor approach or to go back to a situation in which liquidity is regulated to keep the short-term interest rate in the middle of the corridor, as was the case before the Great Recession.

The measures proposed for the institutional setting of central banks are limited in the historical perspective of the changes that impacted central banks over the decades. They are quite incisive, instead, from a legal and institutional perspective. Indeed, they would require changes to the Federal Reserve Act, in the case of the Fed, and to the Treaty on the Functioning of the European Union, in the case of the ECB. They would thus have to overcome a high legal bar to be implemented.

The overall strategy to design the incremental changes that are required is to identify the adaptations needed to confront the issues identified as having impacted central banks during the Great Recession and that we cannot assume will wither away in its aftermath. Four of these issues are left of the six that were mentioned in sections 3.1 and 3.5.[15] In decreasing order of importance, these are:

1. the coexistence of price and financial stability responsibilities for the central bank, creating the risk of dilemmas;

---

[15] This assumes that it should not be difficult to eliminate the reference in the EMS Treaty to the fact that the ECB has to contribute 'in liaison' with the European Commission to troika activities.

2. the risk of a persistent confusion between monetary and fiscal policy, due to the possible need for the central bank to continue using its balance sheet as an instrument of policy;

3. the risk, specific to the ECB, that it would again be called to assure the survival of the euro by acting as a mutualizer of idiosyncratic shocks;

4. the moral hazard consequences of the forceful action of central banks in times of crisis.

The attribution, de facto or de jure, of a financial stability responsibility to the central bank, vying with price stability for the dominance in the hierarchy of its objectives, is the change requiring the most extensive adaptations. A sequencing approach is suggested to deal with this problem.

In normal times, few or no dilemmas emerge between financial and price stability, and what the central bank would do for one purpose would not conflict, and in many cases would coincide, with what it should do for the other. In these times the central bank should continue pursuing its price stability objective and dedicate the interest rate tool, as well as the balance sheet tool if needed, to the pursuit of this objective. The possible concurrent use of macro-prudential tools would also not raise any problem of consistency. However, if the central bank were to identify a dilemma, in which price stability and financial stability considerations would require contrasting actions, say because inflation is too low but there are risks brewing for financial stability, the central bank should undertake the opportune macro-prudential measures, if it has the power to enact them directly, or ask the relevant authorities to undertake them. In any case, the central bank should work in close collaboration with the government in the implementation of macro-prudential measures, as the Fed did with the stress test and not in isolation, as the ECB had to do with its Asset Quality Review.

Of course, the application of macro-prudential measures would influence not only financial stability but also price stability. Starting from a dilemma situation in which, for example, inflation is too low but financial stability is at risk, the general restrictive effect of macro-prudential measures on inflation would be undesirable. To deal with this problem the central bank could even apply a differential strategy, whereby it would, for instance, lower interest rates while applying restrictive macro-prudential measures. This strategy would be complex and would severely test the ability to calibrate the two tools. At least in principle, though, it could work if, as shown in Appendix 1, the effect of macro-prudential measures were stronger on financial rather than on price stability, and the opposite would hold for interest rate changes.

If, notwithstanding the macro-prudential measures, financial stability risks persisted, the central bank could go back to its principal, for instance Parliament, and ask it to prioritize either the price stability or the financial stability objective. Parliament could, of course, ask the central bank to provide its advice on the matter, while retaining its responsibility to decide. The permanence of this state of affairs would depend on the central bank continuing to assess that a dilemma situation persisted. Once the central bank judged that the financial stability issues had subsided, it would return to its normal set-up, re-establishing the priority of price stability.

This hybrid approach recognizes that the occurrence of dilemmas is the exception rather than the rule. Such situations may occur when the financial and the inflation cycles are on divergent phases. Institutionally, the approach also takes into account the fact that an independent central bank can only be given technical discretion (i.e. how to best achieve a given objective), not political discretion (i.e. to arbitrage between different objectives). At the same time, giving to the central bank the exclusive right to decide about the existence of a dilemma avoids the risk that it is distracted from the price stability objective with the excuse of financial stability, when no real dilemma arises. Finally, the recourse to macro-prudential measures as the first line of defence in the event of an inconsistency between price and financial stability is also in line with the view that these measures can help but, given their current degree of development, cannot ensure financial stability. Hellwig (2015) proposes a similar sequencing approach:

In normal times, let monetary policy serve its macroeconomic objectives without paying much attention to financial stability.

If risks in the financial sector are building up, consider the use of macroprudential regulation to restrain the buildup.... In an acute crisis, allow for financial stability concerns to take precedence and support the financial system.   (Page 25)

Should the current development work improve their effectiveness, the occurrence of unavoidable dilemmas would become even more rare.

No neat solution can be identified to deal with the risk of a persistent confusion between monetary and fiscal policy if the central bank were forced to continue using its balance sheet as an instrument of policy. This confusion could arise both when the central bank purchased large amounts of government bonds or when it actively reduced its portfolio to normalize the size of its balance sheet. The only additional protection that one can envisage is that, unlike in the use of the interest rate, decisions relating to the balance sheet tool would require a special majority within the decision-making body of the central bank. Special reporting obligations to justify the use of the balance sheet tool could also be required.

Both special majorities and reporting requirements are relatively weak measures, though. Their strength may be tested if a central bank sought to reduce its imprint in the government bond market at the same time as yields were rising. This relative weakness, however, has to be assessed against the fact that both the Fed and the ECB did not enact QE with the intention of facilitating government financing, but rather in the pursuit of their monetary policy objective, thus lessening the fear that they might succumb to fiscal dominance.

The third point mentioned above, namely the risk, specific to the ECB, that it would be called again to assure the survival of the euro by acting as mutualizer of idiosyncratic shocks, is a specialized version of the moral hazard point covered below. Given its importance, however, this particular version needs a treatment of its own.

The solution to this problem cannot be looked after within the central banking sphere: basically the issue is the incomplete design of the monetary union as established in Maastricht. The completion of the project, as sketched in the so-called Five Presidents' Report (Juncker et al., 2015), is the only way to free the ECB from the task, which clearly does not belong to it and yet was put on its shoulders, to deal with the idiosyncratic shocks that the exchange rate can no longer offset.

It is also difficult to envisage a neat solution against the fourth point recalled above, namely moral hazard created by the fact that, to some extent, central banks bailed out imprudent banks, both in the USA and in the euro-area, as well as imprudent governments, in the latter. Such actions were undertaken, however, because potential damages to the financial system and the real economy by not acting were deemed a greater risk.

A partial solution to moral hazard concerns is to forcefully use the approach employed during the Great Recession: letting imprudent actors bear part of the consequences of their imprudence, following the traditional practice of insurance companies that exclude deductibles from insurance. For banks, this approach took the form of Diamond–Dybvig pricing of central bank facilities, leaving part of the pain on banks that had put themselves in a vulnerable position. For sovereigns, as recalled above, macroeconomic conditionality was the most important tool, complemented by Diamond–Dybvig pricing, to alleviate the moral hazard. Macroeconomic conditionality will be indispensable for any similar actions in the future. From this point of view, the call for the ECB to become the unconditional supporter of fiscally weak governments (De Grauwe, 2013) is completely counterproductive. Overall, it is a reasonable conclusion that, during the Great Recession, both banks and sovereigns have suffered part of the consequences of their imprudent behaviour, and this should teach them a lesson for the future: imprudence has its cost. In addition, if, as it is hoped, the institutional innovations contained in the Five Presidents' Report are eventually enacted, the risk of the ECB having to once again rescue the euro will effectively be dealt with.

The fact that no definitive solution is available against moral hazard is not surprising. Moral hazard is a ubiquitous phenomenon; targeting it at zero is as optimal as forbidding insurance contracts. Moral hazard should be managed

Table 3.2. Summary of the hits to the pre-crisis central banking model and proposed amendments.

Hit to the pre-crisis central bank model	Proposed amendments to the pre-crisis model
Risk of dilemmas between price and financial stability	Sequencing approach in case of dilemmas: • apply macro-prudential measures • ask principal (Parliament) to establish priority between the two goals
Blurred borders between monetary and fiscal policy	Special majority to use the balance sheet tool. Special reporting duties
Moral hazard created by forceful central bank action	Introduce in the statutes of the Fed and the ECB the principle of Diamond–Dybvig pricing for non standard central bank facilities Introduce in the ECB statute the requirement of macroeconomic programmes before any action targeting specific countries
ECB mutualizing idiosyncratic shocks	The solution is outside the central banking area: complete European monetary union

rather than eliminated. Properly used, Diamond–Dybvig pricing and macro-economic conditionality were sufficiently effective instruments in this respect during the Great Recession. It would be useful, however, to reinforce the prudent use of such tools by inserting relevant provisions to this effect in the statutes of the Fed and the ECB.

It may be useful, even if something of an anti-climax, to present the main hits to the pre-crisis central bank model and the proposed amendments requiring changes to the statutes of the Fed and/or the ECB in a tabulated form (see Table 3.2).

Tightening with Macro-Prudential Tools while Easing with Interest Rates

As mentioned in the text, it is in principle conceivable, confronted with a situation in which there are risks for financial stability but no upwards risks for price stability, that macro-prudential tools could be tightened while simultaneously easing interest rates. The following simple equations show under which conditions this tightening/easing combination is, at least theoretically, possible. Of course, the symmetrical problem of risks for price stability without risks for financial stability can be dealt with analogously.

Let's start from an elementary two equations system:

$$f = \alpha r + \beta m \tag{1}$$

$$p = \gamma r + \delta m \tag{2}$$

Where all variables are defined as changes with respect to current values and specifically:

f = change in risk-appetite (an increase in f denotes higher risk appetite)
p = change in inflation
r = change in interest rate
m = change in the macro-prudential tool.

The assumptions are:

$$\alpha < 0;\ \beta < 0;\ \gamma < 0;\ \delta < 0$$

That is, both an increase of interest rates and a tightening of the macro-prudential tool reduce risk appetite and push down inflation.

The problem is that both the interest rate and the macro-prudential tool influence both price stability and financial stability. Of course, for $\alpha = \delta = 0$ there would be two separate objectives and no problems in pursuing them, each with the assigned separate tool, and Tinbergen would be happy.

Let's define Δf and Δp as the desired changes in risk appetite and inflation to regain financial stability and price stability. The dilemma in quadrant I of Figure 1.18 in Section 1.3 occurs because there is too little risk appetite and too high inflation, thus the desired changes are ($\Delta f > 0$) and ($\Delta p < 0$). In contrast, in quadrant III there is a dilemma because inflation is too low and risk appetite too high, hence the desired changes

Appendix 1

are $\Delta p > 0$ and $\Delta f < 0$. The rest of the exposition takes the situation in quadrant III as an example: policies should be enacted to achieve $\Delta f < 0$ (i.e. there is a desire to lower risk appetite towards its optimal level) while inflation is too low and thus there is a desire to engineer $\Delta p > 0$. In fact, for analytical ease, it is assumed below that there is a desire to lower risk appetite but inflation is at the right level and accordingly there is no desire to lower it, that is, $\Delta p = 0$.

The issue is to find which constraints on the four coefficients, $\alpha, \beta, \gamma, \delta$, allow us to obtain $\Delta p = 0$ while obtaining $\Delta f < 0$.

From Equations (1) and (2) we can write the objectives as:

$$\Delta f = \alpha r + \beta m < 0 \tag{3}$$
$$\Delta p = \gamma r + \delta m = 0 \tag{4}$$

the necessary conditions are that:

$$\alpha r + \beta m < 0$$

and

$$\gamma r + \delta m = 0$$

Substituting the equality into the inequality we get:

$$\left(\beta - \frac{\alpha\delta}{\gamma}\right) m < 0$$

and for m > 0, that is, assuming a tightening of the macro-prudential tool, since

$$\beta < 0 \text{ and } -\frac{\alpha\delta}{\gamma} > 0$$

the constraint is:

$$abs(\beta) > abs\left(\frac{\alpha\delta}{\gamma}\right)$$

meaning that the effect of the macro-prudential tool on financial stability is stronger than the effect of the composite parameter given by the effect of the interest rate on financial stability multiplied by the effect of macro-prudential measures on price stability divided by the effect of the interest rate on price stability. More simply, the condition is that macro-prudential policies must have a stronger effect on financial stability, whereas the interest rate must have a stronger effect on price stability.

Of course the ballet consisting in tightening macro-prudential policies while simultaneously loosening monetary policy by reducing interest rate requires, in practice, not only that the constraint above is respected but also that the parameters are known with sufficient precision to calibrate appropriately the complex strategy. Whether this condition prevails in practice is debatable.

Francesco Papadia

Quantifying Survey-Based Inflation Expectations

1. Introduction

The European Commission has collected consumers' opinions on inflation develop-ments on a monthly basis since January 1985. Its Consumer Survey asks respondents the following question:

'By comparison with the past 12 months, how do you expect that consumer prices will develop in the next 12 months? They will...'

The respondents have a choice of five different qualitative answers:

increase more rapidly (++)
increase at the same rate (+)
increase at a slower rate (=)
stay about the same (–)
fall (—)
don't know

Then, an aggregate measure (the so-called 'balance statistic') weighs together the frequency of responses in different classes, providing qualitative information on the change of consumers' inflation expectations.

A similar question is asked about perceived inflation, resulting in a similar balance statistic:

'How do you think that consumer prices have developed over the last 12 months? They have...'
risen a lot (++)
risen moderately (+)
risen slightly (=)
stayed about the same (–)
fallen (—)
don't know

Figure A.2.1 reports the two balance statistics (*expected* in the next 12 months and *perceived* over the last 12 months) as well as actual inflation rates. Before the

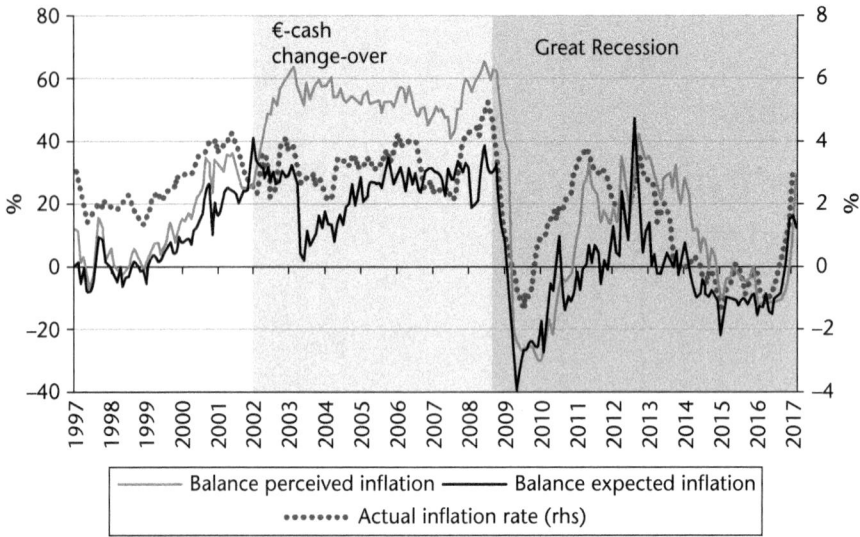

Figure A.2.1 Balance Statistic of Expected and Perceived Rates of Inflation, and Actual Inflation in the Euro-Area (1997–2017)

Note: data availability for the euro-area inflation rate starts January 1997.

Source: European Commission Business and Consumer Surveys and OECD (2017), Main Economic Indicators (database), <http://dx.doi.org/10.1787/data-00052-en> (accessed 27 March 2017).

cash-changeover, the three series followed each other quite closely, but started diverging substantially with the introduction of the euro banknotes and coins at the beginning of 2002. This divergence lasted until approximately the beginning of the most acute phase of the Great Recession in the autumn of 2008. In particular, the balance statistic for perceived inflation surpassed that for actual inflation and even more so that for expected inflation. The peculiar behaviour of the series for perceived inflation has to be associated with the difficulty consumers had in quantifying actual inflation after the change in the monetary metric.[1] In particular, empirical evidence shows that the memory of past prices was particularly faulty after the introduction of the euro (Cestari, Del Giovane, and Rossi-Arnaud, 2007). Another interesting result in the euro-area is that during the Great Recession, particularly in the early years (2008–2012), actual inflation rates tended to be higher than either perceived or expected rates of inflation. However, between 2012 and 2015, perceived inflation tended to be highest. Data from early 2017 suggest that

[1] Del Giovane, Fabiani, and Sabbatini (2008): 'as shown in this paper, consumers interviewed at the end of 2006 reported an average inflation of 18%, as compared to an official rate (measured by the National Statistical Institute, ISTAT) of around 2%.... a divergence of such a magnitude is unlikely to be attributable to the methods used by ISTAT or to their implementation. Moreover, these extremely high evaluations are difficult to reconcile with individual behaviour.... This suggests that what is commonly labelled as "perceived inflation" might capture something more than, and possibly not related to, simply price movements.... "the metrics of perceived inflation is fundamentally unrelated to that of the official statistics, as if the two phenomena were of a substantially different nature".'

perceived inflation closely mirrored actual inflation, both of which exceeded expected inflation.

2. Quantifying inflation expectations

The qualitative responses to the European Commission's Consumer Survey are the basis for the quantitative estimates of the expected change of the inflation rate, based on Papadia and Basano (1981).

In providing the survey information, the respondent is required to transform his/her inflationary expectations into answers to the above questions about inflationary expectations. To do so he/she will have the following transformation function:

$$Y_{it} = h_{it}(p_{it}^e - p_{it}^*) \tag{1}$$

where p_{it}^e is a point estimate of inflation, including a common element to all individuals, which changes over time, and a component that changes over time but also varies between individuals and has a zero mean.

$$p_{it}^e = p_t^e + u_{it}$$

and p_{it}^* is a point estimate of the present (perceived) rate of inflation, again containing a common and an individual component with a zero mean.

$$p_{it}^* = p_t^* + z_{it}$$

To get to this transformation function, we have to make three assumptions. First, we assume that the transformation function is identical for all individuals, so that the differences in the answers given depend only on individual errors (which have a zero mean). Second, we assume that the transformation function is well approximated by a continuous function on average over all individuals. Hence:

$$E_i(Y_{it}) = h_t[E_i(p_{it}^e) - E_i(p_{it}^*)] = h_t(p_t^e - p_t^*) \tag{2}$$

The average answer to the survey is therefore functionally related to the expected change in the inflation rate averaged over individuals. Third, we assume that respondents to the survey divide the range of possible inflationary expectations into five intervals of equal size and choose the interval, and the answer to the survey, in which his/her point estimate of inflation falls. Hence the weights Y_k, attributed to the answers to the survey, are successive values of a function.

Linear transformation

We assume that the h_t function is linear, of the following shape

$$E_i(Y_{it}) = \sum_i f_{it} * Y_{it}, \tag{3}$$

where f_{it} is the frequency of respondents choosing answer Y_i. After some basic algebra, we get the formula for the estimate of the expected rate of inflation, given p_t^* and f_{it}.

$$\dot{p}^e_t = f_2 p^*_t + \frac{p^*_t}{2}(3f_1 + f_3 - f_5) \tag{4}$$

The expected rate is hence a sort of weighted average of today's perceived rate (weighted by the frequency of those who expect no change in the inflation rate) and half of today's perceived rate (weighted by a transformation of the frequencies of the answers which imply a change).

Note that the linear transformation can only accommodate as a maximum an inflationary expectation of 1.5 times the perceived rate.

Logistic transformation

Another way of calculating the h_t function is through a logistic transformation of the general form

$$y = \frac{a}{1 + be^{-cx}} - k, \tag{5}$$

where y and x are the dependent and independent variables respectively, a, b and c are parameters, and k is a constant. Inserting our definitions from above, we derive an alternative estimate of the expected rate of inflation:

$$\hat{p}^e_t = p^*_t * \left(0.5 - 0.4552 * \ln\left[\frac{2 - 2f_1 - f_2 + f_4 + 2f_5}{2 + 2f_1 + f_2 - f_4 - 2f_5}\right]\right) \tag{6}$$

Note that the maximum of the expected rate of inflation is infinity, which occurs when all interviewees choose *Y1* as the answer.

Details about the calculations

We equate the respective 'perceived' rates (p^*_t) to historical OECD data for Italy, Spain, Germany, and France.[2]

To calculate the probability distributions from the survey data, we need to eliminate the 'don't know' answers, assuming that the respondents who answer in such a way have the same average expectation as those who give a definite answer. We add them, pro rata, to the first five answers.

The resulting five frequencies of the survey in each month (which taken together represent the probability distribution of aggregated inflation expectations) are necessary to calculate the estimated expected rate of inflation, using formulas (4) and (6) respectively.

Now we can plot the series. Figure A.2.2 shows the estimated expected rate of inflation, using the logistic transformation, at time t-12 and the actual inflation at time t. In other words, we compare actual inflation with the forecast done 12 months earlier, which allows us to capture the forecast errors.

---

[2] This is the only plausible alternative given that the perceived rate of inflation, at least for a few years after the introduction of the euro, seemed to be disconnected from actual inflation. See also footnote 1.

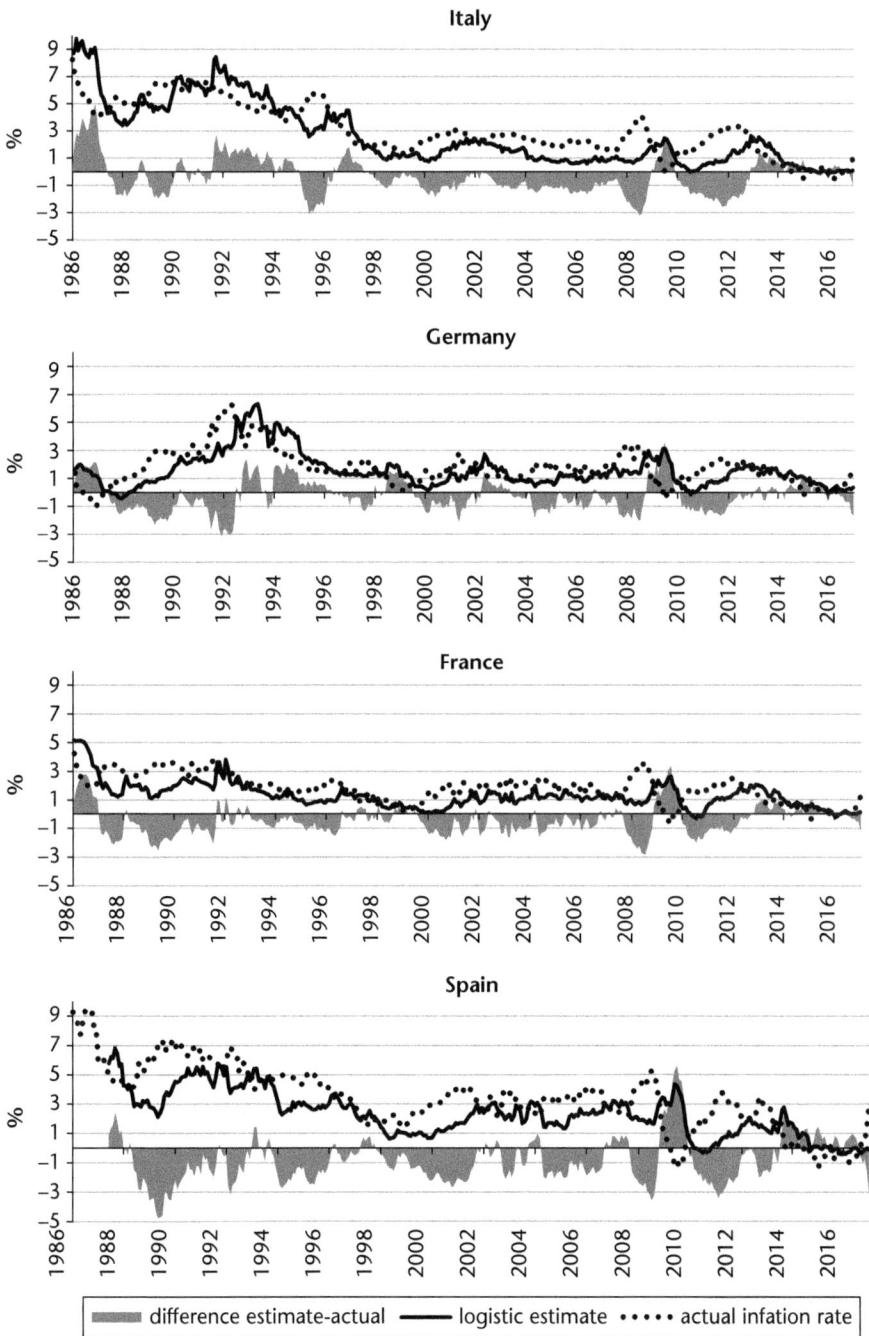

Figure A.2.2 Logistic Estimates of Expected Rate of Inflation and Actual Rate of Inflation in Italy, France, Germany, and Spain (1986–2016)

Note: The actual rate of inflation is defined as annual per cent change on monthly basis. The difference estimate-actual refers to the percentage point difference between the estimated rate of inflation and the actual inflation.

Source: OECD (2017), Main Economic Indicators (database), <http://dx.doi.org/10.1787/data-00052-en> (accessed 27 March 2017) and ECB.

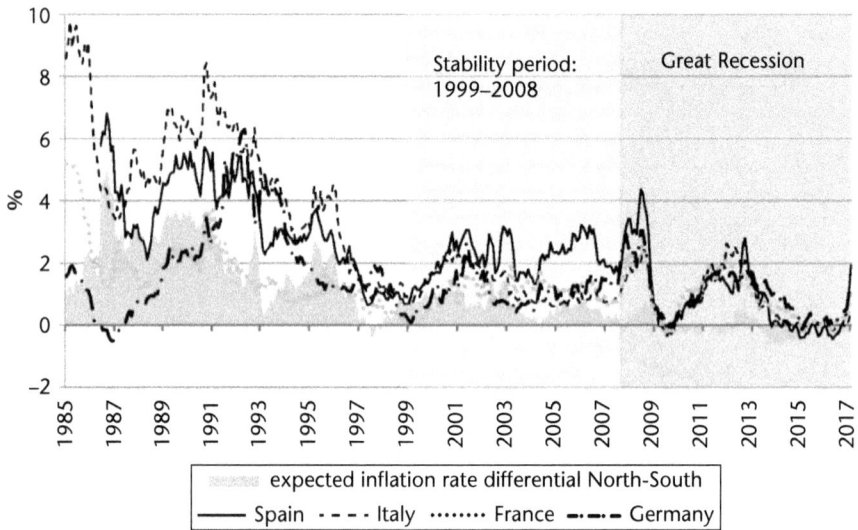

Figure A.2.3 Expected Inflation Rates based on Survey Data Estimates for Spain, Italy, France, and Germany, plus North–South Differential (1985–2017)

Note: South is the unweighted average of Italy and Spain, North is the unweighted average of Germany and France.

Source: Author's calculations based on the EC Consumer Survey and OECD (2017), Main Economic Indicators (database), <http://dx.doi.org/10.1787/data-00052-en> (accessed 27 March 2017).

Without carrying out any formal analysis of the kind carried out by Papadia (1983), two facts clearly emerge from a visual analysis of the figures:

1. Inflationary expectations observed at time t and referring to time t+12 are more clearly correlated to inflation observed at t than to the future inflation at t+12.

2. Inflationary expectations had a downward bias, as they underestimated inflation more often than they overestimated it.

Figure A.2.3 reports the expected inflation rates for the four selected countries showing that they converged as the introduction of the euro got closer, but convergence was not perfect in the first decade or so of the common currency, denoted as the stability period. In particular the expected inflation rate was quite a bit higher in Spain than in Germany and France. Convergence was instead practically complete after the beginning of the Great Recession. The evidence in Figure A.2.3 is consistent with a long learning process.

In peripheral countries, with a memory of high and unstable inflation, there was a lag in recognizing the change in monetary regime brought about by the introduction of the euro, managed with the dominant objective of price stability by the ECB. The quasi perfect convergence of inflationary expectations between peripheral and core countries after the painful experience during the Great Recession seems, however, to indicate that economic agents in the periphery have shed the memory from their unstable, national currencies and adapted their behaviour to a stable euro. This should avoid a repetition of the imbalances that appeared during the first decade of experience of the euro.

Pia Hüttl

Bibliography

Adrian, T., Kimbrough, K., and Marchioni, D. (May 2011). Federal Reserve's Commercial Paper Facility. *FRBNY Economic Policy Review*.

Affinito, M., Albareto, G., and Santioni, R. (2016). Purchases of Sovereign Debt Securities by Italian Banks during the Crisis: The Role of Balance-Sheet Conditions. *Questioni di Economia e Finanza (Occasional Papers)*, No. 330.

Akinci, O., and Olmstead-Rumsey, J. (2015). How Effective Are Macroprudential Policies? An Empirical Investigation. *Board of Governors of the Federal Reserve System, International Finance Discussion Papers*, No. 1136.

Altavilla, C., Giacomo, C., and R. Motto. (2015). Asset Purchase Programmes and Financial Markets: Lessons from the Euro-Area. *ECB Working Paper*, No. 1863.

Altavilla, C., Giannone, D., and Lenza, M. (2014). The Financial and Macroeconomic Effects of OMT Announcements. *ECB Working Paper Series*, No. 1707.

Ando, M. (2012). Recent Developments in US Dollar Funding Costs through FX Swaps. *Bank of Japan*, No. 12-E-3.

Andolfatto, D., Hendry, S., and K. Moran (2008). Are Inflation Expectations Rational?, *Journal of Monetary Economics*, 55 (2), 406–22.

Andrade, P., Breckenfelder, J., De Fiore, F., Karadi, P., and Tristani, O. (2016). The ECB's Asset Purchase Programme: An Early Assessment. *ECB Working Paper Series*, No. 1956.

Angeloni, I. (2017). ECB Banking Supervision Achievements and Challenges. Prometeia conference Europe: Risks and Opportunities, Bologna, 31 March.

Armantier, O., Ghysels, E., Sarkar, A., and Shrader, J. (2015). Discount Window Stigma during the 2007–2008 Financial Crisis. *FRBNY Staff Reports No. 483*, January 2011, revised August 2015.

Atkeson, A., and Ohanian, L. (2000). Are Phillips Curves Useful for Forecasting Inflation? *Federal Reserve of Minneapolis, Quarterly Review*, 25 (1), 2–12.

Baba, N., and Packer, F. (2009). From Turmoil to Crisis: Dislocations in the FX Swap Market before and after the Failure of Lehman Brothers. *BIS Working Papers*, No. 285.

Bagehot, W. (1873). *Lombard Street*. London: Henry S. King and Co.

Ball, L. (2014). The Case for a Long-Run Inflation Target of Four Percent. *IMF Working Paper*, No. 14/92.

Bank for International Settlements (1986). *Recent Innovations in International Banking, Prepared by a Study Group Established by the Central Banks of the Group of Ten Countries* (Cross Report). Basel: Bank for International Settlements.

Bank for International Settlements (2014). *Annual Report*.

Bank of Canada (March 1991). Background Notes on the Targets. *Bank of Canada Review*.

Barro, R. J., and Gordon, B. D. (1983). Discretion and Reputation in a Model of Monetary Policy. *NBER Working Paper* No. 1079, Reprint No. R0448.

Bastasin, C. (2015). *Saving Europe—Anatomy of a Dream*. Washington D.C.: Brookings Institution Press.

Bauer, M., and G. Rudebusch. (2013). The Signaling Channel for Federal Reserve Bond Purchases. *Federal Reserve Bank of San Francisco Working Paper Series 2011–21*. Available at: http://www.frbsf.org/publications/economics/papers/2011/wp11-21bk.pdf.

Bayoumi, T., Dell'Ariccia, G., Habermeier, K., Mancini-Griffoli, T., Valencia, F., and an IMF Staff Team (2014). Monetary Policy in the New Normal. *IMF Staff Discussion Note*.

Bean, C. (2007). Globalisation and Inflation. *World Economics*, 8 (1), 57–73.

Bech, M. L., and Klee, E. (2009). The Mechanics of a Graceful Exit: Interest on Reserves and Segmentation in the Federal Funds Market. *Journal of Monetary Economics*, 58 (5), 415–31.

Beenstock, M. (1989). The Determinants of the Money in the United Kingdom. *Journal of Money, Credit and Banking*, 21 (4), 464–80.

Beirne, J., Dalitz, L., Ejsing, J., Grothe, M., Manganelli, S., Monar, F., Sahel, B., Sušec, M., Tapking, J., and Vong, T. (2011). The Impact of the Eurosystem's Covered Bond Purchase Programme on the Primary and Secondary markets. *Occasional Paper Series*, No. 122. European Central Bank.

Benmelech, E. (2012). An Empirical Analysis of the Fed's Term Auction Facility. *Cato Papers on Public Policy Vol. 2*. Cato Institute.

Bernanke, B. S. (2005). The Global Saving Glut and the U.S. Current Account Deficit. Sandridge Lecture, Virginia. Richmond, VA: Association of Economists, 10 March.

Bernanke, B. S. (2009a). The Crisis and the Policy Response. London School of Economics. Stamp Lecture. London, 13 January.

Bernanke, B. S. (2009b). The Federal Reserve's Balance Sheet. Federal Reserve Bank of Richmond. Credit Markets Symposium, Charlotte, NC, 3 April.

Bernanke, B. S. (2010). The Economic Outlook and Monetary Policy. Federal Reserve Bank of Kansas City Economic Symposium, Jackson Hole, WY, 27 August.

Bernanke, B. S. (2012). The Great Moderation. In: E. Koenig, R. Leeson and G. Kahn eds., *The Taylor Rule and the Transformation of Monetary Policy*, 1st ed. Stanford, CA: Hoover Institution Press.

Bernanke, B. S. (2013). Hearing before the Joint Economic Committee. Congress of the United States. 113th congress, first session. 22 May.

Bernanke, B. S. (2013a). Communication and Monetary Policy. National Economists Club Annual Dinner. Herbert Stein Memorial Lecture. Washington D.C., 19 November.

Bernanke, B. S. (2013b). *The Federal Reserve and the Financial Crisis*. Princeton, NJ: Princeton University Press.

Bernanke, B. S. (2014a). Central Banking after the Great Recession: Lessons Learned and Challenges Ahead. A discussion with Ben Bernanke on the Fed's 100th Anniversary. Washington D. C. Brookings Institute. 16 January.

Bernanke, B. S. (2014b). A Conversation: The Fed Yesterday, Today and Tomorrow. Washington, D.C. The Brookings Institution, 16 January.

Bernanke, B. S. (2015a). *The Courage to Act: A Memoir of a Crisis and Its Aftermath*. London: W.W. Norton & Company.

Bernanke, B. S. (2015b). The Taylor Rule: A Benchmark for Monetary Policy? Blog on the Brookings Website. Available at: https://www.brookings.edu/blog/ben-bernanke/2015/04/28/the-taylor-rule-a-benchmark-for-monetary-policy/ (accessed 11 October 2017).

Billi, R. M., and Kahn, G. A. (2008). What Is the Optimal Inflation Rate? *Federal Reserve Bank of Kansas City Economic Review Second Quarter*.

Bindseil, U. (2004). *Monetary Policy Implementation. Theory-Past-Present.* Oxford: Oxford University Press.

Bindseil, U. (2011). The Theory of Monetary Policy Implementation. In: P. Mercier and F. Papadia, eds, *The Concrete Euro: Implementing Monetary Policy in the Euro-Area.* Oxford: Oxford University Press.

Bindseil, U. (2014). *Monetary Policy Operations and the Financial System.* Oxford: Oxford University Press.

Bindseil, U. (2016). Evaluating Monetary Policy Operational Frameworks. Fed 2016 Economic Policy Symposium at Jackson Hole, 31 August 2016.

Bindseil, U., Dragu, G., Düring, A., and Landesberger von, J. (2016). Asset Liquidity, Central Bank Collateral and Banks' Liability Structure [mimeo], dated 20 March 2016.

Bini-Smaghi, L. (2008). *Careful with (the 'D') Words!* European Colloquia Series, Venice, 25 November 2008.

Blanchard, O., Dell'Ariccia, G., and Mauro, P. (2010). Rethinking Macroeconomic Policy. IMF Staff Position Note. 12 February SPN/10/03.

Blanchard, O., Raghuram, R., Rogoff, K., and Summers, L. H. eds. (2016). *Progress and Confusion: The State of Macroeconomic Policy.* Cambridge MA: The MIT Press.

Blundell-Wignall, A., and Atkinson, P. (2008). The Subprime Crisis: Causal Distortions and Regulatory Reform. Conference Lessons from the Financial Turmoil of 2007 and 2008 hosted by the Reserve Bank of Australia, 14–15 July 2008.

Board of Governors (2000). *Monetary Policy Report to the Congress.* 17 February.

Board of Governors of the Federal Reserve System (2009). *The Supervisory Capital Assessment Program: Design and Implementation.* Available at: https://www.federalreserve.gov/bankinforeg/bcreg20090424a1.pdf.

Boneva, L., Harrison, R., and Waldron, M. (2015). Threshold-Based Forward Guidance: Hedging the Zero Bound. *Bank of England Staff Working Paper*, No. 561. October.

Bordo, M. D. (2007). Economic Commentary: A Brief History of Central Banks. Available at: http://www.clevelandfed.org/research/commentary/2007/12.cfm (accessed 12 January 2017).

Bordo, M. D. (2016). Central Bank Credibility: An Historical and Quantitative Exploration. In: M. D. Bordo, Ø. Eitrheim, M. Flandreau, and J. F. Qvigstad, eds., *Central Banks at a Crossroads: What Can We Learn from History?* Cambridge: Cambridge University Press.

Bordo, M. D., Eitrheim, Ø., Flandreau, M., and Qvigstad, J. F. eds. (2016). *Central Banks at a Crossroads: What Can We Learn from History?* Cambridge: Cambridge University Press.

Borio, C. (2003). Towards a Macroprudential Framework for Financial Supervision and Regulation? *CESifo Economic Studies*, 49 (2), 181–215.

Borio, C. (2009). Implementing the Macroprudential Approach to Financial Regulation and Supervision. *Banque de France, Financial Stability Review*, No. 13—The Future of Financial Regulation, 31.

Borio, C. (2011). Central Banking Post-Crisis: What Compass for Uncharted Waters? *BIS Working Papers*, No. 353.

Borio C. (2012). The Financial Cycle and Macroeconomics: What Have We Learnt? *BIS Working Papers*, No. 395.

Borio, C. (2014a). Monetary Policy and Financial Stability: What Role in Prevention and Recovery? *BIS Working Papers*, No. 440.

Borio, C. (2014b). Central Banking Post-Crisis: What Compass for Uncharted Waters? In: C. Goodhart, D. Gabor. J. Vestergaard and I. Ertürkeds, eds. *Central Banking at a Crossroads, Europe and Beyond*. New York: Anthem Press.

Borio, C. (2015). Macroprudential Frameworks: (Too) Great Expectations? *25th Anniversary Edition of Central Banking Journal. BIS Speeches.*

Borio, C. (2017). Secular Stagnation or Financial Cycle Drag? National Association for Business Economics, 33rd Economic Policy Conference, 5–7 March 2017, Washington, DC.

Borio, C., and Drehmann, M. (2009). Towards an Operational Framework for Financial Stability: 'Fuzzy' Measurement and Its Consequences. *BIS Working Papers*, No. 284.

Borio, C., Erdem, M., Filardo, A., and Hofmann, B. (2015). The Costs of Deflations: A Historical Perspective. *BIS Quarterly Review* (March). Available at: http://www.bis.org/publ/qtrpdf/r_qt1503e.htm (accessed 11 October 2017).

Borio, C., and Filardo, A. (2007). Globalisation and Inflation: New Cross-Country Evidence on the Global Determinants of Domestic Inflation. *BIS Working Papers*, No. 227.

Borio, C., and Lowe, P. (2002). Asset Prices, Financial and Monetary Stability: Exploring the Nexus. *BIS Working Papers*, No. 114.

Borio, C., and Lowe, P. (2004). Securing Sustainable Price Stability: Should Credit Come Back from the Wilderness? *BIS Working Papers*, No. 157.

Brainard, W.C. (1967). Uncertainty and the Effectiveness of Policy. *The American Economic Review*, 57 (2), *Papers and Proceedings of the Seventy-Ninth Annual Meeting of the American Economic Association*, 411–25.

Brunila, A., and Lahdenperä, H. (1995). Inflation Targets: Principal Issues and Practical Implementation. In: A. G. Haldane, ed. *Targeting Inflation*, 1st ed. London: Bank of England, pp. 119–34.

Brunnermeier, M. K., Garicano, L., Lane, P. R., Pagano, M., Reis, R., Santos, T., Thesmar, D., Van Nieuwerburgh, S., and Vayanos, D. (2016). The Sovereign-Bank Diabolic Loop and ESBies. *American Economic Review, Papers and Proceedings*, 106 (5) (May), 508–12.

Brunnermeier, M. K., Harold, J., and Landau, J. (2016). *The Euro and the Battle of Ideas*. Princeton, NJ: Princeton University Press.

Brunnermeier, M. K., and Sannikov, Y. (2014). A Macroeconomic Model with a Financial Sector. *American Economic Review*, 104 (2), 379–421.

Bruno, M., and Easterly, W. (1996). Inflation and Growth: In Search of Stable Relationship. *Federal Reserve Bank of St. Louis Review*, 78 (3), 139–46.

Buchanan, J., and Wagner, R. (1977). *Democracy in Deficit*. New York: Academic Press.

Buiter, W. (2016). *Dysfunctional Central Banking. Global Economics View*. Citi Research Multi Asset. https://www.linkedin.com/pulse/dysfunctional-central-banking-end-independent-banks-return-buiter/

Bullard, J. (2012). Shadow Interest Rates and the Stance of U.S. Monetary Policy. Center for Finance and Accounting Research Annual Corporate Finance Conference, Olin Business School, Washington University in St. Louis, 8 November 2012.

Campbell, J. R., Evans, C. L., Fisher, J. D. M., and Justiniano, A. (2012). Macroeconomic Effects of Federal Reserve Forward Guidance. *Brookings Papers on Economic Activity*, Spring.

Campbell, J. R., Fisher, J. D. M., Justiniano, A., and Melosi, L. (2016). Forward Guidance and Macroeconomic Outcomes since the Financial Crisis. *NBER Macroeconomics Annual 2016*, 31, 283–357.

Carlstrom, C., and Fuerst, T. (2008a). Explaining Apparent Changes in the Phillips Curve: Trend Inflation Isn't Constant. Federal Reserve Bank of Cleveland. Available at: https://www.clevelandfed.org/newsroom-and-events/publications/economic-commentary/economic-commentary-archives/2008-economic-commentaries/ec-20080101-explaining-apparent-changes-in-the-phillips-curve-trend-inflation-isnt-constant.aspx.

Carlstrom, C., and Fuerst, T. (2008b). Explaining Apparent Changes in the Phillips Curve: The Great Moderation and Monetary Policy. Federal Reserve Bank of Cleveland, *Economic Commentary* (February). Available at: https://www.clevelandfed.org/en/newsroom-and-events/publications/economic-commentary/economic-commentary-archives/2008-economic-commentaries/ec-20080201-explaining-apparent-changes-in-the-phillips-curve-the-great-moderation-and-monetary.aspx.

Chen, H., Cúrdia, V., and Ferrero, A. (2012). The Macroeconomic Effects of Large-Scale Asset Purchase Programmes. *The Economic Journal*, 122 (564), 289–315.

Christensen, J., and Rudebusch, G. (2016). Modeling Yields at the Zero Lower Bound: Are Shadow Rates the Solution? In: E. Hillebrand and S. J. Koopman, ed., *Dynamic Factor Models* (Advances in Econometrics, 35). Bingley: Emerald Publishing Group, pp. 75–125.

Chung, H., Herbst, E., and Kiley, M. (2015). Effective Monetary Policy Strategies in New Keynesian Models: A Reexamination. *NBER Macroeconomics Annual*, 29 (1), 289–344. Available at: https://doi.org/10.1086/680629.

Chung, H., Laforte, J.-P., Reifschneider, D., and Williams, J. (2012). Have We Underestimated the Likelihood and Severity of Zero Lower Bound Events? *Journal of Money, Credit and Banking*, 44 (1), 47–82.

Cerutti, E., Claessens, S., and Laeven, L. (2015). The Use and Effectiveness of Macroprudential Policies: New Evidence. *IMF Working Papers*, No. 15/61.

Cestari, V., Del Giovane, P., and Rossi-Arnaud, C. (2007). Memory for Prices and the Euro Cash Changeover: An Analysis for Cinema Prices in Italy. *Banca D'Italia, Temi di discussione*, No. 619.

Claessens, S., and Kodres, L. E. (2014). The Regulatory Responses to the Global Financial Crisis: Some Uncomfortable Questions. *IMF Working Papers*, No. 14/46.

Claessens, S., Kose, M. A., and Terrones, M. E. (2010). The Global Financial Crisis: How Similar? How Different? How Costly? *Journal of Asian Economics*, 21 (3), 247–64.

Clarida, R., Gali, J., and Gertler, M. (2000). Monetary Policy Rules and Macroeconomic Stability: Evidence and Some Theory. *Quarterly Journal of Economics*, 115, 147–80.

Cœuré, B. (2016). Assessing the Implications of Negative Interest Rates. Yale Financial Crisis Forum, Yale School of Management, New Haven, CT, 28 July 2016.

Coibion, O., Gorodnichenko, Y., and Wieland, J. (2012). The Optimal Inflation Rate in New Keynesian Models: Should Central Banks Raise Their Inflation Targets in Light of the Zero Lower Bound? *Review of Economic Studies*, 79 (4), 1371–1406.

Constâncio, V. (2013). The European Crisis and the Role of the Financial System. Bank of Greece Conference The Crisis in the Euro-Area, Athens, 23 May 2013.

Constâncio, V. (2015). The Role of Stress Testing in Supervision and Macroprudential Policy. London School of Economics Conference on Stress Testing and Macroprudential Regulation: A Trans-Atlantic Assessment, London, 29 October 2015.

Constâncio, V. (2016). *The Challenge of Low Real Interest Rates for Monetary Policy*. Macroeconomics Symposium at Utrecht School of Economics, 15 June 2016.

Cour-Thimann, P. (2013). Target Balances and the Crisis in the Euro-Area. *CESifo Forum 14, Special Issue*.

Cour-Thimann, P., and Winkler, B. (2016). Central Banks as Balance Sheets of Last Resort: The ECB's Monetary Policy in a Flow-of-Funds Perspective. In: D. Cobham, ed., *Monetary Analysis at Central Banks*, 1st ed. Basingstoke: Palgrave Macmillan.

Crespo-Cuaresma, J. C., and Silgoner, M. (2014). Economic Growth and Inflation in Europe: A Tale of Two Thresholds. *Journal of Common Market Studies*, 52 (4), 843–60.

Crockett, A. (2000). Marrying the Micro-and Macro-Prudential Dimensions of Financial Atability. *BIS Speeches*, 21.

Crockett, A. (2011). Central Bank Governance under New Mandates In: S. G. Cecchetti, A. Lamfalussy, J. Caruana, M. Carney, A. Crockett, S. Ingves, L. Papademos and D. Subbarao eds, *The Future of Central Banking under Post-Crisis Mandates*. Bank for International Settlements. Ninth BIS Annual Conference, 24–25 June 2010.

Cukierman, A. (1992). *Central Bank Strategy, Credibility, and Independence: Theory and Evidence*. Cambridge, MA: The MIT Press.

Cukierman, A. (2016). Global Crisis in the US vs the Euro-area: Banks and Monetary Policy. VOX CEPR Policy Portal. Available at: http://voxeu.org (accessed 16 April 2016).

D'Amico, S., English, W., López-Salido, D., and Nelson, E. (2012). The Federal Reserve's Large-Scale Asset Purchase Programmes: Rationale and Effects. *Economic Journal*, 122, 516–446.

D'Amico, S., and King, T. (2013). Flow and Stock Effects of Large-Scale Treasury Purchases: Evidence on the Importance of Local Supply. *Journal of Financial Economics*, 108 (2), 425–48.

Darracq-Paries, M., and De Santis, R. (2013). A Non-Standard Monetary Policy Shock: The ECB's 3-year LTROs and the Shift in Credit Supply. *ECB Working Paper*, No. 1508.

Davis, S. J. (2008). The Decline of Job Loss and Why it Matters. *American Economic Review: Papers and Proceedings*, 98 (2), 263–7.

Davis, S. J., and Kahn, J. A. (2008). Interpreting the Great Moderation: Changes in the Volatility of Economic Activity at the Macro and Micro Levels. *NBER Working Paper*, No. 14048.

De Grauwe, Paul (2013). Design Failures in the Euro-Area: Can They Be Fixed? *LSE 'Europe in Question' Discussion Paper Series*, 57.

De Larosière, J., Balcerowicz, L. Issing, O., Masera, R., McCarthay, C., Nyberg, L., Perez, J., and Rudin, O. (2009). *The de Larosière report*. The High-Level Group on Financial Supervision in the EU, Brussels.

De Pooter, M., DeSimone, R., Martin, R., and Pruit, S. (2015). Cheap Talk and the Efficacy of the ECB's Securities Markets Programme: Did Bond Purchases Matter? Federal Reserve Board of Governors, *International Finance Discussion Papers*, No. 1139.

Del Giovane, P., Fabiani, S., and Sabbatini, R. (2008). What's Behind 'Inflation Perceptions'? A Survey-Based Analysis of Italian Consumers. *Banca D'Italia, Temi di Discussione*, No. 655.

Dell'Ariccia, G., Igan, D., Laeven, L., and Tong, H. with Bakker, B., and Vandenbussche, J. (2012). *Policies for Macrofinancial Stability: How to Deal with Credit Booms*. Washington, DC: International Monetary Fund.

Deutsche Bundesbank (2010). Price-level targeting as a monetary policy Strategy. Monthly Report January.

Deutsche Bundesbank (2017). The Eurosystem's Bond Purchases and the Exchange Rate of the Euro. *Monthly Report*, January, 13–39. Available at: https://www.bundesbank.de/Redaktion/EN/Downloads/Publications/Monthly_Report_Articles/2017/2017_01_anleihekaeufe_eurosystem.pdf?__blob=publicationFile.

Diamond, D. W. (2007). Banks and Liquidity Creation: A Simple Exposition of the Diamond-Dybvig Model. *Economic Quarterly*, 93 (2) Spring, 189–200.

Dias, F., Duarte, C., and A. Rua (2008). Inflation Expectations in the Euro Area: Are Consumers Rational?. Banco de Portugal Working Paper 23. Available at: https://www.bportugal.pt/sites/default/files/anexos/papers/wp200823.pdf.

Dickens, W., Goette, E., Groshen, S., Holden, J., Messina, M., Schweitzer, Turunen, J., and Ward, M. (2007). How Wages Change: Micro Evidence from the International Wage Flexibility Project. *Journal of Economic Perspectives*, 21 (2), 195–214.

Dornbusch, R. (1976). Expectations and Exchange Rate Dynamics. *Journal of Political Economy*. Revisited by Rogoff, K. (2002). Dornbusch's Overshooting Model after Twenty-Five Years. *IMF Working Paper*, WP/02/39.

Dornbusch, R., Fischer, S., and Startz, R. (1994). *Macroeconomics*. 8th ed., New York: McGraw-Hill.

Draghi, M. (2017). Monetary Policy and the Economic Recovery in the Euro-Area. The ECB and Its Watchers XVIII Conference, Frankfurt am Main, 6 April 2017.

Dynan, K., Elmendorf, D. W., and Sichel, D. E. (2006). Can Financial Innovation Help Explain the Reduced Volatility of Economic Activity? *Journal of Monetary Economics*, 53, 123–50.

ECB (1999). The Stability-Oriented Monetary Policy Strategy of the Eurosystem. *Monthly Bulletin*, January.

ECB (2007). *Financial Stability Review*, December, p. 9.

ECB (2008). *Financial Stability Review*, December.

ECB (2010). *Financial Stability Review*, June, Box 11, p. 87.

ECB (2012). *Financial Stability Review*, December, p. 10.

ECB (2013a). Exploring the Nexus between Macro-Prudential Policies and Monetary Policy Measures. *Financial Stability Review*, May p. 99.

ECB (2013b). *Monthly Bulletin*, June.

ECB (2014a). Experience with Foreign Currency Liquidity-Providing Central Bank Swaps. *Economic Bulletin*, August.

ECB (2014b). *Aggregate Report on the Comprehensive Assessment*.

ECB (2015a). The Role of the Central Bank Balance Sheet in Monetary Policy, *Economic Bulletin*. 4, June.

ECB (2015b). Statistical Annex of 2015.

ECB (2017). The Targeted Longer-term Refinancing Operations: An Overview of the Take-up and Their Impact on Bank Intermediation. *Economic Bulletin*, 3.

ECB (n.d.) *Survey of Professional Forecasters*. Available at: http://www.ecb.europa.eu/ stats/prices/indic/forecast/html/index.en.html.

ECOFIN (2013). *The November Statement*.

Eggertsson, G. B., and Woodford, M. (2003). The Zero Bound on Interest Rates and Optimal Monetary Policy, Brookings Paper on Economic Activity. No. 1.

Eichengreen, B. (2010). From Great Depression to Great Credit Crisis: Similarities, Differences and Lessons, *Economic Policy*, 62, 219–265.

Eichengreen, B., El-Erian, M., Fraga, A., Ito, T., Pisani-Ferry, J., Prasad, E., Rajan, R., Ramos, M., Reinhart, C., Rey, H., Rodrik, D., Rogoff, K., Shin, H. S., Velasco, A., Weder di Mauro, B., and Yu, Y. (2011). *Rethinking Central Banking Committee on International Economic Policy and Reform*. Washington D.C.: Brookings Institution Press.

Eijffinger, S., and de Haan, J. (1996). The Political Economy of Central-Bank Independence. *Special Papers in International Economics*, No. 19, May. Princeton University, Princeton, NJ.

Eijffinger, S., and de Haan, J. (2016). The Politics of Central Bank Independence. *Discussion Paper*, No. 2016–047, Tilburg University, Center for Economic Research.

Eijffinger, S., and Masciandaro, D. (2014). Modern Monetary Policy and Central Bank Governance: A Story of Two Tales. *Baffi Center Research Paper*, No. 2014–157.

Eisenschmidt, J., and Tapking, J. (2009). Liquidity Risk Premia in Unsecured Interbank Money Markets. *ECB Working Paper Series*, No. 1025.

Engen, E., Laubach, T., and Reifschneider, D. (2015). The Macroeconomic Effects of the Federal Reserve's Unconventional Monetary Policies. *Finance and Economics Discussion Series* 2015–005. Washington: Board of Governors of the Federal Reserve System. Available at: http://dx.doi.org/10.17016/FEDS.2015.005.

Enria, A. (2011). Introduction to *Regole e Finanza* (Italian translation of Padoa Schioppa, T. (2004) *Regulating Finance: Balancing Freedom and Risk*. Oxford: Oxford University Press) Bologna: Il Mulino.

Eser, F., and Schwaab, B. (2013). Assessing Asset Purchases within the ECB's Securities Markets Programme. *ECB Working Paper Series*, No. 1585, September.

European Banking Authority Website on the Single Rule Book. Available at http://www. eba.europa.eu/regulation-and-policy/single-rulebook.

European Systemic Risk Board (2014). *Flagship Report on Macro-Prudential Policy in the Banking Sector*.

Fed (2009a). Board of Governors of the Federal Reserve System. *The Supervisory Capital Assessment Program: Design and Implementation*, 24 April.

Fed (2009b). *The Supervisory Capital Assessment Program: Overview of Results*, Board of Governors of the Federal Reserve System. 7 May.

Fed (2017). Projections for the SOMA Portfolio and Net Income. An Update to Projections. *Report on Domestic Open Market Operations during 2016*, July.

Feroli, M., Greenlaw, D., Hooper, P., Mishkin, F., and Sufi, A. (2016). Language after Liftoff: Fed Communication Away from the Zero Lower Bound. 2016 U.S. Monetary Policy Forum in New York, 26 February 2016. Available at: https://research.chicagobooth. edu/igm/events/conferences/2016-usmonetaryforum.aspx.

Fischer, S. (1977). Long-Term Contracts, Rational Expectations, and the Optimal Money Supply Rule. *Journal of Political Economy*, 85 (1) February, 191–205.

Fischer, S. (1993). The Role of Macroeconomic Factors in Growth. *NBER Working Paper*, No. 456.

Fischer, S. (1995). Modern Central Banking. In: F. Capie, S. Fischer, C. Goodhart, and N. Schnadt, *The Future of Central Banking*. Cambridge: Cambridge University Press.

Fischer, S. (2015). Macroprudential Policy in the U.S. Economy. Macroprudential Monetary Policy, 59th Economic Conference of the Federal Reserve Bank of Boston, Boston, MA.

Fischer, S. (2016). Monetary Policy, Financial Stability, and the Zero Lower Bound. Annual Meeting of the American Economic Association San Francisco, California, 3 January.

Fischer, B., Lenza, M., Pill, H., and Reichlin, L. (2008). *Money and Monetary Policy: The ECB Experience 1999–2006, The Role of Money—Money and Monetary Policy in the Twenty-First Century*. Frankfurt am Main: ECB.

Flemming, M., Hrung, W., and Keane, F. (2010). Repo Market Effects of the Term Securities Lending Facility. *American Economic Review: Papers & Proceedings*, 100, 591–6. Available at: http://www.aeaweb.org/articles.php?doi=10.1257/aer.W0.2.591.

Florio, A., Lossani, M., and Nardozzi, G. (2011). *From the Global Financial Crisis to Global Monetary Rules: A Wicksellian View*. Soveria Mannelli: Rubettino.

FOMC (2012). FOMC Statement of Longer-Run Goals and Policy Strategy, 5 January.

Forsells, M., and Kenny, G. (2002). The Rationality of Consumers' Inflation Expectations: Survey-Based Evidence from the Euro Area, ECB Working paper No. 163.

Fratianni, M., and Spinelli, F. (2000). *Storia monetaria d'Italia. Lira e politica monetaria dall'unita all'unione europea*. Milan: Etas.

Fratzscher, M., Lo Duca, M., and Straub, R. (2014). ECB Unconventional Monetary Policy Actions: Market Impact, International Spillovers and Transmission Channels. 15th Jacques Polak Annual Research Conference, Washington, DC, 13–14 November.

Friedman, M. (1960). *A Program for Monetary Stability*. New York: Fordham University Press.

Friedman, M. (1968). The Role of Monetary Policy. *American Economic Review*, 58, 1–17.

Friedmann, B. M., and Kuttner, K. N. (2011). Implementation of Monetary Policy. How Do Central Banks Set Interest Rates? In: B. M. Friedman and K.N. Kuttner, eds, *Handbook on Monetary Economics*, 1st ed. Amsterdam: Elsevier, pp. 1345–1433.

Gagnon, J., Raskin, M., Remacheb, J., and Sack, B. (2011). The Financial Market Effects of the Federal Reserve's Large-Scale Asset Purchases. *International Journal of Central Banking*, 7 (1), 3–43.

Gali, J., and Gambetti, L. (2008). On the Sources of the Great Moderation. *NBER Working Paper*, No. 14171.

Gamber, E., and Hung, J. (2001). Has the Rise in Globalization Reduced U.S. Inflation in the 1990s? *Economic Inquiry*, 39 (2), 58–73.

Gerlach, S., and Lewis, J. (2010). The Zero Lower Bound, ECB Interest Rate Policy and the Financial Crisis. *DNB Working Paper*, No. 254 July.

Gertler, M., and Karadi, P. (2011). A Model of Unconventional Monetary Policy. *Journal of Monetary Economics*, 58, 17–34.

Ghosh, A., and Phillips, S. (1998). Warning: Inflation May Be Harmful to Your Growth. *International Monetary Fund Staff Papers*, 45, 672–710.

Gibas, N., Juks, R., and Söderberg, J. (2015). Swedish Financial Institutions and Low Interest Rates. *Economic Commentaries*, No. 16.

Giraudo, A. (2016). Tiberius's Experiences with Zero Interest Rates in AD 33. *Central Banking*, June.

Goldberg, L.S., Kennedy, C., and Miu, J. (2011). *Central Bank Dollar Swap Lines and Overseas Dollar Funding Costs. FRBNY Economic Policy Review*, May.

González Cabanillas, L., and Rusche, E. (2008). The Great Moderation in the Euro-area: What Role Have Macroeconomic Policies Played. *European Economy Economic Papers*, 33.

Goodhart, C. (1999). Myths about the Lender of Last Resort. *International Finance*, 2 (3), 339–60.

Goodhart, C. (2004). Introduction to: Padoa-Schioppa, T. (2004). *Regulating Finance: Balancing Freedom and Risk*. Oxford: Oxford University Press.

Goodhart, C. (2010). The Changing Role of Central Banks, Financial Markets Group, London School of Economics. Available at: http://www.bis.org/events/conf100624/goodhartpaper.pdf [28.3.2017].

Goodhart, C., Baker, M., and Ashworth, J. (22 January 2013). *Monetary Targetry: Might Carney Make a Difference?* VOX CEPR's Policy Portal. Available at: http://voxeu.org [6 April 2017].

Goodhart, C., Gabor, D.,Vestergaard, J., and Ertürk, I. (2014). *Central Banking at a Crossroads: Europe and Beyond*. London: Anthem Press.

Goodhart, C., Pradhan, M., and Pardeshi, P. (2015). *Could Demographics Reverse Three Multi-Decade Trends?* Morgan Stanley Research, Global Economics, 15 September.

Gordon, R. (2016). *The Rise and Fall of American Growth: The US Standard of Living Since the Civil War*. Princeton: Princeton University Press.

Greenspan, Alan (1989). Statement before the US Senate Committee on Banking, Housing, and Urban Affairs, 21 February.

Gros, D. (2015). Countries under Adjustment Programmes: What Role for the ECB? *CEPS Special Report*, No. 124.

Gürkaynak, R. (2005). Using Federal Funds Futures Contracts for Monetary Policy Analysis. *Finance and Economics Discussion Series* 2005–29. Board of Governors of the Federal Reserve System.

Gürkaynak, R., Sack, B., and Swanson, E. (2005). Do Actions Speak Louder Than Words? The Response of Asset Prices to Monetary Policy Actions and Statements. *International Journal of Central Banking*, May.

Hagen von, J. (2009). The Monetary Mechanics of the Crisis. *Bruegel Policy Contribution*, August.

Haldane, A. (1995). Inflation Targets. *Bank of England Quarterly Bulletin*. August, 250–9.

Hancock, D., and Passmore, W. (2011). Did the Federal Reserve's MBS Purchase Program Lower Mortgage Rates? *Finance and Economics Discussion Series*. Washington, DC: Federal Reserve Board.

Hansen, H. (1939). Economic Progress and Declining Population Growth (speech for AEA meetings 1938), *American Economic Review*, March. XXIX (1/ I).

Hellwig, M. (2015). Financial Stability and Monetary Policy. *Preprints of the Max Planck Institute for Research on Collective Goods*, 10.

Hofmann, B., and Bogdanova, B. (2012). Taylor Rules and Monetary Policy: A Global 'Great Deviation'? *BIS Quarterly Review*, September.

Hoisington, V. R., and Hunt, L. (2013). Federal Reserve Failures. *Quarterly Review and Outlook* Q3.

Holden, S., and Wulfsberg, F. (2014). Wage Rigidity, Institutions, and Inflation. *Scandinavian Journal of Economics*, 116 (2), 539–69.

Holló, D., Kremer, M., and Lo Duca, M. (2012). *A Composite Indicator of Systemic Stress in the Financial System. Working Paper Series*, No. 1426, Frankfurt am Main: ECB.

Homer, S., and Sylla, R. (1991). *A History of Interest Rates*. 3rd ed. New Brunswick, NJ: Rutgers University Press.

Ihrig, J., Kamin, S., Lindner, D., and Marquez, J. (2007). Some Simple Tests of the Globalization and Inflation Hypothesis. *International Finance Discussion Papers*, No. 891, Federal Reserve Board. Finance, 7, 61–84.

IMF (2006). How Has Globalization Changed Inflation? *IMF World Economic Outlook*, April.

IMF (2007). GFSR of September.

IMF (2008a). GFSR of April, p. IX.

IMF (2008b). GFSR of October.

IMF (2009). GFSR of October.

IMF (2013). *Key Aspects of Macroprudential Policy*, 10 June 10.

Jaumotte, F., and Tytell, I. (2007). How Has the Globalization of Labor Affected the Labor Share in Advanced Countries? *IMF Working Paper*, December.

Jordan, T. (2016). The Euro and Swiss Monetary Policy. Europa Forum Lucerne, 2 May .

Jørgensen, A., and Risbjerg, L. (2012). Negative Interest Rates. *Danmarks Nationalbank Monetary Review*, 3rd Quarter (1).

Juncker, J.-C., Tusk, D., Dijsselbloem, J., Draghi, M., and Schulz, M. (2015). *The Five Presidents' Report: Completing Europe's Economic and Monetary Union*. Available at: https://ec.europa.eu/commission/publications/five-presidents-report-completing-europes-economic-and-monetary-union_en.

Kahn, G. A. (2010). Monetary Policy under a Corridor Operating Framework. Kansas City Fed website. Available at: http://www.KansasCityFed.org, p. 22.

Kahn, James A., McConnell, M., and Perez-Quiros, G. (2002). On the Causes of the Increased Stability of the U.S. Economy. *FRBNY, Economic Policy Review*, 8, 183–202.

Kashyap, A. K., and Stein, J. C. (2012). The Optimal Conduct of Monetary Policy with Interest on Reserves. *American Economic Journal: Macroeconomics*, 4 (1), 266–82.

Keister, T., Martin, A., and McAndrews, J. (2008). Divorcing Money from Monetary Policy. *FRBNY Economic Policy Review*. Available at: https://www.newyorkfed.org/medialibrary/media/research/epr/08v14n2/0809keis.pdf.

Khan, M. S., and Senhadji, S. A. (2000). Threshold Effects in the Relationship between Inflation and Growth, *IMF Working Papers*, 110/2000.

Kindleberger, C. P. (1978). *Manias, Panics, and Crashes: A History of Financial Crisis*. New York: Basic Books.

Kindleberger, C. P. (1988). *The International Economic Order, Essays on Financial Crisis and International Public Goods*. Cambridge, MA: The MIT Press.

Kindleberger, C. P., and Aliber, R. Z. (2005). *Manias, Panics, and Crashes: A History of Financial Crisis*. 5th ed. Hoboken, NJ: John Wiley & Sons Inc.

King, M. (1997). Changes in UK Monetary Policy: Rules and Discretion in Practice. *Journal of Monetary Economics*, 39, 81–97.

Kofoed Mandsberg, R., Lejsgaard Autrup, S., and Risbjerg, L. (2016). Pass-through from Danmarks Nationalbank's Interest Rates to the Banks Interest Rates. *Danmarks Nationalbank, Monetary Review*, Q2.

Kohn, D. (2008). *Implications of Globalization for the Conduct of Monetary Policy*. International Symposium of the Banque de France, Paris, France, March 7, 2008.

Kohn, D. (2012). It's Not So Simple. In: E. Koenig, R. Leeson, and G. Kahn, eds., *The Taylor Rule and the Transformation of Monetary Policy*, 1st ed. Stanford, CA: Hoover Institution Press.

Koo, R. (2009). *The Holy Grail of Macroeconomics-Lessons from Japan's Great Recession*. Singapore: John Wiley & Sons (Asia) Pte. Ltd.

Kortela, T. (2016). A Shadow Rate Model with Time-Varying Lower Bound of Interest Rates. *Bank of Finland Research Discussion Paper*, No. 19/2016.

Kremer, S., Bick, A., and Nautz, D. (2013). Inflation and Growth: New Evidence from a Dynamic Panel Threshold Analysis. *Empirical Economics*, 44 (2), 861–87.

Krippner, L. (2015). *Zero Lower Bound Term Structure Modeling*. New York: Palgrave Macmillan.

Krishnamurthy, A., and Vissing-Jorgensen, A. (2011). The Effects of Quantitative Easing on Interest Rates. *NBER Working Paper*, No. 17555.

Krishnamurthy, A., and Vissing-Jorgensen, A. (2013). The Ins and Outs of LSAPs. Proceedings—*Economic Policy Symposium—Jackson Hole*. Available at: http://www.kansascityfed.org/publicat/sympos/2013/2013Krishnamurthy.pdf.

Krugman, P. (2015). Nonlinearity, Multiple Equilibria, and the Problem of Too Much Fun (Wonkish). Available at: http://krugman.blogs.nytimes.com/.

Kuroda, H. (2014). The Practice and Theory of Unconventional Monetary Policy. 17th World Congress hosted by the International Economic Association, 7 June 2014.

Kuttner, K. N., and Shim, I. (2013). Can Non-Interest Rate Policies Stabilise Housing Markets? Evidence from a Panel of 57 Economies. *BIS Working Papers*, No. 433 Monetary and Economic Department.

Kydland, F., and Prescott, E. (1977). Rules Rather than Discretion: The Inconsistency of Optimal Plans. *The Journal of Political Economy*, 85 (3), 473–92.

Lamfalussy, A. (2010). The Future of Central Banking under Post-Crisis Mandates. 9th BIS Annual Conference Lucerne, 24–25 June 2010.

Laubach, T., and Williams, J. C. (2015). Measuring the Natural Rate of Interest Redux. *Federal Reserve Bank of San Francisco Working Paper*. Available at: http://www.frbsf.org/economic-research/publications/working-papers/wp2015-16.pdf.

Lemke, W., and Vladu, A. (2016). Below the Zero Bound – a Shadow-Rate Term Structure Model for the Euro-Area. *Discussion Paper*, Deutsche Bundesbank, No. 32.

Lim, C. H., Costa, A., Columba, F., Kongsamut, P., Otani, A., Saiyid, M., Wezel, T., and Wu, X. (2011). Macroprudential Policy: What Instruments and How to Use Them? Lessons from Country Experiences. *IMF Working Papers*, No. 11/238, International Monetary Fund. Available at: http://ssrn.com/abstract=21697491, 2.1 (accessed 3 April 2017).

Lucas, R. E. (1973). Some International Evidence on Output-Inflation Tradeoffs. *American Economic Review*, 63 (June), 326–34.

McAndrews, J., Sarkar, A., and Wang, Z. (2017). The Effect of the Term Auction Facility on the London Interbank Offered Rate. *Staff Reports, No. 335*, January.

Maes, I. (2010). Alexandre Lamfalussy and the Origins of the BIS Macro-Prudential Approach to Financial Stability. *PSL Quarterly Review*, 63 (254), 265–92.

Maes, I. (2014). Financial Crises: Will it be Different Next Time? In: P. Clement, H. James, and H. Van der Wee, eds, *Financial Innovation, Regulation and Crises in History*, 1st ed. London: Pickering & Chatto Publishers, pp. 1–3.

Maes, I. (2015). The BIS Macro-Prudential Approach to Financial Stability. In: L.-P. Rochon and S. Rossi, eds, *Encyclopedia on Central Banking*, 1st ed. Cheltenham: Edward Elgar Publishing, pp. 54–6.

Mavroeidis, S., Plagborg-Møller, M., and Stock, J. (2014). Empirical Evidence on Inflation Expectations in the New Keynesian Phillips Curve. *Journal of Economic Literature*, 52 (1), 124–88.

Meaning, J., and Zhu, F. (2011). The Impact of Recent Central Bank Asset Purchase Programmes. *BIS Quarterly Review*, December, 73–83.

Mercier, P., and Papadia, F. eds. (2011). *The Concrete Euro: Implementing Monetary Policy in the Euro-Area*. Oxford: Oxford University Press.

Merler, S., and Pisani-Ferry, J. (2012). Sudden Stops in the Euro-Area. *Bruegel Policy Contribution*, 29 March.

Messina, J., Caju, P., Duarte, C., Hansen, N., and Izquierdo, M. (2010). The Incidence of Nominal and Real Wage Rigidity: An Individual-Based Sectoral Approach. *Banco de Espana Working Papers*, No. 1022.

Minsky, H. P. (1986). *Stabilizing an Unstable Economy*. New Haven, CT: Yale University Press.

Minsky, H. P. (1995). *Financial Factors in the Economics of Capitalism*. Hyman P. Minsky Archive, Paper 64. Available at: http://digitalcommons.bard.edu/hm_archive/64, p. 203.

Minsky, H. P. (2008). *Stabilizing an Unstable Economy*. New York: McGraw-Hill.

Mishkin, F. (2007). Inflation Dynamics. *NBER Working Paper*, No. 13147.

Mitchell, B. (1992). *International Historical Statistics, Europe, 1750–1988*. New York: Palgrave Macmillan.

Morris, S., and Shin, H. S. (2000). *Rethinking Multiple Equilibria in Macroeconomic Modelling*. In: B. S. Bernanke and K. Rogoff, eds, *NBER Macroeconomics Annual 2000, Volume 15*, 1st ed. Cambridge, MA: The MIT Press.

Moselund Jensen, C., and Spange, M. (2015). Interest Rate Pass-through and the Demand for Cash at Negative Interest Rates. *Danmarks Nationalbank, Monetary Review*, Q2.

Neely, C. (2014). Lessons from Taper Tantrum. Economic Synopses 2014 No. 2. Federal Reserve Bank of St. Louis.

Neely, C. (2015). Unconventional Monetary Policy Had Large International Effects. *Journal of Banking and Finance*, 52, 101–11.

Nordhaus, W. (1975). The Political Business Cycle. *Review of Economic Studies*, 42 (2), 169–90.

Nouy, D., and Lautenschläger, S. (2017). Introductory Statement to the Press Conference on the ECB Annual Report on Supervisory Activities 2016 (with Q&A). Frankfurt am Main, 27 March.

O'Donoghue, J., Goulding, L., and Grahame, A. (2004). *Consumer Price Inflation since 1750*. London: Office for National Statistics; Federal Reserve Economic Data.

Officer, L. H. (2015). What Was the Interest Rate Then? Available at: https://measuringworth.com/.

Orphanides, A. (2008). Taylor Rules. *The New Palgrave Dictionary of Economics*, 2nd ed.

Orphanides, A. (2013). Is monetary policy overburdened? BIS Working Papers No 435 Monetary and Economic Department, December.

Padoa-Schioppa, T. (1994). *The Road to Monetary Union in Europe*. Oxford: Clarendon Press.

Padoa-Schioppa, T. (1999). EMU and Banking Supervision. Lecture at the London School of Economics, Financial Markets Group, London, 24 February.

Padoa-Schioppa, T. (2004). *Regulating Finance: Balancing Freedom and Risk*. Oxford: Oxford University Press.

Papadia, F. (1983). Rationality of Inflationary Expectations in the European Economic Communities Countries. *Empirical Economics*, 8, 187–202.

Papadia, F. (2013a). Central Bank Cooperation during the Great Recession. *Bruegel Policy Contribution*, June.

Papadia, F. (2013b). Forward with Forward Guidance! Or Much Ado about Nothing? Money Matters? Perspectives on Monetary Policy website. Available at: http://moneymatters-monetarypolicy.eu.

Papadia, F. (2014). *Re-thinking the Lender of Last Resort*. Workshop at the BIS in Basel, 15 May 2014.

Papadia, F. (2016a). *How Should Central Banks Steer Money Market Interest Rates?* Workshop on Implementing Monetary Policy Post-Crisis: What Have We Learned? What Do We Need to Know? Organized by Columbia University SIPA and the Federal Reserve Bank of New York, 4 May.

Papadia, F. (2016b). *Liquidity Supply and Demand in the €-Area: A Schematic Approach*. Money matters? Perspectives on Monetary Policy website. Available at: http://moneymatters-monetarypolicy.eu.

Papadia, F. (2016c). *Secular Stagnation vs. Debt Super-Cycle: Which One Is Right?* Money Matters? Perspectives on Monetary Policy website. Available at: http://moneymatters-monetarypolicy.eu.

Papadia, F., and Basano, V. (1981). EEC-DG II Inflationary Expectations; Survey-Based Inflationary Expectations for the EEC Countries. *Economic Papers*, No. 1, May.

Papadia, F., and Saccomanni, F. (1994). From the Werner Plan to the Maastricht Treaty: Europe's Stubborn Quest for Monetary Union. In: A. Steinherr, ed., *30 Years of European Monetary Integration: from the Werner Plan to EMU*. London: Longman.

Papadia, F., and Välimäki, T. (2011). The Functioning of the Eurosystem Framework since 1999. In: P. Mercier and F. Papadia eds, *The Concrete Euro: Implementing Monetary Policy in the Euro-Area*, 1st ed. Oxford: Oxford University Press.

Paquet, A. (1992). Inflationary Expectations and Rationality. *Economics Letters*, 40 (3), 303–8.

Phelps, E. S. (1967). Phillips Curves, Expectations of Inflation and Optimal Unemployment over Time. *Economica*, 34, 254–81.

Phelps, E. S. (1968). Money-Wage Dynamics and Labor-Market Equilibrium. *Journal of Political Economy*, 76, 678–711.

Phillips, A. W. (1958). The Relation between Unemployment and the Money Wage Rates in the United Kingdom, 1861–1957. *Economica*, 25, 283–99.

Pisani-Ferry, J. (2011). *Le réveil des démons: La crise de l'euro et comment nous en sorti*. Paris: Fayard.

Pisani-Ferry, J. (2014). *The Euro Crisis and Its Aftermath*. Oxford: Oxford University Press.

Plosser, C. I. (2013). *A Limited Central Bank*. Philadelphia: Federal Reserve Bank of Philadelphia.

Posen, A., and Véron, N. (2014). Europe's Half a Banking Union. *Bruegel*, 19 September.

Potter, S. (2016). Discussion of 'Evaluating Monetary Policy Operational Frameworks' by Ulrich Bindseil. 2016 Fed Economic Policy Symposium at Jackson Hole, WY, 25 August.

Praet, P. (2016). Monetary Policy Transmission in the Euro-Area. SUERF Conference Global Implications of Europe's Redesign, New York, 6 October.

Rajan, R. (2013). A Step in the Dark: Unconventional Monetary Policy after the Crisis. Andrew Crockett Memorial Lecture, Bank for International Settlements, 23 June.

Reinhart, C. M., and Rogoff, K. S. (2009). *This Time is Different*. Princeton, NJ: Princeton University Press.

Reinhart, C. M., and Rogoff, K. S. (2013). Shifting Mandates: The Federal Reserve's First Centennial. American Economic Association Meetings, San Diego, CA, 5 January.

Reinhart, C. M., and Sbrancia, B. (2011). The Liquidation of Government Debt. *NBER Working Paper*, No. 16893. Available at: http://www.bis.org/publ/work363.htm.

Richter, R. (1989). *Money: Lectures on the Basis of General Equilibrium Theory and the Economics of Institutions*. Berlin: Springer Verlag.

Riksbank (2016). Perspectives on the Negative Repo Rate. *Monetary Policy Report*, July.

Roberts, J. (2006). Monetary Policy and Inflation Dynamics. *International Journal of Central Banking*, 2 (3), 193–230.

Rodrik, D. (2011). *The Globalization Paradox: Why Global Markets, States, and Democracy Can't Coexist*. Oxford: Oxford University Press.

Rogoff, K. (1985). The Optimal Degree of Commitment to an Intermediate Monetary Target. *Quarterly Journal of Economics*, 100 (4), 1169–89.

Rogoff, K. (2016). Debt Supercycle, Not Secular Stagnation. In: O. Blanchard, R. Rajan, K. Rogoff, and L. H. Summers, eds, *Progress and Confusion*, 1st ed. Cambridge, MA: The MIT Press.

Saccomanni, F. (2002). *Tigri globali, domatori nazionali*. Bologna: Il Mulino.

Saccomanni, F. (2008). *Managing International Financial Instability: National Tamers versus Global Tigers*. Cheltenham: Edward Elgar Publishing.

Samuelson, P., and Solow, R. (1960). Analytical Aspects of Anti-Inflation Policy. *American Economic Review Papers and Proceedings*, 50 (2), 177–94.

Sargent, T., and Wallace, N. (1981). Some Unpleasant Monetarist Arithmetic. Federal Reserve Bank of Minneapolis, *Quarterly Review*, Fall.

Schmitt-Grohe, S., and Uribe, M. (2010). The Optimal Rate of Inflation. *NBER Working Paper*, No. 16054.

Schularick, M., Ferguson, N., and Schaab, A. (2015). Central Bank Balance Sheets: Expansion and Reduction since 1900, Economic History and International Macroeconomics. *Discussion Paper*, No. 10635. London: Centre for Economic Policy Research, 25 May.

Scott, H. S. (2016). *Connectedness and Contagion: Protecting the Financial System from Panics*. Cambridge, MA: The MIT Press.

Shambaugh, J. C. (2012). The Euro's Three Crises. *Brookings Papers on Economic Activity*, Spring.

Siegele, L. (2004). Germany on the Mend. *The Economist*, 17 November.

Sinn, H. W. (2014). *The Euro Trap. On Bursting Bubbles, Budgets, and Beliefs*. Oxford: Oxford University Press.

Staiger, D., Stock, J. H., and Watson, M. W. (2001). Prices, Wages, and the U.S. NAIRU in the 1990s. In: A. B. Krueger and R. M. Solow, eds, *The Roaring Nineties: Can Full Employment Be Sustained?* 1st ed. New York: Russell Sage Foundation.

Stein, J. C. (2013). Overheating in Credit Markets: Origins, Measurement, and Policy Responses. Restoring Household Financial Stability after the Great Recession: Why Household Balance Sheets Matter research symposium sponsored by the Federal Reserve Bank of St. Louis, St. Louis, MO, 7 February.

Stock, J. H., and Watson, M. W. (2002). Has the Business Cycle Changed and Why? In: M. Gertler and K. Rogoff, eds., *NBER Macroeconomics Annual 2002*. Cambridge, MA: The MIT Press, pp. 159–218.

Strauch, R. (2016). Strengthening Resilience in Europe after the Crisis. ISPI-Milan conference, Milan, 28 January.

Summers, L. H. (1991). How Should Long-Term Monetary Policy be Determined? *Journal of Money, Credit and Banking*, 23, 625–31.

Summers, L. H. (2016). Rethinking Secular Stagnation after Seventeen months. In: O. Blanchard, R. Rajan, K. Rogoff, and L. H. Summers, eds, *Progress and Confusion: The State of Macroeconomic Policy*, 1st ed. Cambridge MA: The MIT Press.

Summers, P. M. (2005). What Caused the Great Moderation? Some Cross-Country Evidence. *Federal Reserve Bank of Kansas City Economic Review*, 3, 5–32.

Svensson, L. (2010). Inflation Targeting. *Handbook of Monetary Economics, Volume 3*, pp. 1237–302.

Sylla, R., and Homer, S. (2005). *A History of Interest Rates*, 4th ed. Hoboken, NJ: John Wiley and Sons, Inc.

Taylor, J. B. (1979). Staggered Wage Setting in a Macro Model. *American Economic Review*, 69 (2), 108–13.

Taylor, J. B. (1993). Discretion versus Policy Rules in Practice. *Carnegie-Rochester Conference Series on Public Policy*, 39. Amsterdam: Elsevier Science Publishers B.V., pp. 195–214.

Taylor, J. B. (1999). A Historical Analysis of Monetary Policy Rules. In: J. B. Taylor, ed., *Monetary Policy Rules*, 1st ed. Chicago: University of Chicago Press.

Taylor, J. B. (2012). The Great Deviation. In: E. Koenig, R. Leeson, and G. A. Kahn, eds, *The Taylor Rule and the Transformation of Monetary Policy*, 1st ed. Stanford, CA: Hoover Institution Publication.

Taylor, J. B. (2016). A Monetary Policy for the Future. In: O. Blanchard, R. Raghuram, K. Rogoff, and L.H. Summers, eds, *Progress and Confusion: The State of Macroeconomic Policy*, 1st ed. Cambridge, MA: The MIT Press, pp. 135–41.

Taylor, J. B., and Williams, J. (2008). A Black Swan in the Money Markets. *NBER Working Paper Series*. Available at: http://www.nber.org/papers/w13943.

The Economist (1999). *The Sick Man of the Euro*. 3 June.

Tinbergen, J. (1952). *On the Theory of Economic Policy*. Amsterdam: North-Holland Publishing Company.

Tobin, J. (1972). Inflation and Unemployment. *American Economic Review*, 62, 1–18.

Trichet, J. (2008). The Financial Turbulence: Where Do We Stand? Economic Club of New York, New York, 14 October.

Truman, E. M. (2009). Lessons from the Global Economic and Financial Crisis. Conference G-20 Reform Initiatives: Implications for the Future of Regulation, co-hosted by the Institute for Global Economics and the International Monetary Fund in Seoul.

Tucker, P. (2009). The Repertoire of Official Sector Interventions in the Financial System: Last Resort Lending, Market-Making, and Capital. Bank of Japan's 2009 International Conference: Financial System and Monetary Policy Implementation, p. 5.

Véron, N. (2014). European Banking Union: Current Outlook and Short-Term Choices. Conference on Banking Union and the Financing of the Portuguese Economy, Portuguese Parliament, Lisbon, 26 February 2014.

Véron, N. (2017). Economic and Financial Challenges for the European Union in 2017. Lecture at the European School of Management and Technology, Berlin, 24 January 2017.

Weinberg, J. (2015). Federal Reserve Credit Programs during the Meltdown. Available at: https://www.federalreservehistory.org/essays/fed_credit_programs.

White, W. R. (2009). Should Monetary Policy 'Lean or Clean'? *Working Paper*, No. 34, Globalization and Monetary Policy Institute, Federal Reserve Bank of Dallas.

White, W. R. (2013). What Has Gone Wrong with the Global Economy? Why Were the Warnings Ignored? What Have We Learned from the Experience? Official Monetary and Financial Institutions Forum Golden Series Lecture, Innholders' Hall, London, 23 October.

Wicksell, K. (1935). *Lectures on Political Economy*. London: George Routledge & Sons Ltd, p. 193.

Wieladek, T., and Pascual, A. (2016). The European Central Bank's QE: A New Hope. *CEPR Discussion Paper*, No. 11309.

Williams, J. (2006). Inflation Persistence in an Era of Well-Anchored Inflation Expectations. *FRBSF Economic Letter*, No. 27.

Williams, J. (2013). A Defense of Moderation in Monetary Policy. *Journal of Macroeconomics*, 38, 137–50.

Williams, J. (2016). *Discussion of 'Language after Liftoff: Fed Communication Away from the Zero Lower Bound'*. U.S. Monetary Policy Forum New York, 26 February 2016.

Woodford, M. (2012a). The Changing Policy Landscape. Jackson Hole Symposium, Columbia University, New York, 20 August.

Woodford, M. (2012b). *Methods of Policy Accommodation at the Interest-Rate Lower Bound*. Columbia University, New York, 19 September.

Wu, C., and Xia, F. (2016). Measuring the Macroeconomic Impact of Monetary Policy at the Zero Lower Bound. *Journal of Money, Credit, and Banking*, 48, 253–91.

Wynne, M. A., and Kersting, E. K. (2007). Openness and Inflation. *Federal Reserve Bank of Dallas Staff Papers*, No. 2, April.

Yates, A. (1995). On the Design of Inflation Targets. In: A. G. Haldane, ed., *Targeting Inflation*. London: Bank of England, pp. 119–34.

Yellen, J. (1996). *Monetary Policy: Goals and Strategy*. National Association of Business Economists, Washington, 13 March 1996.

Yellen, J. (2006). Monetary Policy in a Global Environment. The Euro and the Dollar in a Globalized Economy Conference. U.C. Santa Cruz, Santa Cruz, CA, 27 May.

Yellen, J. (2016). Macroeconomic Research after the Crisis, The Elusive Great Recovery: Causes and Implications for Future Business Cycle Dynamics, 60th annual economic conference sponsored by the Federal Reserve Bank of Boston, Boston, MA, 14 October.

Yellen, J. (2016a). The Federal Reserve's Monetary Policy Toolkit: Past, Present, and Future. At Designing Resilient Monetary Policy Frameworks for the Future, a symposium sponsored by the Federal Reserve Bank of Kansas City, Jackson Hole, WY. 26 August 2016.

Zaniboni, N. (2011). *Report on Globalization and the Phillips Curve*. Georgetown University.

Zürbrygg, F. (2016). Negative Interest Rates: Necessary from a Monetary Policy Point of View—But with what Risks for the Banks? Volkswirtschaftliche Gesellschaft des Kantons Bern, 24 November.

Index

Tables, figures and boxes are indicated by a italic *t, f* and *b* following the page number